The Life and Work of

SAMUEL RUTHERFORD CROCKETT

AUP titles of related interest

THE HISTORY OF SCOTTISH LITERATURE
in four volumes
general editor: Cairns Craig
Volume 1 Origins to 1660, *editor R D S Jack*
Volume 2 1660 to 1800, *editor Andrew Hook*
Volume 3 Nineteenth century, *editor Douglas Gifford*
Volume 4 Twentieth century, *editor Cairns Craig*

THE LUM HAT AND OTHER STORIES
last tales of Violet Jacob
edited by Ronald Garden

THE TRUTH OF IMAGINATION
essays and reviews by Edwin Muir
edited by P H Butter

LITERATURE OF THE NORTH
collection of essays on the literature of North East Scotland
edited by David Hewitt and Michael Spiller

NORTHERN VISION
partner volume to Literature of the North
edited by David Hewitt and Michael Spiller

STRUCTURED THOUGHT
a reassessment of J M Barrie's dramatic art
R D S Jack

A BLASPHEMER AND REFORMER
a study of James Leslie Mitchell/Lewis Grassic Gibbon
William K Malcolm

POPULAR LITERATURE IN VICTORIAN SCOTLAND
language, fiction and the press
William Donaldson

THE JACOBITE SONG
political myth and national identity
William Donaldson

the life and work of
SAMUEL RUTHERFORD CROCKETT

Islay Murray Donaldson

ABERDEEN UNIVERSITY PRESS

First published 1989
Aberdeen University Press
A member of the Maxwell Pergamon Macmillan Group

© Islay M Donaldson 1989

*All Rights Reserved. Except as permitted under current legislation
no part of this work may be photocopied, stored in a retrieval system,
published, performed in public, adapted, broadcast, recorded or reproduced
in any form or by any means, without the prior permission of the
copyright owner. Enquiries should be addressed to Aberdeen University Press,
Farmers Hall, Aberdeen.*

The publisher acknowledges subsidy from the Scottish Arts Council
towards the publication of this volume.

British Library Cataloguing in Publication Data

Donaldson, Islay Murray
　The Life and Work of S R Crockett
　1. A fiction in English. Crockett, S R (Samuel Rutherford), 1859–1914
　I. Title
　　823′.8
ISBN 0 008 0365973

Typeset and printed by AUP Glasgow/Aberdeen—A member of BPCC Ltd

Contents

List of Illustrations		vi
Acknowledgements		vii
Chapter 1	Galloway	1
Chapter 2	Edinburgh to Penicuik	16
Chapter 3	Minister to Writer	29
Chapter 4	*The Stickit Minister and Some Common Men*	52
Chapter 5	*The Lilac Sunbonnet*	71
Chapter 6	*The Raiders, being some passages in the Life of John Faa, Lord and Earl of Little Egypt*	98
Chapter 7	The Historical Romancer	141
	I In Galloway	141
	II Elsewhere	159
Chapter 8	*Cleg Kelly Arab of the City*	186
Chapter 9	*Kit Kennedy: Country Boy*	202
Chapter 10	Scenes of Contemporary Life	217
	I City and Country	217
	II Industrialism and the Day's Work	237
Chapter 11	'Climbing on the Steep Stairs'	253
Chapter 12	Posthumous Achievements	285
Publishers and dates of first editions of Crockett's works		328
Notes		331
Index		351

List of Illustrations

1	Crockett's grandfather and mother, with Crockett as a child	4
2	The Rev S R Crockett in the year of publication of *The Stickit Minister*	39
3	Bank House	48
4	Crockett's letter to Mowat (1896)	144
5	Crockett golfing at St Andrews	145
6	Little Duchrae, The Birthplace of Crockett	254
7	Raiders Bridge, New Galloway Station	254
8	The Murder Hole and the Merrick	255
9	Crockett's 'Kirk on the Hill'	255
10	'The Stickit Minister'	264
11	The Crockett Family abroad, *c*1908	269
12	Memorial erected by public subscription and unveiled in 1932 by Ruth Crockett at Laurieston	283

Acknowledgements

I read S R Crockett over the years, but reference books and histories of literature had nothing to tell me about him except disparaging remarks about the 'Kailyard', which did not square with my impressions at all. Mr J W Vitty, MA, of the Linenhall Library, Belfast, presented me with a copy of the eighth illustrated edition of *The Stickit Minister* and suggested that I look into Crockett for myself. I did. I have not dealt with every book he wrote between 1893 and his death in 1914, but have tried to blaze a trail through those I found significant.

Several Crockett relatives helped me. The late Mrs Margaret Douglas Newman of Altrincham, Cheshire, Crockett's younger daughter, wrote to me describing the family homes at Bank House, Penicuik, and Torwood, Peebles, her sister and brothers, and the servants and gardeners who were devoted friends. She also identified her father's second travelling pupil in Europe as Mr John Bertram Marsden-Smedley; subsequently the Marsden-Smedley family and Miss Joyce Collyer shared with me memories of the young Scot who had so impressed the older generation.

Professor John Crocket Smyth of Glenpark, Johnstone, and Paisley Technical College, grandson of Crockett's cousin William Crocket who became headmaster of Sciennes School, Edinburgh, produced photographs, diaries, letters and traditions so generously that he in person is virtually the old tin trunk of documents, the dream of all biographers. Mr Iain Sproat of London, whose grandmother Alice Sproat was Ruth Crockett's sister, told me about the *Vanity Fair* cartoon which in turn pointed the way to Whistler. In Edinburgh, Miss Joan Hastings, daughter of Crockett's cousin Sam, lent me a letter from Crockett to her father and introduced me to her Auchencairn cousins Eileen and Charlotte Alexander, now Mrs Dobie and Mrs Stewart. All three had memories and photographs, and suggested that Mr Eddie Fisher of Auchencairn might take me in his boat to Heston, 'Isle Rathan', which in due course came about. Mrs Mary McKerrow of Edinburgh, descended from the Smiths of Netherholm, Kirkmahoe, Dumfries, filled in that part of the family tree relating to Crockett's great-aunt Christian; Miss Pearl McDowall of Kirkton, Dumfries, daughter of the Rev William McDowall of Kirkton by a second marriage (his first had been to Crockett's Aunt Janet of Drumbreck) contributed more details, as did her nephew Mr William McDowall of Dunlop, Ayrshire, and elsewhere. Miss Anne Todd of Maxwelltown and Carronbridge, whose mother as a child had met Crockett, drove me to Dunscore to meet the

McKnights, kin to Crockett's grandmother, and put me in touch with Mrs Nan O'Brien of Londonderry whose mother, a niece of Mrs John Crocket of Drumbreck, looked after the old lady in her last years.

Many people in Midlothian remembered Crockett or had heard their elders speak of him. The late Mr James Milroy worked with his father as garden-boy at Bank House and knew where Crockett bought his typewriters and how he used shorthand. Later, as a railway employee, Mr Milroy described Crockett's interest in trains, the affection in which railway-workers held him, and his friendship with Mr David Deuchars, Superintendent of the Line and Mr Paton, station-master at Waverley. The late Mrs Ruth Sandilands, a daughter of the Rev William Thomson, Free Church minister at Auchencairn, lent me her father's manuscript talk on Crockett delivered in 1935 to the Sanquhar Literary Society and two letters to her father in Crockett's last year of life. The letters are now in Edinburgh University Library's Department of Rare Books and Manuscripts, by her request.

Mrs Helen Wallace of Penicuik remembered how Crockett preached. The late Mrs Nellie Kerr of Penicuik, daughter of the Crockett cook, lent me photographs of the family and one of a Sunday School picnic at Brunstane Castle with Crockett a tall black figure encompassed about by pupils and parents arrayed in their Sunday best.

Mrs William Laidlaw, also of Penicuik, told me about Daniel Holt, 'minister's man' to Crockett, and gave me his Bible inscribed and presented by Crockett. Mrs Elinor Tavner, now living in Norfolk, took me through Bank House and its gardens, and with the help of other members of the Penicuik Historical Society identified the personages appearing, under disguised names and unflatteringly, in Crockett's *The Seven Wise Men*, and described the mingled sensations of shock and glee the story aroused in Penicuik when it first came out. Ted Cowan, now Professor of Scottish History at the University of Guelph, Ontario, Canada, passed on to me his discovery of the wealth of cuttings pasted into over one hundred and forty notebooks by R E Black, dealing with every aspect of Penicuik life. Mr William Black generously allowed me free access to his late father's collection, which is now deposited for consultation in Penicuik Public Library as the 'Black Papers'.

Mrs Margaret Christie of Wolverhampton whose mother had been Elizabeth Shanks, one of the Bank House maids, both wrote of and told me in person about her mother's vivid and shrewd reminiscences of the household. The late Mr Laurie Auchterlonie of St Andrews showed me Crockett's left-handed golf clubs, still in his shop, and described his father Willie Auchterlonie's warm golfing friendship with Crockett. Mr James Williams, FSA(Scot) of the Dumfriesshire and Galloway Natural History and Antiquarian Society, helped me with the Crockett family tree and from the very old parochial records of Lochrutton sent me more Crockets than I knew what to do with. Dr H C Weaving of Hartlepool drove me around the little pit towns and villages of Northumberland and Durham, with their rows of back-to-back houses named by numbers or letters of the alphabet, so that I could see them for myself.

The Rev F P Canavan, SJ, looked out and had photocopied for me in New

York Public Library Samuel Picard's article on 'The Student Life of S R Crockett' in a New York *Independent* of the late 1890s. Mr Ian Jackson, antiquarian bookseller of Berkeley, California, searched and found for me a copy of *A Galloway Herd* by Crockett, published in the USA but never as a book in this country. Messrs Hodder and Stoughton most kindly sent me a large envelope bulging with photocopies of their correspondence with A P Watt, Crockett's literary agent—everyone's literary agent—which shed light on Crockett's later years. The late Mr William Blair of the Grange Bookshop, Edinburgh, generously directed me to Crockett references in twentieth-century periodicals which I might never have found without his guidance. Professor John MacQueen, late of the School of Scottish Studies, University of Edinburgh, who supervised the PhD thesis from which this book has grown, not only encouraged me but saved me from unwise excursions into irrelevance and made inspired suggestions from which I have gratefully profited.

Many institutions came to my help. Thanks are due to the National Library of Scotland; the Scottish section of Edinburgh Central Library, George IV Bridge; the Ewart Public Library, Dumfries; the Chambers Institution, Peebles; the Mitchell Library, Glasgow; New College Library, Edinburgh; Register House, Edinburgh; the Department of MSS. and Rare Books, Edinburgh University Library; the Trustees of the Hornel Collection at Broughton House, Kirkcudbright; the Headquarters of the Lothian and Borders Police, Fettes Row, Edinburgh, who confirmed that there had existed a rank of Detective-Lieutenant so that Crockett was not wrong; Ms Caroline Dutton, Archivist of New College, Oxford, who ascertained that Crockett was never a matriculated member of the University; and Cambridge University Library who allowed me to consult the *Book of Gosse*.

Individual men and women, especially in Galloway, wrote to me with cuttings, news items and good wishes; they are too many to mention in detail but they show that Crockett is not forgotten. To all these, named and unnamed, I offer most gladly and gratefully my warmest thanks, not forgetting the kindly staff of Aberdeen University Press, who turned my typescript into this printed book, and Mrs Moyra Forrest who prepared the Index.

Islay M Donaldson
Dunbar
May 1989

To Alf and Chris and Gordon
who suffered long and were kind

CHAPTER 1

Galloway

Though his name will always be associated with his native Galloway, Samuel Rutherford Crockett lived there for only the first fifteen years of his life. Thereafter he visited it frequently, on vacations from University, in forays from his ministry in Penicuik to gather material for one book or another, as a visiting celebrity fêted by fellow Gallovidians, and, towards the end of his days, as an ailing man spending the milder months of summer or autumn at the little village of Auchencairn, but never after he departed to become a student at Edinburgh did he spend any continuous time there.

Nevertheless in another sense he never left it. His imagination was held by the Galloway landscape—the grey rocks and shining lochs, the Solway tides, the winding roads with their abundance of wild flowers, the dark peat mosses, the silent hills which rose above and behind the rest. For him there was also the older Galloway, that of the Black Douglases, rebels against the ruling Stewarts, and of the later, less romantic rebels of the seventeenth century, the Covenanters, facing persecution for what they believed to be the true word of God and Christ's Covenanted Reformation. He was a country boy, more aware than most of the natural beauty which surrounded him, and came of pious Cameronian stock of which he was intensely proud.

His great-grandparents, John Crocket and Ann Milligan, were married in December 1777 at Lochrutton in the Stewartry of Kirkcudbright, a quiet rural parish four miles west of Dumfries; the marriage is recorded in the Parish Register of Lochrutton, Volume One. Three of their children, either themselves or through the next generation, played a part in shaping his creative mind, and he himself, after a life which led him far from the old paths, lies buried as he had desired in the churchyard of Balmaghie, near Castle Douglas, 'among the dear and simple folk I knew and loved in youth'.[1] His epitaph occupies the last inches on one of the red sandstone Crocket family tombstones, close to the grass and clover:

> Also SAMUEL RUTHERFORD CROCKETT
> Minister of the Gospel and Novelist, born at
> Duchrae in this parish on 24th September 1859,
> Died at Tarascon, France, on 16th April 1914[2]

The contrast of 'Minister of the Gospel' and 'Novelist' almost deprived him of his right to lie there. When he died suddenly abroad, many people, some of them from his own family of cousins and connections, questioned whether

1

he should be allowed to rest with his forebears; had he not given up his Free Church ministry in favour of the life of a fiction writer and made himself a backslider from the religion in which he was brought up?[3]

William Crocket, his grandfather, one of the sons of John and Ann, married Mary Dickson, also of Lochrutton, and settled in the small farm of Park in the neighbouring parish of Kirkpatrick Irongray. John and Samuel their sons were born in 1824 and 1826. By 1828 they had moved to another small farm, Bush, still in Irongray parish, where their other children were born— Ann or Annie, Christina, Janet or Jessie, William, Robert and Mary.

Robert Crocket, William's younger brother, with his wife Janet Clark, set up his household at the farm of Killylour in Irongray; their children, approximately a decade younger than William's, were born there—John, David, Robert, William and Mary.

An elder sister, Christina or Christian, married John Hyslop of Lochrutton-gate, later renamed Southpark. She comes into Crockett's life only indirectly through her children and grandchildren; her marriage made her socially a little above her brothers. The entry of her daughter's birth in the Lochrutton Parish Register in 1818 describes her husband as a 'Proprietor'; William and Robert were only tenant farmers.

Irongray is known as a Covenanting parish. Its minister John Welsh, descended from John Knox, was one of the leaders and inspirers of the Pentland Rising of 1666 crushed at Rullion Green by Bloody Dalyell. In Irongray the rebels gathered before marching on Dumfries against Government dragoons, and the infamous persecutor Grierson of Lag came from a nearby parish. Memories of the Covenant were strong; one of the greatest conventicles had been held in 1678 in the hills above Irongray Church and a polished granite memorial was erected by public subscription in 1870. All these things must have been familiar to the Crockets and talked of round their hearths; young Sam must have listened.

At some time between the Census dates 1841 and 1851, both William and Robert Crocket moved farther into the Stewartry, deeper into Covenanting country, and settled at farms in the parish of Balmaghie. William became the tenant of Little Duchrae, a farm on the road between Laurieston and New Galloway, where in 1851 he and his eldest son John are recorded as farming 108 acres jointly. John had married the daughter of the farmer at Mains of Duchrae, a little to the east on an unclassified road running past Balmaghie Church, and was living there with his father-in-law, his mother-in-law, his wife and young family. William's other children were employed in traditional country ways, Samuel apprenticed to a joiner, the girls out at service, William and Robert helping on the farm at Little Duchrae.

Robert Crocket and his wife Janet leased Drumbreck, a larger outlying farm on the Duchrae estate consisting of 143 acres south of Laurieston village. In the 1851 Census they are there with another son, James, born at Balmaghie, and a daughter Janet, also born there. Robert and Janet, with two of their sons David and William, were to die either before or shortly after young Sam's birth, but the two other sons, John and Robert, continued to farm Drumbreck, and Robert in particular was to be a close and good friend to Sam.

Thus during the 1840s the two brothers William and Robert Crocket were living on farms near one another, with the same landlord on the same estate (now known as Hensol), taking a keen interest in one another's affairs. The Drumbreck Crockets were members of the Free Church of Scotland which in 1843 had broken away from the Established Church at the Disruption; Robert was an elder[4] of Laurieston Free Church, and his son John was to follow him in this position. The Little Duchrae Crockets were of an older secession; they were Cameronians, a sect which remained aloof when the Revolution Settlement in 1688 failed to impose Presbyterianism on the whole country; they took their name from Richard Cameron, a Covenanting martyr, and regarded both Established and Free Churches as Erastian, under the yoke of secular government; they themselves were the only true heirs of the Society Men or Hill Men who had died for their pure faith at the hands of the redcoats.

Samuel Crocket, whom readers were to know as Samuel Rutherford Crockett (the single or double 't' seems to have been optional among different branches) was born on 24 September 1859 at Little Duchrae to Annie Crocket, William and Mary's daughter, who described herself on her son's birth certificate as a dairymaid. The identity of his father is not known, though there is evidence that he was no stranger to the family. Annie's brother Samuel, who had emigrated to the United States and was farming near Rochester, Minnesota, wrote home with quiet anger at hearing the news—anger at the wrong done his sister.

> I was very sorry to read the account you sent me about Anne (sic), all of you must be as kind to her as you possibly can, for he that thinketh he standeth must take good heed lest he fall, he must be a miserable wretch to act as he has done, but vengence (sic) is mine I will repay saith the Lord, if no earthly tribunal will punish him for his conduct. I am glad that he did not marry her, I never thought highly of him and the longer the less.[5]

This warmhearted attitude gives a kindly picture of the family and perhaps explains why S R Crockett was never troubled by his illegitimacy in the way that George Douglas Brown was by his. Sympathy for the unfortunate sister is paramount. There is no suggestion that she should for the sake of respectability have married a man who had proved himself unworthy. Uncle Samuel wrote later the same year regretting that he was too far away to send his little namesake a present: 'he will be running all over by this time I expect'.[6]

Sam was brought up at Little Duchrae by his mother, his aunts and uncles, but chiefly by his grandparents, the prominent figures of his childhood; the only child on the farm, much loving and much loved, he was surrounded by affection, though in the undemonstrative, unexpressed way typical of Scots country people. It was Crockett who first in fiction made a child ask Peter Pan's question 'What is a kiss?', though there is no nonsense thereafter about thimbles. It appears in an early story 'A Galloway Herd'[7] and is repeated by little Hugh in *Cleg Kelly*, a book dedicated to Crockett's friend J M Barrie.[8] One suspects that Sam himself may have innocently asked the question

1 Crockett's grandfather and mother, with Crockett as a child—even then he could not sit still.

for kisses were not mentioned at Drumquhat. It was not thought menseful to do so.[9]

But the affection between Sam and his elders was deep and lasting on both sides, and there were plenty of elders. His mother and aunts were often out at service but two uncles Bob and Willie were at hand on the farm, he had Uncle John at the Mains and two second-cousins John and Robert at Drumbreck. Uncle Samuel came back from America and settled at Glenlochar, near Laurieston, with his family; he became a respected joiner and undertaker and was followed in this trade by his son William, Sam's favourite cousin. But the grandfather and grandmother were the closest and best of all.

Growing up in Balmaghie, it was inevitable that Sam's mind should be full of Covenanting beliefs and stories—chiefly stories. Most of his reading was concerned with them in his early days; few secular papers came to Little Duchrae—Cameronians did not vote and were little interested in an uncovenanted government—and news came from meeting other farmers and farmers' wives at the church. They travelled on Sundays to Castle Douglas in their red farm cart to the Cameronian church which Crockett has called the 'Kirk on the Hill', though it is hardly worthy of that name, only a few steps above street level in Queen Street.

Stories of the Covenant were presented to Sam not as dead history or even theology but as thrilling events, captures and escapes and summary executions, examples of quick-witted courage shown by men and women, heroes and heroines who had lived in the places he knew. Claverhouse and Grierson of Lag were dark familiar villains; the simple country folk who had defied them were of his own kind. He rejoiced in the wildness of Galloway's past.

> The parish of Balmaghie is the *Cor Cordium* of Galloway. It is the central parish—the citadel of Gallovidian prejudices. It was the proud sanctuary of the reivers of the low country before the Reformation. Then it became the headquarters of the High Westland Whigs in the stirring time that sent Davie Crookback to watch the king's forces on the English border. From its Clachanpluck (Laurieston) every single man marched away to Rullion Green, very few returning from the dowsing they got on Pentland side from grim long-bearded Dalyell. It was the parish that for many years defied, indiscriminately, law courts and Church courts, and kept MacMillan, the first minister of the Cameronian Societies, in enjoyment of kirk, glebe and manse in spite of the invasion of the emissaries of Court of Session and the fulminations of the Erastian Presbytery of Kirkcudbright.[10]

Solitary as many other only children, he played with his dogs or occasional visiting cousins or friends at Covenanters and Dragoons as later generations were to play at Cowboys and Indians, surrounded by the scenes which had witnessed the reality. The stories he found in the approved family reading—Simpson's *Traditions of the Covenanters*, Howie of Lochgoin's *The Scots Worthies*, Wodrow's *History of the Sufferings of the Church of Scotland*, Bunyan's *Pilgrim's Progress*, Josephus' *History of the Jews*. Secular fiction was forbidden to Cameronians, but these close-packed volumes provided fighting and excitement in plenty, and there was oral tradition to be picked from grown-ups at Little Duchrae:

> By that fireside sat night after night the original of Silver Sand, relating stories with that shrewd beaconing twinkle in the eye which told of humour and experience deep as a draw-well and wide as the brown-backed moors over which he had come.[11]

Smugglers, reivers, gipsy cairds—all these must have mingled with the more sober Covenanting annals to make Galloway one glorious scene of colour, movement and hair-raising adventure.

It had natural beauty too. 'Such a heavenly place for a boy to spend his youth in!' Crockett exclaims in *Raiderland*,[12] listing its delights, road, hedgerow and Woodhall Loch near his home (which should have kept its old name, Loch Grenoch, just as Laurieston should have remained Clachanpluck[13])—the 'paradise of pebbly shadows and reedy pools', the 'water-meadows rich with long deep grass that one could hide in standing erect', the 'little brook that rippled across the road (now, I fear, ignominiously conveyed in a drain-pipe), at which the horses were watered night and morning, and where I got myself muddied and soaking—but afterwards well warmed'.

'Well warmed'—there was no notion of corporal punishment perhaps damaging the child's ego. 'Lickings' were part of life; if one misbehaved, tore one's clothes, threw stones at the minister's hens, came home sopping and dirty, one got what one expected and deserved. 'Warm backs, guid bairns'[14] was a saying of Grandfather Crocket's mother, and he approved and had applied it to his sons as well as his grandson;

> Life was paternal in the Galloway uplands, and many a son took a thrashing from his father after he was 'man-muckle' and thought himself all the better for it ... It was his father's duty (for which he had to answer to the minister) to discipline his family.[15]

Religion was far removed from Sunday School piety; cause led to consequence with remorseless logic; one knew and respected this rule and took no harm because under it lay affection, concern and justice.

The longest account of his country upbringing is given by Crockett in *A Galloway Herd*, his first serial story in the *Christian Leader*.[16] Young Walter Anderson who lives with the McQuhirrs of Drumquhat is young Sam living with his grandparents.

> It is a thousand pities if in this chronicle Walter has been represented as a good boy. He was seldom so called by the authorities about Drumquhat. There he was usually referred to as 'that loon', 'the *hyule*', 'Wattie, ye mischieevious boy'. He was a stirring lad and restlessness frequently brought him into trouble. He remembers his 'grannie's' Bible lessons on the green turn of the road, and he is of the opinion now that they did him a great deal of good. It is not for an outside historian to contradict this, but it is certain that his 'gran' had to

exercise a good deal of patience to induce him to give due attention, and a modicum of suasion that could not be called moral to make him learn his verse and his psalm.[17]

Mary Crocket his gran had a sharp and biting tongue, as M McL Harper says in *Crockett and Grey Galloway*[18] and Crockett confirms.

> Shrewd, kindly, clever, managing, with a 'clip in her speech' that the stranger might mistake for ill-temper ... Mary ... was a 'kenned women' through all the parish. She kept the whole of the *personelle* of the establishment up to the mark, and her mark was a mark a little higher than that of anybody else ... Yet, though the service at Drumquhat could not be called an easy one, it was performed with such a birr and cheerfulness that there was not a heart-somer place in all the countryside than the moorfarm under the brow of the peat-hags.[19]

Young Sam/Walter was near her heart, for all his mischief, even when he took eggs from the nests of virtuous hens and pretended that they had been 'laid away' to earn the fee for their retrieval.[20]

Such a bustling figure was not always completely in accord with her husband's 'slow, thoughtful, book-reading ways'[21] but for all that,

> snell and sharp-tongued as Mary McQuhirr was, she yielded loyally in all great matters to the silent, great-hearted man who was her husband.[22]

Crockett's grandfather was the patriarchal head of the family, earnest and devout.

> My grandfather always had an hour of private devotion, early in the morning, going to a particular corner of the house outside, which was a little sheltered from the winds. This was known to all the house as 'grandfather's corner', and was held sacred from rude intrusion. There many a time I have stood in wonder at the sight, so mysterious to me, of my grandfather speaking with someone, who was unseen, yet was as real and near to him as I was. This silent testimony to the power of prayer, in one to whom I looked up with all the devotion of a childish hero-worshipper, will remain with me while life lasts. Then, when he came out, I was always at hand to ask questions—an operation at which youth is always distinguished.[23]

William Crocket had strong old-fashioned views. He did not

> hold with the new-fangled Sunday Schools at all. He was born before them ... and his father ... taught him the *Westminster Confession* and the *Psalms in Metre*, by Francis Roos. Just that and nothing more ... hymns about 'little pilgrims' who cannot get within the kirk door without taking off their tall hats—my grandfather could not away with! ... A fine upstanding, sinewy man was my grandfather ... and much respected by everyone. He could fell a tree with any man, and once he even came near to felling me—just for a little slip of the tongue which he mistook (but not so very much either) for impudence.[24]

He would have his children taught only the Lord's Prayer for their private devotions and warned them that they should be brief and to the point.

> HE is the most High—to be feared and reverenced. If you want to know His will, go and read His book. But let your prayers be few and your words well-ordered. Don't chatter to your Maker ... And when you do pray, see that you want something that you can't do for yourself. HE is the hearer of prayer, but you will get more if you don't be forever deafening HIM with vain repetitions as the heathens do.[25]

Independent, strong-willed, idiosyncratic, William Crocket and his family gave Sam security—the Shorter Catechism tempered with humour but accepted as guidance through life. The work of the farm accorded with its theological ethos; Sam's very early babyhood memories are of his elders busy about their tasks—the scent of fir and pine chips as his mother and uncles gathered them after the felling of trees; the warm smell of baking as his grandmother padded softly about the stone-flagged kitchen making oatcakes on a girdle—oatcakes, potatoes and milk were their staple fare, with cheese and soda scones; the sounds of an early September day with the low sweep of a scythe and the sharper cut of the reaping-hook breaking

> that silence in comparison with which the hush of a kirkyard is almost company—the silence of a Scottish farmyard in the first burst of harvest.[26]

Very soon Sam himself was involved in this busy, energetic striving, making bands for the sheaves of oats in harvest, taking tea to the haymakers,[27] rising at five in the morning to slice turnips for the sheep in winter, often brushing the snow from his coverlet where it had drifted through the rafters of the loft where he and his uncles slept.[28] He remembered being wakened at night by the sudden cry that the Dee was in flood; the family had to brave the dark waters to save their precious hay.[29] Such minor hardships, and the rats rustling in the hay or behind the plaster (he learned to kill them with his catapult)[30] were all part of the reality of farm life. The pictures that stayed in his mind were not idyllic, nor were the adults in this hardy community; laziness for them was the worst sin, with heather and peat-bog threatening always to encroach on arable and pasture field and having to be fought; they were dour, strong and harsh even in their looks:

> tall, stoop-shouldered men ... of shaven upper lips and bristling beards, the most unpicturesque fashion, barring the mutton-chop whisker, which has yet been discovered.[31]

Family, friends and early acquaintances appear over and over again, with minor variations and different names, in Crockett's fiction. Saunders McQuhirr and his sharp-tongued wife, favourite narrators of Galloway stories, are his grandparents; so are the Armours in *Kit Kennedy*. Mary Crocket is Mary Lyon in *The Dew of their Youth*:

grandmother came in wiping her hands ... whenever she does make an entry into the story I always feel I must write yet another page about the dear, warm-hearted, tumultuous old lady ... [32]

Aunt Janet, trusted servant at Airieland, between Gelston and Kirkcudbright, orders her mistress about with the familiarity of long faithful service;[33] she is the prototype for Lady Grizel Maxwell's outspoken Jen in *The Raiders*; Winsome's Meg Kissock in *The Lilac Sunbonnet*; Betty Landsborough in *Kit Kennedy*; perhaps even, caricatured a little, Megsy Tipperlin in *Cinderella*; outspoken affectionate servants wherever they appear. Muckle Alick, the huge strong railwayman in *Cleg Kelly*, is based on Uncle Bob.[34] The Stickit Minister is taken, in character and tastes though not in situation, from Robert Crocket of Drumbreck—which farm, in its lively farm-servants and practical jokes, suggests some of the features of Nether Neuk, the farm in *Lads' Love*.[35] George Breerie, the packman in *Kit Kennedy*, was recognisable to Galloway readers— and in his habit of frightening off dogs by looking at them through his legs may have given an idea to Barrie for the Lost Boys.

Part of his popularity in his native province was due to these familiar local touches. He shared rough country jokes against the Stewartry's neighbours; Stranraer is

> a long, clarty, Irish-looking street with pigs and bairns running about it, set on the shore of a fine loch[36]

although this is in the seventeenth century. Dumfries does not get off so easily in a contemporary picture of its inhabitants as ignoramuses:

> There's nae run on the dead languages in Dumfries. Bibles are drug stock, and even Shakespeare—man, I dinna think we hae selled yin o' him for twenty year, except a big bound copy to Bob Veitch, the hosier, that he uses to keep the letters doon on his desk, and to throw at the dogs that come snuffin' aboot the wicks o' his shop door.[37]

But, above all, in affectionate nostalgia, he goes back to Little Duchrae, kept small or enlarged as the story demanded. It is Craig Ronald, Drumquhat, Dornal, Lesser Duchrae, the farm of farms for the man who had grown up in it. The pattern of its days remains always in his mind and is repeated with variations.

The 'Taking of the Buik' morning and evening made the framework. Each morning

> ... the whole family was collected at family prayers, 'The Book', as it was always called. The psalm was reverently given out, two lines at a time, and sung to the old tunes of Coleshill, Martyrdom or St Paul's, then followed the reading of the 'Portion' and the simple earnest prayer ...
>
> Then in the evening the same course of worship was followed, and so every evening till the Sabbath came with its sense of another world altogether. Clearer than almost anything else there comes back to me the remembrance of these

Sabbath morns at the farm, when the sense of 'hallowed days' was in the very air. I seem to get my clearest hints of what the solemn gladness of the New Jerusalem will be from these sweet still Sabbath mornings of my youth.[38]

Solemn this gladness may have been but it was always gladness; a feeling of simple happiness pervades Crockett's writings about childhood. He was not always expected to go with the red cart to the Kirk on the Hill on Sunday. When he did go, his errings and strayings after wild flowers were tacitly ignored,[39] but often he was left at home, to

> relieve his mind in a rough-and-tumble with the collie dogs, which wearing like himself accurately Sunday faces, had been present at the worship, but now the red cart once out of the way, were very willing to relapse into such mundane scufflings, grippings and scourings of the countryside as to prove them no right Cameronians of the blue.[40]

Crockett stresses the kindliness that underlay the Cameronian austerity, so that

> not only was his path strewn with 'let-ups' from too much gravity by sympathetic seniors, but he discovered 'let-ups' for himself, in everything that ran or swam or flew, in heaven or earth or the waters beneath.[41]

His lively mind found even the Catechism, that formal expression of Presbyterian doctrine learned by heart and gone through as question and answer in the evenings, grandfather putting the questions, an exciting intellectual exercise. Sometimes the minister came to go through the 'Questions'; this was a special occasion.

> Saunders sat with his wife beside him, the three sons—Alec, James and Rob—on straight-backed chairs, Walter with his hand on his grandmother's lap ... Question and answer from the Shorter Catechism passed from lip to lip like a well-planned game in which no one let the ball drop. It would have been thought as shameful if the minister had not acquitted himself at 'asking' the questions deftly and instantaneously as for one of those who were answering to fail in their replies. When Rob momentarily mislaid the 'Reasons Annexed' to the second commandment, and his reason reeled in the sudden terror that they had gone from him for ever, his father looked at him as one who would say 'Woe is me that I have been the means of bringing a fool into the world!' But his mother looked at him wistfully, in a way that was like cold water running down his back, while Mr Cameron said kindly, 'Take your time!'
> Rob recovered himself gallantly, reeled off the 'Reasons Annexed' with vigour, and promised himself under his breath a sound thrashing to his model brother James, who, having known the Catechism perfectly from his youth up, had yet refused to give a leading hint to his brother in his extremity. Walter had his answers as ready as any of them ...
> After the catechising the minister prayed. He prayed for the venerable heads of the household, that they might have wisdom and discretion—that in the younger members the fear of the Lord might overcome the lust of the eye and

the pride of life.—and for the young child, that he might be a Timothy in the Scriptures, a Samuel in obedience, and that in the future, if so it were the will of the Most High, he might be both witness and evangelist of the Gospel.[42]

So far there was little sign of this hope's being realised; it was Sam/Walter who when a minister preached too long asked in a sleepy shrill whisper 'Will that man no sune be dune?'[43] When he played at Covenanters, 'listening with a tremulously mingled joy and fear to the crackling of the leaves under the imagined horse-hoofs of Claverhouse'[44] all the enjoyment was in the adventure. Even playing out scenes from *The Pilgrim's Progress* could not be regarded as awakening piety; his fellow-actors

> always decided to be Christian and Faithful, or some distinguished and respectable persons of that sort. But not such for me. These allured me not. Upon a hill I stood in lurid dignity as Apollyon, a bundle of darts in hand, and regularly falsified the allegory by making Christian weep bitterly, while Faithful made his best time in the direction of home.[45]

When he was five, Sam, having been taught the alphabet by his mother on her floury baking-board,[46] went to the Free Church School at Laurieston, three and a half miles from Little Duchrae, walking there and back morning and afternoon by the side of the loch. His natural quickness helped him at school, especially since the education was elementary, based on the Bible and the Shorter Catechism. There were few airs and graces taught—lickings from the master, playground fights, trippings up, knockings on the head were taken as normal. Possibly Laurieston Free Church School's chief contribution to his development was the discovery that he could hold his own when schoolmates demanded 'Can ye fecht?'[47] Fight he could, first of all savagely and instinctively like the collies, then, with experience, more orthodoxly. This schoolboy creed of rough violence remained with him in the enjoyment with which he wrote of horseplay and comic rough-and-tumble, making genteel readers find him rather vulgar in some aspects of his work; he always relished humour about wives handy with 'tattie-beetles' and 'besom-shanks', and the primitive amusements of boys:

> Whenever we met a boy belonging to the Established Kirk (who learned paraphrases), we threw a stone at him to bring him to a sense of his position. If, as Homer says, *he* was a lassie, we put out our tongue at her.[48]

In 1867 William Crocket retired from farming and moved with his family to 24 Cotton Street, Castle Douglas. It was probably at this time that his eldest son John likewise changed his trade; at any rate, now or later, he became a City Missionary at Liverpool. His two sons William and James were educated there but returned to Edinburgh; William shared for a while Sam's student life at Edinburgh University and rose to become headmaster of Sciennes School, Edinburgh, and James became Free Church minister at Yester Church, Gifford, near Haddington. The Crockets were clever chiels.

The move to Castle Douglas, the 'Cairn Edward' of his books, meant a busier, more populated, more bustling scene for Sam. In Castle Douglas there were markets, fairs, the coming and going of carriers' carts, perpetual activity. For the first time he lived in a street. Life centred on the Cross, where farmers met to exchange views and drive hard bargains. Irish drovers came and went, sober or drunk—the foot of the town was called 'Little Dublin'. There was also Carlinwark Loch, dotted with small islands, round which to row and have adventures, and Gelston estate near Dalbeattie offered rich woodlands in which to bird-nest, botanise or gather hazel-nuts, to the wrath of the gamekeepers.

Castle Douglas may have been little more than a village then, but the railway from Dumfries had opened its line and its station there in 1859, the year of Sam's birth. His two uncles became porters, introducing to him a life-long interest in trains. Tradition has it that he worked as a booking-clerk at Castle Douglas station during University vacations; certainly he was fascinated by the steam train with its chugging roar and trail of white smoke and smuts—it crops up often in his books. The romantic past came to him also in Threave Castle, the square fourteenth century fortress of the Black Douglases whose ruins stand on an island in the River Dee a few miles from the town. It introduced him to the feuds of the Douglases and the Stewarts, history of a new mediaeval kind.

Once more it was a Free Church school which he attended—Cowper's school called after its master. Crockett writes of both school and town with great affection, though it was only for a few years that he lived there.

> Little town, once built at the foot of a hill and ever since running a race up it—I do not know whether you are very proud of me, but at any rate I am proud of you.
> To me you are still 'the toon'—*my* town. I came to you as a boy, and found in you the best of schoolmasters, the best of schoolmates, the snellest, sharpest-tongued, kindliest-hearted folk in the world.[49]

Three boys were to be his particular friends—Andrew S Penman, later to be the founder of a prosperous firm of coach-builders and motor mechanics in Dumfries; William MacGeorge, later a professional artist and ARSA; and William Maxwell, later editor of the *Aberdeen Daily Journal*; Penman's lively description of Crockett, given at length in Harper's *Crockett and Grey Galloway*,[50] shows a vivid picture of the adolescent.

He looked soft, Andrew Penman says, but 'he had a marvellous long reach and a style of fighting, like an infuriated windmill, which was most disconcerting. This, and the fact that he had wonderful stores of information about such interesting subjects as "Knights Errant" and "Red Indians" and that he was a perfect genius at devising new games' made the others his followers and admirers. They read 'Penny Dreadfuls' together, but Crockett discovered the Waverley Novels and by his command 'the "Penny Dreadfuls" were collected into a bon-fire and burned. He was always a propagandist, and a little bit of a tyrant in matters of literary opinion. If we did not admire his latest hero . . . we got punched until we rendered lip service at least.'

Holidays were spent roaming the countryside and Crockett was the leader in all such dare-devil expeditions. 'He was absolutely fearless. I have seen him go up the chimney of Threave Castle ... right up to the top of the walls, walk round them and get down straddle-legged on the hanging stone, while we stood below and held our breaths'. Saturday was the day for battles at Threave; the boys chose sides, and one group defended the castle while the other besieged it, capturing and recapturing it over and over again. 'Mr Crockett has told all this in a slightly glorified form in "Sir Toady Lion" [one of his books for children]. Every boy in the story was at either Cowper's or Johnstone's school, and to contemporaries the names are only a thin disguise.'

How did Sam, in a Cameronian household, learn about Knights Errant, Red Indians and the Waverley Novels? The answer lies in one of his 'let-ups'.

> I used to get my books from the Mechanics' Institute, and was always careful to take two books at a time. One was a biography or a history, and that was to show at home. The other was a novel, and that was smuggled into the house, under my waistcoat ... I used to hide them away under my bed. My mother knew of it, but said nothing.[51]

Robert Crocket of Drumbreck improved his taste in reading; at Drumbreck Sam was a visitor and his time was his own, no work being expected of him; he spent summer holidays there and Robert, a reader and collector of books, twenty years older and with the experience of having travelled to Canada and back, encouraged him to read Shakespeare, Milton, Tennyson, Macaulay, Longfellow, Dante in Cary's translation, and Carlyle[52]—and probably Scott. Sam read avidly, hour after hour, in his perch up a tree, forgetting the time, deep in Chambers' *Edinburgh Journal*, Hogg's *Instructor*, Chambers' *English Literature*. Robert encouraged him to discuss what he read:

> To him I propounded all the various crude theories and beliefs that I was constantly having; and even now I can hear the sound of his voice, at once amused, pleased and shocked, when I laid down the law in a manner very far from the received opinion, and, indeed, very far from any real sense or merit.[53]

Other summer holidays were spent at the farm of Borland in Colvend above the Solway, at 'the house of a distant connection ... already an old man' whose name Crockett disguises. The Colvend censuses suggest that he was Robert Hyslop, father of Uncle Samuel's first wife, a kindly man still fresh and hearty who lent Sam and a Hyslop grandson a large three-decker telescope. His wife, 'a tall gaunt woman apparently clothed in old corn sacks and with a poke bonnet you could have stabled a horse in— a woman terrible to me as fate'[54] was as sharp-tongued as Mary Crocket but kindly too. From Borland, Sam and his friend explored the headlands and beaches, sustained by soda scones and whangs of cheese, watching the sloops and schooners 'beating up the Solway or making a long tack to avoid the deadly pea-soup of Barnhourie Sands'. They walked along the heathery cliff-tops and scrambled down to the little seaport of Scaur, now Kippford, from where they walked along the beach to Satturness. It is easy to see where the early chapters of *The Raiders* came from; Sam, Penman, MacGeorge and Maxwell in their teens spent a memorable holiday on Rough Island,[55] providing the source for the squabbling household of youngsters.

In Cowper's School, Sam acquitted himself well; John Cowper won respect as well as obedience from his pupils. Sam stayed on as pupil-teacher and at the same time was coached for the Bursary awarded annually by the Edinburgh Galloway Association to the pupil most worthy of promotion to Edinburgh University—Crockett describes the ordeal of the examination in *Kit Kennedy*. Like Kit, he won the Bursary, and in the autumn of 1876 the raw country lad, tall, erect and broad-shouldered, with a ruddy complexion and a tangle of chestnut hair, set off by train to Edinburgh and a University career, the £20 annual Bursary almost his only support.

This was the end of his Galloway boyhood. Death gradually removed one by one the people who had made it so happy. His grandfather had died in 1875, the year before the Bursary. Robert of Drumbreck died in 1877 of tuberculosis. Sam's mother and his Aunt Janet died in 1879, his mother also of tuberculosis. His grandmother died in 1884 when Sam was abroad. His Aunt Mary died in 1892. Uncle Samuel retired to the little fishing village of Auchencairn looking over the Solway to Heston Island, the Isle Rathan of *The Raiders*, and died there in 1901. Uncle Bob and Uncle Willie retired there also, and their now famous nephew inherited from them the two-storied semi-detached granite 'cottage' and liked to spend the milder months of autumn or summer there. But the little household of Balmaghie and Cotton Street had gone forever except as a bright perpetual memory.

In 1895 Crockett wrote a foreword to the Rev H M B Reid's history of Balmaghie church, *The Kirk Above Dee Water*, in which he said

> I am not often there, save when the beat of the passing bell calls another to the long and quiet rest.

He is exaggerating only a little.

The degree to which the past was distanced from him, though kept vividly alive in his imagination, is shown by the letter he wrote to Mrs John Crocket of Drumbreck after her husband's death in 1898. He had been in St Andrews, unable to attend the funeral.

> The necessities of the world have taken us far asunder, but if you have read my books you will know that I have never ceased to think lovingly and warmly of John and you, and of my first and dearest friend Robert, the brother whom he has gone to join.[56]

There is no estrangement, and the novelist S R Crockett wrote verses for John

Crocket's 'In Memoriam' card, but we feel in his letter regretful acknowledgement that he has travelled far in time and circumstance from his kinsfolk. If they have read his books, they will understand that he remembers them, but he knows that he has moved into a different and alien world.

CHAPTER 2

Edinburgh to Penicuik

Sam Crockett arrived in Edinburgh for the first time in October 1876, hanging out of the carriage window in the train from Carstairs Junction.

> Smuts flew in his eyes. Weird illuminations from paraffin shale mines challenged his sidelong regard. But he saw them not. He was looking for Wallace, and Bruce, and John Knox, and Queen Mary, and Claverhouse (but him he hated) riding out of the West Bow with all his troopers behind him.[1]

His cousin William Crocket, already a student, met him at the Caledonian Station at the west end of Princes Street; all that remains of it now is its hotel. William, as befitted the son of the City Missionary, escorted Sam and his wooden country-joiner-made box (Uncle-Samuel-made box?) to the lodgings they were to share in the St Leonards district on the South Side, telling his country cousin not to talk to policemen as if he were still in Galloway; this was a city full of strangers.

> We lived next to the sky in a many-storied grey house, but one of our two windows, by God's grace, looked up to the mural battlements of the Salisbury Crags and across the valley to the western shoulder of Arthur's Seat. That seemed in some far-off way to suggest home. But from the other window, looking down on the twinkling lamps receding into the distances by the city dusk—frankly, to go near them, they made me giddy.[2]

A *Christian Leader* story,[3] reprinted in *Bog-Myrtle and Peat*, suggests that he quickly found his feet. The country student whom it describes

> went up to Edinburgh one windy October morning, and for the first time in his life saw a university and a tramcar. The latter astonished him very much; but in the afternoon he showed four new comers the way to the secretary's office in the big cavern to the left of the entrance of the former, wide-throated like the portal of Hades.[4]

This quick settling in and taking over the office of guide to a place as new to him as to the innocents he was guiding is so like Crockett that it surely must be autobiographical. But the student, Ebenezer Skinner, whom he is describing in 'The Biography of an Inefficient' is very different from the author. He takes a lodging in Simon Square, and his educational progress is 'as bare of interest as a barn without the roof'. He reads his set texts and nothing else. He takes down all the dates in the English Literature class lectures but

> he did not attend the class on Fridays for fear he should be asked to read, so he never heard Masson declaim
>
> > 'Ah, freedom is a noble thing!'
>
> which some of his contemporaries consider the most valuable part of their university training.

He laboriously memorises all that he is told to study. He talks only to one contemporary,

> the youth next to him on Bench Seventeen, who had come from another rural village, and who lived in a garret exactly like his in Nicholson Square.
> Sometimes the two of them walked through the streets to the General Post Office and back again on Saturday nights to post their letters home, and talked all the while of their landladies and of the number of marks each had got on Friday in the Latin version. Thus they improved their minds and received the benefits of a college education.

Crockett mocks Ebenezer for his closed mind and timid outlook; his studies like a mackintosh shut out the buffeting winds of wider experience. Many students are like this, Crockett says, and they generally go into the church.

Crockett was very different, or so he would have us believe in an interview with R H Sherard in 1895; he boasts that he read widely whatever books and in whatever subjects he found interest. He did not attend all the lectures;

> I did not work very hard at my studies but read vastly, reading anything and everything; a constant visitor to the University Library. I do not think that there ever was so omnivorous a reader. I read ravenously, but without judgment.[5]

He not only disparages poor Ebenezer in the story written long afterwards but plumes himself on daring to cut lectures and suggests to Sherard that he was unique in his idiosyncratic attitude—no one else was like him.

Crockett always exaggerates. He may well have attended more lectures and listened more carefully than he admits to the London journalist. It sounds well to present oneself as a careless student whose brilliance had made him independent of his professors, but if he had behaved as he describes, he risked throwing away all that his Bursary had brought him. He was probably not as foolish as he sounds. Though not an Ebenezer with tunnel-vision, he was neither rich nor secure enough to despise a moderate competence in examinations. No doubt the University Library gratified his passion for reading on a scale never met before; he was able enough to keep his studies going and yet spend much time reading; looking back, the reading is what he remembers most prominently—or affects to remember most prominently. It must have been tempting to show off to Sherard in the heady success that had come to him as recently as 1893.

There were two terms in a session in the 1870s, a summer one for Medicine and tutorial classes in Arts from May to July, and a winter one—the important one for all four faculties, Arts, Medicine, Law and Divinity—which began in November and ended in April. Matriculation was in October. A degree in Arts took four winter sessions unless students sat an Entrance Examination in Latin and Greek stiff enough to satisfy the University that they could be allowed to complete their Arts degree in three winter sessions, entering the higher classes in their first year. Cousin William Crocket's diary[6] records that Sam sat his Greek examination, and we may presume that he passed this and the similar hurdle in Latin.

The Faculty of Arts consisted of seven chairs held by their several Professors—Barrie has sketched some of them in *An Edinburgh Eleven* but Crockett wrote little about his University days except for a few scrappy references in *Kit Kennedy*. He mentioned Professor Masson in connection with Ebenezer; a chapter in *Kit Kennedy* tells how the personage representing the eccentric Professor of Greek John Stuart Blackie calls Kit a 'porridge-fed Gallovidian' but relents and begs Kit's pardon when Kit continues to stand in protest. Could this have happened to Sam? It sounds possible. On the whole, however, University life seems to have made as little impression on Sam as he did on the University. He was awarded a Certificate of Merit as 48th equal in the class of Natural Philosophy in session 1878–79 and was Highly Commended for work in the Physics Laboratory.[7] This may show that his interests were not narrowly literary but is hardly brilliance.

There was a reason for this more cogent than the airy-fairy disregard of humdrum learning with which he regaled R H Sherard—the problem of finance. Crockett shared an attic room for a while with his cousin, but they were never close friends; later he shared a room with William MacGeorge, his artistic friend from Castle Douglas:

> we each paid three shillings and sixpence a week for rent, including coal and gas. For breakfast and supper we used to have oatmeal porridge; our dinner never exceeded sixpence each. When I was saving up to buy a book, I would content myself with a penny roll and a glass of milk.[8]

His Bursary of £20 a year—£11 of which went in University fees[9]—was not enough even for this frugal living. During his first year, Sam, like so many other needy students, supplemented his income by coaching. He had three pupils, one near St Mary's Cathedral, another at Leith Links and another beyond Regent Road. He walked from one to the other in the evenings, making £1 a month, then had to return to his attic room and his own studies for the next day. This does not make for scholarship.

It did not satisfy Sam. After the first year, he tried another expedient.

> In the second and following years I did journalistic work, my first contributions, paragraphic reports, soon being printed in the *Edinburgh Daily Review* ... I was so busy, forced as I was to work very hard at journalism, writing anything and everything, and sending articles everywhere. At that time I contributed with

> some regularity to *Lloyd's* and the *Daily Chronicle*. I was also writing verse in those days, contributing to the magazines and to the local papers.[10]

Much of this early verse is said to have appeared in the Dumfries and Castle Douglas newspapers.[11] He even tried art criticism; MacGeorge had induced him to try his hand at water-colours while still at school[12] and no doubt introduced him to art students in Edinburgh.

> I began as art critic for the *Daily Chronicle*. But when I got to know a little about art, I gave it up.[13]

For once there is a becoming humility. But he continued to pour out notes, paragraphs and articles 'on anything and everything'.

Harper comments 'Mr Crockett tells us that he has never been able to write slowly. That if he does so he loses spirit and *verve* and grows dull.'[14] Much of the criticism levelled at his later writing attacks his haste, his signs of hurried composition, and his slapdash style in his stories. This almost frenzied journalistic activity as a student must have created these very faults. Impetuous by temperament, by dashing off quick topical comments or instructive paragraphs of information he must have accentuated his liking to work at top speed. Not only did his journalism divert his attention from serious academic work, it would also make him prone to carelessness. Moreover all his paragraphs, articles and lengthier comments on current affairs were printed anonymously; they brought him an income but no literary reputation.

Crockett does not seem to have worried about this or about the lack of friends, another result of his journalism. He liked solitary activities. One of these, begun at Castle Douglas, he continued enthusiastically—book-collecting.

> All the forenoon I poked from Wynd to Port, and from Bridge to Raw, with a shilling to spend on a book, a pamphlet, or a rare print ... The memory of these 'traipsings'—my landlady's word—were more to me than the University and its Library—more than the Professors and their classes, better than the fellowship of men ... After practising the bookchase for years in Edinburgh, I hold even the quays by the Seine in light esteem, and as for London—there never was anything worth carrying home.[15]

Exaggeration again: one does not pick up the volumes which made up his vast and exotic library with shillings to spend in second-hand book-boxes, even in the 1890s, but his cheerful dismissal of professors and the need for friends is probably near the mark—his miscellaneous journalism absorbed him almost completely. During vacations he went back to Galloway, staying for long periods at Drumbreck where he still read 'omnivorously'—a favourite word—and tried to write.

> I sketched out plays and wrote a *Marie Stuart*—every Scotch fellow does that.

My idea was that Darnley was really a woman. My favourite author at this time was Dumas and I was constantly reading him in translation.[16]

It is a pity that this remarkable *Marie Stuart* is lost to us; Darnley as a woman is ominously bizarre and would make it difficult to account for James VI.

In the summer of 1878 Crockett spent the whole of the six months vacation in London, keeping himself by his writing.[17] It may have been his hope to find permanent employment with some periodical (why did he not look for advertisements like Barrie?) but he returned empty-handed to complete his MA degree in April 1879. Without waiting to graduate formally, he went, it seems, to Oxford: he was in Castle Douglas that autumn when his mother died, then to Oxford again where he made, in some completely unexplained and incomprehensible way, the acquaintance of Dr Jowett, Master of Balliol, and of Vice-Chancellor Bacon.

It is not clear why he went to Oxford, or for how long he stayed, or what he did there. His entry in the 1901 *Who's Who* says that he was educated at Edinburgh, Heidelberg and New College, Oxford; Heidelberg can be accounted for, as we shall see, but he was never enrolled at the Oxford New College or at the University of Oxford at all. The editors may have confused New College, Edinburgh with its older Oxford namesake. But Margaret Oliphant was in Oxford in 1879 and her two sons at Balliol;[18] could he have visited her? Neither party records such a meeting. The Oxford sojourn is shrouded in mystery.

According to Harper,[19] through Jowett and the Vice-Chancellor, Crockett was recommended as a travelling tutor to a rich young American doing a nineteenth century Grand Tour, with letters of recommendation from J R Lowell. Crockett described his journey with relish to Sherard:

> We travelled all over Europe, and, knapsack on back, tramped a long way in Northern Italy. We were travelling for nearly two years—visited Siberia, and sailed from Archangel to Novaia Zembla (sic). While so travelling I wrote poetry, but chiefly, and most copiously, notes and descriptions which I intended to use in a book ... Shortly after my return to England I obtained another tutorship, and this time went to Switzerland, and afterwards to Heidelberg. Altogether, we were abroad for a year, and during that time I wrote many verses. Perhaps one third of my book of poems *Dulce Cor* was written during that year.[20]

The identity of the young American is not known, but the Englishman, Crockett's second charge, was John Bertram Marsden-Smedley, considered too delicate to go to Harrow like his brother and sent instead to the Continent with the tall young Scot. Family tradition among the Marsden-Smedleys agrees that the tutor was a good and abiding influence on the young man, who had lost his father at the age of three; he never forgot their long discussions on religion and philosophy in the evenings after their day's climbing. It may have been with this pupil that Crockett encountered Bismarck.

> My pupil and I were mountaineering in the Tyrol and had climbed the Gross Glockner. When we came down, we learnt that Bismarck was staying in the

> little Tyrol village where we put up. Everyone was talking about the 'mad Englanders' who climbed hills in the winter, and Bismarck sent an *aide* to ask us to call on him, just as we were, ice-axes and all. He was extremely civil, and when he heard that we were thinking of going to Heidelberg to study he gave us a letter of introduction to 'all officials of the German Empire' asking them to do all they could for us. We first proved its efficacy in crossing the frontier into Germany. My pupil was lying ill in our travelling-carriage, and the officer of the guard on the frontier insisted on his turning out and allowing everything to be examined, though it was night. I produced the Chancellor's letter, and it acted like oil on waves, turning the officer's demands into the civilest excuses and the offer of hot coffee and cognac.[21]

There is an ironic twist to the relationship. Delicate young John Marsden-Smedley survived to be the chairman of the family firm, John Smedley Ltd, until he was ninety-three. Miss Joyce Collyer, his nurse and companion during the last twenty years of his life, describes a holiday they spent in Galloway in the summer of 1946 or 1947:

> Mr Marsden-Smedley and I went on a nostalgic tour of the Crockett country. We found his grave, but I regret to say I do not remember where ... I sat reading *The Raiders* amidst the original country. ... I think it must have been a beneficial association and J B M-S always spoke of him with great affection.[22]

Mr Marsden-Smedley outlasted his vigorous companion by almost fifty years, in spite of his delicate health.

These years of travelling (which did not last for as long as Crockett or his interviewer suggest: Crockett was vague and untrustworthy about time) were much to his taste and provided material for many articles and settings for future novels, but travelling tutorships are not stepping-stones to a secure career. Crockett returned to Edinburgh in no way more definite about his intentions. He attended science classes, helped in the arrangement of Professor Tait's museum at New College and worked in his laboratory, but remained undecided.

> My intention, at that time, was to try for a BSC (sic) degree, but I eventually drifted back again into writing. It was an aimless two years, spent in reading, teaching, writing, and, in the summer time, in wandering about Galloway. And I always continued my journalism, more for amusement, as I made plenty of money by tuition.[23]

The feeling of aimlessness, which possibly made the time seem longer in memory than it was, was accentuated by Crockett's making the acquaintance through his writing and reviewing of Mr George Milner of Manchester and, more relevantly, of his third daughter Ruth.

Mr Milner was a Manchester mill-owner who lived with his family at Moston House, then in the countryside near the city. He was a leading philanthropist with a particular interest in Sunday Schools, prosperous, kindly, a typical Victorian amateur naturalist, *littérateur* and public figure, sitting on the boards of hospitals, schools and colleges. He was an authority on Lancashire dialect and for many years was President of the Manchester Literary Club. Crockett may have reviewed favourably some of Mr Milner's writing and was invited to visit Moston House. There he met Ruth and fell in love with the enthusiasm he devoted to all his activities. *Dulce Cor*, his volume of poems,[24] narrates in faded Tennysonian measures the progress of their relationship—Ruth's portrait as *The Lady Beatrice*, done in sepia by William MacGeorge, forms the frontispiece.

Memory Harvest tells how Crockett journeyed to Manchester by train one cold bitter December; the poem is dated 1883.

> From out the dark one gloaming shineth bright,
>   When in Fate's door Love placed his golden key—
>   A dull December day with spurts of hail,
> And fine frost garniture on bush and tree.
>   O'er a white land had raved the southern mail,
>   And now through early night
> The city lights flash past, and all my youth
>   Stirs in my heart to greet one in the hall—
>   A grey-eyed maid, as comely, sweet, and tall
> As in Judean field the gleaner Ruth.[25]

The young writer became an accepted family friend, spending holidays with them in Arran; the two wandered hand in hand, their love presumably declared, although it was marred by partings. Crockett in Edinburgh, he says, will be haunted by Ruth's shadow and the hope of their ultimate union, for God

> ... will not let
> Slip from His hand two lives, that He hath brought
>   Together by strange ways ... [26]

The poems of travel in *Dulce Cor* echo with the sighs of a lover sundered from his lady, longing for the 'mystic union' of loving hearts, yearning for her presence in the High Alps or wherever he finds beauty, hopefully dreaming of the 'hearth-fire' which they will one day share. It is probable, therefore, that when in the autumn of 1881 Crockett brought his aimlessness to an end and entered New College as a divinity student preparing himself for the ministry of the Free Church, it was partly because that settled profession would be eminently secure in the eyes of a future father-in-law, especially one so interested in religion and Sunday Schools.

Yet it would not be fair to regard this as his only motive. He had moved far from the simple Cameronianism of his youth, but he retained enough of its ethos to be able to enter sincerely upon this new vocation, to which his mother had looked forward for him. Ruth would never know his family, but they were all alive in his memory, kindly and beloved, with sufficient strength to make the ministry a welcome answer to his questionings. There is no doubt that there was duality in his nature, and that he was aware of it. Writing in 1891 about Dr Whyte of Free St George's Church, Edinburgh, he could remember the examination of conscience one sermon had called up in him years before.

> 'Yes! Yes!' comes the acknowledgment winched like tooth-drawing from an unwilling heart, fiercely fighting for the lust of the eye and the pride of life, 'that is my very self, I know it, but I cannot—I will not—give it all up; what right has he—' ... As the congregation disperses that young man walks away with a sharp chill in all his veins and a feeling as though the air he breathed had suddenly turned to some rarer medium.
>
> Dimly he heard the people saying about him that the preacher had been very severe that day; but he only knew that never had he been dealt with in this way before, and his soul quailed at being alone with itself.
>
> Yet he took the bare side of Arthur's Seat that night, and the sheets of his lodging-house bed (first floor from the sky) knew him not till the great battle had been fought out, and the lad knew that for good or ill, he could never be the same man who had entered with the easy insolence of youth that left-hand gallery of St George's Church in Edinburgh town.[27]

There is no doubt that this reaction is honest and sincere, even if it be only a passing one. Crockett the divinity student, Crockett the minister, embodied contradiction; he had a relish for the good things of this world, an enjoyment of luxuries, a knowledge of his own power and a desire to use it which, when he thought about these things, were totally unsuited for a Free Church minister. He had known and needed 'let-ups' from his childhood and would go on needing them. Yet his nature was extrovert, finding release in action. He was too energetic a personality to torment himself with long solemn self-examinations such as afflicted the heroes and heroines of C M Yonge and were to afflict those of Mrs Humphrey Ward. It was typical of Crockett that his theological studies at New College were carried on with more seriousness than one would have expected from his University record, but simultaneously with continued journalism and excursions to the Continent, and that during term-time he threw himself into strenuous missionary work in the Edinburgh slums, cheerless, ugly and dangerous, but for all that enjoyable to his optimistic temperament that liked to be doing things.

The ignorance and vice prevalent in industrial slums had prompted the Free Church to make Home Missions one of its pressing concerns, and Edinburgh was foremost in the field.

> The districts chosen for aggressive work were amongst the poorest in the city,— Fountainbridge, the Cowgate, and the Pleasance.[28]

The Pleasance, which derived its cruelly inappropriate name from a convent of St Mary of Placentia which had stood there in mediaeval times, was next to St Leonards where Crockett lodged; he chose to work there. He found himself understanding what drove slum-dwellers to vice and crime; he had known poverty in the country but that of the city was infinitely worse because it denied human dignity. He could face danger and violence because of his height and physical strength; there is no doubt that danger and violence were there. Thomas Cochrane of the Pleasance Territorial Church had worked there in the mid nineteenth century and described it as a 'rookery ... where a missionary dared not enter without the company of a policeman', such were the grim possibilities lying await in those rat-infested alleys of brawls and drunken attacks.[29] In the 1880s conditions were very little better; missionaries still ventured into the Pleasance, armed if not with a policeman at least with a stick. But Crockett saw the brutalising effect their sour and clammy background had on its victims, took their iniquities for granted and even won the confidence of a few, like the suspicious street urchins on whom his tales of Cleg Kelly are based. He talked to them in their own Scots tongue, did not take himself too seriously—and did not distribute tracts.

He has given us in *Cleg Kelly* a hilarious account of himself as a Pleasance missionary—'Big Smith'.

> On this occasion he was addressing his weekly open-air meeting on the ground underneath one of the great houses in the Pleasance. The Knuckle Dusters [a gang of young toughs] thought it good sport to ascend to the window of the common stair, and prepare missiles both fluid and solid. This was because they belonged to the Sooth Back and did not know Big Smith.
>
> Big Smith's mode of exhortation was the prophetic denunciatory. He was no Jeremiah among preachers—a Boanerges of the slums rather. He dealt in warm accusations and vigorous personal applications. He was very decidedly no minor prophet, for he had a black beard like an Astrakhan rug, and a voice that could outroar a Gilmerton carter. Also he was six feet high, and when he crossed his arms it was like a long-range marker trying to fold his arms round the target.
>
> 'Sinners in Number Seventy-Three!' cried Big Smith, and his voice penetrated into every den and corner of that vast rabbit warren, 'You will not come out to hear me, but I'll make ye hear me yet, if I scraich till the Day of Judgment. Sinners in Number Seventy-Three, ye are a desperate bad lot. I hae kenned ye this ten year—but— '
>
> Clash! came a pail of dirty water out of the stair window behind which the Knuckle Dusters, yet completely unregenerate, were concealed.
>
> Big Smith was taking breath for his next overwhelming sentence, but he never got it delivered. For as soon as he realised that the insult was meant for him, Big Smith pushed his hat firmly down on the back of his head, and started up the stair. He had his oak staff in his hand, a stick of fibre and responsibility, as indeed it had need to be.

The tallness, the black beard and the countryman's gesture of settling his hat back on his head ready for battle identify him completely; but most characteristic is the gusto with which he describes his roaring evangelism and his weekly 'open air meeting' to which no one had come or perhaps ever came. He routs the boys as they run down to escape; he joyfully trips them up one after another

> with a foot like a Sutton's furniture van ... till quite a little haycock of Knuckle Dusters was formed at an angle of the stair.
>
> Then Big Smith, in a singularly able-bodied way, argued with the heap in

general for the good of their souls; and the noise of the oak stick brought out all the neighbours to look on with voluble approbation ...

'Lay on till them, Maister Smith!—bringin' disgrace on oor decent stair,' cried a hodman's wife from the top landing, looking over with her brush in her hand ...

'It'll learn them no to meddle wi' oor missionary,' they said, as they retired to drink the syrup, which had been stewing on the hearth since morning ... The Pleasance was naturally proud of its missionary, and offered long odds on him as against any evangelist in the town. 'He could lick them a' wi' his hand tied ahint his back,' said the Pleasance in its wholly reasonable pride.[30]

In 'Big Smith' are traces of the boy who could 'fecht' and punched his cronies until they agreed to read the Waverley novels, but there is also a likeable lack of illusion about his own efficacy as a saver of souls. His value to the Pleasance was as a free entertainment; they take bets on his ability to fight other missionaries; they retire to drink their stewed tea serene in their self-approving sinfulness, and Crockett knows all this, and writes of it with ironic amusement, knowing that he is making little impression of the 'decent stair' and that the impression he does make is not the one a mission worker would have hoped for. Yet the scenes he presents in *Cleg Kelly* and *Kid McGhie* have an underlying anger beneath the reality; he took to heart the plight of the poor in Christian middle-class Edinburgh and was what the 1980s would call a 'caring' person.

Part of his ability to be detached enough to see the comic side of his missionary labours came from his wider experience. Several of his contemporaries at New College have commented that he was no ordinary lad up from the country; he had seen much of the world and had acquired a certain degree of sophistication.

> When Mr Crockett came to the New College, Edinburgh, as a student of theology, writes one of his fellow-students, 'he was a stranger to his fellow-students as much as to the professors. He lived a life of his own, devoting more time to hack literary work than to college exercises. He had obtained a connection with the London Press, and practically maintained himself from the proceeds of his daily paragraphs. He rarely had any time to spare to mingle with his fellow-students. To all save his few intimates he appeared to be a man who took his studies too easily, and whose bill for the students' midnight oil must have been very small indeed. But he was at work early and late to find the means necessary to support him during his college courses. Dr Walter C Smith was his minister, and with him he formed a lasting friendship.'[31]

Crockett improved his name during his years as a divinity student. He signed the New College Enrolment Book in 1881 as plain Samuel Crocket as he had been born. In 1882 he is still Samuel Crocket but in 1883 he is a tentative Samuel R Crockett. In 1884 he was abroad and did not sign at all, but in 1885, the beginning of his final year, he is S Rutherford Crockett. Even such a trifling change suggests that he had felt a growth of confidence, a movement towards literary as opposed to mere journalistic writing. 'Rutherford' points back to Samuel Rutherford, the Covenanting saint of Anwoth, near Gatehouse of Fleet; the whole name has a fine man-of-letters ring to it, like the names of William Robertson Nicoll and Robert Louis Stevenson.

And he could not have been entirely solitary. In October 1882 he wrote to the American Quaker poet John Greenleaf Whittier expressing admiration for his poems and telling him that in distant Edinburgh he has appreciative readers:

> Here live seven of us students of God's Word and human wisdom, and every heart of us warms at the mention of your name.[32]

Whittier replied and for a while the two corresponded, though the letters have not survived. Who were the other six students so fervent in admiration for the aged American sage?—or was Crockett inventing them to make the admiration more pleasing to its recipient? There is a reference in the same letter to 'a long illness ... from which I have recovered by the blessing of God'. Robertson Nicoll's obituary of Crockett in the *British Weekly*[33] mentions the dark shadow of an illness which hung over him but was mercifully dispelled. Was Crockett perhaps threatened with the tuberculosis which had carried off so many of his relatives? And did this illness contribute to the vividness of his depiction of the Stickit Minister's discovery of his condition? It is significant that health should have troubled so early in life a man who to all outward appearance seemed a giant of strength and physical wellbeing.

Vacations were spent abroad, or in Galloway, or with the Milners in Arran, or with relatives in Dumfriesshire, descendants of his grandfather's elder sister Christian Crocket. Her daughter Margaret had married Edward Smith of Netherholm, a prosperous farm in the parish of Kirkmahoe of 216 acres. They lived in what amounted to a mansion compared with Little Duchrae or even Drumbreck, employed four indoor servants, seven outdoor labourers and a boy. They kept their own carriage and a coachman to drive it. Although members of the Established Church, they made the young Free Church student welcome; he spent happy weeks at Netherholm, enjoying the green meadows and lush countryside of Nithsdale.[34] Dumfries he liked in spite of the 'raw beef sandstone' of its villas[35]; it was near the green braes of Cluden and Cargen, the parish of Irongray from which his grandparents had come, and Sweetheart Abbey down near the Solway was to give the title to his book of poems, *Dulce Cor*.

The company he kept in Dumfriesshire was more varied and cultured than his Galloway kin. The Smiths had eleven children, some older, some younger than Crockett. One son was a doctor in Dumfries, living in professional and exclusive Castle Street. Another was a bank manager. One daughter had married first a schoolmaster and, after his death, the local solicitor and Registrar. They had an assured and comfortable place in the community and could add polish to his manners. In 1885 another link with Kirkmahoe was added; his aunt Jessie, the youngest of the Drumbreck family, a teacher, married the Free Church minister of the parish; as a young minister Crockett was occasionally to preach there for his cousin-by-marriage, the Rev William McDowall.

A daughter of Mr McDowall by a second marriage remembered a local tale about Crockett.

> I know SRC and Smith were seeing Mrs Crawford (née Smith) home to Gallaberry along the back road in front of Carzield when a 'ghost' appeared. SRC and Smith took Mrs Crawford home and on the way back waylaid the 'ghost' and thrashed it. The ghost was dressed in white sheets. The next day a quarryman in the village could not go to his work in Locharbriggs Quarry, and ever since that road has been known as 'the Bogey loaning'.[36]

In 'A Midsummer Idyll', one of the stories in *The Stickit Minister*, this incident is reproduced; Crockett draws on his own experience and is still 'fechting'.

In 1886 he completed his course at New College, and marked the occasion by a brief poem in pamphlet form, *Valete Fratres*, dedicated to his fellow students 'by the author of *Dulce Cor*', and published by David Douglas, Edinburgh. It bids farewell to the collegiate halls,

> ... our prison-house
> Of pleasant prisoners ...

and rejoices that he and his fellows were now free to enter upon their careers and go their ways,

> ... flying
> Far upon the winds or waiting with
> The good seed for sowing in good soil.

Crockett did not fly very far; he went to the Free Abbey Church in Dunfermline as assistant to the minister there.

In the meantime, members of the Free Church in Penicuik, Midlothian, were having trouble in choosing a new minister.

> When the Rev H A Stewart resigned his charge of the Free Church in 1885, there were over forty applications for the vacancy, many of whom preached to the congregation. Considerable diversity of opinion as to the merits of the various candidates existed for a time, but at the last moment the name of Mr Samuel Rutherford Crockett, who was not one of the candidates, was put forward and at a congregational meeting, held on 11th October 1886, it was evident that the preponderance of feeling was in his favour. Mr Crockett had been licensed a few months, and was acting as temporary assistant to the Rev Mr Shiach of the Free Abbey Church, Dunfermline. He had the most favourable recommendation not only from prominent office-bearers of the congregation but also from such eminent leaders of the church as Dr Rainy and Dr Whyte.[37]

Dr Rainy was Principal of New College and Dr Whyte the revered minister of Free St George's in Edinburgh; Crockett in spite of his journalism had clearly made a favourable impression if two such men sponsored him.

The call from Penicuik was unanimous—perhaps the thought of all those trial sermons contributed to agreement—and in November 1886 he was inducted to the charge. The Free Church in Penicuik—now the South Church—is a creation of the Gothic Revival architect Pilkington, who also designed the Barclay Church in Edinburgh. Squatting strong and lowering, with an abundance of carved leaves and fruit above heavy arches guarding its entrance porch, it shows his originality but lacks a spire. The Barclay Church has a spire but its capitals are incomplete, and it has one half-finished angel. The architect's vision of his creation had exceeded the finances of both churches.

The text of Crockett's first sermon in Penicuik was 'Who is on the Lord's side, let him come unto me'. Exodus 32:26. In his address, 'my first words as your minister' he declared that 'the disease of which the Church of Christ is sick is indifference. Indifference is more abhorred by God than open enmity'.[38] Both as man and minister, Crockett had many weaknesses but indifference was never among them. He could not have chosen a more appropriate theme.

As one would have expected, his establishment in the Free Church Manse in West Street was followed within a few months by his marriage to Ruth Mary Milner at the parish church of Harpurhey in Lancashire on 10 March 1887, Crockett giving as his father's name on the marriage certificate 'David Crockett, farmer', an inexactitude for which he may be forgiven, surrounded as he was by Milners and their kin. The couple went to the Continent for their 'marriage Tour' of six or seven weeks, during which Crockett was no doubt able to introduce Ruth to many of the beauty-spots in which he had poetically lamented her absence. Thereafter they returned to their longed-for 'hearth-fire' in the Manse and began their married life under the happiest of auspices and with the good wishes of all.

CHAPTER 3

Minister to Writer

As a young minister in his first and as it happened his only charge, Crockett was a whirlwind of activity. In addition to the normal ministerial duties of preaching, prayer meetings and regular pastoral visiting, he began programmes of extra-ministerial activities, as if he were bursting with ideas which he must share with as many as he could persuade to listen.

He instituted a course of Tuesday evening lectures in Valleyfield School in which he took his audiences through the first dozen books of the Old Testament, commenting on their content as religious history and their style as literature.

> One read the finest English in the Bible, the worst in the newspaper. He (Mr Crockett) knew that for he used to write it himself.[1]

So reported R E Black, the local newspaper correspondent, passing over the sweeping condemnation for the sake of the lively remark.

Crockett likewise began a series of 'Free Church Weekly Lectures' on Friday evenings during the winter of 1887; he himself spoke on 'Alpine Mountaineering' to start the course, which was to raise money for a Bible Class Library. Other speakers were Mr Dickson of the Ben Nevis Observatory who discoursed on 'Weather', Crockett himself on 'The Geology of Scotland' and J A Thomson, lecturer in geology at Edinburgh University on 'Shifts for a Living among the Lower Animals'.

By February 1889 the *Christian Leader* was able to report approvingly on this Free Church phenomenon, six feet three inches tall, poet, traveller, raconteur, with thick auburn hair, blue eyes and limitless energy.

> Having an ardent and genial temperament he has the faculty of making and keeping friends, especially in literary circles, and the special favour and honour is his of having as a regular correspondent his gifted and versatile countryman Robert Louis Stevenson ... At Penicuik ... he has been instrumental in infusing new life into the various departments of congregational activity, and has added over 100 members to the roll.
>
> This winter's syllabus shows an extraordinary amount of work, especially among young men and women. Besides a senior Bible Class with a membership of 127 and a junior class with 91 members, there are classes meeting weekly for the study of English literature, geology, English history, all conducted by himself. One criticism of the syllabus made by a Free Church minister was that

there was 'little of the Gospel in it', but it would be a pity to suppose that Mr Crockett is lacking in evangelical fervour.

Mission work is being vigorously carried on, especially in the out-lying districts of the town among the mining population; and the mission schools as well as the congregational Sabbath schools secure a share of his attention and help. A good preacher, he is like nearly all who have the poetic instinct a little unequal in the pulpit, but his powers in that direction are undoubtedly developing.[2]

With regard to his appearance, the *Leader* had been less than flattering the previous week:

Mr Crockett of Penicuik conducted the services in the McCrie-Roxburgh church last Sabbath and gave much satisfaction, especially in the morning. His head from the eyes upward strongly resembles Mr McNeill's but his cheeks are larger. The Scottish Spurgeon with an incipient gumboil might be taken for Mr Crockett.[3]

His preaching style was unconventional; he talked eagerly, holding on to his lapels with both hands. He liked to stride up and down as he talked and found the pulpit constricting so he not only dispensed with his gown but had the pulpit replaced by a platform which gave him the space he liked.[4]

Stevenson and Crockett never met but their friendship flourished through letters. Crockett began it. He sent Stevenson a copy of *Dulce Cor* and a separate letter to say he had done so, using the elegantly looping signature he had developed for himself just as he had improved his name into Samuel Rutherford Crockett. In the spring of 1888 Stevenson wrote from Saranac Lake lamenting that the book had never arrived, in a letter which began

DEAR MINISTER OF THE FREE KIRK AT PENICUIK,—for O, man, I cannae read your name![5]

This was a good start for writers who had the same boyish delight in the ridiculous. For Stevenson there was the nostalgic attraction that Penicuik was near his beloved Glencorse. Writing from Vailima in 1893, Stevenson asked a favour of Crockett.

Do you know where the road crosses the burn under Glencorse Church? Go there, and say a prayer for me: *moriturus salutat*. See that it's a sunny day; I would like it to be a Sunday, but that's not possible in the premises; and stand on the right-hand bank just where the road goes down into the water, and shut your eyes, and if I don't appear to you! Well, it can't be helped, and will be extremely funny.[6]

Crockett was proud of the correspondence and derived, he says, much good from Stevenson's advice—none of it could have been better than the letter which said firmly 'Write ... my Timothy no longer verse, but use good Galloway Scots for your stomach's sake—and mine'.[7] What better service could Stevenson have done for his friend than divert him away from the feebly derivative verses of *Dulce Cor* towards the fresh nervous strong prose in which he could write with originality and his own voice, in Scots and English? Unfortunately, most of Stevenson's letters were lost in the removal from one house to another,[8] probably from Penicuik to Peebles, and only a few survive in Colvin's collected edition.

In 1889 Crockett lectured on Stevenson at a public meeting in Penicuik Town Hall, singling out Stevenson's eagerness, the quality which he and Stevenson shared and had liked in one another. Courses of lectures for the congregation continued. The year 1891 brought to the Bible Class a series on the Bible—the Bible as History, The Bible as Philosophy, the Bible as Science, and the Unity of the Bible. Crockett added for good measure one on 'Jewish History as a Key to our Own' and another on the light shed on the Old Testament by the discovery of the embalmed bodies of the Pharaohs in Egypt.

A talk on Tennyson (who, it was reported in the *British Weekly* in February 1887 had commented favourably on *Dulce Cor*, as well he might) was followed by others on the religious faith of various literary figures; listeners were whisked through the beliefs of Bunyan, Longfellow, Scott, Burns, Carlyle, Browning and Whittier, Crockett crowning the last with readings from letters he had received from the American poet—these too seem to have disappeared.

In addition to all these, Crockett maintained his preaching duties, presided at soirées and socials, held evangelical meetings for the miners at the Townsend and Valleyfield missions and made regular visits to his flock in their homes; one must know one's people. Occasionally he preached or gave talks for Dr Whyte of Free St George's, Edinburgh; Dr Whyte had been one of his sponsors and had a considerable influence upon him. As a student he had been moved by Dr Whyte's strong but compassionate sermons; as a minister, Dr Whyte's programmes of half-religious, half-literary lectures to his well-known Young Men's and Young Women's Bible Classes must have been in his mind as models for his own similar courses in Penicuik.

Dr Whyte had a broad catholicity of interests. His 1923 biographer G F Barbour says that his broadness and tolerance sometimes aroused protest among more conservative Free Church members since he chose new and not necessarily Presbyterian subjects. He rejoiced in the truth wherever it was found. He was a friend and admirer of Cardinal Newman and wrote of him appreciatively. In the 1870s he gave lectures on Dante, whose soaring imagination must have stretched the minds of his audiences. He lectured on such men as St Augustine, Socrates, Erasmus and the English mystic William Law; he admired mystics like St Teresa, Thomas à Kempis, Bishop Andrews and Father John of Kronstadt and authors like Sir Thomas Browne. He prayed for Christian unity in its most liberal sense and was a friend of George MacDonald, the Scottish novelist who was too universal in his Christianity for any one church to hold.

This encouraged Crockett, already interested in so many things beyond the everyday scope of a minister's parish work, to draw on his own experience and his own reading to make his sermons penetrating and his lectures direct expressions of his own beliefs. He loved nature; at St George's on 4 May 1893 he talked on 'Some Evangelists of Nature and their Gospel', finding in Ruskin the love of nature which was the love of God. This was followed on 24 September 1893 by 'The Gospel in Richard Jefferies'; nature was God and God nature. On 24 December 1893 he talked on 'Jesus the Observer', pointing out how Christ in His deepest meditations is wholly out of doors and uses ears of wheat and seeds sown by the roadside to illustrate His teaching.

> I never saw in Eastern land a dreamy, dark-faced boy leaning upon the lintel of a doorpost, looking on the broad glow of the sun on the fields, or watching the shadows creep across the plain, without thinking that in him I saw Jesus of Nazareth at the door of the carpenter's shop, when a halt was called from work, and His mother in the little living-room was preparing the evening meal ...

This technique—more than a technique, an imaginative sharing of personal experience of the Divine—he learned from Dr Whyte. These and other of his talks were printed as they were given in the *Christian Leader*—the wider audience he had hoped for in his writing.

In 1892 the *Leader* reports that

> Mr S R Crockett of Penicuik has been evangelising for three weeks in England, and his mission closes this week. He has been addressing meetings in Keswick, Bolton, Liverpool and in Southport, and also in Castle Douglas.[9]

Crockett enjoyed these invigorating excursions. He declared that there was nothing better for a settled minister, growing stale after a winter's work, than to take to the road.[10] He could attach himself to an organised evangelical group or simply set out on his bicycle and draw his hearers from wherever he found them. It may have been on one of these expeditions that Dr W Robertson Nicoll first saw Crockett

> in the pulpit of a Presbyterian Church at Hampstead. He was then vaguely known as a Free Church minister with literary ambitions and capacities ... The only sign of a literary man perceptible in the sermon was a beautiful quotation from Ruskin.[11]

Robertson Nicoll, though not impressed by Crockett as a preacher, would keep him in mind as a potential protégé, just as later he seized upon the Rev John Watson and turned him into Ian Maclaren.

In 1892 also Crockett introduced his congregation to the magic lantern, one borrowed from Glasgow; he loved mechanical gadgets. Slides were shown of The Prodigal Son, a favourite subject, with comments from himself and songs and solos from Mrs Crockett and the choir. A series of other slide-shows followed—an illustrated talk by Crockett on the Emir Pasha expedition, in the Town Hall, a talk on Scotland 'Land of the Mountain and the Flood' and another on 'A Tour to the Holy Land' given by Crockett and accompanied by slides made from his own photographs. The church later got its own lantern.

A particular *tour-de-force* came in his talk 'From Penicuik to London', illustrated once more by his own slides, in the Town Hall.

> The views in the first part had a strictly local interest, comprising scenes about Penicuik and views of the streets as well as a number of well-known faces, all of which were loudly applauded as they appeared on the screen. The scenes were pithily described by J J Wilson, Penicuik's local historian, who gave a short and pointed historical sketch of the district as seen on the pictures. Mrs Crockett gave a most delightful song—Dae ye ken Penicuik?—which was repeated over and over again by the audience. Mr Crockett then went on with the Journey to London, Mr W G Brown ably managing the lantern.[12]

This kind of informal entertainment to Penicuik's mixed population of miners, workers in the paper mills, iron-workers, church members and shopkeepers goes far to explain Crockett's popularity; he probably made up the song himself to the tune of 'D'ye ken John Peel'. Friendly, athletic, willing to talk to anyone—in broad Scots if that were appropriate—and ready to help from his own pocket those most in need, he was a likeable personality.

> 'He's a gran' man Mr Crockett' declared one of his flock, 'an' he's weel liked hereaboots. He often comes into ma hoose, sits doon beside me, an' cracks awa', speerin' hoo I'm gettin' on, an' askin' if I've read a' the books he's lent me. He's no yin o' the kind that's eye spoutin' aboot religion, but he always acts up to it, oot an' oot.'[13]

He never stood on his dignity as a minister because he never felt any special dignity in himself which could come between him and those to whom he ministered. Even in his dress he seemed to be trying to make no distinction between himself and ordinary men.

> The first time we saw him was on a day of stir and noise in the General Asssembly, when the mob of young divines was crowding back into the house after a division; rising half a head above the crowd was the author of 'Dulce Cor', as different from his neighbour ministers as from the conventional amatory poet, a proper man, with fresh colour telling of country breeding and large easy movement, not like a country elder either, who would have laid off those grey tweeds and donned the careful black to do honour to Edinburgh and her Assembly—a man not easily classified, but fit for manifold work and much enjoyment.[14]

'Manifold work and much enjoyment': that sums it up, and for Crockett the two were the same.

In *The Cairn Edward Church Militant* he describes a minister like himself who insists on wearing knickerbockers, riding a bicycle and doing as he pleases in spite of complaints, though when the 'scaffie's wife' asks him, he goes home, gets into his blacks and brings his pulpit robe and bands to christen her baby—there never was such a christening. There is a drunken fight between two notorious sinners, and oot of the grund there raise a great muckle man in grey claes, and took fechtin' McKelvie an' me by the scruff o' the neck, and dauded oor heids thegither till we saw a guano-bag fu' o' stars.

'Noo will ye shake hands or come to the lock-up?' says he. We thocht he maun be the chief o' a' the chief constables, an' we didna want to gang to nae lock-ups, so we just shook haun's freendly-like. Then he sent a' them that was lookin' on awa' wi' a flee in their lugs.

'Forty men,' says he, 'an' feared to stop two' men fechtin'—cowards or brutes, either o' the twa'!' says he.[15]

This sounds very like Crockett, fechting again.

In darker times, he entered into Penicuik's sorrows. When the Mauricewood pit disaster in 1889 claimed the lives of sixty-three men and boys, he and his workers in the mission areas comforted the bereaved, providing winding sheets for the dead and daily necessities for the living. On the Sunday after the mass funerals, sermons were preached in local pulpits about the little town's loss. In the *Scotsman* reports on the Monday, Crockett's words stand out for their grief and for a note of anger that such a calamity should not have been foreseen and provided for—that there should have been no second exit for the miners' escape. In Penicuik Free Church,

> In the midst of the universal grief, he said, they, as a congregation, had more cause for it than any, for no other religious body had closer ties with the bereaved, and it was upon them and upon their Fieldsend mission that the heavy end of the work must fall. There were few houses in the stricken districts where they did not bless the work which the mission had carried out and even in their deepest sorrow they could catch a glimpse of a future blessing through that great calamity.
>
> The printed list of the dead which he held in his hand was the emblem of a world of desperate grief and grim suffering, but would there not be good fruit from that bitter flower if the law, or the administration of the law, became so strict that never more, legally or illegally, would more than half a hundred men be left to die with no chance of safety, without even a Man's poor consolation of a fight for life and wife and little ones?
>
> God forbid that they prejudge or apportion blame on insufficient knowledge. There might be no blame, but the hard fact remained that these men died because there was no other way to life save that which was barred by fire and deadly vapour—no other way to reach the air save that which a repeated accident made impossible.
>
> He would impresss upon them that these terrible and extra-ordinary risks must cease, and that the inspection of the mines must be a much more frequent and real thing. If the Mauricewood disaster did nothing else it would at least make that certain, for he knew that that question would assuredly be brought to the front in the highest councils of the nation.[16]

Crockett has not merely gone to comfort the sorrowing in a professional capacity but has listened to the talk in the rows of miners' cottages, has questioned the survivors and heard the bitter grievances they have felt for a long time about lack of safety measures. He is not afraid to speak out on their behalf, using his pulpit to express their indignation and his own.

This mining disaster lay heavily in Crockett's memory. He used his recollection of it in a short story 'The Respect of Drowdle' in which a young minister makes his way down 'the second exit' although it was blocked with steam pipes and brings up two boys through the fire and fumes to show that escape is possible.

> The minister sat in the cage with a couple of boys in his arms. The rough wet brattice cloths that had been placed over them were charred almost to a cinder. Dairsie Gordon's face was burnt and blackened.
> He handed the boys out into careful hands.
> 'I am going down again,' he said; 'unless I do the men will not believe that it is possible to come alive through the fire. Are you ready, Walter? Let her go!'
> So a second time the young minister went down through the furnace. Presently the men began to be whisked up through the fire, and as each relay arrived at the pit-bank they sang the praises of Dairsie Gordon, telling with Homeric zest how he had crawled half-roasted down the narrow throat of the steam-pipe-filled shaft, how he had argued with them that the fire could be passed, and at last proved it with two boys as volunteers. Dairsie Gordon, BD, was the last man to leave the pit, and he fainted with pain and excitement when all Drowdle cheered him as they carried him home to his mother.[17]

The description shows that Crockett too, as part of his duty as missionary to a mining community (and to satisfy his endless curiosity about how things work) had gone down a mine to learn what it was like, what the technical terms were and what were their dangers. The story is given a happier ending than Mauricewood but has Crockett's wry realism; the respect of Drowdle for a minister whom they had regarded, with reason, as a mere 'mother's boy', a milksop, is won not by his theology or his eloquent preaching but by his selfless courage. Example, not fine words, is what counts.

In 1894 Crockett was invited to contribute to a Christian Socialist publication, *Vox Clamantium*; he wrote for it a short story describing a mine disaster and castigating greedy mine owners and managers whose sole interest was their profits.[18] Still later, in *Vida*[19] published in 1907, he used his memory of Mauricewood as part of the plot; the lack of a second exit is again stressed, though the cause of the fire is wildly sensational.

Busy with all his ministerial duties, it is remarkable that he found time to continue his free-lance writing. He rose early in the morning at five o'clock as he had done at Little Duchrae and as Scott had done at Abbotsford and wrote quickly, sometimes by typewriter, so as to have his writing finished before breakfast at nine, when his work as a minister commenced. He edited and probably contributed much of the material to a periodical for Sunday School teachers, *The Workers' Monthly*,[20] thriftily reprinting many of his talks to the Bible Class and the congregation; he commented on current church affairs, directed his readers' attention to books, devised competitions for children which would make them explore the Bible for answers, and used his own photographs to illustrate a series written by himself on the Holy Land. One of his more personal articles was 'Stray Memories of a Galloway Farm'.

He contributed most copiously to the *Christian Leader*, a Glasgow penny weekly funded in 1882 and edited by the Rev W Howie Wylie. His contributions were unsigned, but we know from a book of cuttings pasted into a notebook by Crockett himself, that he wrote some of the 'Penportraits of Eminent Divines'[21] which ran intermittently in it. Among them were portraits of ministers he had known personally, including Dr Rainy, Dr Whyte, and Canon H D Rawnsley of Crossthwaite, pioneer of conservation in the Lake District, whom he had met at the Keswick Convention, on which there is also a descriptive article. Robertson Nicoll described Crockett's pen-portraits as 'frank and penetrating studies'.[22] Some were perhaps too frank; the minister of Liberton wrote protesting against his remarks about Principal Rainy's inaudible prayers; this too is pasted into the notebook of cuttings—Crockett was not too disturbed by his critic.

The contributions of most interest are those called 'The Ministers of Our Countryside' and 'Congregational Sketches'. He tells Sherard exactly how they began, at the same time as the sober religious articles which he was turning out regularly.

> At the same time I wrote sketches and stories which I thought might come to something, and kept these lying by me. It was in this way that the first half of *The Lilac Sunbonnet* was written. At that time I was also writing editorials on theological subjects for religious periodicals, and one day the editor of *The Christian Leader* wrote to me and asked me to send him an editorial which was wanted at once. I had no time to write one, and I told him so, but at the same time I sent him one of the sketches which I had in my drawer, and asked him if he could use that instead. It was the story called 'A Day in the Life of the Reverend James Pitbye', which is in *The Stickit Minister*.
>
> I didn't think that the editor would use it. However, he wrote me: 'Never send me anything else.' So I continued writing him these sketches, and they met with a great deal of appreciation, and were widely copied into the papers, especially in Canada and Australia. Almost all the tales in *The Stickit Minister* appeared in this way in *The Christian Leader*. I used to get as much as a guinea apiece for them.[23]

It is little wonder that Crockett did not altogether expect the editor of the *Leader* to use his sketch of the Rev James Pitbye, for it deals, in the sarcastic Galloway Scots of a disillusioned elder, with a minister who is lazy and bone-idle, spending his day eating his meals, smoking his pipe, reading the *Scotsman*, talking to any passers-by and retreating every afternoon to prepare his sermon in the study with the blinds drawn.

> 'For twa 'oor he works hard there,' declares the narrator, 'an' disna like to be disturbit nayther, for yince afore we fell oot, when I gaed to see him aboot some sma' maitter, the lass pit me in raither sharp, an' the sofa gied an awfu' *girg*, an' there sat the minister on's ain study chair, blinkin' an' no' weel pleased, like a hoolet, at bein' disturbit at the studyin'.'[24]

When one turns to the sober pages of the *Christian Leader* in the early 1890s full of douce respectable improving contents, one can appreciate the freshness and originality of Crockett's sketches, presented within the framework of a pseudonymous 'Saunders McQuhirr of Drumquat'. The lively biting sketches of country parishes, parishioners and ministers leap out of the page at the reader from among the worthy but not especially exciting News of the Churches, Temperance Notes, reprinted sermons, obituaries of ministers and missionaries, reviews of books on the Hittites and pious poems on subjects ranging from 'Bluebells' to 'The Second Coming'. A 'Minister of Our Countryside' became a regular feature, often given pride of place on the front outside page. October 1891 saw the opening chapter of a serial *A Galloway Herd* 'By the Author of "Ministers of Our Countryside"'; after this the Ministers appeared intermittently while the serial ran, interspersed with a new series, *Congregational Sketches* 'by the Author of "Ministers of Our Countryside", "A Galloway Herd", etc'. As Crockett's contributions to the *Pen-Portraits of Eminent Divines* came at the same time, one wonders whether in the last years of the Rev Howie Wylie's life and the first of his son's editorship, Crockett may have carried most of the literary side of the *Leader* on his own shoulders—and when he found time to write his sermons.

Another series, *The New Naturalists*, addressed to young readers, sprang from his interest in birds and the countryside. It was not necessary to be scientific to study nature; patience and sharp eyes were what were needed. Books were suggested for consultation and amateur naturalists were advised not to mind the weather but wait quietly and watch. The series gradually became lighter and more anecdotal—the writer has watched jackdaws nest and bring up their young among the brewery chimneys in St Leonards—and slid into stories of the author and his small daughter 'Sweetheart' travelling, observing and talking to one another about what they saw.

Literary Vignettes made its way through a list of authors which the Bible Class and the Free Church at Penicuik would have recognised—Longfellow, Burns, Browning, Whitman, Carlyle, Tennyson, Whittier, George MacDonald; Crockett was never averse to using his material twice, like ministers with sermons. *Laureates of Labour* shows his sympathy with working-class people; it is a very mixed bag, beginning with 'William Morris, Socialist, Poet and Writer' and working its way through 'Alexander Anderson, the *Surfaceman* Poet' (remembered today for 'Cuddle Doon', not for the 'Songs of the Rail' which Crockett had in mind), James Thomson's 'City of Dreadful Night', 'Ebenezer Elliott, Corn Law Rhymer and Poet of the Poor', to dwindle away into very minor versifiers forgotten today and perhaps forgotten in Crockett's time until he disinterred them—who was 'Shipsey the Poet of the Pitfolk'?

Meanwhile, back in Hampstead, William Robertson Nicoll had been taking note. He knew who was the 'Author of Ministers of Our Countryside, A Galloway Herd, Congregational Sketches, etc'; few things escaped him. With a keen eye for the market, he suggested to Crockett (as Crockett tells R H Sherard in his interview) that he gather together a selection of his stories and sketches and offer them to T Fisher Unwin. Twenty-four of them, under the title *The Stickit Minister*, were collected and published on 20 March 1893 and revealed to the readers of the *Christian Leader* that the author of all these things was the Rev S R Crockett of the Free Church, Penicuik, and to a wider world that a new talent had arrived for their entertainment. The book was immediately successful—extravagantly successful, too much so for Crockett's good; it was greeted with enthusiastic uncritical praise. Its author became famous overnight.

Its appearance was timely. The public in the nineties craved above all novelty. The great figures of the Victorian era were nearly all dead. The sense of high purpose which had informed serious literature had relaxed. Thomas Hardy was at his peak; Henry James firmly established on both sides of the Atlantic; but neither of them was remarkably entertaining for the ordinary reader. Stevenson was to die the next year with *Weir of Hermiston* uncompleted. A new kind of 'popular author' was in demand, created by the many magazines with short stories catering for travellers on the rapidly expanding railway services. John Buchan summed up the situation well in the *Glasgow Herald* in 1895:

> In a time when the prosperity of a country is considerable, when no great war is on hand, when no burning questions, social or religious, are stirring its heart and bringing to view hidden powers or hidden weakness, when no writers of surpassing greatness are among us, it is no more than natural that the heart of the people should go after strange gods, and our younger writers vie with one another in seeking for the odd, and, when found, proclaiming its magnitude.[25]

People wanted to be 'taken out of themselves' by light, clever, exciting but not demanding fiction, and they were provided with what they wanted by Anthony Hope, Arthur Conan Doyle, H Rider Haggard, Max Pemberton, F Marion Crawford, H G Wells, Rudyard Kipling, H Seton Merriman, Stanley Weyman—not all of the same quality but serving the same public.

The 'Scotch' stories of J M Barrie were part of this proliferating new fiction. Thrums was 'different', its men and women articulate in their own terse vivid way and their communities and values a world away even in church-going from Trollope's Barchester and Mrs Oliphant's Carlingford. The English-speaking world was charmed. And with Crockett came more of these stories from an unfamiliar area of Scotland, belonging to the same tradition as Barrie but adding the freshness of Galloway, its hills and lochs and white-washed cottages, and an author who could be both astringent and moving in a way distinct from Barrie.

The *Christian Leader* welcomed the fame its contributor had achieved and reprinted in April 1893 the *Daily Chronicle* review which had hailed a 'New Scottish Master' and had remarked, with great acumen, that not Barrie but Bret Harte was Crockett's closest parallel. From now on, some of his work began to appear over his signature and his lectures for Free St George's were reported. On 14 June 1893 came the old *Workers' Monthly* essay 'Stray Memories of a Galloway Farm.' 'A Summer Day in Ap Jones Land by R M and S R Crockett' appeared on 3 August; Crockett and his wife had been in Wales. Later the same month readers were offered three signed articles by Crockett

2   The Rev S R Crockett in the year of publication of *The Stickit Minister*.

on aspects of Whittier, one after another; his enthusiasm had not been exhausted by the anonymous 'Personal Reminiscences of John Greenleaf Whittier' contributed by Crockett in September 1892 to mark the poet's death.

In the third of the signed articles, 'Whittier on Nature and Love'[26] Crockett quotes one stanza from a personal poem 'Memories' in which the poet in old age, the 'Indian Summer of the Heart', looks back to a lovely hazel-eyed girl he had loved in his youth but whose life and beliefs had moved far from those they had shared together:

> Thine the Genevan's sternest creed,
> While answers to my spirit's need
>   The Derby Dalesman's simple truth.
> For thee, the priestly rite and prayer,
>   And holy day, and solemn psalm;
> For me, the silent reverence where
>   My brethren gather, slow and calm.[27]

The 'Derby Dalesman' was George Fox, founder of the Society of Friends whose first recorded meeting was in Derby and whose nickname 'Quakers' was given them by a judge in that county. The Free Church could not be said to have much elaborate 'priestly rite' but its creed was stern and solemn; this verse with its rejection of Calvinism in favour of Quaker quiet and calm is not what one would have expected a Free Church minister to have singled out.

On 1 May 1894 Crockett was the Guest of Honour at a meeting of the Pen and Pencil Club of Edinburgh, the toast of 'Our Guest' being proposed by Professor David Masson and the printed menu card including a portrait of Crockett, scenes of Galloway, a sketch of Cleg Kelly, and a poem by Alexander Anderson in praise of *The Raiders*,[28] Crockett's story of adventure in eighteenth century Galloway, published by this time and almost all copies sold out on the day of issue.[29]

By August 1893 the eighth illustrated 'de luxe' edition of *The Stickit Minister* was in the press, lavishly illustrated by artists in their different styles; they gave their services without any charge to honour the new author. It also carried a facsimile of Stevenson's poem 'To S R Crockett' which had been inspired by the rhythm of Crockett's dedication to him as one who knew

> that grey Galloway land
> where about the graves of the martyrs
>   the whaups are crying—
> his heart remembers how.

By one of those comic twists with which literary history is fraught, the dedication as Crockett had originally written it and as it appears in the first edition of *The Stickit Minister* has as its final line

> his heart has not forgotten how

which seems well enough. It was Robertson Nicoll who declared that it would not do and insisted that it be changed to 'his heart remembers how' in all future editions; Stevenson must have been sent an amended one. Nicoll relates this in his obituary article on Crockett.[30] It is unlikely that over the years he had been reflecting glumly that the poem by rights should have been addressed 'To W Robertson Nicoll', but an obituary is an odd place to reveal such a trifling incident.

Two shorter books by Crockett came out in 1894. *Mad Sir Uchtred of the Hills*, serialised in the *St James's Gazette* from March to April was inspired by a dream in which Crockett had seen a wild creature prowling and ravening in the Galloway hills.[31] Out of it he created a tale of Sir Uchtred (a name borrowed from the ancient Douglases) who for his brutality towards Covenanters is cursed by a Covenanting minister and turned into a beast, ranging the moors like Nebuchadnezzar with slavering mouth and claw-like talons until church bells sounding over the moorland silence bring him to repentance. Readers of the *St James's Gazette* must have been startled. The description has power, but the book's main importance is that it showed Crockett turning towards Covenanting times as splendidly suitable for historical romance and also that, in the 'beast man', he relished and could conjure up horror for its own sake.

In book form, *Mad Sir Uchtred* was one of the small oatmeal-coloured volumes in Unwin's *Autonym* series which was advertised by an orange and black poster by Aubrey Beardsley. In the same series came the second shorter Crockett of 1894, *The Play-Actress*. It had appeared as a serial in the *Christian Leader* from 7 September to 16 November 1893 but under the title *A Great Preacher*. Such an astonishing change demands explanation.

The 'Great Preacher' of the story—of both versions for they are identical—is the Rev Gilbert Rutherford of the Cameronian Kirk on the Hill in Cairn Edward. His son Willie has gone to London and fallen into evil ways. One Sunday morning after the morning service, a girl dressed in black brings a golden-haired child to him, his granddaughter Ailie. Willie is dead and his divorced wife Elsa, a drunken dissolute actress, is not a fit person to look after the child. The girl is Bessie Upton, also an actress, Elsa's sister; she has looked after Ailie since Willie's death but though her heart breaks to part with the child, she now hands her over to Rutherford. She will be safer in Scotland.

Rutherford is appalled at the responsibility of a child from that sink of iniquity, London, and a theatre! But he finds that Ailie has been taught to say her prayers by Aunt Bessie and is as pure as any in his flock. He must go to London and find out more. By a series of coincidences he finds the Siddons Theatre. Elsa is an alcoholic drug-addicted wreck; he begs Bessie to come to Scotland with him but she rebukes him; Christ would not wish her to abandon her sister. Conveniently, Elsa suffers a stroke as a result of her debauched life and dies, in the end repentant and peaceful, as Rutherford sits by her bedside.

Bessie gladly returns to Scotland and Ailie, and her young man Johnny (from Annan, and he says his prayers too) comes north also; the happy ending is complete.

This would be little more than an improving sentimental story from a tract were it not for the exactness of its detail—the smell of hot oil and tin from a policeman's lamp at the end of his night beat, a street urchin whistling with his hands in his pockets, the gassy cold smell of the draught in an empty theatre, the tawdry cheap finery and stale scent of Elsa's rooms, her sheepish 'aristocratic' sleazy admirers. *A Great Preacher* is the primary character for the *Leader* but *The Play-Actress* is the greater draw as a title for T Fisher Unwin. For Crockett the change signifies that he has made a deliberate step into dangerous territory for Free Church members; he has been in a theatre, to see plays and to visit backstage, witnessing shrill brawls and drunken fights, but he does not think actors and actresses utterly immoral. The congregation were horrified—a maid who worked for the Crocketts, Elizabeth Shanks, still recalled years later just how horrified they were.[32] Crockett was an unusual minister, but was this not too much?

He had forseen this and expressed their reaction himself, through Mr Rutherford's housekeeper, Girzie, who listens at the bedroom door the night Ailie is taken in and reports what she hears to Mrs MacClever over the manse dyke, in outrage.

> 'Weel, he talked to the bairn aboot plays and playactors, aboot giants an' fairies, an' siccan balderdash—on the Sabbath nicht, too, mind ye, after preachin' twice! An' then, to crown a', what did the man do but licht a bit stick that was in the grate, and made reed *Ingry-Doories*, waving the burnt stick in the gloamin' o' the chamber!'
>
> 'Ye dinna tell me!' said Mistress MacClever. 'Heard I ever the like o' that? Dear sirs!'
>
> Manse Girzie stayed her with her hand.
>
> 'There's faur waur to come,' she said solemnly. 'That's nocht.'
>
> 'Waur canna be,' said Mrs MacClever. 'What wull the tailor's wife say?'
>
> Girzie of the Manse went on:
>
> 'Then when the bairn was tired—mind you, it was far by buik-time—gin the misguided man didna pit her to sleep, singing—
>
>> "Katie Beardie had a coo,
>> Black and white aboot the moo;
>> Wasna that a dainty coo?
>> Dance, Katie Beardie!"'
>
> There was silence for two clock ticks over the manse dyke.
>
> 'He mauna win aff wi' the like o' that,' said Mistress MacClever with emphasis. 'It behoves that it shall be brocht to the notice o' the session!'
>
> 'Aye,' said Manse Girzie, 'an' a bonnie, unfaceable-like story ony way for a lass to step up to a minister and leave a bairn on his hand at the kirk door!'[33]

One can feel the mischief running through Crockett as he created this dialogue with its mention of the tailor's wife and the session, and his choice of an old nursery rhyme involving dancing, that most wicked of activities, and the final slanderous comment from Girzie who should have known better.

To conclude the work of 1894 *The Lilac Sunbonnet* ran as a serial in the *Leader* and came out in October as a book. Its first edition numbered 20,000 and was sold out in a few days; the *Dumfries and Galloway Standard* reviewer had to make do with a second edition.[34] Crockett was booming as a popular writer.

This brought problems. The new celebrity, though still a full-time minister, was much in demand as a public speaker, a contributor to periodicals, a writer of prefaces to other men's books. To one request he acceded in good measure—*Vox Clamantium* the collection of essays by Hall Caine, the Dean of Ely, Henry Arthur Jones, Richard le Gallienne and others, brought together by Andrew Reid as a Christian socialist blast against the rich who oppress the poor.[35] To it he contributed a short story 'In the Matter of Incubus and Co', a hard-hitting attack, based on the Mauricewood disaster, on mine-owners and managers who, professing to be Christians, are both greedy and inhuman. Completely forgotten today, it is worth examining.

Crockett's two villains are Mr Grindlay, a worldly man with a fine watch-chain, a member of the Hill Kirk but in secret a drunkard, and Hector McKill, a hypocritical ruling elder of the Valley Kirk. They are partners in the Incubus mines and their one aim is to do things as cheaply as possible even though this may endanger the safety of their workers. A new minister comes to the town, David Oliphant, and greatly offends:

> 'He said to me in the smoking-room,' said Hector McKill to his wife, 'that there was no doubt that Jesus was a working-man and his followers socialists.'

McKill 'lifts his lines' and leaves the church after such blasphemous sentiments, but David Oilphant,

> cleared of Incubus and Company and all their works, preached the Gospel as it was given to him, and instructed his people, among other things, that the fatherhood of God meant the brotherhood of man.

It is hard today to conjure up the shock and horror in the idea that Christ was a socialist but in 1894 it verged on the revolutionary. As for the brotherhood of man, Grindlay and McKill are by no means of the opinion that the workers are their brothers, nor do the workers feel any brotherhood towards them. Crockett expresses angry sympathy with the miners below ground leading a dark unnatural life; the waving cornfields in the sun above are all left behind.

> The pit hummed like a hive, and there was little enough time for thought. The door-boys heard the whistle of the men running the truck-loads through the dark passage, and threw open each their doors. Then with a yell and a gust of wind a long line of cars rushed through the open doorway. Sometimes one of the men upon them would wave a hand kindly to the lonely boy, left by himself in the darkness. And the flames of their hat-lamps streamed back like the smoke-tract behind a railway engine.

When disaster struck in the shape of fire, the airshaft was found to be blocked up with steam pipes; there was no escape.

> They were no better than rats caught in the trap set for them by Incubus and Company, and baited with thirty shillings a week. But the senior partner was a pious man, and had often prayed for them—only he had not finished the second exit.

The Rev David Oliphant speaks his mind in words very like those of the Rev S R Crockett in 1889, only more strongly:

> I do not stand here to apportion blame or decide legal quibbles; but I say that the men who are responsible for failing to provide a way of escape for these men are responsible for the loss of these hundred lives, and one day shall have to answer for the murder before the bar of God.

Incubus and Co could not be reached by earthly law; they 'got clear in the Government inquiry' says Crockett in one of those contemptuous colloquialisms by which he can demolish the pretensions of the respectable, but McKill will not escape;

> ... the Great Court of Appeal has not done with him yet. There is a certain white throne to be set up, and even if there be no hell, as the new-fangled folk say, God is going to set about making one specially for Hector McKill.

The story illustrates an aspect of Crockett which is often overlooked—his concern for the poor and oppressed, the down-trodden and ill-paid. In politics he was a Liberal, as were many Free Churchmen, and his anger flared at the rich sitting at ease in mansions paid for by the misery of helpless victims.

He wrote two articles on Galloway during 1894, 'Galloway Bygones' and 'Galloway Fastnesses' published in the *Leisure Hour* and thriftily reprinted in *Raiderland* in 1904 as the chapter called

> The Raiders' Country:
> I   Why we are what we are and
> II What we see in Raiderland

A third essay, entitled

> III   What we say and how we say it

completed the chapter. It had travelled far. It was delivered as a talk on 'Scottish National Humour' to the Edinburgh Philosophical Society; then it became one of the Armitstead lectures in Dundee; then it served as a talk to the Glasgow Athenaeum; and finally it was published in the *Contemporary Review* for April 1895. His praise of John Galt, in Edinburgh, led to William Blackwood's inviting him to edit the new edition which he had said was something to be hoped for. He replied regretfully that he had no time for such work. This was just as well; he had neither the patience nor the accuracy for an editor; but he offered to write an introduction to each volume as it came out if they thought of publishing. Blackwood found an editor in D S Meldrum and 1895–6 saw an edition of eight volumes of Galt, with breezy personal introductions by Crockett which, no matter how readable and pleasant, are far from scholarly. In the introduction to *Annals of the Parish*, for instance, he remarks cheerfully that he never could get through Galt's *Ringan Gilhaize* and does not expect ever to be able to,[36] and when talking of the author's personality comments later that

> Of course it is a commonplace that all novelists become their own good and bad characters for the occasion.
>
> As the poet sings—
>> I am the batsman and the bat,
>> I am the bowler and the ball,
>> The fielders, the pavilion cat,
>> The pitch, the stumps, and all.
>
> Or words to that effect.[37]

It is absurdly like Crockett to use his friend Andrew Lang's poem *Brahma*[38] as a neat epitome of his sentiments without troubling to verify the quotation so that he trails off into 'words to that effect' to cover what he did not precisely remember. Yet the manuscripts of his Introductions to the volumes of Galt, preserved in the Hornel Collection in Broughton House, Kirkcudbright,[39] are carefully worked over with corrections, underlinings and emendations to the drafts; he really was trying to write slowly and with care. His articles on Stevenson, Barrie and Kipling for the *Bookman* all show the same breeziness; he wrote personally, anecdotally, idiosyncratically, but never as a sober critic. Editors grew to realise this and ceased to invite him to contribute this kind of work.

Crockett's letters to his friends John and Marion MacMillan, also preserved at Broughton House in the Hornel Collection, are an index to the changing nature of his life. He wanted to explore farther into the uplands of Galloway—the Merrick, Benellary, Loch Enoch, the Dungeon of Buchan, Loch Macaterick—and John MacMillan, an experienced hill sheep farmer, with first-hand knowledge of these distant hills, was the obvious guide. He and his wife were tenants of the farm Glenhead of Trool; he made their acquaintance through John's brother, the Rev Anthony MacMillan of Kirkcaldy[40] and met them first on a hot August day in 1893.[41] The three immediately took to one another; in them Crockett recaptured something of the simple homely kindliness of Little Duchrae. He learned from them both and always kept in touch by letter, letting them know how his work was progressing. He sent them a copy of *The Stickit Minister*, which they had not seen, later that August:

> puir laddie, you will treat him kindly and gie him a place by the fireside, a guid horn spoon an' a sonsy cogful o' brose. The author has had some buttermilk since he cam doon here, but it's gye an' wersh stuff to the grand meat an' drink o' the Mistress o' Glenhead.

The Raiders may bring tiresome visitors and journalists to them; he hopes they will not be pestered; he is full of gratitude for John's having taken him to see Loch Enoch.

> All the rest I had seen before on the Kells range & Loch Dee side, but not Enoch and the Wolf's Slock. I knew *Slack* was right but Slock was the better word for writing ... I have to come down again to get stuff for a great book (in size) about the Galloway Covenanters. So John must be picking up all the tales he can for me ... This Covenanting story Men of the Moss Hags is bought by *Good Words* to be their leading story next year, running through the whole year. So I must come to you, if you can stick me in somewhere—a shakedown will do, & if I am in the way you must tell me just to march ... I must see the Dhu Loch, Loch Macaterick, and get over into Shalloch-on-Minnoch, perhaps John can get a day off to go with me.[42]

He visited these friends as often as he could, but running through the letters are his regrets that he cannot come as often as he would like. There is a lecture to be given in Manchester, a week to be spent with Ruskin—Crockett never divulged in print how he fared in Coniston during Ruskin's last sad silent days; were they able to talk about Ruskin's Galloway forebears?—a lecture to be given in Dundee, a week to be spent in St Andrews with Andrew Lang, a visit to Dr Whyte on holiday in Aviemore. He is busy with *Men of the Moss Hags*, and has had an invitation from Sir Herbert Maxwell of Monreith:

> I have to go down to stay a day or two with Sir Herbert; but one day at Glenhead and the parritch and milk thereof is worth all the Monreiths in the world. But I suppose I'll hae to gang an' see the body![43]

Sir Herbert Maxwell of Monreith was a man of consequence in Galloway and elsewhere; to say that a day at Glenhead is worth all the Monreiths in the world is a high compliment; and to remark that he supposes he 'must gang an' see the body' is so cheerfully ridiculous that it expresses his pride; the MacMillans will understand this indirect Scots way of expressing it.

Periodicals of many kinds besieged him for contributions—*Woman at Home* edited by Annie S Swan, the *Bookman* edited by Robertson Nicoll, the *Graphic*, the *Leisure Hour*, the *Christian Leader*, of course, *Ladies' Realm*, the *Pall Mall*, the *Windsor*, the *People's Friend*—these are only some of those who received work from him at their own request sooner or later. 'S R Crockett seems to be ubiquitous these days' said the *Dumfries and Galloway Standard*.[44] The new writer had entered upon a period of hard work but financial prosperity; his work was in demand and paid for highly.

His two friends at Glenhead were close to him and in his confidence; he had no secrets from them: 'I was sorry to leave you, as sorry as if you had been brother and sister. I never got so near to any folk in such a short time. I seem to have known you all my life'.[45] When he wrote early in 1894 to say that we are just flitted from the Manse, *not yet* from the Kirk, and going into a larger house.[46]

the emphasis on *not yet* is significant; they, and probably Ruth, know what is in his mind; he is already facing the possibility of giving up the ministry.

It was indeed a larger house to which they had flitted, Bank House, in its own grounds with its own drive, a large sandstone house leased from Sir George Clerk of Penicuik, overlooking the River Esk and with access to the woods and paths of Penicuik House nearby.

> It is a comfortable, prosperous house, and, from the very moment that the threshold is crossed, it shows itself a bookman's house. Books in the hall, in serried ranks, and above the shelves are portraits of familiar bookmen.
> As for the study, which may be directly entered from the hall, it is all books. Books from the floor to the ceiling, with space only for a door, a fireplace and the window. Against the smaller window which overlooks Penicuick (sic) with its towering chimneys, is set Crockett's writing-table. In the bow of the larger window, from which one sees the Esk and its timbered yonside, is a table. But here also there is an invasion of books. The drawer of the table is full of maps, old and elaborate maps of Scotland, while underneath it stand in folio volumes the records of the State Trials of Scotland. Away in a corner is a small typewriting machine.[47]

It was to this large comfortable house that the visitors came—Andrew Lang in October, J M Barrie, his wife and their dog in November, Dr and Mrs Robertson Nicoll on their way south from their summer holiday at Lumsden in Aberdeenshire. The Crockett children—three in number, and another was to be born at Bank House—were able to become familiar with birds and the shy animals of the woods. Crockett and his eldest daughter Maisie— 'Sweetheart'—explored every path, talking about animals and their habits, braving rain and snow, looking especially for birds. He enjoyed passing on his knowledge and his pleasure was increased by the candid remarks of Maisie who spoke her mind when it was necessary and was not to be told birds were sparrows when she knew they were chaffinches.

In time the house was not large enough for the books; a wooden annexe was built on to it with gas light and fireplaces and comfortable chairs; it had proper library stacks for the books and a revolving dome for a telescope through which Crockett could study astronomy. There was a dark room for his photographs and a study well supplied with several typewriters, reference books and an Edison-Bell dictaphone. Finance for the moment was no problem; his time for as far forward as he could see was taken up with books he had contracted to write. But there was looming large in Crockett's mind the other problem of his ministry. His literary talks, his literary journeys to Galloway, Ayrshire and Northern Ireland (for the Isle Rathan cave, taken from one on the Antrim Coast)[48] were eating into his time. He could not combine them with ministerial duties, yet, having gone so far, how could he, being human, turn back? His writing had given his wife a house similar to the one from which he had taken her in Manchester; she was its happy

3 Bank House.

mistress, and his children were growing up in just such an environment as he would have wished for them. He himself was in his element, his mind full of ideas, projects, plans—but all of them would involve further absences form his pulpit in search of background material. *The Grey Man* was already in his mind, necessitating time spent in Ayrshire to see Ballantrae, Culzean Castle, Ailsa Craig and Auchendrayne, to say nothing of reading up Ayrshire folklore.

He must choose one or the other; he could not keep the two halves of his life running side by side. Elizabeth Shanks described to her daughter how often Mr Crockett went down to the Church alone, to wrestle with the problem on his knees.[49] It was not easy; he had not chosen the ministry lightly, although perhaps his parish duties had been more noted for energy than for spirituality, but to put it aside once it had been chosen was a different matter. He would be sharply criticised—he would be attacked. He had always been a little at odds with the Free Church and its narrowness and had not hesitated to criticise his fellow ministers, but to turn his back on it needed courage and strength.

The decision was forced upon him and he faced it squarely. Early in January 1895 Crockett, having first informed his Kirk Session, announced to a packed church, while the snow fell outside, that he must give up his ministry; there was no other way he could conscientiously take. His statement was worded carefully, in a curious mingling of pride and regret.

Most sincerely do I believe that the same Lord who sent me here to preach the

Gospel has revealed to me the possession of a talent which He desires and intends me to use. I did not seek this literary work—it found me. I have only followed on, wondering often, doubting often, and yet sure that to every faithful servant there is given no tool which the Master Workman does not intend him to use.

Brethren, my resignation is accompanied with this unusual circumstance, which I think robs it of any bitterness, that if it be the Lord's will it is not to be accompanied by separation. I mean to become a humble and loyal member of the congregation to which I have tried faithfully to minister for eight years. I shall remain yours in all affection, sympathy and the bond of one desire. Only I feel that it is in the best interests of the congregation that another teaching elder should take over the responsibility. A congregation of the size and importance of Penicuik requires a man for its minister who can give his whole time and his entire strength to the work. This I cannot do, without, as it seems to me, hiding some of the entrusted talents in the ground.

Moreover, I think the matter should be faced now at the beginning of this year. So far as I know, the congregation was never in a better state. It was never, I think, larger in numbers. The young communicants at the last two communions have been exceptionally numerous. The whole people are, I believe, in good heart. It is thus that I should desire to hand my charge over to a worthy successor, whose hand, when you choose him, I shall loyally and cordially uphold.

In resigning my charge, I desire to put on record that I hold, and shall teach to the wider audience, the same vital truths that I have taught to you—the virtue, the praise, the sacrifice and the atonement. Literature has need of believing men to hold aloft the banner of belief. I am, it is true, but a humble soldier in the army, but I trust that in the day of battle I shall not be found wanting.

With regard to more immediate interests, I desire to hold myself responsible for the supply of the pulpit till such time as it shall be your wish to begin the hearing of candidates, or the using of other means to fill the vacancy. I shall preach as often as I can during the period of preparation, and constantly be at your service for all counsel and help. I desire at all times to continue to serve the congregation; but in the future free from wearing responsibility and anxiety, lest one part of my work should unduly encroach upon that other, for which I am responsible to you.

Finally, brethren, 'Pray for me,' for I have a sore heart this day. I have not done all I ought. I have been an unprofitable servant. But this I do say, that I have given this people my heart. I have never spoken a word among you for the sake of praise, or in order to please you. I have never, as God sees me, been silent because of the fear of man. I have declared the whole counsel of God as I have known it. No man ever had a more loving and faithful people; none ever kinder or more loyal office-bearers.[50]

The controlled tone, mingling sincere emotion with practical arrangements for the 'supply' of the pulpit at his own expense (he must have been well practised in this from his absences during the past two years) makes it the more decisive and final. The resignation created a considerable stir, being so unprecedented. For the most part, reaction was sympathetic; his own congregation had been partially expecting it. This being an imperfect world, there were bound to be exceptions, and although Crockett said nothing at the time, in 1907 he wrote a story 'The Seven Wise Men' as a supplement to *Sunday at Home*[51] which harked back to back-biting in an imaginary Free Church; this would not have mattered if he had not tied it firmly to Penicuik and himself.

A young minister comes to Longwood to preach a trial sermon, tall and burly, of humble stock with two uncles working on the railway. He had been forking sheaves from a cart to a cornstack when the invitation came. He is appointed in spite of strong opposition from the wealthier members of the congregation, 'proprietors who have been ennobled by having a bank account for at least a generation and a half, or bankrupt landowners with unblemished pedigrees and no bank account at all.' He remembers what the Principal of his college had said to him: in every congregation there are the 'Seven Wise Men' who do nothing but criticise and complain; do not preach to them but to

> the ignorant, the weary, the sinful and the poor. Preach unto these and never mind 'the Seven Wise Men' ...

Whether Principal Rainy ever gave this advice is doubtful; it sounds very like Crockett himself. The story goes on to specify by social position, occupation or a play upon a name who the Seven Wise Men in Penicuik had been—or who Crockett thought they had been. It was taken by a gleeful but shocked Penicuik to be Mr Crockett getting his own back. To this day, some people of the town can identify each individual; Mr Black who compiled the Penicuik Cuttings wrote 'Least said best' in the margin. After twelve years, some buried resentment must have surfaced, but it would have been better if Crockett had not given way to it. It was not like him to bear grudges.

The wonder really is that he was able to do as he wished—become a member of the congregation he had once ministered unto. He remained an elder until ill health forced long absences. He was on good terms with his successor, the Rev Robert T Jack. The late Mr Milroy testified that 'Mr Jack was never out of Mr Crockett's house; he was always in and out consulting and discussing'; others who remember bear this out. That Crockett, the congregation and Mr Jack remained on friendly terms in a difficult situation speaks well for all concerned.

Many Free Church members, in his own Galloway as well as the rest of Scotland, considered that he had betrayed a holy trust. Members of his own family disapproved of his writing; Aunt Marion, wife of the Liverpool City missionary, wrote to her son in scathing terms:

> ... that was a very foolish thing of Sam's. I am sure neither Penman nor

> MacGeorge will like to see it at this date and I think he very seldom dined on herring. I wonder he does not think some poeple (sic) knows him better than to believe the things he says. Aunt Aggie said how the Castle Douglas people talked about his queer things in the C. Leader, but you and me must hold our tongues and make him no worse than he is.[52]

The reaction of this lady and others like her to the news that Sam had announced in church that he was going to spend his life writing little better than 'queer things in the C. Leader' may be imagined. Even Robertson Nicoll was perturbed.

> Crockett did right to resign whatever happens, when he felt his main interest elsewhere, it was not for his soul's health to keep a pastorate. What he will do and where he will turn 'being let go' is a serious problem; but I hope for the best.[53]

As the years went by and commercial constraint compelled Crockett to write to please publishers rather than his God or himself, he may have looked back upon the ingenuously hopeful words of his resignation and felt a measure of disillusionment. One thing is certain; as things stood in January 1895, the decision was not a foolish one. The auspices were good; success had been so great that faith in the future was justified. He had reason to trust his individual talent; not to have done so would have been a turning aside from what he believed to be his true vocation.

J M Barrie, in a letter to Sir Arthur Quiller-Couch a year after this crisis in Crockett's life, gives a glimpse of his abounding delight in its outcome.

> Crockett was here with us for a week-end. 'His terms are'—'he sells'—'Watt says'—'his publishers say'—'his terms'—'his sales'—but otherwise he is all right and kindly, and, oh, he is happy.[54]

Crockett's happiness at what is to him the heady novelty of being a full-time author is wryly amusing to one more experienced in the literary game, but he is 'all right'. Barrie, like all the others, waits with interest to see what will happen next.

CHAPTER 4

The Stickit Minister And Some Common Men

Barrie, Crockett and Ian Maclaren are regarded as the leaders of the so-called 'Kailyard School', though they did not work together like the Pre-Raphaelites. Barrie's early titles—*Auld Licht Idylls* (1888), *A Window in Thrums* (1889) and *The Little Minister* (1891) have a homely appeal which suggests sentimental kindliness towards the country people he was describing—deceptively so. Maclaren sounds even gentler—*Beside the Bonnie Brier Bush* (1894), *The Days of Auld Lang Syne* (1895) and *Kate Carnegie and Those Ministers* (1897). Between them, and contrasting with them, come the harsh thumping consonants and sibilants of Crockett's *The Stickit Minister and Some Common Men* (1893) which hammer home the difference between him and the other two writers.

By the time that 'A Day in the Life of the Rev James Pitbye' appeared in the *Christian Leader* Crockett had been Free Church minister at Penicuik for more than six years, long enough to have experienced the drawbacks as well as the advantages of his position and to have a fund of anecdotes from and about ministers, not always to their credit. The sketches he had begun for his own pleasure had served as an outlet for the mingled amusement and irritation which his colleagues and their congregations provoked in him. Some went as far back as his student days as a missionary in the Pleasance—the two Cleg Kelly tales which exposed the reality behind some mission Sunday Schools, their tough little pupils, and the sentimental middle-class ladies who condescendingly distributed tracts to the poor who did not particularly want them. Many of the 'Ministers of Our Countryside' were unflattering portraits and probably pleased the readers among the congregations more than the ministers, though he could occasionally turn his caustic attention to congregational failings as well.

They were not written by someone looking out of 'the windows of the Presbyterian manse' as George Blake suggests[1] but by a man with a keen sense of justice and of the ridiculous who went here and there out of his manse and was very well aware of what was wrong with ministers, manses and churches. The many styles of the stories show a man writing as the moment took him, critical, laughing, sometimes angry, often shrewly ironic; the common denominator is that he wrote as one at the same social level as his most homespun characters. Barrie's narrator is an imaginary schoolmaster, a little above the people he is describing. Maclaren has a slightly superior attitude, so that he comments on his farmers and their wives from a distance—

affectionately but still from a distance. Crockett is down among the events he chronicles, recording the people whose side he takes as if he were one of them.

This must account for his initial popularity. He is not one of the 'establishment' but has been brought up as a Galloway farm lad, and whether in Galloway Scots or formal English makes the scathing remarks and forms the same sharp judgements as his readers may have formed themselves. He says what the congregations would like to say, and may have said themselves many times in private, but have never before seen in print. He shows ministers quarrelling among themselves, almost coming to blows, so that in 'Trials for License by the Presbytery of Pitscottie' the unfortunate young candidate says that 'he was glad he was gaun awa' to the Cannibal Islands, and no settling in oor pairt o' the country'. In the same story his narrator comments that the lad was 'gaun oot to be a missionar' to the haythen. So afore they could let him gang they bood examine him on the Hebrew an' Latin, an' ither langwiges that naebody speaks noo'—an irresistibly ridiculous proposition that stands quietly by. The ministers of whom he writes with approval—Thomas Todd the probationer, Allan Fairley of Earlswood—are of humble stock like himself, not ashamed to talk broad Galloway Scots and proud of their origins.

The Stickit Minister and Some Common Men is as significant in content as it is rough in sound. With twenty-four stories to choose from, Crockett selects for his title a failure, a 'stickit minister' who had not succeeded in getting as far as ordination, and 'common men'—and women—who are looked down upon by the well-to-do for their very commonness. He is on the side of the under-dog, suspicious of comfortable men and women who have achieved worldly success in material terms. Failure and commonness may be virtues when looked at with the truer vision of human sympathy and in the sight of God. Yet his stories do not preach; they expose, usually through laughter, the true state of affairs to which the merely successful are blind, insulated by the thick cotton-wool of respectability.

It is easy not to notice what he is about. 'Ensamples to the Flock', its title a Biblical phrase,[2] as if for a conventional improving tale, introduces a determined young girl Leeb and the low repute in which she and her brothers are held in the community.

> Leeb had gone to Sabbath school every week, when she could escape from the tyranny of home, and was, therefore, well known to the minister, who had often exercised himself in vain on the thick defensive armour of ignorance and stupidity which encompassed the elder M'Lurg, her father. His office-bearers and he had often bemoaned the sad example of this ne'er-do-weel family which had entrenched itself in the midst of so many well-doing people. M'Lurg's Mill was a reproach and an eyesore to the whole parish, and the M'Lurg 'weans' a gratuitous insult to every self-respecting mother within miles. For three miles round the children were forbidden to play with, or even speak to, the four outcasts at the Mill. Consequently their society was much sought after.[3]

The paragraph reads innocently, but Crockett has embedded in it the cleverness of Leeb, the ineffectualness of the minister, the useless complaining—'bemoaning', a delicately chosen word—in which he and his elders had indulged without doing anything to set things right, the materialism which made their chief complaint the disgrace to a 'well-doing' parish—'well-doing' meaning rather 'prosperous' than the doing of good, least of all to the luckless children, ostracised by the whole community—and the final deft anticlimax whereby their forbidden and unseemly ways brought them popularity among the local youngsters

Most of the stories come from the 'Ministers of Our Countryside' series.[4] The Rev James Pitbye we have already met. 'The Three Maister Peter Slees' derives from the habit ministers have of preaching old sermons; the third Maister Slee carries this to extreme by preaching a sermon his grandfather had used to celebrate Waterloo. 'Trials for License' tells of a clever young candidate who sets the Presbytery at odds by showing up their ignorance and their prejudices. 'The Probationer' describes the wet dark miserable non-welcome extended to a 'supply' preacher by the minister and elders whom he is obliging by his preaching.

There are two ministerial love stories. One, 'The Courtship of Allan Fairley of Earlswood', has a conventional happy ending; Allan refuses to turn his humbly-born mother out of his manse because his parishioners think that, as she once knitted his father's socks, she is unfit for their wives to associate with; by his defiance he wins the love of Miss Gordon of Earlswood, one of the local gentry. The other, 'The Minister of Scaur Casts Out With his Maker' is less conventional but happy in its own way; an odd unbalanced minister yearns madly after a fine young lady who has rejected him for a rich man, until he meets her later as a fat and wealthy widow and returns to his manse, cured.

'Congregational Sketches'[5] provides a variety of tales. 'The Split in the Marrow Kirk' shows a contumacious elder stirring up feeling against the minister because he is liberal enough to take part in services outwith the rigid Marrow Kirk, a sect Crockett invented and was to use again in the *The Lilac Sunbonnet*. He and his cronies are prepared to resort to violence but the two small sons of the elder and the minister prevent them from barring the minister out of his kirk and the plot is foiled, though the elder's son is almost killed by his own father's ignorant brutality. The point is taken; the elder is repentant; and the two boys are friends for life.

'John Black, Critic in Ordinary' deals with a pleasant Sunday School outing punctuated by John Black's complaints that they should have gone to the field near his auntie's farm instead—so that she could have made money out of supplying milk. 'The Candid Friend' depicts with deep feeling a visitation a minister receives from a busybody who feels it his duty to tell of all the complaints made against him until routed by the minister's strong-minded wife and servant.

The two 'Cleg Kelly' stories are set in the slums of Edinburgh. 'A Knight-Errant of the Streets' comes from the 1891 Christmas and New Year number of the *Leader* and the urchin proved so popular that three more of his adventures were written and made into one story, 'The Progress of Cleg Kelly,

Mission Worker'. 'Ensamples to the Flock' and 'The Siege of M'Lurgs's Mill' take us back to Galloway; M'Lurg's Mill was taken from a ruin Crockett had passed on his way to school in Laurieston. 'Ensamples' shows us Leeb M'Lurg dragooning her brothers into cleanliness and school attendance after her father's death, and the 'Siege' shows us how she deals with a drunken uncle who comes back hoping for money—the water from the mill-wheel is turned on him in a rollicking tale of country rough-and-tumble. 'The Lammas Preaching', the last 'Congregational Sketch', seems to have strayed from the 'Minister' series; a too enthusiastic visiting minister from Wigtownshire ignores all warning of floods as he insists on preaching at Cauldshaws and is saved from drowning only by Providence and the local ne'er-do-weel.

'A Midsummer Idyll' is about a wilful young girl who agrees to marry three bridegrooms on the same day but in the end has to go and fetch the one she wants. 'The Tutor of Curleywee' depicts an English Minister of Education who finds out how isolated families in lonely cottages 'keep' a student during the summer vacation in exchange for his teaching their children, and is much astonished. 'The Heather Lintie' is very different; a lonely woman old before her time has ambitions to be a poet, but the volume of poems she has printed is so bad that a clever reviewer covers it with ill-natured ridicule. She has time to read only the first mock-heroic praise before death frees her from this cruelty.

'The Stickit Minister' and 'The Tragedy of Duncan Duncanson' are tragedy of different kinds. 'The Rev John Smith prepares his Sermon' is a mere sketch; he is full of his own grumbles and embarks on a discourse about them until shamed by the trust three simple folk have in his power to teach and sustain them. 'Why David Oliphant remained a Presbyterian', shows a young Presbyterian divinity student tempted for a moment by the urbane charm of Oxford and the Church of England until he remembers his Cameronian grandfather's staunch and stubborn Cameronian faith. 'The Glen Kells Short Leet' presents three candidates for a ministerial vacancy; the one who is appointed is the shy, modest, pleasant one who still 'preaches from the shoulder' and will love and marry the late minister's daughter; neither she nor her invalid mother will leave the manse. The strangest of the ministers is the subject of 'Accepted of the Beasts', a saintly young man too good for this world, far less a Presbyterian congregation, who sings like an angel, and dies. The most unpleasant is the one in 'Boanerges Simpson's Encumbrance', on whom Crockett unleashes the full force of his scorn.

The variety of themes and the variation in treatment are wide, even although ministers and congregations feature so often. No two stories are alike in style, not even the two about Cleg Kelly or the two about Leeb M'Lurg. Some are entirely in Scots, some are entirely in English, some are in a blend of the two. The English can vary from light bantering amusement to heavy newspaper prose. The Scots can be satirical or it can be moving in its strong simplicity. Crockett was at home in many areas of language. He had been brought up among Scots country folk, speaking broad Scots and knowing it by heart. His ear was attuned to the cadences of the Authorised Version. He had grown up with *The Pilgrim's Progress* and Covenanting histories and pamphlets. He had listened to the homely talk of dairymaids and ploughmen and learned 'all the mirth of farm-ingles and merry meetings under cloud of night'.[6] At school and university he had been drilled in nineteenth century formal English, the solid prose into which his Latin and Greek texts would be translated, and he was used to 'sermon English' both in country and city pulpits. He had mastered journalistic English in his contributions to a range of newspapers and periodicals, and had travelled with an American and an Englishman of education and wealth. He was more practised in varying styles than most young men who come to the profession of writer.

Whatever the style, Crockett could maintain his sharp edge of observed speech to an exact degree. He can delineate in a few words spoken by a sceptical woman that there is little she does not know about her minister; we hear her very voice, in 'The Lammas Preaching':

> 'Janet,' said the minister to his housekeeper, 'I am to preach tonight at Cauldshaws on the text "Whatsoever thy hand findeth to do, do it with thy might"'
> 'I ken,' said Janet, 'I saw it on yer desk. I pat it ablow the clock for fear the wun's o' heeven micht blaw it awa' like chaff, an' ye couldna do wantin' it.'
> 'Janet MacTaggart,' said the minister, tartly, 'bring in the denner and do not meddle with what does not concern you.'[7]

The suggestion that the sermon might be blown away like chaff is a sly deliberate insult, compounded by the additional suggestion that the winds of heaven might do the blowing as a hint of what God thought of the sermon; she put it away safely because she knew that he read his sermons from written notes and cannot preach extempore—read sermons were not thought much of in Presbyterian Scotland. The minister picks up every *nuance* of what she says; that is why he is irritated.

It is often in side-comments that the sting comes; the Rev Allan Fairley mentions in passing that there is a

> big colony o' dreadfu' respectable gentry in oor pairish—retired tradesfolk frae Glasgow and Edinburgh wi' a pickle siller and a backload o' pride.[8]

There is cutting comment on the youngest of the three Maister Slees:

> His sermons were like himsel', like pease brose made o' half a pun o' peas to the boilerfu' o' water—rale evangelical, ye ken, but meat for babes, hardly for grown folk.[9]

One can imagine ministers wondering uneasily whom Crockett had in mind. He can be equally cutting in English; the Rev Boanerges Simpson—Boaenerges means 'son of thunder'—had a 'bland, vague, upward-looking eye' intended to convey holiness, and an admiring group of

> rich old ladies who were known to have Mr Simpson in their wills, and these followed him about wherever he preached, like Tabbies following a milk jug.[10]

The comparison to a 'milk jug' puts him firmly into his category of one purveying smooth soft easy nourishment.

Very different from this, although using English for the narrative, are the two Cleg Kelly stories. Crockett must have known a youngster like this cheeky street urchin when he was working in the Pleasance, or perhaps Cleg is a combination of several urchins. He is bare-legged and ragged, putting in an appearance at five mission Sunday Schools because it is the season of 'trips' and he wants to go to them all. On his way home he meets three clean well-dressed good little children coming from a congregational Sunday School; they have stockings and come from good Christian homes. Cleg demands their 'gundy', their toffee, but is seen by a raw young policeman who, instead of just shouting at him as his colleagues who knew Cleg would have done, decides to 'take him in'. Cleg eludes him by his skill in climbing crumbling walls, running up common stairs and out of windows into others in the rabbit warren of the slums, until he finds himself at his own particular 'Mission for the Poor' Sunday School, Hunker Court. Its pupils and teachers are just coming out. Cleg sees with approval boys throwing clods at the more unpopular teachers, but Archie Drabble is about to throw 'glaur' at Cleg's own beloved teacher, Miss Celie. Leaping down from a first floor window, he flattens Archie and escorts the mystified Miss Celie home—a Knight Errant indeed.

This is not exactly an improving story, but a second had to be written by public demand; the public and, according to Malcolm Harper, Stevenson himself, liked Cleg for his liveliness and his cheerful demeanour. Cleg himself, says Crockett, has been keeping out of his way; a too earnest Sunday School superintendent has read aloud the 'Knight Errant' story to his senior division and Cleg, disgusted, has left Hunker Court for good. The second story probes more deeply into Cleg's circumstances. He hates ladies who drive in carriages giving tracts to the 'lower classes' for the good of their souls; when one such lady gives him a tract, he runs, gathers an unsavoury collection of objects only too easily found in the Pleasance—an eggshell with herring bones, rotten cabbage, something so dead that it cannot be identified—and hands them up to her with a paper round them saying 'With thanks for yer traks'.

But Miss Celie is not like the tract lady. Miss Celie is genuinely concerned about the waifs and gives up time to help them. Cleg finds a room and benches for her to hold an evening class, and fights off the louts who try to wreck it. They lie in wait for him; he joyfully sees his chance to fulfil a dream, blocks the entrance to the police station with a brewery barrel and conducts a gang fight under the noses of the trapped 'poliss' who laugh even while they struggle to get out.

At the end of the day, Cleg must steer his drunken father home from the public house, with a strong, heavy forked stick with which he pushes him along at a distance safe from vicious kicks and blows. He reaches the foot of the common stair up which he must somehow haul his father to their 'home'. His father slumps into a hoggish snoring sleep. Cleg has to ask for help, and the first passerby is the policeman whom he had most cheekily abused.

>A policeman came round the corner, flashing the light of his bull's-eye right

and left. Cleg's heart stopped still. It was the lengthy officer whom he had called 'Langshanks' and invited to come through the bung. He feared that he was too kenspeckle to escape. He went over to him, and taking a tug at his hair, which meant manners, said:

'Please, officer, will ye gie me a lift up the stair wi' my faither?'

'Officer!' says he, 'Officer! Be the powers, 'twas "Langshanks" ye called me the last time, ye thief o' the wurrld!' said the man, who was of national kin to Cleg.

So they twain helped their compatriot unsteadily to his den at the head of the stairs.

'Ye're the cheekiest young shaver I ivver saw,' said Langshanks, admiringly, as he turned away; 'but there's some good in yez!'[11]

His reaction shows that the police had more understanding of Cleg's problems with a drunken father than any number of 'tract ladies'; they appreciated the struggle of the poor simply to stay alive, far less live a 'good' life and liked Cleg's courageous cheerfulness, cheeky though it may have been. 'Knight Errant of the Streets' is a light sketch; encouraged by its popularity Crockett in 'The Progress of Cleg Kelly, Mission Worker' goes more fully into his hero's background and leaves him with the kindly tolerance of the police. He is later to be given a full-length book to himself.

'Ensamples to the Flock' takes us back to Galloway again, and country outcasts, the M'Lurgs. A different face of respectability is shown. The thirteen-year-old Leeb by threats and a hazel stick persuades her three younger brothers to be useful. The older two look after the cows and pasture them by the roadside, keeping a look out for policemen, while the youngest, eight years old, helps her to scrub the floor, wash the walls and clean the dirty furniture of their house. She makes it as clean as cold water and whitewash will make it; she does not beg for the whitewash either; she barters for it with eggs from her few hens.

Leeb got the whitewash that very night and the loan of a brush to put it on with. Next morning the farmer of the Crae received a shock. There was something large and white down on the lochside, where ever since he came to the Crae he had seen nothing but the trees which hid M'Lurg's Mill.

'I misdoot it's gaun to be terrible weather. I never saw that hoose o' Tyke M'Lurg's aff oor hill afore!'[12]

It might have been just an improving moral story extolling the virtues of cleanliness but Crockett recounts each detail with such amused and affectionate realism that there is no moralising. The magnitude of Leeb's achievement is brought out by a comic glimpse of a very real farmer in strong Scots darkly foretelling bad weather, but completely wrong and unexpected and funny. The house is made complete by Leeb's pinning a piece of muslin over the window and setting a jug of heather and wild flowers as decoration so that when the minister happens to pass he stands 'aghast' with astonishment. Leeb is equal to the occasion. 'Will ye be pleased to step ben?' she says happily, using the pleasant old-fashioned greeting she has heard in the mouths of other housewives. On her small heroic scale, by her own ingenuity, she is uniting her brothers and her self to the decent self-respecting country community, achieving the true respectability which is based on effort and not mere show. Crockett admires this kind of respectability. There is a slight irony in the minister's complacent reflection as he goes on his way that 'Tyke M'Lurg's children may yet be ensamples to the flock'; we know that, through no help of his, they are that already. When Uncle Tim M'Lurg, released from prison, comes home drunk in a cart to 'look after' the children and see what money there is to be got out of them, Leeb barricades the house and the now repaired mill, and all that Tyke gets is his share of the water from the mill-wheel turned on to sweep him away, more water than he had ever had in his life. 'The Siege of M'Lurg's Mill' is totally different from the first Leeb story; she is older now and respected and Crockett can enjoy a shout of laughter in rough horseplay and her continued ingenuity in defence of her little world.

In 'The Tragedy of Duncan Duncanson' a sterner note emerges. Duncan is an alcoholic; he had been a minister but had fallen down drunk at the front door of his manse on a Sunday morning and so been deposed; now he is a schoolmaster but still an alcoholic. Crockett hated drunkenness but realised that Duncan is not like Cleg Kelly's father or the M'Lurgs; he is a sick man unable to help himself but not a cruel one. On the other hand, the colleagues who had deposed him were not without fault:

> ...the presbytery of that day adjourned to the Gordon Arms to wash down their presbyterial dinner with plentiful jorums of toddy, and Duncan Duncanson sat for the last time in his study at the manse of the Shaws, sipping and filling the demon bottle which he carried like a familiar spirit in his black bag ... There were those in the presbytery who had often fallen down at their back doors, but then this made a great difference, and they all prayed fervently for the great sinner and backslider who had slidden at his front door in the sight of men. The moderator, who in the presbytery had called Duncan everything he could lay his tongue to, reflected as he drove home that he had let him off too easily. Then he stooped down and felt in the box of his gig if the two-gallon 'greybeard' from the Gordon Arms were sitting safely on its own bottom. So much responsibility made him nervous.[13]

Cold narrative English registers the distaste Crockett feels for those who are no better than Duncan but have not been found out, for a moderator who is anxious about his whisky but not about a ruined fellowman. He is not sentimental about Duncan—he shows him to us drinking himself stupid in the manse—but the sudden drop in style to the colloquial 'called Duncan everything he could lay his tongue to' registers contempt for the moderator in the slack ugly vulgar phrase he uses of him, just as the 'plentiful jorums of whisky' hammer home guilt of the sin which the Presbytery have condemned in Duncan Duncanson; the only difference is that they are discreet enough to hide it. They contrast with Duncan's daughter and her husband, the pupil he had narrowly escaped killing with a poker when drunk; the two care for Duncan in their home and when he dies the verse they select for his gravestone is St Luke 7:47: 'To whom little is forgiven, the same loveth little',[14] the words Christ uses of the sinful woman with the alabaster box. Crockett is not afraid of the challenging text.

He had a keen ear for Scots. In 'The Stickit Minister' he uses it at three levels. The narrative is in what Professor Kurt Wittig called 'Scots-English' when writing of Burns,[15] English with Scots pronunciation, Scots vocabulary and constructions. The speech of Fraser, the ex-divinity student, is in educated English with Scots undertones which grow stronger as his feelings run more deeply. For Saunders McQuhirr, Crockett turns to strong colloquial Scots, not mean as the English colloquialisms can be, but warm-hearted, vigorous and earthy.

The scene is set in Scots-English

> The crows were wheeling behind the plough in scattering clusters, and plumping singly upon the soft, thick grubs which the ploughshare was turning out upon an unkindly world. It was a bask blowy day in the end of March, and there was a hint of snow in the air—a hint emphasised for those skilled in weather lore by the presence of half a dozen sea gulls, white vagrants among the black coats, blown about by the south wind up from the Solway—a snell, Scotch but not unfriendly day altogether.[16]

Fraser comes in from ploughing and explains to Saunders for the first time why he gave up his college career.

> I have not spoken of it to so many; but you've been a good frien' to me, Saunders, and I think you should hear it. I have not tried to set myself right with folks in the general, but I would like to let *you* see clearly before I go my ways to Him who seeth from the beginning.[17]

Saunders interrupts impulsively:

> 'Hear till him,' said Saunders; 'man, yer hoast is no' near as sair as it was i' the back-end. Ye'll be here lang efter me; but lang or short, weel do ye ken, Robert Fraser, that ye need not to pit yersel' richt wi' me. Hev I no' kenned ye sins ye war the size o' twa scrubbers?'[18]

Fraser's quiet narrative continues; he uses purely English expressions as he describes how Sir James at the Infirmary recognised that this student who had come to consult him had lungs badly affected with tuberculosis, because this belongs to the Edinburgh world he had long left behind and is naturally told in the language of that world.

> 'He told me that with care I might live five or six years, but it would need great care. Then a great prickly coldness come over me, and I seemed to walk light-headed in an atmosphere suddenly rarefied. I think I know now how the mouse feels under the air-pump.'
> 'What's that?' queried Saunders.
> 'A cruel ploy not worth speaking of,' continued the Stickit Minister.[19]

THE STICKIT MINISTER AND SOME COMMON MEN

Fraser's sense of shock is well conveyed as he remembers and relives it; Crockett is good at rendering emotion in terms of physical sensation. But once the mouse and the air-pump—how exact a comparison for Fraser's situation—are brushed aside as self-pitying and irrelevant, his Scots grows stronger as he explains his decision.

> 'I must come home to the farm and be my own "man"; then I could send Harry to the college to be a doctor, for he had no call to the ministry as once I thought I had. More than that, it was laid on me to tell Jessie Loudon that Robert Fraser was no better than a machine set to go five year ... I worked the work of the farm, rain and shine, ever since, and have been for these six years the "stickit minister" the world kens the day. Whiles Harry did not think that he got enough. He was always writing for more, and not so very pleased when he did not get it. He was aye different to me, ye ken, Saunders, and he canna be judged by the same standard as you and me.'
> 'I ken,' said Saunders McQuhirr, a spark of light lying in the quiet of his eyes.[20]

The compression is sharply effective; 'it was laid on me' expresses a strong sense of duty almost religious in intensity; 'no better than a machine set to go five year' carries a peasant's contempt for his own physical weakness; and his deliberate use of 'stickit minister' shows how well he is aware of the low opinion in which he is held, and how it hurts him. The increasing use of simple Scots indicates that we are near the heart of his trouble, the unworthiness of his brother—an unworthiness which he will not admit to because of his affection for him. Saunders' apparent agreement in the sardonic 'I ken' implies exactly the opposite and brings to our attention the ambiguity of 'different' and 'canna be judged by the same standard as you and me'. The gleam of anger in Saunders' eye impresses on us, if we have not thought it already, that Harry is different in being infinitely less of a man than his 'failure' of a brother.

> 'He doesna come here much,' continued Robert, 'but I think he's not so ill against me as he was. Saunders, he waved his hand to me when he was gaun by the day!'
> 'That was kind of him,' said Saunders McQuhirr.[21]

We are instantly reminded of the smoothly prosperous picture of Harry we have been shown early in the story, smart in his gig driven by a man in livery, and giving 'a careless wave of recognition over the stone dyke'.

The climax is reached by the three levels of Scots interacting. The farm has been mortgaged to buy Harry a practice, and repayment is nearly due.

> 'I got my notice this morning that the bond is to be called up in November,' said Robert. 'So I'll be obliged to flit.'
> Saunders McQuhirr started to his feet in a moment. 'Never,' he said, with the spark of fire alive now in his eyes, 'never as lang as there's a beast in Drumquhat,

or a poun' in Cairn Edward Bank'—bringing down his clenched fist upon the *Milton* on the table.

'No Saunders, no,' said the Stickit Minister very gently; 'I thank you kindly, but *I'll be flitted before that!*'[22]

The different elements are handled with dexterity—the flat legal terms which Fraser uses to describe the financial crisis which has been in his mind all day and has led to these confidences which are foreign to his reticent nature, the impulsive warm reaction of the simpler older Saunders, the *Milton* on the table reminding us of Fraser's rich promise so cruelly frustrated, and the repetition of the Stickit Minister to remind us of the mean jibe in the same moment as we realise his stature as a man, aware of his doom but unafraid. Above all there is the concentration of several layers of meaning in 'I'll be flitted before that'—one could have wished that Crockett had omitted the italics; they are not necessary. The verb is a common Scots one derived from Norse and not found in English; it means to move house, brief, casual and concrete. In the context it has a dry effectiveness of meiosis, a calm acceptance of what is to come, a hint of triumph that he is soon to be beyond the reach of brother, lawyers and all, and a humour especially Scottish in the laconic equation of death with a mere change of abode, which to the believer it is. It could have been said sardonically—there is a hint of this in its gleam of amusement—but it is said gently because it is said to Saunders. All this is packed into one simple sentence; Crockett has used the commonplace to extract the full significance from the situation.

Yet for all the skill of the telling, for all the realism of the speech and the setting, the story is flawed. Seven years earlier Fraser has had a tubercular cough and has been told that with care he may live for five or six years. He has in fact lived for longer than that, and done the work of a labourer on the farm 'rain and shine'. Crockett knew from his own experience of at least three deaths in his own family that tuberculosis was a swift destroyer; his mother died of it in twelve months; his Uncle Robert of Drumbreck in six months; his literary cousin Robert in five months.[23] Nevertheless, in order to point Robert Fraser's sacrifice, we are asked to believe that he performed hard manual labour for this incredibly long time so that his brother Harry should qualify as a doctor. His sense of the dramatic has made him strain probability beyond belief and write melodrama instead of tragedy. The honest homely detail with which the story is told blinds us to this until we examine it later; we want to believe it because Robert and Saunders are so convincing and Harry so vividly selfish, but we have been cheated for the sake of dramatic effect and a better story.

Elsewhere Crockett uses death as a similarly dramatic conclusion, though never so well expressed in careful gradations of Scots. 'Accepted of the Beasts', handled in a more elevated English style, tells of young Hugh Hamilton, blue-eyed and ethereal, a minister misunderstood, slandered, mystical, cast out by his congregation; he dies singing Handel to a group of cows in a quarry, appropriately 'he was despised and rejected of men'. Even Crockett could not have invented this ending; he knew the story of William Nicholson, the

Galloway packman and poet who played the fiddle to colts in a quarry, a tale current in Galloway and repeated by Dr John Brown in *Horae Subsecivae*.[24] It was injudicious to make use of such a bizarre ending in a story which already strained credulity. It is hard to depict a character too fine for ordinary humanity. Crockett wisely never lets his saintly young minister utter a word but suggests his fineness by stylised references to unseen music and the seventh heavens glimpsed as he walked along the street, entranced, with faint echoes of Coleridge and Wordsworth. What we do hear and remember are the mean voices of the congregation behind the minister's back. The wife of a well-to-do merchant, a Bailie, affronted when the minister passes her by without seeing her, complains

> an' him had his tea in my verra hoose on Wednesday three weeks, nae further gane, the prood upstart![25]

The 'theological postman' grumbles gloomily after Hamilton's first wonderful sermon

> He was ayont the cluds afore we could get oor books shut, oot o' sicht gin we gat oorsel's settled in oor seats, an' we saw na mair o' him till he said 'Amen'.[26]

Hugh Hamilton might have been a success in the Garden of Eden, says Crockett drily, but not in Cowdenknowes. 'He's far ower the heids o' the fowk,'[27] grumble the wiseacres. Only the children love him, but that too is a fault. He tells them Bible stories and sings to them in his clear flute-like voice.

> 'I like nae siccan wark' said some, 'how is he to fricht them when he comes to catechise them if he makes so free wi' them the noo, that's what I wad like to ken.'[28]

Christ said 'Suffer the little children to come unto Me', but the Catechism, taught by fear, is more important.

> 'Na, an' another thing, he's aye sing, singin' at his hymns. Noo, there nay be twa three guid hymns, though I hae ma doots—but among a' that he sings, it stan's to reason that there maun be a hantle o' balderdash'[29]

It is not that there is—they don't know, not having investigated—but it 'stan's to reason' that there must be. This ungenerous, carping criticism is the only lively thing about 'Accepted of the Beasts' and the chorus of Presbyterian whines reminds us of the 'bodies' of Barbie in George Douglas Brown's *The House with the Green Shutters* (1901) and is just as forceful. Hugh Hamilton has no chance when a false charge of immorality is brought against him. He is so shadowy that we read of his strange demise, singing Handel to the cows, with total disbelief. Reality breaks in when the mean-minded congregation

> buried him at his own expense in the deserted kirkyard at Kirkcleuch, a mile

or two along the windy brow of the sea cliff, looking to the sale of his books to defray the cost.[30]

The farmer of Drumrash who had seen him among the cows and heard his song makes the drunken stone-cutter add to the name on the plain gravestone 'He was despised and rejected of men', likening him to Christ Himself. Crockett does his best for Hugh, but a saint is too delicate and static for him—and for most authors; the wicked are more lively and picturesque, like Milton's Satan.

Contrast with Hugh Hamilton the high-flown foolishness of the Rev Douglas Maclellan of 'The Lammas Preaching'. He too is a stranger in the midst of his flock; he comes from Wigtownshire and is not familiar with the ways of the Stewartry. He had thanked the Lord that morning for

> 'the bounteous rain wherewith He had seen meet to refresh His weary heritage.'
> His congregation silently acquiesced, 'For what,' said they, 'could a man from the Machars be expected to ken about meadow hay?'[31]

That 'silently' is masterly in its evocation of mingled resignation and despair; there is more life in it than in all the strained effort to create poor Hugh Hamilton.

The minister is to preach that evening at Cauldshaws, and his text, as he keeps telling everyone, is to be 'Whatsoever thy hand findeth to do, do it with thy might.' Stubbornly set on having his own way and carrying out the precepts he would no doubt have elaborated upon in his sermon, he disregards all warnings about the wild weather and the dreaded Skyreburn in flood, plunges obstinately into the tempest and the drowned fields, and even after he has had to be pulled half-drowned from the water by the local ne'er-do-weel (who was moved to prayer for the first time in twenty years by the danger 'and to infinitely more purpose than the minister') insists on pushing on and having to be rescued again. He is a living text on the perils of too literal interpretation of Scripture. 'The Lammas Preaching', the best story of the twenty-four, is brilliantly, sardonically comic from beginning to end; the minister's voice argues as strongly as do his frustrated well-wishers, the landscape roars energetically in windswept hostility, the simple are proved over and over again to be more wise than the learned man who ends tucked up in bed in Cauldshaws farm-house still rambling on about his text but quietened by the stout red-cheeked good wife who suggests a better text: 'He sent from above, He took me and drew me from out of many waters.' Every point is made neatly and skilfully; this is Crockett at his comic best because there is so much of himself in the story. From what we know of his temperament we can hazard a guess that 'Whatsoever thy hand findeth to do, do it with thy might' may have been one of his own favourite texts.

In 'Boanerges Simpson's Encumbrance' and 'The Heather Lintie', death is again a convenient climax. The Rev Boanerges is a self-satisfied town minister very much at home in Zion who preaches wonderful sermons; it is only after the death of his wife, his 'encumbrance', that the Provost by an ingeniously simple chance discovers that it is she who has been writing them for him, including the one—deeply moving—preached on the Sunday after she dies. Crockett opens with a paragraph in heavy English thick with reported speech and the jargon of church reports.

> Every one said that it was a pity of Boanerges Simpson, the minister of St Tudno's. This was universally recognised in Maitland. Not only the congregation of St Tudno's but the people of other denominations knew that Mr Simpson was saddled with a wife who was little but a drag upon him. They even said that he had been on the point of obtaining a call to a great city charge, when, his domestic circumstances being inquired into, it was universally recognised by the session of that company of humble followers of Christ that, however suitable the Rev Boanerges Simpson might be to receive £1,200 a year for preaching the Carpenter's gospel to it, Mrs Boanerges Simpson was not at all the woman to dispense afternoon tea to the session's spouses between the hours of three and six.[32]

Crockett puts us on our guard with the facile phrase 'Every one said ... ' so often the herald of unkind judgements and lies and follows it with the mean colloquialism using the generous 'pity' in a shallow sneering way: 'It was a pity of Boanerges Simpson'. We hear their uncharitable voices spreading their cheap gossip that 'Mr Simpson'—(that 'Mr' is worth thinking about)—

> that Mr Simpson was saddled with a wife who was little but a drag upon him

The ugliness of the imagery, of a cart held back by a heavy brake, is an index to the delicacy of their minds. Once more we are reminded of the 'bodies' of Barbie.

The long final sentence introduces a series of jarring contradictions which show up the commercial values of Maitland; Mrs Simpson has been such a handicap to her husband that she has actually deprived him of material advancement, surely the greatest sin she could commit.

> They *even said* that he had been on the point of obtaining a call to a great city charge

when his wife's unworthiness came to light. The session of the great city charge are referred to as 'that company of humble followers of Christ' who decide that, though the Rev Boanerges would have been a good financial investment for them, worth a lavish salary (for those days) of £1,200 a year for expounding the goodness and beauty of poverty, 'preaching the Carpenter's gospel', his wife is simply not good enough for their wives to take tea with. Their lack of Christianity is laid bare; their middle-class respectability is shown in their ponderous phrases: 'his domestic circumstances being inquired into', 'dispense afternoon tea', 'on the point of obtaining a call to a great city charge'—this last being surely the greatest unconscious revelation of the session's and Mr Simpson's qualities, since 'obtaining' suggests a degree of intrigue and backstairs wangling grossly inappropriate to Christ's humble simplicity. Crockett by manipulating the simple colloquialisms of the gossips and the heavier jargon of the Kirk Session has loaded his factual opening paragraph with the very phrases which surround the situation, giving us an insight into the forces at work which suggests that he has hit upon the technique which Lewis Grassic Gibbon was to use in *A Scots Quair* many years later. It is also significant that the only man who can see through the Rev Boanerges is the Provost, a direct forthright man whose homely Scots speech is apt to 'cut through the pretentious unction of the cleric like a knife through soap'.[33]

In 'The Heather Lintie', the setting and circumstances are filled in realistically—Janet Balchrystie is a lonely ageing woman, the motherless daughter of a foreman platelayer on the Port Patrick Railway who is much given to getting drunk. After his death she lives on in isolation in the cottage at the back of Barbrax Long Wood, her one ambition to win recognition as a writer of poetry. She sends anonymously her poems to local papers, which print them after cutting and mangling them to suit the space available. Finally she decides to have them printed at her own expense by a provincial printer, under the title *The Heather Lintie*. Here Crockett could have been sentimental but he is far from that; the title is appalling, the verse matches it, and the book itself when it comes out is

> a small rather thickish octavo, on sufficiently wretched grey paper which had suffered from lack of thorough washing in the original paper-mill. It was bound in a peculiarly deadly blue of a rectified Reckitt tint which gave you dazzles in the eye at any distance under ten paces.[34]

Crockett, collector of books, knows all about volumes of verse produced provincially at their author's expense, and has not lived near paper-mills without learning something of their processes.

The book goes up to Edinburgh for review, and a clever young reporter seizes on it with glee. He begins by affecting to praise it:

> This is a book which may be a genuine source of pride to every native of the ancient province of Galloway. Galloway has been celebrated for black cattle and for wool—as also for a certain bucolic belatedness of temperament, but Galloway has never hitherto produced a poetess.

He then falls into the mocking style of satirical literary magazines, a style which Crockett catches perfectly—the style of the *Saturday Review*. A poetess, he says

> has arisen in the person of Miss Janet Bal—something or other. We have not an interpreter at hand, and so cannot wrestle with the intricacies of the authoress's name, which appears to be some Galwegian form of Erse or Choctaw. Miss Bal—and so forth—has a true fount of pathos and humour

which he illustrates by scraps of Janet's sadly vulnerable verse. Then

> The authoress will make a great success. If she comes to the capital where

genius is always appreciated, she will, without doubt, make her fortune. Nay, if Miss Bal—, but again we cannot proceed for the want of an interpreter—if Miss B., we say, will only accept a position at Cleary's Waxworks and give readings from her poetry, or exhibit herself in the act of pronouncing her own name, she will be a greater draw in this city than Punch and Judy, or even the latest American advertising evangelist who preaches standing on his head.[35]

A situation of excruciating horror for the lonely woman awaiting her newspaper has been built up, but Crockett shirks the harsh ending it demands. Janet has been ill for some months, and a friendly woodman from Barbrax brings the paper to her late one evening. Janet has time to read only the first sentence. She takes its mock approval for praise, and in the darkening light leaves the rest for the morning, shedding tears of happiness. But before morning the Angel of the Presence comes to her and she dies without ever knowing the truth. 'God' says Crockett portentously, becoming a preacher in the final sentence, 'is more merciful than man'.

In four stories, death has been manipulated so as to move us. In 'The Stickit Minister' it has been postponed beyond credibility for the sake of a strong dramatic conclusion. In 'Accepted of the Beasts', 'Boanerges Simpson's Encumbrance' and 'The Heather Lintie' it has been made a convenient literary device. There may be some excuse in that Crockett was writing short sketches and stories, but he has in each case built up a strong situation, then shirked its strong conclusion; it would have been more honest (if more difficult) if Hugh Hamilton had been made to face his congregation squarely instead of dying among the cows; more revealing (if harder to work out) if Boanerges Simpson's personality had been made worthy of his wife's devotion—as it is, she remains a vague exasperating shadow; it would have been more like real life (if crueller) if Janet had read the whole review. In each case the careful realism of the settings deserved better; the Great Presence has been diminished. In at least one instance, that of Boanerges Simpson, it may be that another writer caught up the idea and worked it out in terms of politics most successfully; Maggie Shand in Barrie's *What Every Woman Knows* takes a hand in writing her husband's speeches, and we believe in her wholeheartedly. But Crockett was content with the melodrama and left the stories imperfectly worked out.

It may be objected that 'A Midsummer Idyll' with Meg letting three different men notify the Registrar that they were to marry her on the same day, or 'The Three Maister Slees' with a minister in the 1890s carelessly preaching his grandfather's sermon giving thanks for Waterloo, are equally improbable, but we let this pass in comedy and laugh at the exaggeration without any sense of jarring discord. Crockett has a surer touch in comedy; tragedy unbalances him and makes him uneven and at times almost shrill. He grows not so much sentimental as sensational.

But there was a freshness, a vigour, an originality about these short stories which took him to the top of his publisher's list in 1893. The form suited him; it compressed and concentrated his ideas. He could write variously and sincerely, he could adopt a wide range of voice and manners, he could be angry as well as amusing, compassionate as well as comic. He was obviously a young man, interested in trying out different devices and effects, willing to depict a saint as well as he could, even if that were not very well, in addition to his amusing collection of sinners. He was not afraid to be critical of his colleagues and had a healthy scorn of what Burns called the 'Unco Guid'; and though not a politician or a reformer, he could depict the scenes and characters of his native countryside with telling implied criticism, at his best when his weapon was ridicule. He could build up a scene with carefully marshalled effects, could catch a mood or a landscape in brief flashes of colour, and could parody and catch the common clichés of his time to good purpose. Underneath everything runs the sense of humour—that dancing commonsense—which was his greatest quality; and allied to it is indignation with the pompous, anger at cruelty and scorn of hypocrisy. He can laugh at himself as well as at others; in 'The Three Maister Peter Slees' he makes the Established Church beadle ramble on about his minister:

> '...he's a graun' naiteralist, the body,' said the minister's man, 'an' whan the big Enbra' societies come doon here to glower an' wunner at the bit whurls and holes in the rocks, he's the verra man to tak' them to the bit; an' whan the Creechton Asylum fowk cam' doon to a picnic, as they ca'ed it, it was Maister Slee that gied them a lectur' on the bonny heuchs o' Couthy. An' faith I couldna tell ye what yin o' the twa companies was the mair sensible.'[36]

The Rev S R Crockett, enthusiastic lecturer on geology, does not mind likening himself to a minister of whom he is making fun; he has a good idea of how his flock regard him and does not mind in the least. In the story of the Sunday School picnic which John Black so deplored, he tells an anecdote which is surely against himself. Children and teachers are wandering happily among the rocks and on the sands; others are having a swim; it is time to relax.

> All was peaceful and happy, and the minister was the happiest of all, for his sermons were both done, and lying snug within his Bible in the study of the manse. He talked to the superintendent at intervals, sucking meanwhile the ends of some sprays of honeysuckle. Then he crossed his legs, and told tales of how Rob Blair and he lived on ten shillings a week in their first session at college. The superintendent took mental notes for the benefit of his own boys, two of whom were going up to college this winter with quite other notions.[37]

This is nothing but sheer warm humour, the minister stretching himself at ease, talking about the past (as Crockett did himself in interviews) without its dawning on him that his boasting of how thriftily he and his friend had lived at college years ago is going to bring down upon the superintendent's sons lectures on that thriftiness which they are not going to enjoy at all. He is dooming them, quite unconsciously, to a measure of penury. Here Crockett is attacking no one and nothing, merely enjoying the comedy of his own tactlessness.

Critics like Robertson Nicoll and William Wallace hailed Crockett as yet another writer on the Scottish scene[38] but confessed themselves puzzled by where to place him. He was no imitator but had a tart flavour all his own. Sir George Douglas was the most acute. He praised his speech and the Galloway speech of Saunders, but struck a warning note about the stories in general.

> All are vigorously written; indeed, where fault is to be found, it is rather on the ground that restraint rather than force is wanting. For instance, that blow from a poker that falls on a boy's head in 'Duncan Duncanson'; that incident with the powderflask in 'The Split in the Marrow Kirk'—do they not savour somewhat too strongly of Mr Kipling's manner to be perfectly in place among quiet tales of a country parish?[39]

This criticism is percipient. Even if Galloway parishes were not as quiet as Sir George supposes (and they were not); even if one suggests that Crockett was not trying to write 'quiet tales' but was writing from experience without any attempt to sentimentalise any aspect of his scene, least of all his ministers and his congregations; even if one recognises the element of social criticism, almost socialist criticism, which Crockett turned into stories without taking it into any more specific rebellion, one has to admit that in *The Stickit Minister* there are elements of melodrama which reveal a defect in Crockett's taste. He could manage his styles but not his imagination, and as time wore on this fault, forgivable in the early work, was not corrected. He was inclined to let himself go too far in engineering quick drastic endings; he was writing for a public which craved the strongly dramatic and by that craving encouraged his worst qualities. His humour was his redeeming virtue; he could write plainly and forcibly without it when his anger was roused; but when his imagination was set free without either humour or quiet anger, he wrote shrilly and at times without balance.

Sir George Douglas dismissed 'The Heather Lintie' as 'the false sublime', and this Crockett should have noted and taken to heart. Sir George advised him to curb his exuberance—'in his next book let Mr Crockett tell his plain tale with no thought in his head but to get it told'. He could handle a plain tale like 'The Lammas Preaching' with energy, enjoyment, stylistic exactness and point, and should either have given up his saintly ministers and ethereal minister's wives, or have worked at them honestly and hard so as to give them intelligible, credible and sensible personalities. Above all, he should have tested all he wrote, even when it was not comedy, against the salt astringency of his ridicule; his humour, that other name for a sense of proportion, would have kept him rooted firmly in reality.

Ironically, the success of *The Stickit Minister* made this hard to do. What he could do easily had brought him easy fame. He was caught up into faster writing and hastier production. Four books in the next year, even when two of them were *The Lilac Sunbonnet* and *The Raiders*, were too many—and both of these would have benefited from hard pruning and longer consideration. For *The Stickit Minister* he deserved praise but not the wild acclaim he received. He himself was delighted and surprised by the popularity which his twenty-four tales—light quick contributions to a minor religious periodical—brought him. He should have been warned by the surprise; they were not as totally brilliant as readers thought, and he must himself have known it. Nevertheless, *The Stickit Minister* revealed a new and original talent, one to be watched and to be reckoned with, in popular Scottish writing.

CHAPTER 5

The Lilac Sunbonnet

The Lilac Sunbonnet, though published some six months after *The Raiders* appeared in the spring of 1894, was begun before and completed after it. The *Sunbonnet* ran first of all as a serial in the *Christian Leader* from 4 January to 27 September 1894, and came out in book form in October. Its narrative proceeds more purposefully than did that of *A Galloway Herd*, its predecessor as a *Leader* serial (which begins in Crockett's childhood Galloway and ends surprisingly and dramatically in Paris during the Commune) but still at first reading seems to ramble, with chapters about minor characters that are almost separate stories. This is perhaps natural since Crockett while he was writing it was also contributing short stories and sketches anonymously nearly every week to the *Leader* and was at home in that form.[1]

On closer examination, the rambling chapters which appear to wander away from and even hold up the plot are all related to it in some way, however tenuous, and by their diversity provide a lively picture of Galloway country life at widely differing levels. They also ensure that the serious plot dealing with matters of creed and belief is not too prominently didactic. Without the many digressions—the comic wooing of Meg Kissock by Saunders Mowdiewort the gravedigger, his battle with the Established Church, his ludicrous views on matrimony, the eldritch singing of Jock Gordon the 'natural' about the devil, young Andra Kissock guddling in the river for trout, the Greatorix gentry in their mouldering castle—the story would be too simple and obvious, not to say too short. The apparent irrelevancies give it roots in country life and customs and enable clues to a central mystery to be planted here and there for the reader to find if he looks. Every character relates to and by his or her mere existence and conversation sheds light on some aspect of the lovers. They are grouped round Winsome and Ralph like a very odd Greek chorus. Moreover, by wrapping his theme up in innocent-looking rustic fun and incident drawn from his own Galloway upbringing, Crockett is able not only to provide variety and humour but also to disguise what exactly he is about. There is more to *The Lilac Sunbonnet* than a love-story set against the activities of a farm community, though it is the love-story which carries in its fabric the serious theme.

The public received *The Lilac Sunbonnet* enthusiastically; its first issue of 10,000 copies was sold out on the day of publication, according to its publisher's advertisement in the *British Weekly* on 11 October 1894, and a second printing was on the way. Robertson Nicoll, in his weighty personage as

'Claudius Clear' and editor of the *British Weekly* reviewed it favourably.[2] He called it

> a sweet, slow idyll of Scotch love-making,

very different from *The Raiders* but not on that account to be despised:

> the background is commonplace, and how happy and enviable does the commonplace sometimes appear. Mr Crockett tells a pure and fresh love-story ... I think he has done a great deal for us all in writing a story so full of inspiring faith in womanhood.

The 'New Woman' had been invading fiction; was this why Robertson Nicoll went out of his way to hint that Crockett's heroine—a most competent young woman—also possessed the goodness and sweetness of the older ideal? He may have felt that her unwomanly competence needed a blessing from him before it could be allowed to be approved of. And he voiced one other complaint:

> I will own to some disappointment that religion plays so poor a part in the story. There is a real danger that Mr Crockett may dwell too much on what is external and grotesque in the faith of his men and women. Better leave religion alone than use it merely for comic effect.

The serious Free Churchman feels that Crockett, in his farcical scene of Saunders called up before the Kirk Session, may have gone too far. There is a suggestion of the headmaster telling the pupil that he will forgive him once for the sake of the love-story but hopes he will not do it again.

The *Sunbonnet* met with harsher treatment elsewhere. J H Millar's article 'The Literature of the Kailyard' in W E Henley's 'New Review' was the first to use the derisive nickname 'kailyard', taken from an old Scottish song which Ian Maclaren affixed as motto to his first collection of Scottish rural tales, *Beside the Bonnie Brier Bush*:

> There grows a bonnie brier bush in our kailyard,
> And white are the blossoms on't in our kailyard.

Millar, six years younger than Crockett, classical scholar from Balliol College, Oxford, son and grandson of Scottish judges, was eager to make his mark in the old vituperative *Maga* style. He blamed Barrie for inventing the kailyard, passed scornfully over Maclaren, but poured out the vials of his wrath upon Crockett. *The Lilac Sunbonnet* was, he declared, a 'warm' book, exceeding the limits of good breeding. Its love-making was a mixture of coyness and explicit sexuality that 'opened the sluices to an irresistible flood of nauseous and nasty philandering', a 'slough of knowing archness, of bottomless vulgarity'. It is hard to define what he meant by kailyard; he seems to have intended some kind of ungentlemanly coarseness—certainly not the sentimental parochialism it has come to mean today. He belonged in spirit to the law and to the eighteenth century; he was to become Professor of Constitutional Law at Edinburgh University and concurrently for two years lecturer in and expert on eighteenth-century literature at Glasgow. In both he was considered eccentric.[3] Even in his salad days he was perhaps the most inappropriate critic for a deceptively simple tale of rural love.

The young John Buchan in the *Glasgow Herald* in November 1895 was equally scathing, but in a totally different direction. He did not sense any salaciousness but rather its opposite; he complained that Crockett was too wholesome.

> Mr Crockett hates the sickly and the grimy with a perfect hatred. He is all for the wind and the sunshine, hills and heather, lilac and adventure, kisses and well-churned butter. He is clamorous over their beauties; he is all for the great common things of the world—faith and love, heroism and patience. But it seems to us that in this also there is a danger; mere talking about fine things does not make fine literature, and Mr Crockett at his worst is only a boisterous talker.[4]

Crockett's energy and enthusiasm are what damn him; he does not toil and moil, polish and perfect sufficiently. Once again the critic is a classics man, out of sympathy temperamentally with Crockett—though *Sir Quixote of the Moors* and *John Burnet of Barnes*, written at approximately this time, show that Buchan was not above taking hints from Crockett, without equalling his vividness of description.

In our own century, George Blake in his inaccurate and intemperate *Barrie and the Kailyard School*, set about the *Sunbonnet* with cudgels:

> It is hard for any reasonably literate adult of the mid-twentieth century to read *The Lilac Sunbonnet* without nausea ... Crockett's air of jaunty realism conveys the impression that he really believed this mass of sludge to be pretty good and almost possible.[5]

Crockett did think highly of the *Sunbonnet*; he called it 'the best expression of my youth'[6] and dedicated it to his English wife. It is a happy book, its author delighting in the life and sunshine of the countryside, whole-heartedly on the side of the lovers, and critical right from the start of the Marrow Kirk whose narrow doctrines for a time over-shadow their happiness. The root of Blake's objection to the so-called 'Kailyard' writers was their over-emphasis on the manse, the minister and the religion of the kirk. It is odd that it did not occur to him that Crockett's message was much the same. The lovers are in the foreground and behind glowers the Marrow Kirk, stern, humourless and puritanical. The hero is a divinity student destined for the ministry of this small but severe sect; it is the beauty of nature and his love for the heroine that liberate him. The Marrow Kirk is the villain of the piece, and the business of the story is to free the hero and heroine from its grip.

Crockett is open to criticism for loading the dice too heavily against his imaginary sect. It is small, consisting of only two congregations and two ministers who have 'come out' against all larger Presbyterian churches and cut themselves off in righteousness and rectitude. The Rev Gilbert Peden in Edinburgh and the Rev Allan Welsh in Galloway are distinctly strange— stranger than any of the ministers Crockett has mocked in *The Stickit Minister*. Gilbert Peden lives in a sunless flat in James's Court in the Edinburgh Lawnmarket, looked after by John Bairdieson, an ex-sailor who expresses his fervour as a convert to the Marrow Kirk by refusing to allow any woman to enter. Peden's son Ralph, whose mother is long since dead, has led a restricted and narrow life; his experience comes from books and study—he has known nothing at first hand. He has met no women except the old wives of his father's flock, and has been brought up to believe that women are necessary but on the whole inferior and ill-advised creations of the Almighty.

The Rev Allan Welsh of Dullarg in Galloway is strange in a different way. Gilbert Peden is allowed to be austerely well-favoured, but Welsh is harsh and repellent, his body bent and twisted, his huge head top-heavy with sombre learning so that when he walks he looks perpetually as if he were about to topple over. He broods darkly at all times. His gloomy Manse of Dullarg is so full of death-watch beetles that he imagines he hears them all the time ticking in his brain. Neither of the two ministers is a testimonial for their gospel.

Among Welsh's Galloway flock are Walter Skirving and his wife, well-to-do and prosperous, owning the rich farm of Craig Ronald—but they too are far from ordinary. Walter Skirving is semi-paralysed, and sits silent all day looking out of the window across his fields, the shattered remnants of a man. His wife, in strong contrast, is talkative to the point of garrulousness, but she too has been stricken by life; she is confined to her chair by a stroke. The farm is managed for them by their granddaughter Winifred Charteris, known as Winsome, a lively fair-haired young beauty who combines efficiency with attractiveness. Many young men have sighed for her, but she is heartwhole. She appears a normal happy girl, but her background is as strange as Ralph's in its own way. She has lived as a child in Cumberland before being brought to Craig Ronald to comfort her grandparents after the accidental death of their only son. She has almost forgotten that part of her life. Her mother's name has not been spoken in Craig Ronald for twenty years, and she does not know who her father is.

Ralph Peden is sent down by his father to continue his studies during the summer vacation under the supervision of Allan Welsh in Galloway. Ironically, the first task set this youth who has met no women is to summarise and pronounce judgment upon the nature of a virtuous woman as set out in the Book of Proverbs. When he encounters the reality of Winsome, he falls in love with her. She finds him oddly attractive, and as they gradually get to know one another, she too falls in love, but she forbids him to think of her. She will never marry, she declares. Some mystery hangs over her birth; it has darkened the lives of her grandparents and she does not wish it to darken his.

Inevitably, Ralph begins to doubt his vocation as a Marrow Kirk minister. Even in Edinburgh, before he came to Galloway, he had been tempted to write poems and articles unknown to his father, knowing that they would be forbidden. The rich sensuous beauty of Galloway and his love for Winsome increase his doubt. When he is called back to Edinburgh to stand his 'trials for license' as a minister, he writes to Winsome asking her to meet him the night before he leaves. A scheming servant-girl Jess Kissock, who covets Ralph for herself, not for the first time intercepts his letter, and contrives that he keeps a false tryst with her, while Winsome goes to the arms of the local seducer, Agnew Greatorix. The plot almost succeeds in the darkness, but in failing brings them even closer together.

Allan Welsh has noted Ralph's love for Winsome. He intervenes and forbids Ralph to have anything more to do with her. Twenty years before, he, Allan Welsh, had won the heart of Gilbert Peden's betrothed and run off with her to an unsanctified marriage at Gretna Green, one not recognised by the Marrow Kirk. Winsome is his daughter, and as the child of a sinful union is no fit bride for a Marrow minister. Ralph refuses to give her up, and is turned out of the Manse forthwith—Welsh cannot have an unbeliever under his roof. Ralph and Winsome, their love now plighted, take a sad but not altogether hopeless farewell, but when Ralph reaches Edinburgh, he finds himself similarly condemned by his father and turned away from James's Court. His uncle, Professor Thriepneuk (presumably the brother-in-law of his late mother, and not a Marrow adherent) makes him his assistant at the College and gives him a home so that he can find his true bent as a poet.

Meanwhile, Walter Skirving has sent Winsome to Allan Welsh with her mother's miniature and the love-letters Welsh had written twenty years before. These soften his heart. When the two Marrow ministers meet at their Synod in Edinburgh, Welsh deliberately makes no complaint about Ralph and declares him a satisfactory candidate. Peden immediately accuses him of withholding the truth. Welsh retorts that Peden twenty years before for the sake of the Marrow Kirk had withheld the truth of his unsanctified marriage. They depose one another from office, so that, to the horror of John Bairdieson listening at the keyhole, the Marrow Kirk ceases to exist. Fortunately, by the next day John has thought of a procedural loophole. Peden accepts reinstatement as a serving minister, but Welsh refuses, knowing himself to be unworthy. The two men, formerly held together only by their allegiance to the Marrow Kirk, renew their old friendship and are reconciled through the memory of the woman they had both loved.

Welsh returns to Galloway to seek forgiveness from Walter Skirving whose hospitality he had abused by eloping with his daughter. Skirving yields it freely, but Welsh, worn out by stress and the guilty brooding of years, dies in receiving it. Skirving, for so long a sick man, dies only hours later. The two are buried in the August sunshine of the same day. Their legacies of money and land to Ralph and Winsome signify their tacit consent to their marriage. Ralph's poems in any case are a success; they are married an unspecified time later, and we leave them on a bright day of harvest and fulfilment with two happy children playing around them.

It can be seen clearly in summary how the two elements, warm human love and cold doctrine always work against each other. In the telling of the story this is less obvious. Crockett adopts the tone of an older, wiser man who can watch the lovers with amusement as well as sympathy—this is presumably why Millar found 'coyness' and 'archness' in the book—and dwells on the beauty of the midsummer landscape more than in any of his later books. This is not without reason; if Ralph is to be so deeply moved by the richness of summer, the reader must be made to feel it too. In any case, Crockett delights in revisiting in imagination the scenes of his own boyhood. Craig Ronald is a rich and prosperous version of the much smaller bleaker farm on which he was born, Little Duchrae, loch, stream, bridge, loaning, gate, craigs and all. He does not describe it idyllically—his ploughman wash in tin basins outside the door of the farm, his servants are sharp-tongued and caustic as they knit in the evening at the gable-end of the house, his small boy Andra has been known to keep worms in the milkflask which he takes to school, a detail which may have come from Crockett's own mischievous boyhood. The play of light and shade on the fields and the loch, the day to day life of the farm, the genial deliberate slowness with which the tale is told all serve to complicate the theme and give it truth to life.

In addition, we are not presented with the narrative directly. It comes to us through hints and clues strewn through the chapters as if it were a detective story. Ralph brings Welsh a letter in which his father talks of the solitariness of their life in James's Court and adds 'to you I do not need to tell the reason of that',[7] he asks Welsh to examine Ralph well, 'dig deep and see if the lad has a heart. He shows it not to me'. The Marrow Kirk has made its student cold and distant even to his father. The handwriting 'A Welsh' on the minister's Hebrew Bible seems strangely and pleasantly familiar to Winsome, a fleeting memory of her Cumberland childhood, though she does not realise it.[8] When Winsome takes Ralph to meet her grandparents, they welcome him warmly as his father's son; on his second visit, Mrs Skirving asks him about his father whom she has known well in the past; she makes the curious comment 'When I kenned yer faither, he wad hae been nocht the waur o' a pickle mair o' the auld Adam in him.'[9] The Skirvings are wholeheartedly glad that Ralph loves their granddaughter; his father had been 'sorely used' by this house and 'it wad maybes be some amends' if he won her in the end.[10]

Winsome too refers to the past and the mystery that hangs over her birth. She asks Ralph if his father could be unkind; she suspects, though she has never been able to wheedle the whole story out of her grandmother, that her mother and his father have been in some way connected and says that her grandmother possesses a miniature of Gilbert Peden as a young man, with her mother's maiden name written on the reverse side. She wonders if perhaps his father had been unkind to her mother.[11] Ralph answers that his father is silent and reserved 'as I fear I too have been till I came down here', but never unkind except on matters connected with the Marrow Kirk. He would like to have said of himself that his reserve had lasted only 'till I met you, dear' but cannot find courage to utter the words—yet.[12] They realise that their parents have been involved in some far off sadness which is never spoken of.

Allan Welsh furtively kisses the handwriting on a packet he finds left carelessly lying by Andra Kissock at the Grannoch Bridge addressed by Winsome to Ralph[13] and roundly takes Agnew Greatorix to task for his frequent visits to Craig Ronald. He knows him as the ruin of several local girls already, and sternly orders him to leave Winsome alone, as if he had some peculiar interest in her.[14] And once Mrs Skirving, irrepressible as always, tells Winsome in Ralph's hearing that 'the faither o' him there cam as near bein' the daddy o' ye . . .' but has to break off at her husband's stern reproof.[15] A half-forgotten secret has been stirred up by Ralph's appearance in Galloway, one which has been bitter but is so no longer.

The comedy provided by the rustic characters counteracts the melancholy suggested by the old sadness. Saunders Mowdiewort, Allan Welsh's servant as well as Established Church gravedigger, reports to the Craig Ronald servants on Ralph's behaviour. He is very learned, but also inexplicably restless—seldom can a young man in love have been described so unsentimentally:

> He's for a' the world like a stirk wi' a horse cleg on him that he canna get at. He comes in an' sits doon at his desk, an' spreads oot his buiks, an' ye wad think that he's gaun to be at it the leeve-lang day. But afore ye hae time to turn roon' an' get at yer ain wark, the craiter'll be oot again an' awa' up to the hill wi' a buik aneath his oxter.[16]

Saunders, a 'seeking widower', is trying to win the affections of Meg Kissock, Winsome's maid, but is making little progress. He gives Meg a page on which Ralph had written a poem

> cuttit intil lengths like the metre psalms, but it luikit gye and daft like, sae I didna' read it.[17]

Winsome, listening at the window where she sits in the evenings, later demands it from Meg and lies awake until dawn to read it; there is a gentle vulnerable side to her, for all her sharpness.

Saunders is grossly stupid; coming to court Meg, he is easily tricked by her sister Jess into giving her Ralph's letters to Winsome, the letters which enable her to devise her plot. She wants Ralph herself and knows that Agnew Greatorix wants Winsome, but despises him as too foolish to be a real blackguard:

> Ye'll do the young mistress nae hurt

she says to herself

> for she wad never look twice at ye, but I canna let her get the bonny lad frae Enbra'—na, I saw him first, an' first come first served![18]

But she underestimates Greatorix; he is less foolish than she thinks.

Saunders is also used for the one completely irrelevant piece of comedy in the book. He has been summoned to appear before the Kirk Session of the Established Church for drunkenly miscalling the minister and his office-bearers, and brings with him his formidable mother to speak in his defence. She is the church cleaner and by listening at keyholes and surreptitiously reading the session records knows far more than she should about the church's affairs, particularly its discipline. Others have sinned as well as her son; others have sinned far more gravely; yet they have not been punished, and she will know the reason why. The minister maintains pompously that the law of the kirk is no respecter of persons, but even as he says this a heritor, a landed proprietor in the parish, interjects an exception—'... unless they are heritors', a member of session puts in 'Or members of session' and the schoolmaster adds 'Or parish dominies'.[19] This chapter, reminiscent of Scott's Cuddie Headrigg and his ranting mother, does nothing to forward the plot. It is mischievously included by Crockett as a sly dig at the Established Church, which it strips of all pretensions to fairness and impartiality. Excellent as caricature, it is still shrewd enough to hurt. One sees why Robertson Nicoll had reservations about using religion merely for humour.

Saunders and Meg, Jess and her clumsy ploughman swain Ebie Farrish, Meg's undemonstrative solid relationship with Jock Forrest and to some extent the oddly-matched Skirvings who seem so unsuited to be man and wife, are used to throw into prominence the more subtle level at which Ralph and Winsome live and fall in love, just as their speech is educated and free of local colloquialisms. They have a delicacy of feeling which is their own, and their tentative approaches to one another, though at times absurd as all young love is at times absurd, are yet touching in their puzzled fluctuations of feeling.

Their first meeting is utterly comic. Ralph, on his first day in Galloway, is lying on a hillside above Loch Grannoch trying to keep his mind on the Book of Proverbs and its views on virtuous women. Already the beauty of the countryside is distracting him, lulled by the *chirring* of the grasshoppers and 'that heather scent on which the bees grew tipsy'.[20] He falls asleep, then is suddenly and alarmingly wakened by the sound and sight of Winsome and Meg preparing to wash blankets in the old-fashioned Scottish way in huge wooden tubs by the riverside. Meg is the first to step into a tub and begin to tramp the blankets therein, then Winsome appears, wearing a lilac sunbonnet and carrying water in pails to be heated in the black gipsy pot hung on a tripod over the fire. When she sits down and begins to remove her shoes and stockings before kilting up her skirts to the thighs like Meg, Ralph is seized with adolescent embarrassment and confusion. He runs off to the Manse for safety.

Winsome sees the black figure just as it disappears and looks after it with some amusement as well as curiosity. She finds the books he has left behind in his flight, and is particularly interested in a notebook in which, in his neat small handwriting, there are several strictures upon modern women. His criticism angers her a little, but she is mollified by a sleepy scrawl to the effect that he loves lilac above all colours—this is different. She takes the books, meaning to return them if she meets him the next day, but by then, the notebook has disappeared. She has tucked it into the bosom of her dress, where it remains for the rest of the story, Ralph never knowing what has become of it but Winsome acutely aware of what is near her beating heart. When their love is declared, she thinks with delicious pleasure that she will perhaps tell him one day.

The notebook shows Winsome's immediate sexual attraction to the stranger. Ralph's attraction to her is shown in a more ludicrous way, one matching his sudden retreat. As he answers Allan Welsh's questioning on the subject of his study, he does so, remembering the woman he has seen, 'with a fluency in fervour and exposition to which he had been a stranger', and having got himself well through his oral examination, ruins all in a moment by answering that the badge of beauty in woman is 'A LILAC SUNBONNET!'—a truly Freudian error.[21]

The sunbonnet, the notebook and other trivial everyday objects are used by Crockett as symbols of growing sexual involvement in precisely the same way as D H Lawrence uses simple things—a pound of butter and a bunch of daffodils—to indicate the progress of the erotic relationship between Brangwyn and Anna Lensky in *The Rainbow*. Jess the interloper puts a flower in Ralph's buttonhole in a gesture of apparent intimacy, and Winsome chances to be watching unseen. Later, when the flower falls unregarded to the ground by the stream, she firmly stamps it into the grass with her foot.

'This indicates, like a hand on a dial, the stage of her prepossession', comments Crockett, consciously using this symbolic technique.[22]

In other ways Crockett is unexpectedly like Lawrence. The colours are different; Lawrence sees sex in terms of dark atavistic forces smouldering deep and troubled, like fires burning deep in his tormented characters, whereas Crockett, lighter and more optimistic, thinks in bright clear colours, cool as the blue sky and the green meadows. Yet it is possible to place passages from *The Rainbow* alongside similar passages from *The Lilac Sunbonnet* and see parallels.

The Rainbow[23]

The Lilac Sunbonnet

He felt the fine flame running under his skin, as if all his veins had caught fire on the surface. And he went on walking without knowledge. (p 32)

Time and again the blood rushed to his temples, for he was sure that he heard her coming to him. But it was only the sound of the blood surging blindly through his own veins, or some of the night creatures fulfilling their own night trysts, and seeking their simpler destinies under the cloud of night. (p 238)

Then she looked up at him, the wide young eyes blazing with light. And he bent down and kissed her on the lips. The dawn blazed in them, their new life came to pass, it was beyond all conceiving good, it was so good that it was almost like a passing-away, a trespass. He drew her suddenly closer to him. (p 46)

Winsome drew a happy breath, nestling a little closer—so little that no-one but Ralph would have known. But the little shook him to the depths of his soul. Thus it is to be young and for the first time mastering the geography of an unknown and untraversed continent. ... There is nothing new under the sun, yet to lovers like Winsome and Ralph, all things are new. (p 290, p 293)

Brangwyn went up to his room and lay staring out at the stars of the summer night, his whole being in a whirl. ... There was a life so different from what he knew it. What was there outside his knowledge, how much? What was this that he had touched? What was he in this new influence? ... Where was life, in that which he knew or all outside him? (p 25)

Yet it seemed that in that contact, light as a rose-leaf blown by the winds of late July against his cheek, all his past life had been shorn clean away from the future as with a sharp sword ... This, however, was wholly a new thing. His breath came suddenly short. He breathed rapidly as though to give his lungs more air. The atmosphere seemed to have grown rarer and colder. Indeed it was a different world altogether, and the blanket-washing itself was transferred to some deliciously homely outlying annex of paradise. (p 53)

He had her in his arms, and, obliterated, was kissing her. And it was sheer, blenched agony to him, to break away from himself. She was there, so small and light and accepting in his arms ... that he could not bear it, he could not stand. (p 46)

Ralph Peden's heart stopped beating for a tremendous interval of seconds. The dammed-back blood-surge drave it thundering in his ears. He swayed and would have fallen but for the parapet of the bridge and the clinging arms about his neck. (p 241)

A shiver, a sickness of new birth passed over her, the flame leaped up him, under his skin. She wanted it, this new life from him, with him, yet she must defend herself against it, for it was a destruction. (p 40)

Winsome faltered. She had not been wooed after this manner before. It was perilously sweet. Little ticking pulses drummed in her head. A great yearning came to her to let herself drift out on a sea of love. That love of giving up all, which is the precious privilege, the saving dowry or utter undoing of women, surged in upon her heart. (p 211)

But a sunshiny day came full of the scent of a mezeron tree, when bees were tumbling into the yellow crocuses, and she forgot, she felt like somebody else, not herself, a new person, quite glad. But she knew it was fragile, and she dreaded it. The vicar put pea-flower into the crocuses, for his bees to roll in, and she laughed. Then night came, with brilliant stars that she knew of old, from her girlhood. And they flashed so bright, she knew they were victors. (p 54)

In Winsome's soul the first flushing glory of the May of youth was waking the prisoned life. But there were throbs and thrillings too piercingly sweet to last undeveloped. The bursting bud of her healthful beauty, quickened by the shy reticence of her soul, was shaking the centres of her life, even as a laburnum-tree mysteriously quivers when the golden rain is in act to break from the close-clustered dependent budlets. (p 109)

Crockett, like Lawrence, is rendering sexuality in sharp physical terms; his lovers are part of nature, with the simple direct innocence of nature beneath their conventional behaviour—very unlike Lawrence, it is part of his humour to show the two in conflict. Writing for the *Leader*, he must observe the remnants of Victorian taboos, but the prim Millar was perhaps nearer the truth in 1895 when he called him 'nasty' than Blake was in calling him sentimental in 1951, though neither is right. Crockett had been brought up in the country, as a Galloway peasant, and knew country lads and lasses and their assignations under hedges and by haystacks; in writing of Ebie Farrish he remarks unromantically that 'Galloway ploughmen are the most general of lovers. Ebie looked upon it therefore as no disloyalty to Jess that he should display his watch-guard and other accomplishments to the young maids at the Crae'.[24] That 'accomplishments' covers, as Crockett intended it should, a wide range of amorous activities. He was no ordinary peasant; he had read Hardy, Meredith, Flaubert, Zola, Balzac—he was no ordinary Free Church minister either.

The lilac sunbonnet itself is the strongest of the sexual symbols. Ralph becomes obsessively aware of it on the morning when he and Winsome meet in the summer dawn and walk up the hill together. Winsome teases him about kissing her grandmother's hand, and swings her bonnet carelessly but provocatively by the strings.

> But she had presumed just a hair-breadth too far on Ralph's tenderness. He snatched the lilac sunbonnet out of her hands, tearing, in his haste, one of the strings off, and leaving it in Winsome's hand, from which it fell to the ground. Then he kissed it once and twice outside where the sun had shone on it, and again inside where it had rested on her head.
> 'You have torn it,' she said, complainingly, yet without anger.
> 'I am very glad,' said Ralph Peden, coming nearer to her with a light in his eye that she had never seen before.
> Winsome dropped the string, snatched up the bonnet, and fled up the hill as trippingly as a young doe towards the herd's cottage. At the top of the fell she paused a moment with her hand on her side, as if out of breath. Ralph Peden was still holding the torn bonnet-string in his hand.
> He held it up, hanging loose like a pennon from his hand. She could hear the words come clear up the hill.
> 'I'm very—glad—that—I—tore—it—, and I will come—and—see—your—grandmother!'[25]

This is very close to Lawrence's method of illustrating through external objects the tension between the sexes. The swinging of the bonnet and the teasing reference to the kiss drive Ralph beyond the point of safety; he loses control and not only snatches but tears the bonnet, symbolically violating Winsome. Her answer 'complainingly, yet without anger' might have come from Miriam in *Sons and Lovers*, it is so similar in tone and manner; she is half-willing to be mastered. Ralph is unashamedly triumphantly masculine: 'I am very glad' he says twice. Winsome snatches up the bonnet and runs off with it up the hill, appearing to escape, but stops only 'as if out of breath'. She is waiting for the next move in the sexual game. Ralph holds up the string like a pennon, a flag captured from an enemy in battle, and cries 'I will come and see your grandmother!' They both know that he will do no such thing; he will come to see Winsome.

She, pretending anger, sets her bonnet carefully back on her head, but sees that Ralph is putting the string that remains in his possession carefully away in his book. He waves, and goes off, leaving her to proceed up the hill, telling herself that she will never speak to him again, but at the same time smiling. She wistfully looks at her ravaged bonnet with one string missing, but says after some thought, unconvincingly, 'I can easily sew another on anyway!'[26] The interval of thought shows that something irrevocable has happened; the bonnet, and by inference Winsome, will never be the same again.

This is the bonnet's moment of glory in the tale. It reappears now and again, as if to remind us, but ends in the final chapter in a way which Lawrence would never have tolerated; the erst-while sex symbol has become a faded and frayed adornment on the head of one of the children. For Crockett it is no longer relevant; the battle is over and peace declared in the happy unity of marriage, lit by the autumn sunlight of harvest-time.

This final tableau of parents and children in warm harvest sunshine is typical of the way Crockett uses nature as imagery to illustrate his lovers' moods and actions. It accompanies them and marks their progress in a carefully orchestrated background, unobtrusively manipulating the reader's response. When Ralph lies sleepily trying to read on the hillside above Loch Grannoch, the scene is peaceful and quiet, the inviting white sand on the far side not yet touched by the morning sunshine under the shadowing pine trees. Ralph has not yet met Winsome; the scene waits.

When they meet and make friends on the second day of the blanket-washing, they walk silently together towards Craig Ronald through a sensuous but homely landscape of loaning and stream, the air full of a warm fecundity. The farmhouse seems asleep, except for the hens

> chuckling and chunnering low to themselves, and nestling with their feathers spread balloon-wise, while they flirted the hot summer dust over them.

A distant mower sharpens his scythe, the sound harsh, so that it

> cut through the slumberous hum of the noonday air as the blade itself cuts through the meadow grass. The bees in the purple flowers beneath the window boomed a mellow bass, and the grasshoppers made love by millions in the couch grass, *chirring* in a thousand fleeting raptures.[27]

The voluptuousness in these tiny animal pleasures and matings foretells Ralph's movement toward natural life and vigour and the girl walking by his side.

The false trysts to which Jess sends them, Ralph to the bridge, Winsome to the hill gate, are heralded by sinister sounds and images;

> ... under the cloud there was a great solitariness—the murmur of a land where no man had come since the making of the world. Down in the sedges by the lake a blackcap sang sweetly, waesomely, the nightingale of Scotland. Far on the moors a curlew cried out that its soul was lost. Nameless things whinnied in the mist-filled hollows.[28]

We are made to feel their mingled fear and expectation—fear of the new unknown experience, expectation of the delight it may bring them. We also, knowing the deceit that has been practised upon them, share their feeling of loneliness and strangeness.

When the lovers meet to say farewell as Ralph is to set off for Edinburgh, once more at dawn, they kiss for the first time and their love is acknowledged. Rich warm colours move onward in a vast landscape.

> The sun was rising over the hills of heather. League after league of the imperial colour rolled westward like flame as the level rays of the sun touched it.[29]

Their joy is followed by Crockett's comment a little later upon that joy, again in terms of landscape and colour.

> The heather was dark rose purple, the 'ling' dominating the miles of moor; for the lavender-grey flush of the true heather had not yet broken over the great spaces of the south uplands.[30]

Finer happiness, greater and more mature, is still to come for them; the former was only the beginning.

Throughout *The Lilac Sunbonnet*, light and darkness pursue one another, the ancient Biblical symbols of good and evil. The Marrow Kirk is seldom mentioned without a hint of darkness and cold—the claustrophobic Manse of Dullarg, the narrow flat in James's Court, both dwellings obsessed by the past and by dark theology. Jess Kissock is a swarthy girl, the opposite of her red-faced laughing sister Meg; her hair is black and tangled; she is 'a daughter of the Picts', 'dark-browed Egypt',[31] who hides away to read Ralph's stolen letter in a dim cobwebbed byre by lit lantern which casts tiny flecks of light on to the walls from its perforations. She loves bright flowers, but only to arrange them in twisted decorations and nosegays with the barbaric taste of a savage and for her own ends. She is stealthy and cunning, but not physically strong, so that Winsome will not allow her to do heavy work—she has been a lady's-maid in England. She goes to meet Ralph at the tryst clad in a dark shawl.

Winsome is light and energy combined, her fair hair 'crisping and tendrilling ... scattering and wavering over her shoulders, wonderingly'.[32] Some critics have found this passage sickly and embarrassing; it is really an onomatopoetic device to identify Winsome with sunlight and movement. Love comes to her suddenly, surprisingly, shaking her to her depths and making her uncertain, gentle, soft, as in her white bedroom wrapped in a great white shawl she waits for the dawn to read Ralph's poem, her golden hair no longer crisp but now an aureole round her head, glimmering in the shadow like 'pale Florentine gold'.[33] Even so, she is described in terms of light. At most times she is brisk and efficient, carrying shining pails of water with dextrous skill, whistling to the dogs with two fingers in her mouth like a boy. She can be teasing and mischievous, but she is 'a veritable Napoleon of finance and capacity',[34] her lawyer proud to serve her. She bakes good bread and is famous in Dumfries market for the quality of her butter, very like the New Woman of whom Robertson Nicoll is wary, very like the virtuous woman of the Book of Proverbs. Her moods vary. When Meg wakes her at daybreak (the sunbonnet and the notebook upon her pillow) to send her to say farewell to Ralph, she is almost tearful in her shyness, but when she dresses and goes out to meet him she has regained control and gives passion for generous passion in her kiss. And what sickly heroine would have been practical enough, and strong enough, to make him take money from her for his journey?

Ralph at first is pale, stooped and colourless except for his ministerial black clothes, but he learns rapidly. When Winsome reminds him teasingly of his ridiculous flight on the first day of the blanket-washing, he laughs at himself and says 'I am not sure that I should feel quite the same about it now!'[35] Love to him brings confidence, with knowledge; he grows towards Winsome into the light. Significantly, it is in the shadowed rooms of Craig Ronald, so heavy with the past, that he feels himself cut off from Winsome. Only when they are outside in the sunshine again, guddling trout in the bright stream with Andra Kissock, do they feel at ease with one another. Mrs Skirving understands this well. 'Hoot awa', two young folk! The simmer days are no lang ... Tak' them while they shine, bankside an' burnside an' the bonny heather ... Awa' wi' ye, ye're young and honest. Twa auld cankered carles are no fit company for twa young folks like you.'[36]

The love-story runs its course, with hesitations and misunderstandings like all such. There is one near disaster, when Winsome is tricked into the greedy arms of Agnew Greatorix, thinking him to be Ralph. He insolently kisses her cheek, forcing her body against his with masculine roughness. We are safe in assuming that he is about to rape her—'take his will of her lips'[37]—but such things cannot be made explicit in the *Christian Leader*. She struggles in terror, afraid of fainting, but before she does lose consciousness from shock, she is able to call out loudly and desperately for Ralph. Before Ralph reaches her, Jock Gordon the 'natural' comes to her aid, dragging Greatorix from her body in half-animal, half-human rage and gripping him by the throat with his teeth.

The outcry has been heard. Lanterns appear from Craig Ronald, and Meg runs to her mistress, asking Ralph fiercely who has done this thing. He points to Greatorix, and pulls Jock's hands away from the seducer before murder is committed.

Winsome gradually recovers, sobbing childishly, and is comforted by Meg's kindly soothing words. Ralph kneels by her with loving whispers, but when he tries to kiss her she puts him aside. 'Not tonight. I am not able to bear it.'[38] That simple 'Not tonight' shows that she will kiss him one day, and knows it, but not now, not after another man's brutal attack. The realism of this reaction to attempted rape is acute and exact. Crockett knew what a fastidious young woman would feel. A sickly heroine would have fallen weeping romantically into Ralph's arms. Winsome, a real woman, walks home unsteadily, clinging to the arm of another woman, Meg, temporarily unable to endure the touch even of the man she loves. Ralph understands and will wait; meanwhile he takes charge of Jock Gordon, who must be quieted, fed and sent off to the hills for his own safety. The whole incident has been couched in details of the utmost realism, with no hint of romance or sentimental vapouring. A final faintly comic touch comes when a messsage arrives the next morning from Castle Greatorix to say that Captain Greatorix has been shot in an accident and requires Mrs Kissock as a nurse. Jess sees her chance and goes instead. She has lost Ralph, but Agnew Greatorix will make a good second best for the lady's-maid who wants to be a lady.

We know now that Ralph and Winsome are not far from expressing their love to one another. It is only a matter of time and their next meeting. At this point the Marrow Kirk intervenes, in the shape of the Rev Allan Welsh.

Crockett's first reference to the Marrow Kirk has been to say that Ralph was

> trysted to the kirk of the Marrow, that sole treasure-house of orthodox truth in Scotland, which is as good as saying in the whole wide world—perhaps even in the universe.[39]

The quiet ripple of amusement in the definition hints at what is to come. Thereafter the Marrow Kirk is mentioned always with either mockery or outright criticism. Ralph in his reading by Loch Grannoch has shaken his head dubiously over Luther's credentials as a theologian; he is 'well enough for Germany, a country of great laxity, where as in prelatical England, they drank beer.'[40] We expect some grave defect in Luther from the serious student; instead we are given the anti-climax 'they—drank—beer'. The priggish Ralph is shown in all his priggishness.

All Bibles in his experience have had the paraphrases torn out of them, and the great Bible in the Kirk of Dullarg has had them pasted up, 'so that no preacher in a moment of demoniac possession might give one out'.[41] The Marrow Kirk is mocked once more for being puritanically opposed to poetry and art, even in so innocent a form as paraphrases which are unscriptural, unlike the psalms. It is on this point that Ralph has been doubtful even before coming to Galloway; it is this point that he has defied in writing his poems and articles. As he thinks things over, he realises that in the past he has consented to serve his father's jealous God, even though 'his heart leaned to the milder divinity and the kindlier gospel of One who was the Bearer of Burdens.'[42] The Marrow Kirk adheres firmly to the Old Testament, not the New. One suspects here that Crockett, writer and poet, is speaking for himself as well as Ralph. He too leans to the milder divinity and the kindlier gospel; one of his idols and correspondents as a divinity student was the American Quaker Whittier. In an article in the *Leader* evoked by the aged poet's death, the writer, who though anonymous can be identified by internal evidence as Crockett, quotes approvingly a letter sent him by Whittier:

> I am ... an orthodox friend, profoundly convinced that the Almighty Maker who took the responsibility of bringing so many thousands of millions into the

world will never divest Himself of responsibility for any one individual of them but that Somewhere and Somehow, He will work out their salvation exactly, with no remainder of human souls eternally devoted to destruction.[43]

The man who can admire and treasure this sentiment is no Calvinist.

The dogmatic assertion by Allan Welsh that Winsome, his own daughter, the child of an unsanctified marriage, is through no fault of her own unfit to marry him if he is to be a Marrow Kirk minister makes no impression on Ralph.

> My heart and life, my honour and word, are too deeply engaged for me to go back.

The tone has changed from amusement to complete seriousness. Welsh had declared that

> the kirk of the Marrow overrides all considerations of affection or self-interest

but Ralph will have none of it. When Welsh tells him to think of the poor folk who have saved the money to pay for his college fees, he says honestly

> It is true what you say ... I mourn for it every word, but I cannot and I will not submit my conscience and my heart to the keeping even of the Marrow Kirk.

Welsh retorts that he should have thought of this sooner. Ralph states his new belief and creed, cutting himself off from the old:

> God gave me my affections as a sacred trust. This also is part of my religion. And I will not, I cannot in any wise give up hope of winning this girl whom I love, and whom you above all others ought surely to love.[44]

He has carried the war into the enemy's camp; his behaviour is very different from Welsh's twenty years ago. This marks the end; he is a declared 'unbeliever' and must not be allowed to remain in the Manse.

Ralph leaves, regretfully, respectfully, but sure that he is right. When he steps out into the night air, it seems to meet him with chill like a wall, emphasising the magnitude of the step he has taken; but almost immediately there comes cosmic applause:

> The stars had come out and were shining almost frosty-clear, though it was July.[45]

Light has broken through the darkness, however tiny its form.

He bids farewell to Winsome high above Loch Ken and makes his way to Edinburgh and his father. Opening the door to him, John Bairdieson is aghast, especially when he hears that Ralph has quarrelled with Allan Welsh. Bairdieson implores him to lie to his father—to say it was merely some minor offence, like staying out too late with a girl, anything rather than a dispute over doctrine. Ralph admits that Welsh has turned him out as an unbeliever.

> Then it's doctrine—wae's me, wae's me! I wuss it had been the lasses. What wull his faither say? Gin it had been ill-doin', he micht hae pitten it doon to the sins o' his youth; but ill-doctrine he canna forgie. O Maister Ralph, gin ye canna tell a lee yersel', wull ye no haud yer tongue—I can lee for ye, for I'm but an elder—an' I'll tell him that at a kirn ye war over persuaded to drink the health o' the laird ... [46]

Ralph smiles and declines this kindly offer; even in Galloway they do not have harvest feasts until the harvest is in.
John will not be dissuaded.

> Aweel, can ye no say, or let me say for ye, gin ye be particular, that ye war a wee late oot at nicht seein' a bit lassie—or ocht but the doctrine?

The zealous John is willing to tell any lie to save his young master and save the one and only divinity student the Marrow Kirk can boast. He is able to tell any lie for he is one of the Elect and can commit no sin, according to the Calvinist doctrine of Election. 'Indeed' comments Crockett drily, 'to start with the acknowledged fact of personal election sometimes gives a man like John Bairdieson an unmistakeable advantage'.[47] Once more Crockett is placing himself outside a fundamental dogma of the Calvinist creed and in a situation fraught with comedy too, as if he thought it a matter of little importance.
Ralph could perhaps have maintained without departing from the truth that his offence was over 'a bit lassie', but that lassie was at the mercy of the doctrine; the two are irrevocably intertwined. He again declines John's well-meant offer and goes to face his father. He cannot and will not tell his father the reason for his expulsion from the Manse of Dullarg because it involves Welsh's confession and his own love for Winsome; he finds him as stern as Welsh had been. He cannot be received under his father's roof because he has been, in some way, guilty of doctrinal offence. The irrepressible John offers to hide him away without his father's knowledge.

> It's an awfu'-like thing to be obleegit to tell the hale truth! O man, couldna ye hae tell't a wee bit lee? It wad hae saved an awfu' deal o' fash! But it's ower late now; ye can juist bide i' the spare room up the stair, an' come an' gang by the door on the Castle Bank, an' no yin forbye mysel' 'ill be a hair the wiser. I, John Bairdieson, will juist fetch up yer meals the same as ordinar'. Ye'll be like a laddie at the mastheid up there; it'll be braw and quate for the studyin'![48]

These scenes, so full of John's hearty rough kindliness, are robustly comic, but demonstrate how hard a Marrow adherent finds it to square his austere faith and his kindly heart. For all John's ingenious hypocrisy, willing to cheat and deceive his own respected minister and his own creed, he shows once again that human affection is more likeable than Marrow Kirk sternness. We would have thought less of John if he had gone by the letter of the law and joined with Peden in expelling Ralph so coldly.

As Ralph leaves the flat which has been his home all his life, he makes the strongest declaration of all against his former allegiance. If the Marrow Kirk is too narrow to contain the love which is enriching his whole existence, then the Marrow Kirk is wrong. He uses a Biblical construction to say so:

> God do so to me and more also if I ever seek again to enter the Marrow kirk, if so be that, like my father, I must forget my humanity in order worthily to serve it![49]

He goes sadly, but Crockett impishly adds a humorous touch. When his son has gone, Gilbert Peden turns to the Bible to seek for guidance, but the parable of the Prodigal Son is not relevant to this prodigal son: our Lord's prodigal 'was not under trials for license in the Kirk of the Marrow!'[50]

The meeting of the Synod follows, at which the two ministers fall out over Ralph's defection. Welsh refuses to condemn him. Peden cannot understand why. They hurl accusations of sin at one another, sins of contumacy and contempt, sins of person and life, sins of unfaithfulness, complicity and compliance; the Marrow Kirk is well equipped with sins. They solemnly depose one another, the *reductio ad absurdum* of Presbyterian disruption, and John Bairdieson, listening at the door, is so shattered by this disaster that he runs out and, to relieve his feelings, knocks over a man coming to sell coal, crying out 'There's nae kirk o' God in puir Scotland ony mair!'[51]

One may object—many did in 1894—that this is not truth to life, or even satire, but mere broad farce, ruining any serious criticism by going too far into the ridiculous. In fact, as often in Crockett's unlikeliest tales, the incident is based on a real situation, as an article in the *British Weekly* declared[52] a month after the book appeared.

> It is interesting to know that the much criticised incident of the ministers' mutual deposition in Mr Crockett's 'Lilac Sunbonnet' is not only based upon authority, but is (allowing for the diferences between fiction and fact) actually true.

There existed a denomination of Scottish Presbyterians which consisted of only two congregations and two ministers, the Rev James Wright of Lauriston Street Original Secession Church in Edinburgh and the Rev Andrew Lambie of the Original Secession Church in Pitcairngreen near Perth.

In May 1842, a Union took place between the Original Seceders and the Original Burghers, but these two ministers and their flocks stood out from the Union, forming themselves into

> the True Blue Original Seceder Secession Synod, as they were called, though probably not by themselves. They were the only members of that court, save their several elders, and they made up for the sparseness of their members by the multitude and fervency of their protests against all and sundry.

They had one divinity student, who one Saturday went to Pitcairngreen to preach on the following Sunday. He and the Rev Mr Lambie fell into theological discussion on the Saturday night.

> The evening was spent agreeably between the hot peats of the parlour fire and the hotter fire of the minister's catechising. Suddenly, however, it was revealed to the Eli of Pitcairngreen that his young Samuel was unsound in the faith. Whereupon he told him (as in the story) that he must take his departure, the Scriptures expressly declaring that the 'faithful' must not keep company with unbelievers.

The student was thrust out into the cold of a Saturday night eleven miles from Perth with snow upon the ground, to find lodgings or otherwise make his way as best he could.

In due course the two-member Synod met to discuss the case, and in the process they discovered grave causes for censure in one another;

> both were 'zealous unto slaying'. So without more said, Mr Wright solemnly deposed his erring brother Lambie, and Mr Lambie with equal solemnity deposed his colleague Wright.
>
> Thus was truth vindicated, and in this little Armageddon of two renowned champions of denunciation, the 'True Blue' Original and Only Secession divided itself finally like a split pea, to unite no more.

The amused tone of the article, the mild derision of that last remark, and the fact that the writer mis-spelled Lauriston as Laurieston, the village where Crockett first went to school, all suggest that he was the author. Readers were referred for corroboration to the Rev Walter Smith of the Free High Church in Edinburgh, who possessed the relevant documents; the truth of the matter is beyond dispute. Any lingering doubt was dispelled by a further article in the *British Weekly* the following January.[53] The Rev Andrew Lambie was misguided enough to write to the Editor and defend his Scriptural rectitude, enclosing a pamphlet, no doubt denouncing someone or other; this not only confirmed the actuality of the dual deposition but established its date as 'in the end of August, 1894'. Crockett had been following the affairs of the sect with interest and was in the process of nearing the end of his serial; immediately he whipped the incident into *The Lilac Sunbonnet* almost as soon as it had happened. The chapter in the *Leader* entitled 'The Meeting of the Synod' appeared on 30 September 1894. It was no whimsy of his own devising but an actual event of the present, not of the past, and richly comic ready for his pen.

Crockett therefore in the Marrow Kirk was deriding a minor sect of which he had known for some time. Can it be assumed that he was in no way reflecting on the Free Church of Scotland? It too had reservations about poetry and art, fiction and paraphrases, and held to a stern code of fundamentalism for its members. Crockett gives us the unobtrusive answer himself in *The Lilac Sunbonnet*, an answer so unobtrusive that it is easily missed completely.

In two places, one at the beginning and one near the end of the *Sunbonnet*, he refers briefly to the view from the Peden flat (or house—the terms are synonymous in Scots usage) in James's Court. In Chapter I he says that Ralph had lived all his life

> in an old house in James's Court, Edinburgh, overlooking the great bounding circle of the northern horizon and the eastern sea.[54]

In Chapter XXXVIII, when Ralph is before the accusing gaze of his father, he could

> see through the window the light fading off the Fife Lomonds, and the long line of the shore darkening under the night into a more ethereal blue.[55]

Both these details, the only references in the book to this view, can be taken simply as descriptions contrasting the interior darkness with the vast and colourful panorama outside, so much wider and more splendid. This indeed they are; they evoke the richness of the world outside compared with the narrowness within, exemplifying Crockett's use of imagery to illuminate the situations of his characters. Ralph in the second example is seeing the view over his father's shoulder, so that Gilbert Peden is significantly sitting in his chair, once a Reformer's pulpit, with his back to the light.

They are, however, rather more. They indicate with exactness the position of the Peden residence; it is in the north range of James's Court looking over the Forth to Fife—that north range which was demolished in the nineteenth century and built up in the years between 1850 and 1860 to house the central offices of the Free Church of Scotland.[56] They are there today, looking down the Mound to Princes Street. The leading minister of the Marrow Kirk therefore lives on the site of the nerve-centre of the Free Church; this is probably as close an identification as Crockett could decently make while he was still a serving minister in that church. Readers who picked up the reference might draw their own conclusions and perhaps chuckle. Most were probably too taken up with the 'slow, sweet idyll of Scotch love-making' to notice.

Crockett therefore has freed his lovers from the trammels of the Marrow Kirk and also the Free Church—and the Established Church too, to some extent, if we count the Mowdieworts' rebellion against it. He has not freed them from God. Professor F R Hart has called the *Sunbonnet* 'a late Victorian neo-paganism'[57] but Crockett was never a pagan. Later and elsewhere Professor Hart elaborates, pointing out the unVictorian uniqueness and frankness of Winsome's passionate kiss of surrender and Crockett's

> indiscriminate vitalistic naturalism, with God on the side of youth and love,

but regretting that this should be softened into idyllic unreality.

> Crockett's lovers are young adults whose innocence is inseparable from their fleshliness... He starts out with a neo-pagan vision of youth and love, suggests

strong passions in combat (murderousness in the idiot Jock, Jess's sexual war for Ralph), opposes it all to the foolish rigidities of an old kirk—and there is no evil whatsoever. This later Eden is without the fall or the serpent, and sadness and parting are momentary. It is all real, ripe, yet intensely idyllic, a dream of sinlessness; what starts out as Eliot or Hardy drops the darker possibilities of both.[58]

The image of a sinless Eden has been used frequently throughout the book; it is in this, thinks Professor Hart, that Crockett lays himself open to the charge of sentimentality.

This is fair criticism; the anti-kirk theme demanded some such violent contrast and Crockett is intent on his symbolism. In his other novels we find wickedness, murder, Grand Guignol horrors of all kinds, but in this he is writing his one and only novel of ideas. The lovers are distanced from the other earthier characters; they are sent out to the light by Mrs Skirving; they are separated even from Meg and her quiet understanding with Jock Forrest when she sends Winsome out to give herself to Ralph's kiss, saying 'O I wush it was me!'[59] Closer to one another out of doors, they are likewise closer to God when they find themselves outside all man-devised ecclesiastical institutions in the glory of His creation. For a while Ralph and Winsome are isolated in a simple Christian mysticism which they find with delight and surprise that they share.

This emerges when they meet on that dawn morning on the hillside and see the freshness and loveliness of a newly-created day—a day that is meant as spiritual as well as a unit of time. They talk easily and without formality to one another, gradually opening their hearts like a new-made Adam and Eve.

Winsome makes a characteristically teasing comment that perhaps Ralph has again lost his books. He replies that he does not always study through them; though he is town-bred he loves living things that grow in the country, the animals, the woods, the birds, the flowers,

> the little green plants that have no flowers, yet which all have a message if I could only hear and understand it.
> The sparkle in Winsome's eyes quieted into calm.
> 'I too——' she began, and paused as if startled at what she was about to say. She went on, 'I never heard any one say things like these. I did not know that any one else had thoughts like these excepting myself.'
> 'And have you thought these things?' said Ralph, with a quick responsive joy in his heart.
> 'Yes,' replied Winsome, looking down on the ground and playing with the loose string of the lilac sunbonnet. 'I used often to wonder how it was that I could not look on the loch on Sabbath morning without a feeling as if I were about to cry. It was often better to look upon it than to go to Maister Welsh's kirk. But I ought not to say these things to you,' she said, with a quick thought of his future profession.
> Ralph smiled. There were few things that Winsome Charteris might not say to him. He too had his experiences to collate.
> 'Have you ever stood on a hill-top as though you were suspended in the air,

when you seem to feel the earth whirling away from beneath you, rushing swiftly eastwards towards the sunrise?'

'I have heard it,' said Winsome, unexpectedly.

'Heard it?' queried Ralph, with doubt in his voice.

'Yes,' said Winsome, calmly, 'I have often heard the earth wheeling round on still nights when I stood out on the top of the Craigs, where there was no sound, and all the house was asleep. It was as if some Great One were saying "Hush!" to the angels—I think God Himself!'[60]

Having felt themselves alone in their unorthodox perception of the divine, they now find they are so similar, so distinctively alike, that no minor misunderstanding, like the tearing of the sunbonnet which immediately follows, can separate them. And Crockett, amateur naturalist and astronomer, who in his childhood felt that the Sabbath calm at Little Duchrae was foretaste of the calm of heaven, presents through them his personal religious belief. He too has been alone on hill-tops and felt the presence of God. And once he has done this, once he has affirmed the divine immanence in all things, he can mock sessions and synods to his heart's content; they have no part in his reverent Christian pantheism akin to that of Vaughan, of Wordsworth, and, more relevantly, of George MacDonald. Religion, though by no means that of Dr William Robertson Nicoll, is at the heart of *The Lilac Sunbonnet*.

Crockett does not leave this sense of the divine pervading all things in the possession of only Winsome and Ralph. He repeats it through a character at the other end of the social and intellectual scale, the rough sensual thoughtless Ebie Farrish the ploughman. Returning from an evening's amorous dalliance at another farm, Ebie stops on Crae Bridge and stands looking at the loch's beauty in inarticulate wonder. Up to this moment he had been an unimaginative farm labourer, with few aspirations, but the evening coolness made him feel a better man than he was.

When Ebie Farrish came to the bridge, he was no more than a

> material Galloway ploughman, satisfied with his night's conquests and chewing the cud of their memory.
> He looked over. He saw the stars, which were perfectly reflected a hundred yards away on the smooth expanse, first waver, then tremble, and lastly break into a myriad delicate shafts of light, as the water quickened and gathered. He spat in the water, and thought of trout for breakfast. But the long roar of the rapids of the Dee came over the hill, and brought a feeling of stillness with it, weird and remote. Uncertain lights shot hither and thither under the bridge, in strange gleams and reflections. The ploughman was awed. He continued to gaze. The stillness closed in upon him. The aromatic breath of the pines seemed to cool him and remove him from himself. He had a sense that it was the Sabbath morning, and that he had just washed his face to go to church. It was the nearest thing to worship he had ever known.[61]

He sees shadows pass over the water like breath from a new knife blade; he chews the cud of memory; he thinks of trout for breakfast; he spits into the water; he feels as if he has washed his face for church—his impressions are appropriately couched in terms less lyrical, more mundane than those of Ralph and Winsome, but he too has felt the presence of God.

The matter and even the manner are those of George MacDonald. Ebie Farrish's experience can be paralleled with one which came to the young Robert Falconer, and Falconer's holds a hint of Ralph and Winsome:

> He lay gazing up into the depth of the sky, rendered deeper and bluer by the masses of white cloud that hung almost motionless below it, until he felt a kind of bodily fear lest he should fall off the face of the round earth into the abyss. A gentle wind, laden with pine odours from the sun-heated trees behind him, flapped its light wing in his face: the humanity of the world smote his heart; the great sky towered up over him, and its divinity entered his soul; a strange longing after something 'he knew not nor could name' awoke within him ... Strange though it may seem to those who have never thought of such things save in connection with Sundays and Bibles and churches and sermons, that which was now working in Falconer's mind was the first dull and faint movement of the greatest need the human heart possesses—the need of the God-man. There must be truth in the scent of that pinewood; someone must have meant it.[62]

Once the idea of George MacDonald enters one's mind, many things fall immediately into place. Lady Florimel putting on her stockings in Chapter V Vol I of MacDonald's *Malcolm* (1875) reminds us of Winsome taking hers off. Malcolm's power over the wild stallion in Chapter I Vol I of *The Marquis of Lossie* (1877) may have suggested Ralph's ability to attract and manage the colt in Chapter XII of the *Sunbonnet*. The crumbling Gothic antiquity of Greatorix Castle may owe something to *Castle Warlock* (1882). Above all the 'natural', the 'daftie' Jock Gordon, shrewd for all his lack of wit, bringing a touch of the supernatural in with his song about the devil like the fool in Lear is a character after MacDonald's heart. It is he who is allowed to be the 'instrument of God'[63] even in his most animal rage because he loves Winsome and is able to save her from Greatorix. He later guides Ralph on his journey to Edinburgh, cunning in his knowledge of the best and loneliest tracks over the moors and wise in his refusal to enter the evil city, knowing it, as Sir Gibbie did, to be a place of danger and cruelty for such as he.

The *Sunbonnet* has occasional brief paragraphs of comment and religious musing, never as long as those MacDonald permitted himself but very much in his manner of kindly sermonising.

> It was a marvellous dawning, this one that Winsome waited for. Dawn is the secret of the universe. It thrills us somehow with a far-off prophecy of that eternal dawning when the God That Is shall reveal Himself—the Morn which shall brighten into the more perfect day.[64]

> It were a good place to look one's last on the earth, this wooded promontory, which might indeed have been that mountain, though a little one, from which was once seen all the kingdoms of the earth and the glory of them. For there are no finer glories on the earth than red heather and blue loch, except only youth and love. And these four go well together.[65]

George MacDonald was skilled in constructing novels in which real men and women move through stories which are more allegorical than realistic—fairytales in which there are no fairies but living human beings inhabiting vividly and minutely described rooms and cottages and castles who act out plots that verge on the miraculous and yet convince us momentarily that they are possible. Their power comes from the Christian spirit that fills them. The structure of *The Lilac Sunbonnet* is so creaking and unlikely, when one thinks about it critically, that perhaps Crockett was aiming at some such effect without possessing the skill of his master. What had happened to Ralph's mother? Surely she merited more of a personality than a mere mention from Mrs Skirving that she had been a Gilchrist of Linwood. Why, after having married and begotten a son, is Gilbert Peden living such an inexplicably solitary life in James's Court which Allan Welsh alone will understand? We may consider it possible that for the sake of the Marrow Kirk Peden should remain silent over the unsanctified marriage, but is it likely that he would send his son down to Galloway to the care of the man who had deceived him and to the place where he will meet that man's daughter? Is it likely that Winsome, teasing and determined, could not have wheedled the whole story out of a grandmother who seems only too willing to talk and chatter about the past? These things, we can understand, are necessary so that Ralph, inexperienced, priggish and totally ignorant of women should meet and so ludicrously run away from Winsome at first sight, but the framework which supports this situation is incredible. The timing of the story, too, is inconsistent. Mrs Skirving is reading the novels of the Great Unknown as they appear, between 1814 and 1826. Meg Kissock can taunt Saunders with having his first wife's virtues inscribed on her tombstone by Robert Paterson—Old Mortality—which places the story back in the eighteenth century. Old Mortality died in 1801 and was buried in Caerlaverock graveyard in Dumfriesshire, a fact and place which Crockett in all probability knew. If the day of the 'Great Apostacy' referred to in the novel took place in 1842 as the *British Weekly* article suggests, and we are now twenty years later than that, the date is 1862, yet Crockett says vaguely that Walter Skirving was a type of bonnet-laird better known in Galloway sixty years ago than now—when is 'now'? And if the dual deposition is based on an event that took place in 1894, are we in the present time of the readers in 1894? It is easy to pick holes in the plot and complain about inconsistencies in the time-scheme; the only way to read *The Lilac Sunbonnet* properly is to take it as a semi-allegory, with the realism of the detail and the liveliness of the characters acting together to make a theological point. This is what Crockett was trying to do, without being a George MacDonald.

The worst discrepancy is Ralph's turning to his uncle Professor Thriepneuk for advice and help. The early chapters have stressed Ralph's austere youthful life utterly without feminine companionship; now we discover that he has three cousins, Jemima, Kezia and Keren-happuch who, though named after Job's daughters, are lively affectionate girls a little in love with Ralph who has played with them throughout his childhood and boyhood, both in their house near the castle and in their new mansion at Sciennes, a privileged brother. They welcome him with kisses, but are clever enough to tell that in the meantime Ralph has kissed another girl in a manner far different from mere cousinly salutes. He has no peace until he has told them about Winsome, and in their delight at his happiness they forget any girlish dreams they may have had, quite without jealousy. Jemima hopes that 'she' is of a serious disposition; Kezia that 'she' is pretty; and Keren-happuch, shyly, that 'she' will love her. When their father comes home, they seize upon him in a rush of words, insisting that Ralph be cherished in his breach with the Marrow Kirk and that their father 'see it the right way', or else offend all three and risk destroying the peace of his home.

Writing in serial instalments before the story is complete affords flexibility to the writer—Crockett is able to insert the Meeting of the Synod almost as soon as Mr Wright and Mr Lambie have shattered their True Blue Original and Only Secession Church—but it has dangers; Crockett is so set on showing the freedom and happiness Ralph has gained that he contradicts facts emphasised and essential in the early chapters, written long before and perhaps forgotten in his enthusiasm. But the three girls fulfil their function well, bringing sweetness and light in full measure to counter the darkness of Ralph's doubts, expressing the spirit of the story even if they do not adhere to the letter of the plot. And Professor Thriepneuk, thinking how with Ralph as his assistant he will be able to give more time to his learned treatise on 'The Abuses of Ut with the Subjunctive', adds that touch of the totally ridiculous which Crockett always enjoyed. 'Ut with the Subjunctive' is so basic a Latin construction that not even the most solemn of pedants could have fabricated a book out of it.

It is George MacDonald, however, who must be blamed for the anti-climax of the ending—'Threads Drawn Together' Crockett calls one chapter, as well he might; 'hauled' might be a better word. MacDonald believed in universal salvation, contradicting orthodox Calvinists for whom damnation was necessary to make sense of God's plan. The last chapters of the *Sunbonnet* are swamped with forgiveness, rather to the disappointment of the ordinary reader looking for something more exciting. Welsh and Peden are reconciled to the point of tears over the miniature portrait of the first Winsome whom they had both loved. Jess is forgiven and indeed rewarded by marriage with Agnew Greatorix and the position she wanted in life. Agnew is forgiven his offences and handed over to a woman cleverer than he who will manage him wisely and allow him only one glass of sherry after luncheon. Welsh is forgiven by Walter Skirving, and as if their reconciliation had been the summit of life for them they are rewarded by a kind and gentle death. At a lower level Saunders is forgiven by realising that he will be happier with his mother than with a wife who might not suit him. Meg requires no forgiveness, but is given her reward by marrying Jock Forrest, who becomes Winsome's grieve. Even Gilbert Peden is involved in the general aura of kindliness; he writes often to his son and daughter-in-law telling how his church is prospering and has now several students coming up for its ministry—and has had a 'repeating tune' in a service; paraphrases will be with the Marrow Kirk in no time. And the picture of Winsome and Ralph at Craig Ronald, bathed in sunshine some years after their marriage, with Winsome efficiently running the farm and Ralph allowed to write his poetry in a blossom-strewn study in the garden (a poetic version of the wooden annexe Crockett had for his library at Bank House?) is very clearly being written by a man who has said all he wants to say and wants to reach the end of the story as soon as he can. The fact that Ralph's poetry has made him famous, on the strength of the one poem we are shown in the *Sunbonnet*, is quite the most impossible, incredible fact of all. That same poem, incidentally, may be found on page 72 of Crockett's own early book of poetry, *Dulce Cor, Being the Poems of Ford Berêton* (1886), providing additional proof that Crockett was to some extent using Ralph as an imaginative and distant parallel to himself, externalising his own self-questionings in those of his hero.

Three months after the publication of *The Lilac Sunbonnet*, Crockett, in January 1895, resigned his ministry of the Free Church in Penicuik. In this too he was following, consciously or unconsciously, the example of George MacDonald, whose unorthodox beliefs and liberal theology made it impossible for him to continue as a minister of the Congregational Church in England. He too had laid down his charge and taken to literature, forced to this step by the disapproval of his congregation. Crockett was never in such unpleasant circumstances as MacDonald, but when the writing, method and manner of the two men are so similar, it is tempting to suggest that Crockett's resignation was a move in MacDonald's footsteps.

Be that as it may, once Crockett had written *The Lilac Sunbonnet*, he had left himself no choice. The tendency to be irritated by fellow-ministers, sessions and ladies with tracts which had shown itself in *The Stickit Minister* and had grown sharper in the Christian socialism of 'In the Matter of Incubus and Co', erupted into the joyful unorthodoxy of the *Sunbonnet*. Though it was a popular novel written by a man who knew what his readers liked—a love story set in the Galloway scene he had introduced for the first time (if we except Scott's *Guy Mannering*) to a public eager for fresh glimpses of Scottish landscapes with figures—it was in fact that man's farewell to a ministry which he had entered sincerely eight years before and served enthusiastically but had in the end outgrown. The only honest course was to go.

The literary work which was making so many demands upon his time and his energy enabled him to resign without much ill-feeling and with none of the theological squabbling which he so much detested. *The Lilac Sunbonnet*, if examined sympathetically, honestly and with understanding is a kind of *Apologia Pro Vita Sua* in advance. It is unwise to judge it by standards of ordinary truth to life or try to fit it into any precise period. It is best read as a conflict between sunlight and shadow, between life and denial of life—an uprush of liberal opinion freeing itself from rules and dogmas and carrying its author out of the Free Church and its monthly stipend (which had for two years been only a small part of his income) into the greater freedom of life as a freelance writer—a dangerous freedom for a man with a wife and four children accustomed to a safe, well-to-do, almost luxurious Victorian existence. At first Crockett revelled in it, and even later he did not regret it. It was imposed upon him by his own temperament. One can only regret that he did not have in real life what he bestowed upon his fictional self Ralph, the generous legacies of money and property to cheer him on his way.

Chapter 6

The Raiders, Being Some Passages in the Life of John Faa, Lord and Earl of Little Egypt

The Raiders remains Crockett's best known book. Faces that look a little puzzled over *The Stickit Minister* and *The Lilac Sunbonnet*—and even *The Men of the Moss Hags*—light up with recognition when it is mentioned. It is full of Crockett's energy; it is set in his native Galloway; it was written with that happy trust in his own abilities which must come to any author whose first efforts have found high favour. It is a 'yarn' with no strong moral but the everyday ones of fair-dealing, courage and loyalty implied rather than stated. Its only purpose is to cram as much varied excitement as possible into its forty-eight chapters. Thrilling events, not static self-questionings, are the mainsprings. Crockett is pleasing himself and writing colourful adventure such as he enjoyed in Scott and Stevenson. One would expect it to be both simpler and more extrovert than the *Sunbonnet* and so it is, but by the pleasant irony of circumstance *The Raiders* works in the opposite direction. In *The Lilac Sunbonnet* Crockett had used the rich beauty of midsummer to free his too studious, over cerebral hero from the constrictions of puritanical religion; in *The Raiders* a common-place thoughtless young lad, through conflict with evil men and the terrifying majesty of the mountains against which it is played turns gradually towards conventional religion, though not in a narrow form.

There is little explicit history in *The Raiders* despite its period setting. Crockett hooks his narrative here and there to events and people; George I is on the throne remotely in London; his customs officers appear in early chapters since the Act of Union in 1707 had stimulated the contraband trade on the Solway; Sheriff Agnew of Lochnaw is mentioned only to show how little he counts for with wild Galloway families.[1] The Faas and the Maxwells and the hill gipsies who constitute the major part of the 'raiders', are regarded as akin to and to some extent direct continuations of the Highland Host that was marched down into Galloway against the Covenanters in the late 1670s,[2] before the Killing Time. The 1715 rising is only recently over, and two branches of the Maxwell family have been on opposite sides; Richard Maxwell of Craigdarroch, the heroine's father, is a Whig, and as he dies, shot by the smugglers, utters curses and Biblical texts alternately,[3] whereas Lady Grizel Maxwell of Earlstoun, her elderly cousin, is of the old religion and makes her first appearance in a coat whose velvet collar is 'a wee rusty' because her father the Earl was wearing it when beheaded for his part in the Jacobite cause.[4] These particular Maxwells are fictitious, but the situation is true;

Kenmure and Derwentwater, the leaders of the rebellion, were executed, and Lord Nithsdale, another Maxwell, would have gone the same way had his quick-witted wife not engineered his escape.

The Killing Time, when the Covenanters were persecuted most cruelly by Royalist dragoons under Claverhouse and Grierson of Lag, remains alive in the memories of the older characters. Patrick Heron's father and Silver Sand, the mysterious pedlar, have ridden with the king's troops against the Covenanters, and then, through disgust at the cruelties and butcheries committed under orders, have both changed sides and been hunted in their turn along with the persecuted saints. John MacMillan, the minister of the parish of Balmaghie, is spoken of several times, and it is to him that the hero proposes to go for counsel about the state of his soul.[5] But historical events and personages are like twigs and branches supporting the spider's web of the narrative; they give a framework of actuality to Crockett's plot which he constructs with imaginary characters passing through experiences he has read of in places with which he is familiar. From local traditions he has heard orally and from local sources like Nicholson's *Historical and Traditional Tales*,[6] the *Castle Douglas Miscellany*,[7] the *Scots Magazine*[8] and Simpson's *Traditions of the Covenanters*[9] he draws his knowledge of smugglers and excisemen, of gipsies and hill folk, of the Murder Hole and the evil house of Craignairney, and weaves them into his tale.

The plot is of elementary simplicity, one incident following another with untiring gusto. Because of an old quarrel, Captain Yawkins and his smugglers burn down Craigdarroch, the homestead of the smuggling Maxwells and their sister May. Hector Faa, one of the leaders of the gipsies, takes the opportunity to carry off May to make her his wife, according to the Faa custom; her father is killed in the fighting. Patrick Heron, the young laird of nearby Isle Rathan, and his friend Silver Sand the gipsy set off to rescue her while the Maxwell brothers pursue their stolen cattle. At Clachanpluck (Laurieston, where Crockett went to school) the hero and Silver Sand separate, and Patrick makes his way to the Bridge of Dee just in time to be involved with the terrified cattle as the gipsies drive them up into the hills.

Tired and bruised, he seeks shelter at the small farm of Mossdale and is befriended by Sammle and Eppie Tamson; after a night's rest he is guided by Sammle over the hills towards the outlaws' lair, hearing as he goes of the disappearance a few years back of Sammle's little daughter Marion. Sammle leaves Patrick to complete his journey alone and make his way through the Wolf's Slock, the pass that leads through the crags above Loch Enoch to where the outlaws may be found. He is overtaken by mists and a storm and seeks shelter in what he takes to be a shepherd's cottage. In fact, it is one of the robbers' headquarters. He is taken prisoner. Just as he despairs, he discovers that May Maxwell is also a prisoner there, along with a little girl who is Sammle Tamson's Marion. May and Patrick escape, but are pursued by the outlaws and two bloodhounds. They are run to earth beside the dreaded Murder Hole in Loch Neldricken, where Silver Sand and his dog Quharrie arrive in the nick of time to save them.

Down in the lowlands again, May is welcomed by her cousin Lady Grizel to the Great House of Earlstoun and Patrick returns to Rathan, where he lies ill for a while, tended by Silver Sand and the Tamsons, who have moved there from Mossdale for fear of the outlaws. An attack by the outlaws and their band on Earlstoun in the autumn is beaten off by the Maxwells, aided by local support (Patrick is wounded in the leg), and it is decided that a punitive expedition must go up and drive the raiders away once and for all. Patrick is one of the party, which sets off in December, when the treacherous bogs are frozen and can be traversed safely. After the outlaws have tried to destroy them by engulfing them in the waters from Loch Valley whose dam they break down, Patrick volunteers to go forward and spy out the land on his skates. He finds the enemy encamped on the island in Loch Enoch, and Silver Sand is with them. To his horror, he finds that Silver Sand is really John Faa, Lord and Earl of Little Egypt, the king of the Faa clan and leader of all the gipsies. But he is nevertheless Patrick's friend still; after warning the gipsies of their danger both from the lowland party and from an approaching snowstorm, Silver Sand takes Patrick to an old Covenanting hiding-place where they shelter from the storm, having rescued little Marion Tamson from her captors. For sixteen days they are snowed in and pass the time in explanations; when they emerge they find that only the Faas have escaped destruction. The remainder of the outlaw tribes lie dead in a vast pit of snow. All that remains is for the three of them to make their way down to Earlstoun and the happy ending.

This is very ordinary stuff, reminiscent of the *Boys' Own Paper*, yet it swept Crockett even farther up into the list of popular writers and went into edition after edition. Possibly even the publishers were taken by surprise; in T Fisher Unwin's regular advertisements in the *Academy* and the *Bookman* the first appearance of *The Raiders* announces that the second edition is now ready, the first having been sold out on the day of issue. Clearly it was not the subtlety of the plot that brought this about, but some unique attractiveness in the characters and the writing. It was the book that the time demanded.

Patrick Heron, the lad who tells the story, is a mere bonnet-laird, his Isle Rathan a not very useful island in the Solway Firth, in actuality the island of Heston in Auchencairn Bay. Crockett may have deliberately placed him in this rather middling position in society so that Patrick can express a social point of view near his own. Patrick is a small land-owner, on friendly terms with the sons of Dumfries shopkeepers, ordinary Galloway herds like Sammle Tamson, and a pedlar like Silver Sand, yet sufficiently secure in status to be recognised by Lady Grizel Maxwell (who had known and liked his grandfather) and to be acceptable as a brother-in-law to the Maxwells of Craigdarroch. His is a democratic outlook, independent but integrated into the social pattern of Galloway life; he is educated enough to understand why things are arranged as they are but has no desire to alter them; he respects himself but does not think himself far above the Tamsons who are his friends as well as servants. Crockett was a fatherless peasant from a small farm who by his talents had made himself known and respected in the community and has a secure status as a Free Church minister but does not think himself far above the members of his congregation. There is enough of a parallel to suggest that Patrick is a projection of Crockett's own personality—Patrick's clumsiness and naiveté represent stages through which Crockett is aware of having been himself as he has risen in the social scale. When he allows Patrick to give himself away in his narrative so that we laugh at his slowness, he is actually laughing a little at his own younger self. In this sense, Patrick is Crockett; but in another sense Patrick is not Crockett because in the course of the book we see Patrick grown into a conventional Galloway landowner, unimaginative and respectable, accepting the social pattern more thoroughly than Crockett ever did.

Patrick is Crockett *minus* because although for the purposes of the story he has Crockett's intensity of sensation and sharpness of impression, he is duller and more ordinary than his author. Part of Crockett's temperament responded eagerly to the strange and the bizarre, things which Patrick instinctively distrusts; this part of Crockett is expressed through the free and mysterious Silver Sand who has a charm, a dignity and an authority which Crockett aspired to but never acquired. Silver Sand is Crockett *plus*, a kind of wish-fulfilment figure of exotic foreignness and romantic pedigree, sophisticated as Crockett would have liked to be but never was.

The full title of the book suggests the importance of Silver Sand in Crockett's mind: *The Raiders, being some Passages in the Life of John Faa, Lord and Earl of Little Egypt*, and to underline this he quotes at the beginning in an abbreviated form the writ of the Scottish Privy Council by which James V in February 1540 conferred this exalted title upon the John Faa of his time. After this small show of learning, we move into the Foreword, supposedly written by Patrick in his thirty-seventh year[10] (although he sounds decades older, just as Crockett sounded a wise old man in the Prefaces and Introductions he furnished for the books of others when he was still comparatively young). Patrick looks back on his adventures with a quiet satisfaction that they are over, and then begins to tell his story in the style of the young Patrick about to plunge into them. These two voices are a neat device; the Foreword gives us a picture of a canny rather prosaic man settled solidly into material prosperity and thankful to Providence for it, but the younger Patrick has a naiveté, a clumsy innocence, a simplicity that comes of raw inexperience. The two at first sound very different, but Crockett skilfully manipulates young Patrick's words telling the story so that we can see right from the beginning elements of the older Patrick he is going to become. Gradually as time goes on he changes and becomes more and more like the person who wrote the Foreword. Reminders along the way plot this progress—young Patrick thriftily picking up the candlestick which Silver Sand has thrown away and preserving it to stand on the stone shelf of the milkhouse at Rathan Tower 'to this day';[11] young Patrick telling Silver Sand priggishly that 'I did not care for wine, and indeed never used it';[12] young Patrick announcing to Silver Sand at the beginning of their adventure that 'as for me, I am at *all* times on the side of the law' but admitting with the older Patrick's voice that he must have spoken 'with a self-righteousness that I wonder Silver Sand did not kick me for';[13] young Patrick having his meal with the Tamsons and noting with approval that his coat had been neatly brushed and a patch put on the hole where the bullet had cut it the night before.[14] Crockett wants us to notice the counterpoint.

The Foreword is pious and prosy, fixing the story in a realistic setting of comfort and security. The writer thanks God for the good harvest; one can feel his hearty satisfaction in the comfortable fat phrases:

> throughout all this realm, both hill-land and valley-land, the crops of corn, Merse wheat, Lowden oats, and Galloway bear are in the stackyards under thack and rape by the second day of September.

Things are very different now from what they were at the time of the outlaws; his mind is at ease and 'prices rising', so he has time to write his account of

> those strange years when the hill outlaws collogued with the wild free-traders of the Holland traffic

which were for him the time of

> wild oat sowing when the blood ran warm—

though the Laird of Rathan must defend his youthful self and point out that these days were

> the graceless, unhallowed days after the Great Killing, when the saints of God had disappeared from the hills of Galloway and Carrick, and when the fastnesses of the utmost hills were held by a set of wild cairds—cattle reivers and murderers, worse than the painted savages of whom navigators to the far seas bring us word.

A masterly touch of respectable middle-age comes in his concern for decorum;

> now in any talks of the old days and of all our ancient ploys there are the bairns to be considered.[15]

The children must not be allowed to know too fully what their parents did in their wild youth. This sinks us deep in eighteenth-century Scottish domesticity.

Then suddenly comes Chapter I and the change of voice.

> It was upon Rathan Head that I first heard their bridle-reins jingling clear. It was ever my custom to walk in the full of the moon at all times of the year.[16]

Unknown riders passing at night with their harness ringing in the silence, a hero who wanders romantically by moonlight, a headland above waters— the picture with its light suggestion of sound has the magic quality of a ballad:

> About the middle of the night
> She heard the bridles ring ... [17]

Patrick was pleased with his opening; he repeats it with slight variation farther down the page:

> So it was in the height of the moon of May, as I said, that I heard their bridle-reins jingling clear and saw the harness glisten on their backs.[18]

We are off, it seems, into the land of glamourie, with perhaps a hint of Keats'

> Magic casements opening on the foam
> of perilous seas, in fairy lands forlorn

to speed us on our way. Even the touch of Patrick's pomposity blends with the setting—'It was ever my custom to walk in the full of the moon at all times of the year'—how delightfully poetic! He even has a little boat—a skiff—in which to row away from Isle Rathan and float on the silvery waters.

But Crockett is just playing with us. He has given us a first static scene which appears like a setting for old romance, until we notice the staginess, the contrived conscious felicity and brightness which remind us of a musical comedy's painted backcloth. He has with tongue in cheek built up the beauty and the moonlight; thereafter he just as carefully demolishes them as soon as movement begins.

Patrick is lying back, indulging in boyish dreams about smugglers and how splendid it will be to 'go out to the Free Trade among the Manxmen like a lad of spirit.'[19] All of a sudden his illusions and the silence are shattered. The smugglers are using him for target-practice, with derisive yells. He has to row back into the shadow to escape. His first thought is to go home at once (the older Patrick is felt behind this), then curiosity makes him follow the smugglers to the ruined churchyard of Kirk Oswald to see what they are up to. They are hiding their cargo in one of the graves. Just in time to stop Patrick from striding out of cover into the revealing moonlight, the heroine appears, May Maxwell of Craigdarroch, as curious as Patrick but considerably more prudent.

> I had almost set my foot on the edge of this white patch of moonlight to strike across it, when, with a rustle like a brown owl alighting swiftly and softly, some one took me by the hand, wheeled me about, and ere I had time to consider, carried me back again into the thick of the wood.[20]

Together they watch the men at work and listen to their coarse jesting, until 'From the waste came the baying of a hound—long, fitful, and very eerie.'[21] These are the 'Loathly Dogs', the 'Ghaistly Hounds', as the smugglers call them. 'The Black Deil hunts himsel' the nicht, I'm gaun hame'[22] declares one of the men, and soon the group are up and away in a great clattering of stirrup-irons. Even May is afraid.

> Over the wall at the corner farthest from us there came a fearsome pair. First a great grey dog, that hunted with its head down and bayed as it went. Behind it lumbered a still more horrible beast, great as an ox, grim and shaggy also,

but withal clearly monstrous and not of the earth, with broad, flat feet that made no noise, and a demon mark in scarlet upon its side, which told that the foul fiend itself that night followed the chase. May Mischief clung to my arm, and I thought she had swooned away. But the beasts passed some way beneath us, like spirits that flit by without noise, save for the ghostly baying which made one sweat with fear.[23]

The tension slackens. May and the hero are left to let go of one another's hands. He can think of nothing to say, though May is waiting for something. She gives up in the end.

'Guid e'en to ye,' she said, dropping me a curtsy; 'virtue is its ain reward, I ken. It's virtuous to do a sheep a good turn, but a kennin' uninteresting. Guid e'en to ye, Sheep!'
With that she turned and left me speechless, holding by the wall. Yet I have thought of many things since which I might have said—clever things too.[24]

Off May goes, leaving Patrick to row home and decide that he dislikes her even more than he had thought before this incident.

The splendid smugglers with their ringing bridles turn out not to be romantic figures as in Kipling's 'Watch the wall, my darling, while the gentlemen go by!' but coarse rough brutes who would have shot Patrick without thinking twice about it; he is foolish in his romantic notions and foolish in his actions; once he sees what they are doing he says that he would have run away if May Maxwell had not kept hold of his hand.

In most romantic stories, the heroine is a timid trembler seeking protection; here she is the decisive one, the one with the brains who keeps the hero out of danger, pulls him nearer the smugglers to see what they are doing, yet prevents him from showing himself. She knows what she is about, very much in the tradition of Leeb M'Lurg. May is a very Scottish heroine, full of commonsense; the frank comradeship she offers to the slower-witted boy, her later mockery and the boy's hostility, are in the tradition of a Scots wooing. The only true romantic trapping which is left to us is the eerie vision of the 'Loathly Dogs', and they are part of the puzzle; if we remember the details, especially the 'demon mark in scarlet' we will guess who they are later when we meet Silver Sand who sells keel or raddle in winter to mark sheep in red, and has a huge wolf-hound Quharrie as his constant companion. We have been given a fair clue to their identity.

However, in case the romance should still not be sufficiently countered by reality, Crockett supplies us with two additional counterweights before swinging into the heart of his story—the personality of Patrick's father, and the little community of boys on Isle Rathan when Patrick is left his father's heir. On first reading, these two elements seem an unnecessary hindrance; we have been lured into the story by smugglers, supernatural apparitions and the boy and girl who are to be the lovers, and are all agog to get on with the plot. Instead we are treated to five chapters of rambling disquisition—but at the end of them the Galloway background has been filled in with affectionate ordinariness and we know Patrick very well indeed. Its very garrulousness is part of Patrick's character.

Patrick's mother has died long before the beginning of the story; she had been a Galloway girl, strong and sensible, who had been carried off by one of the visitations of plague which ravaged the country from time to time. He, like Ralph Peden, has been brought up by his father alone on Isle Rathan, the family inheritance, and knows little of women. His father, John Heron, plays no part in the story; he is introduced in one chapter merely to die at the end of it and make way for his son. The idea of a dying father may have been suggested by the death of Jim Hawkins' father at the beginning of *Treasure Island* and of David Balfour's at the beginning of *Kidnapped*, but Crockett utilises the father figure to much greater purpose, perhaps to compensate for the father he himself had never known. John Heron is 'humoursome' and whimsical, with values that reflect Crockett's own and apt, memorable sayings which all tend to uphold a philosphical acceptance of the weaknesses and inadequacies of man and his world. He has been shrewd as the father of Robert Burns was shrewd, and has taught his son surveying and land measurement, foreseeing how important these skills are to be in the future, as well as Latin, English and Euclid. He has led an active life, going out with the smugglers in his wild youth but not with the Black Smugglers of Yawkins' band 'with whom, as my father used to say quaintly, no honest smuggler hath company.'[25] He had ridden with the royalist forces in the Killing Time, and had also been one of the hunted, but he is not a deeply religious man; he sympathises with John MacMillan and the Society Men rather than the parish ministers and encourages Patrick to attend their services but does not go himself. He doubts whether the truth can be found in any one religion or any one minister.

> My advice to you, Patrick, is no to be identified wi' ony extremes, to read yer Bible strictly, an' gin ye get a guid minister to sit under, to listen edently to the word preached. It's mair than your faither ever got for ony length o' time.[26]

The burden of his advice is caution, scepticism, moderation in all things—almost the balanced philosophy of the Enlightenment, of Johnson's *Vanity of Human Wishes* which was one of Scott's favourite poems, the outlook of a man whom life has disappointed but who has thought his way through to a whimsical wisdom; seeing a gull flash down to the water from the blue sky he declares

> Even thus has my life been, Paitrick. I have been most of my time but a great gull diving for herring on an east-windy day. Whiles I have gotten a bit flounder for my pains, and whiles a rive o' drooned whalp, but o' the rale herrin'—desperate few, man, desperate few.[27]

He feels he has handed on to his son, if not a rich inheritance, at least 'a pickle siller' and a quality of mind worth having:

> ...gin I can leave ye the content to be doing wi' little, an' the saving salt o' honour to be kitchen to your piece, that's better than the lairdship o' a barony.[28]

Above all, he leaves him his freedom, the chance to 'try all ways o't'. His intention, as expressed to and carried out by Matthew Erskine the Dumfries lawyer, is that his son should, in Patrick's words, 'neither be hampered in well-doing nor in ill-doing, but do even as it seemed good to me.'[29]

All this, from the point of view of Crockett, is interesting. His growing doubts about the narrowness of any one belief—the narrowness which gives the illusion of height—are strongly echoed by John Heron, and the negative constrictions of religion are lifted for Patrick as they had been, after much soul-searching, for Ralph Peden. His father makes this crystal-clear.

> 'When I was a lad,' he used to say, 'I was sore hampered in coming and going, and most of the evils of my life have come upon me because I was not really left to myself to choose right and wrong, nosing them for myself like a Scent-Dog after birds. So I will even leave you Paitrick, as says the Carritches, to "the freedom of your own will."'[30]

This sounds like Crockett awarding to his hero what he himself in his Cameronian upbringing had not received except through the connivance of kindly uncles, had later won through his travelling and writing, and was while this was being written thinking of winning again by laying down his ministry. It forms only one chapter in *The Raiders* but one would not be without it.

The second counterblast against romance is the inconsequential rambling life the boys lead on Isle Rathan after John Heron's death, when Patrick is putting 'try all ways o't' into tentative practice. He has imported some young cronies to live with him in the old tower, and, if one is honest, tiresome boring company they are. Their youthful squabbling and horseplay are based on Crockett's holidays at the Scaur and Colvend, made more lively perhaps by a reminiscence of R M Ballantyne's *The Coral Island* (1858) and its trio of boyish adventurers Ralph, Peterkin and Jack. He admits that he alters facts; in *The Raiders* it is May Maxwell who brings them the pie to eke out their diet of flounders, but in the reality it was one of the kindly mothers.[31] He lets himself go on too long in happy recollections, but these chapters fulfil two functions— they bring us down from John Heron's philosophical observations based on experience to homely ordinariness, showing us that Patrick was without experience, an irresponsible high-spirited boy, fond of his own way, inclined to bully his friends, contented with an idle carefree existence, oiling the firearms at Isle Rathan because he likes to see them clean and shining, not because he expects to use them. He is a decent young lad but take away the decentness and there is little left. He likes to tease his friends' mothers according to his father's recipe from the Scriptures—

> Mind ye, a soft answer's aye best. It's commanded—and forbye, it makes them far madder than anything else ye could say.[32]

and the appearance of May Maxwell with these indignant mothers links these rambling chapters with the sharply-defined incident in Kirk Oswald churchyard at the opening of *The Raiders*; May Maxwell in Chapter V and Silver Sand in Chapter VI herald the beginning of the adventure.

Mystery was a popular feature of light literature in the 1890s, and Silver Sand provides it. He is, as Patrick says,

> a problem like those they give to the collegers at Edinburgh, which the longer you look at, grow the more difficult. To begin with, there seemed nothing uncanny about Silver Sand more than about my clogs with their soles of birk. But after you knew him a while, one strange and unaccountable characteristic after another emerged and set you thinking.[33]

Silver Sand is a pedlar, selling sand for sharpening scythes in summer, sand from Loch Skerrow, from Loch Valley, and the silver sand from Loch Enoch which gives him his name. In the winter he sells keel, or raddle, for marking sheep. This second trade of raddle-seller or reddleman may have been suggested by Thomas Hardy's Diggory Venn in *The Return of the Native*;[34] it seems a prosaic occupation but as Hardy presents him Venn leads a strange wandering lonely life, held in superstitious awe by the villagers; he is a 'red ghost', a 'fiery mommet' who reminds them of the devil and fills them with fear. Hardy had originally conceived him as

> a sort of benevolent, mysterious spirit, who appears, from no one knows where, to save Thomasin at the crises of her fortune, and then, once more, vanishes into obscurity.[35]

In the end, on the advice of his publishers, Hardy provided a happy ending for Diggory and Thomasin, but the reddleman's weird trick of appearing just when wanted and then quietly disappearing certainly belongs to Silver Sand also. He flits in and out of Patrick's fortunes for the first forty-one chapters of *The Raiders*, coming and going throughout all Galloway and Carrick unhindered either by gipsies or outlaws, with a mysterious power which puzzles the reader and baffles poor simple Patrick, and he is not finally identified as John Faa until Chapter XLII.

It has been suggested that the original of Silver Sand was Johnny Morgan,[36] a pedlar of Irish origin who travelled Galloway and Ayrshire as a rag and bone man when Crockett was a boy, with a donkey called Tommy and dog named Quharrie, dealing in rabbit skins, gossip and scythe sand. He died in 1901 and is buried in Morton churchyard. The donkey and Quharrie may have been borrowed from him, but the photograph of this drab and uninviting Johnny Morgan shows how far Crockett's imagination had transformed him—if it is he, and we must remember that Crockett in *Raiderland* said that the original of Silver Sand used to tell tales by the fireside at Little Duchrae. But there are no rags and bones for his wandering enigma. Silver Sand is proud and cryptic, knowing all and foreseeing all, talking Galloway Scots but with overtones of a wider experience, and a knowledge of men and affairs undreamed of by even the most gossiping of Johnny Morgans. He can produce a bottle of wine and sweet cakes to cheer Patrick—wine 'that comes from whaur the swallows gang in the winter time'[37]—and a purse of golden guineas such as Patrick had never seen in his life before. He is a solitary figure, coming and going as he pleases:

> all Silver Sand's movements were so still and secret that no one could have been much astonished at any hour of the day or night had he appeared at their door or suddenly vanished from their sight.[38]

He dislikes boys, but Patrick has won his trust by rescuing his donkey from the village tormentors at Orraland—a trust of which Patrick is rightly proud;

> In these troubled times to be a third with Silver Sand and Quharrie was better than to be the Pope's nephew.[39]

a comparison which in its sophistication is oddly vivid. He has a strong gipsy element in his character but one from which all squalor and lowness are removed; his skills are many and conveyed in imagery which has dignity and sometimes beauty.

> Whenever I think of Paradise, to this day my mind runs on gypsy poles, and a clear stream birling down among the trees of birk and ash that cower in the hollow of the glen from the south-west wind, and of Silver Sand frying Loch Grannoch trout upon a skirling pan.[40]

or else perhaps

> a red speckled trout fresh out of the pan, which the night before had steered his easy way through the clear granite-filtered water of Loch Skerrow. It was hardly food for sinful mortals.[41]

He has 'a queer, smileless humour of his own'[42] and an authority over Patrick and the others which he exercises quietly or sharply as seems appropriate, never questioning that he will be obeyed. Rather than any itinerant Johnny Morgan, it seems likely that in the back of Crockett's mind was the ballad of 'The Gyspy Laddie' and the countess, the high-born Lady Cassillis who ran off with a sweetly-singing Egyptian, forsaking her horse and her feather-bed for the roving life.

> Sae take from me my silk mantle,
>   And bring to me a plaidie,
> For I will travel the world owre
>   Along with the gypsie laddie.
>
> I could sail the seas with my Jockie Faa,
>   I could sail the seas with my dearie;
> I could sail the seas with my Jockie Faa,
>   And with pleasure could drown with my dearie.[43]

As the story proceeds we are given clue after clue to Silver Sand's identity; Patrick puts them down without comprehending them (in keeping with his guileless honesty of character) but the reader picks them up as he is intended to do and, long before Patrick does, realises that Silver Sand is John Faa, leader of the most powerful and aristocratic of the gipsy tribes, and that he has chosen to be a pedlar rather than condone the crimes of his mother and brother Hector.

Picking up the clues is part of the pleasure of the narrative, whether they be verbal, as Sammle Tamson's description of John Faa as he guides Patrick up towards the outlaws' country—

> He's a kind o' pope among them ... Faith, they say that Billy Marshall is feared o' the Faa himself'. Johnny Faa is no canny. He comes an' gangs like a wraith, or like the wind—no man knoweth whither he goes or whence he comes.[44]

—which echoes precisely those things which Patrick himself has earlier written of Silver Sand; or part of the action, as when Lady Grizel Maxwell's servant recognises Silver Sand's horse as John Faa's,[45] or when Lady Grizel herself in quick surprise words first speaks to him.

> It was at Silver Sand she looked first.
> 'Preserve us, man!' she said; 'surely hemp's no sae dear that ye can afford to risk the tow. What do ye in this country?'
> Silver Sand was manifestly put out.
> 'I think your ladyship is mistaken,' he said.
> 'Mistake here!—mistake there!—Grizel Maxwell kens a—'
> 'Wheesht, wheesht, my Leddy! There's names that's no for cryin' at ilka lodge-yett.'[46]

Silver Sand is a splendid figure, weaving in and out of the story with mysterious omniscience; he is John Faa, Lord and Earl of Little Egypt by the patent bestowed by King James on his ancestor; he may choose to be a pedlar but that is his own business, and he defends the Faas every time they are criticised—they are aristocrats among gipsies, far above *canaille* like the Macatericks and the Marshalls. It is easy for Crockett to convey this side of his character, the strangeness, the kissing of hands, the way he

> never was comfortable inside a room for more than half an hour together. The wide lift was his house, and sun or shine, rain or fair, made little difference to him.[47]

Hardy's Diggory Venn may have suggested the superstitious reverence in which he is held; Stevenson's incident of the Black Spot in *Treasure Island* probably suggested the metal token which Silver Sand is so strangely startled to find among his Loch Enoch sand;[48] Scott's Meg Merrilies and Rob Roy surely provide a few hints, and there may even be a dash of Robin Hood. But

Crockett does more than make him a romantic gipsy leader; he knits him firmly into the religious life of Galloway as well as its social structure.

Early in the story, just after the death of Richard Maxwell, a quiet paragraph brings out a side of Silver Sand which we had not expected, at the same time showing Patrick unconsciously revealing his solid down-to-earth realism.

> On the sandy knowe behind the cave at the farthest end of Rathan we laid Richard Maxwell to rest. As we came out the seagulls clanged about, and a rock dove flew down and perched on the prow of the boat above the dead body, which was strange, and mightily admired, for never did any of us see such like before. But the Maxwells took it as a sign not of this world, so they all of them took off their bonnets and put them in the bottom of the boat; for which I thought none the worse of them though I kept mine on (for, indeed, it was but a pigeon and a young bird that was tired flying, which presently was gone), and so we drew to the shore. We buried him with haste and without ordered preparation, but with all reverence, and Silver Sand put up a prayer that moved me strangely, for I knew not even that he was a man who held religion in honour. Then I bethought me on many things I had said to him that were no credit to me to say, and I wished that I had not said them. Yet I remembered that he had never rebuked me as a strict professor would have done.[49]

This is carefully composed in contrast to the noise and tumult of fighting which preceded it; Silver Sand's prayer stands out with dignity, emphasised by the comic schoolboy chagrin which seizes Patrick as he remembers past indiscretions. We can believe that Silver Sand is 'no strict professor' and yet a man of faith in his own way.

The relationship between Patrick and Silver Sand is finely worked out in the course of the story. It may remind some readers of that between David Balfour and Alan Breck in Stevenson's *Kidnapped*, which might initially have been in Crockett's mind when considering a friendship between a young lad and an older man, but it has much more variety and depth than the alternate sulkiness and sentiment of that touchy pair. Silver Sand has none of the childish vanity of Alan Breck and Patrick has none of David's weak selfishness; the two are held together by a strong attraction of opposites which holds even in the moment when Patrick at last realises who Silver Sand really is, and with a sore heart believes him to be an enemy.

Silver Sand has no illusions about Patrick; he makes fun of his mental slowness:

> Preserve us a', Paitrick, but ye mauna pit sic a strain on your uptak. It's no human to understand a' that! Aye, as ye say, it's the cave, and nocht else but the cave.[50]

He makes fun of his worldly pretensions:

> Ye needna turn up your een at me like tea-dishes. I am neyther thief nor robber, though I bena a laird wi' an island that I can nearly cover wi' my breeks when I sit doon on it.[51]

—showing, incidentally, how clearly he knows what Patrick is suspecting about him. Yet he has a delicacy which understands why Patrick stands on his dignity when May Maxwell is spoken of; he is able to explain that there is no need for desperate hurry in pursuit of her, and accords Patrick his full title in affectionate amusement—the mocking amusement of an older man at a young lover.

> 'Silver Sand, I ask ye no to speak o' the young lass like that.'
> 'Aweel, aweel, Rathan, then I'll no; but dinna fret, I'm kind o' sib to the gypsies mysel', an' I can tell ye that till the marriage is by at the end o' the three days o' feastin', May Maxwell will be attended and "kuitled" like a leddy— an' after that mair nor ever, for she'll be a Faa hersel'.'
> 'God forbid!' said I fervently.
> 'Amen to that!' said Silver Sand. 'We'll e'en make her a Heron, though the Herons are but lang-nebbit paddock-dabbers to the Faas.'[52]

The emotion which perpetually zigzags between the two suddenly comes out after this exchange. Patrick in his relief that they have three days in hand feels impulsive gratitude; he looks at Silver Sand's twisted arms, with a stab of quick compassion, seeing

> the joints ... set the other way, either naturally or through some extraordinary torture

and asks his forgiveness for doubting him, for

> O' Man, I like ye—I like ye![53]

For a moment Silver Sand holds back in angry pride, but it is so boyish, so honest, so affectionate an apology that his heart is touched; he

> suddenly laid his face between his hands and sobbed as if he would tear his throat. It was terrible. I knew not what to do in that lonely place, but I laid my head on his shoulder to see if that would comfort him.
> 'O man Paitrick!' he cried out at last, 'ye hae given me back my manhood. I have been treated like a beast. I have been a beast. I have lived wi' the beasts, but you are the first that has drawn close to me for thirty years. Paitrick, ye may want a friend for you and yours, but it shallna be as lang as Silver Sand can trail his auld twisted banes after ye. Man, I wad gang for ye into the Ill Bit itsel', that's fu' o' brimstane reek, the reed lowe jookin' through the bars, and the puir, puir craiters yammerin' ahint.'[54]

This outburst of emotion between the two friends could have been embarrassing, but Crockett needed to make clear how deep the relationship was between the two so that later, when they are sheltering in the Cave of the Aughty, it will seem natural that the proud Faa should humble himself to this lad of so little experience and tell him in anguished confession the story of his involvement with Lag and the persecutors.

This passage foreshadows it; the mystery of Silver Sand deepens as he talks of having lived like a beast and been a beast, and his picture of the hell through which he will follow his friend is a very Covenanting hell, aflame with brimstone and the nether pit, the damned crying behind the black bars as they burn in eternal flame. We feel that whatever dark past lies behind the gipsy pedlar, it is in some way connected with religion, which we already know him to revere. Any embarrassment we may feel at his sudden breaking down into tears is dispelled because Patrick himself gives expression to it and shares it: 'It was terrible' he says, in frightened uncomprehending dismay; he does not know what to do and tries to comfort him like any small boy comforting any grown-up whose grief he cannot understand or share. He moves closer and puts his head on Silver Sand's shoulder, to see if that helps. The loving intimate movement is so natural that the awkward moment achieves firm reality, and Silver Sand recovers his poise in a by now familiar way which is equally convincing.

> 'But this is no what we are here for,' he said, with one of his quick changes ... [55]

and in a second they are back laying plans for May Maxwell's rescue. Silver Sand has deeper roots than a gipsy figure of romance; his love for Patrick has grown because of his need for human friendship, because Patrick alone has reached out to him without fear. But he remains for Patrick still a figure of mystery,

> a man with more secrets of his own, and dangerous ones to boot, than I had cared to carry about without a steel jacket over.[56]

The older Patrick seems to speak here, but the younger one only occasionally wonders about Silver Sand's timely appearances and disappearances, until on the second expedition up into the hills there comes the sudden shock of finding Silver Sand and Quharrie among the enemy, apparently a leader among them. It is for this moment's sake that Crockett has kept Patrick from guessing the truth. He must for this moment think himself betrayed by his friend, so that his personal courage, his simple honest bravery, can be shown. Crockett expresses it through anti-romance by making Patrick adopt a pose like an operatic hero, theatrical and verbose. Silver Sand looms menacing as he walks towards him with the lantern but Patrick is ready.

> I took the dagger by the point and offered it to him, saying 'Silver Sand, true friend; here is a knife; strike quickly at my heart and make a swift end. Thou knowest where to strike, for thou hast lain against it many a time.'
> This I thought mighty fine at the time, and original; but now I know that I had heard my father read somewhat like it out of an old book of stage plays.[57]

To these stilted, fustian heroics,

> 'Patrick!' was all he said,

that one word, his friend's name, conveying so many shades of meaning—a little reproach, a little amusement, kindliness, affection, understanding and forgiveness, then the quick business-like question 'Can you walk?' The moment of high drama, which another author might have treated with solemnity, is turned by Crockett into comedy, funny yet touching—funny because of the heroics, touching because Patrick really thought he was facing betrayal and death and faced it without flinching. It is a delicate original treatment of what could have been a scene from *The Scarlet Pimpernel* if approached conventionally.

Silver Sand, in the speeches he makes to the Faas, thunders eloquently in Biblical English.

> 'Silence, hound!' said Silver Sand, with consuming vehemence. 'Well you know who I am. I am John Faa, of the blood royal of Egypt. Well you remember why I left you, because I am not of them that do murder. Well you know that I have kept free not from the danger but from the plunder. Now that the plunder is done with, and the danger come, I am here. Is it not so? ... I will hunt you with the Loathly Beasts. I will press on you with the Faa's curse. I will dwine your flesh on your bones, for I am your king, John Faa, and the power is mine, alone and without bound among this people of Egypt ... There shall be no assault delivered by your enemies, but one more sure and terrible by the Almighty. The judgment for murder and crime comes swiftly. Go not back to to take part in it, for I foresee that no one shall escape.'[58]

This is rich roaring stuff; but Crockett throws it away for the deliberate calculated rodomontade that it is; in the Cave of the Aughty, when the crisis is over, Patrick asks Silver Sand if he really could have carried out the 'warlock threats' he had uttered. Silver Sand smiles.

> They believed I could, which is the same thing.[59]

The secret of John Faa's power is no romantic mysterious magic but merely the clever politician's manipulation of a dangerous crowd. He plays on their superstition, which he is both too sophisticated and too Christian to share; he uses his wits as a cunning realist, almost a cynic; he is not deceived by his own oratory but uses it to play on those who are. He has no illusions about the divine power of a king but draws on the illusions of others to control them by deliberate unromantic lies for the sake of their safety.

When Silver Sand opens his heart to Patrick in the Cave of the Aughty, his speech is quite different; he speaks from the heart, in harsh Scots which almost wrenches his mind as he relives the agony he has felt in being part of Lag's brutality.

> He wad ride up to a farmhouse an' chap on the door wi' the basket hilt o' his broadsword.
> 'Is the guidman in?' says he.
> 'Deed, he is that—' says the mistress: 'he's gettin' his parritch.'
> 'Haste him fast, then,' says Lag, 'for the Archangel Gawbriel (nae less) is

waitin' to tak' his fower-'oors wi' him, an' it's a kittle thing to keep the likes o' him waitin'!'

Then in ten minutes that wife's a weedow, an' gatherin' up her man's harns in a napkin!'[60]

He forces himself to tell of the murder of the little boy at Crichope Linn, and his speech takes on another rhythm, the slower and more measured style of the Covenanters and Patrick Walker.

'So that day,' continued Silver Sand, 'made me a believing man—that is, so far as a gypsy and a Faa may be a believing man.'[61]

But when the Killing Time was over, every man's hand was against him, for the Faas were outlaws.

So I took to the hills and to the trade of selling the bonny scythe sand and the red keel for the sheep. And though I have not where to lay my head, I am a better and a happier man, than the man who witnessed that sight by the Linn of Crichope ever deserved to be. But I have dwelt with my Maker and humbled myself before Him in secret wood and lonely fell. The men of the hills ceased their abiding in the mosses and moors nearly forty years gone—all but one, and he a persecutor, a heathen man, and one whose hand had been dyed in the blood of God's saints. For forty years I have dwelt where God's folk dwelt, and striven with the devil and the flesh in many a strange place—often not sure whether indeed I had gotten me the victory.[62]

As he continues, we can feel his ironic self building itself up again after the pain of confession, the whimsical Silver Sand who has to delight in his own cleverness and enjoys playing tricks.

'My arms which were twisted in the torture of the Star Chamber before James, Duke of York, have served me in that I can run like a beast, and when we hunt as the Loathly Dogs, Quharrie and I fear the foolish folk out of their wits.'

'Indeed, I think you are no that canny mysel',' I said, with a kind of awe on my face.

'Weel,' said Silver Sand, 'I doubt not that gin some o' the landward presbyteries got me, I micht burn even at this day, as did Major Weir. Yet is all my magic of the simplest and most childish—even as simple as keel and scythe sand.'[63]

The penitent is not so permanently or obsessionally repentant that he cannot enjoy his own mischief. He plays kindly tricks on the country folk to mystify them—stooking their corn, herding their sheep and lambs into the buchts when a storm is coming, playing bogles with the girls round the corn-stacks, playing at being the Brownie who works for the cotmen. This aspect of Silver Sand was prompted by Crockett's reading of James Hogg. In a letter to Hogg's daughter he claims to have been strongly influenced by him.

I have reverenced your father all my life and his stories were those best known to be in my youth ... in *The Raiders* you will see traces of Hogg's influence perhaps stronger than any other. Of course the sapient critics led away by the fact that I tell a romantic story cry 'Stevenson' or 'Scott'; but they miss the cardinal fact that I am herd and herd's son and (like James Hogg) was reared upon the hills of sheep.[64]

Writing to Hogg's daughter, Crockett exaggerated a little; he read Hogg among others at Drumbreck, but only among others. Nevertheless the Covenanting strain in Silver Sand, and certainly his mischievous Brownie tricks, are very like those of Hogg's *Brownie of Bodsbeck* (1817), most significantly in the deformity and eeriness of the Brownie.

The welding together of the two elements, the gipsy Earl and the humble believer, is the most audacious part of *The Raiders*. It was too much for the *Scotsman* critic; 'Mr Crockett overstrains the reader's powers of faith'.[65] Nevertheless, Crockett prepares us right from the beginning for this revelation; Patrick's father has changed sides from dragoon to a hunted man with Peden—Silver Sand is not unique; and Silver Sand prayed over Richard Maxwell's body. Moreover, in the Cave of the Aughty Patrick asks the questions the reader would like to ask, and Silver Sand answers well.

> 'Content?' said Silver Sand: 'what for shouldna I be content? I ken nane that has mair cause to be. I look on the buik o' God a' the day under His wide, high lift for a rooftree, an' often a' nicht forbye, gin the storms keep aff. I hae God's Word in my oxter—see here!'
>
> He pulled out two dumpy little red-covered Bibles, with the Old Testament divided at Isaiah, and the Psalms of David in metre, very clean, but thumbed yellowish like a banknote at the end.
>
> 'What mair could a man want?' he said.[66]

The voice comes through so authentically and the dumpy books are so convincing that we are compelled to believe; we feel sure that Crockett the collector of books had seen those very volumes and has pinned us down neatly as Silver Sand produced them.

Silver Sand has the same reality as Edie Ochiltree in *The Antiquary*. He knows all that is going on in the country around and comments in as sardonic a way. He knows that the Maxwell brothers have been making use of Patrick in their smuggling activities without his knowledge:

> gin I war you I wad pit my fit doon again them using the cellars o' Rathan for their caves o' storage[67]

and Patrick reacts with righteous indignation, as Silver Sand knew he would. The older Patrick shows himself for a moment. Silver Sand also knows that May Maxwell has been trying in vain to penetrate Patrick's density, going down to the shore to gaze at Rathan but finding no response from its dunderhead of a laird.

> 'Whatna cuif was the lad she likit to bide in the Rathan when the bonniest

lass in the countryside cam' doon to keep tryst wi' nocht but the bit fardin' candle in the Hoose o' Rathan?'

'But I never jaloosed—hoo was I to ken?' I say, for I am indeed ashamed.

'Hoots awa', man! Ye surely wore your e'en in the tail o' your coat! Ye micht hae kenned by the way she flyted on ye!'[68]

Patrick is a very reluctant hero, quite apart from his slowness with May. He enters upon his adventures with perpetual doubt. Scott and Stevenson had already used this type of unheroic hero thrust into events which he fails hopelessly to understand, but Crockett adds Galt's technique, which is to let a character reveal his nature unconsciously in the self-satisfaction with which he chronicles his affairs. Patrick is never wholehearted in being a hero; he is never wholeheartedly sure that he wants to be in love. We pick up his comments as clues to his state of mind just as we pick up the clues to Silver Sand's identity. His initial remarks about May Maxwell as he floats, dreamily in his skiff show this self-revelation.

> A lad's mind runs naturally upon the young lasses, but as yet I had none of these to occupy me. Indeed there was but one of my standing in the neighbourhood—that Mary Maxwell who was called, not without cause, May Mischief, a sister of the wild Maxwells of Craigdarroch—and her I could not abide. There was nothing in her to think about particularly, and certainly I never liked her; nevertheless, one's mind being contrary, my thoughts ran upon her as the tide swirled southward by Rathan—especially upon a curious way she had of smiling when a wicked speech was brewing behind her eyes.[69]

He has no lass to think of—but May Maxwell, whom he cannot abide. His mind does not run on any lass—except May Maxwell, 'one's mind being contrary'. There was nothing in her to think about—yet he thinks of her as the tide pulls him southward, an interesting accompaniment to his thoughts which Freud might find significant. He assures us twice that he does not like her, then describes minutely the look in her eye and her smile before she makes a cutting remark, revealing not only that he has noticed these things but has remembered them, which surely he would not have done if completely indifferent as he really believes he is. Patrick may not be aware of his feelings during this half-sleeping, half-waking stream of consciousness, but the reader has a good idea.

After the burning of Craigdarroch, Patrick pesters Silver Sand with questions about where they are going and is anxious about Rathan Tower,

> for though I was willing enough to take part in the quarrel of the Maxwells, now that I was in for it, I did not want all my earthly possessions burned within half a mile of me without doing my best to save them.[70]

That 'now that I was in for it' removes all the value of the brave willingness to take part in the quarrel; he has no choice, and saying that he was willing enough is grudgingly making a virtue out of necessity.

As the boat enters the high narrow entrance to the cave and the green glimmer of its darkness, May is quiet, all her mischief gone. When she takes Patrick's arm in fear, all his dislike vanishes—and indeed, when he thinks about it, he never really disliked her as much as all that. He is gradually learning. He picks some white heather from a rock for her; she thanks him with tearful eyes and says he is too good to her, she does not deserve it.

> I meant to have said something exceedingly fine and appropriate, but all that I could get out was just 'Aye, but ye do!'
> And even that I stammered. However, I am not sure that I could have much bettered it after a week's consideration.[71]

The older Patrick looks back approvingly on his own honest tongue-tied self; fine speeches could not have improved on his sincere homely phrase, and he may well be right.

After the second attack by the raiders, May is kidnapped to be a bride for Hector Faa. Silver Sand urges action upon Patrick if he wants his lass; but Patrick touchily resents the inference—only to repent later when they find her shoe in the sand with its 'little wet silver buckle'.[72] He is moved to sentimental tears. He vacillates in all the inconsistencies of calf-love; even when high above the Dungeon of Buchan he is still berating himself for involving himself in what is really none of his business.

> What right had I to be here—I that might have sat safe and smiling on my Isle Rathan? Had any meddled with me there, that I must go and take up a stranger's quarrel? What a fool to bring myself to the dagger's point—and that for a girl who had no thought or tenderness for me, but only scoffs and jeers! ... What had I, who might have been sailing in the tall ships to see strange lands (for so my revenues permitted)—eating of the breadfruit and drinking of the coco brew that is as wine and milk at once—to do here on this Hill Perilous on such a desperate quest among desperate men?[73]

The smooth soft 'sat safe and smiling' is nicely chosen for the material comfort that floods Patrick's imagination, and it is like him that the fine voyages he might have taken (how solid his revenues sound—revenues from Rathan!) should end as prosaic pictures of eating and drinking strange food and drink. But he banishes these thoughts and goes on, as indeed he has to, reflecting that by the grace of God—and by taking great pains—he may yet accomplish his task and commenting (in the elder Patrick's style) that

> it is ever the nature of Galloway to share the credit of any victory with Providence, but to charge it wholly with any disaster. 'Wasna that cleverly dune?' we say when we succeed. 'We maun juist submit,' we say when we fail—a comfortable theology, which is ever the one for the most feck of Galloway men, whom chiefly dourness and not fanaticism took to the hills when Lag came riding with his mandates and letters judicatory.[74]

This reflection, inserted unobtrusively but giving a fresh view of Covenanting fervour, is relevant to Patrick but also to Crockett; not fanaticism but dourness—we note it with interest in the passing.

Patrick finds May in the evil hut at Craignairny by the unheroic means of being made prisoner himself. Once he and May have made their way to freedom, Kirk Oswald is repeated; it is May who thinks to bring the two knives; as they go in headlong flight down the rocky terrain, the outlaws after them with lanterns and two bloodhounds, it is Patrick who, though he does his best to assist May, falls over a heap of stones and knocks himself unconscious. May defends the hero and herself against the dogs and kills them both. When Patrick regains consciousness he finds they are near Loch Neldricken and its dreaded Murder Hole—May points it out to him,

> level as a green where they play bowls, and in daylight of the same colour, but in the midst a black round eye of water, oily and murky, as though it were without a bottom, and the water a little arched in the middle—a most uncomfortable place to look upon.[75]

The outlaws are near now, and we have a moment of romantic defiance—if they are to lie in the Murder Hole, they will not lie without company. But is May who utters this brave speech, not Patrick, and when the Loathly Beasts appear she is once more afraid.

> 'Oh, the Beasts—they are not of this earth,' cried May, holding my hand tightly. 'Oh, Patrick, do not faint away again and leave me all my lone.'[76]

This is surely the least romantic plea that ever heroine made to hero.

But the Beasts are simply Silver Sand and Quharrie; the outlaws flee in terror but May and Patrick are in safe hands. They are content and happy to be riding down to safety on horses that Silver Sand mysteriously has waiting at the Gairland Burn. As they ride alongside one another, with May leaning over now and then to wipe Patrick's brow, he takes the opportunity to kiss her when Silver Sand is not looking;

> she took it exceedingly sedately, which I liked best of all. Indeed, she kissed me back again fair and frank, without shame, a good true-hearted kiss, which I am proud of ... Now I vow and declare that this was all our love-making. Which is strange, considering the coil that is made about the affair in verse-books and ballads.[77]

Poor May! she at least has a kiss; Patrick is heartily glad not to have to bother with story-book love; not for him and May any nonsense about wooing which wastes time and gives so much trouble. From now on he is confidently possessive. When May learns that her father is dead, she tries to tell Patrick he must not think of marrying her; the Maxwells are too wild and her brothers are likely to want bloodshed in revenge.

> 'My lass,' I said,'I did not think of marrying your brothers.'[78]

When Patrick sets off with the party up Glen Trool for his second visit to the Wolf's Slock, May bids him farewell with tearful but good advice.

> See an' keep your feet dry. There's a pair of socks in your left pistol holster.[79]

She is exactly the wife that Patrick wants. They have grown up in the course of the story and already are looking to the future—the refurbishing of Rathan Tower and settling down to their life together. Patrick's reluctance to set off on this dangerous expedition shows that having 'tried all ways o't' he has chosen a quiet domestic life. He has also grown more serious; God and His Providence are strongly present in his mind. But even in this Crockett inserts a touch of the ridiculous. High above the desolate wastes of Loch Enoch, Patrick is moved to examine his conscience in the most exemplary manner.

> I blamed myself that I had been so slack and careless in my attendance on religion, promising (for the comfort of my soul as I lay thus breathing and looking) that when I should be back in Rathan, May and I should ride each day to church upon a good horse, she behind me on a pillion—and the thought put marrow into me.[80]

Who but Patrick would solace himself in a crisis with such humdrum domestic resolutions? Who but Patrick would think of his lady with such solid practicality sitting firmly behind him on a good horse, on her way with him to church? Who but Patrick would comfort his soul with such homespun conclusions? Patrick the narrator is now of the same mind exactly as Patrick of the Foreword, though Crockett allows him in the next two sentences a shrewd appraisal of his own motives:

> but whether grace or propinquity was in my mind, who shall say? at any rate I bethought myself that God could not destroy a youth of such excellent intentions.

May Maxwell is much more conventionally the Scottish heroine, charming, tomboyish and teasing, quicker-witted than her lover—in this she resembles all Crockett's heroines—yet tender and vulnerable when off guard. She kisses Patrick while he is unconscious beside her by Loch Neldricken, reflecting sadly that this may be her only chance. She is courageous in the face of pain. When she fights off and kills the raiders' bloodhounds, she has been badly bitten, but without fuss or complaint she herself burns the bite-marks in her arms. As a counter-part to the Foreword's picture of Patrick in his late thirties, we catch quick glimpses of her as the comfortable Mrs Heron, looking over his shoulder to make sure he is writing it all down properly, reminding him that people like to hear what the characters in stories are wearing—judicious and feminine at the same time—and complaining when he uses her precious empty sugar-bags to write his tale upon; they are needed for her garden seeds.

These three characters have been examined carefully because it is easy to overlook their solidity in the colour and movement and sound of *The Raiders* considered merely as a story. Its energy tends to be the main impression it leaves with a reader, obscuring the care with which the principal characters have been drawn. Even the minor ones have a realistic humour about them which sets *The Raiders* apart from the average historical romance popular during the 1890s and later. Richard Maxwell, for example, dying with exemplary piety but exhorting his sons not to be pious and forgiving until they are as near death as he is, has a macabre humour which is far removed from the conventional dying speeches of Covenanting tradition. Sammle and Eppie Tamson have a vivid voluble grotesque comedy in the same vein as Mowdiewort the gravedigger in *The Lilac Sunbonnet* but with a warm-heartedness which that crabbit fellow lacks. Lady Grizel Maxwell is an elderly *grande dame* in the tradition of Scott's Mrs Bethune Baliol and Stevenson's Lady Allardyce in *Catriona*. She has her dog and cat and parrot and monkey, and her outspoken servant Jen with whom she delights to argue and bicker; in her eccentricity she matches the ancient house of Earlstoun and provides a sharp-voiced touch of aristocratic independence. The circumstances in which all these characters move are wild and romantic in the extreme and even larger than life, but the people who live through them and take part in them are real and human, unromanticised, unsentimentalised and kept warmly memorable because all of them are comic in the sense that we are all a little comic since we are erring and foolish human beings. Crockett's sense of the ridiculous keeps his characters always fresh and alive.

Nevertheless it is true to say that it is the adventure, the scenery, the landscape, the rocky crags and wide airy vacancies above the bogs and among the peaks of the mountains, which captivated the first readers.

> 'The Raiders' is alive and throbbing with the Gallowegian spirit; the strong and wholesome air of the hills and seas of the Stewartry blow through it

said the *Scotsman*;[81]

> So-called nature description is not much insisted on in 'The Raiders' but the whole book is steeped in the open air. However thick may have been the walls of the room that shut in the writer and his manuscript, while he wrote the wind over a moorland county was in his ears, and in his eyes the glory of morning on the Solway.

said the *Bookman*;[82]

> 'The Raiders', when all allowance is made for its defects, is indubitably a fine book and this is the 'psychological moment' for its appearance surely; sick of incompetent diagnosis of unimportant aspects of neurosia (sic) and allied diseases, the public will eagerly welcome this clean and virile romance.

said the *St James's Gazette*.[83]

By telling the story in the first person, by dwelling on what interested him in Galloway and its past, by remembering what the scenes of his early days had looked and felt and smelt like and finding the exact words to set these impressions down, Crockett succeeded in conveying to a public sated with comfort and Oscar Wilde, the sheer freshness and excitement of youth. Through the personality of Patrick his narrator, perhaps slow in his mental processes but acutely aware of the world in which he lives, Crockett involves the reader to an extraordinary degree in the varied physical experiences which Patrick passes through—the movement of sunshine and shadows across great spaces, the textures of rocks and sand and boggy moorland, the tiny plants growing among the rocks above the cave, the sound of sheep cropping the short turf as they move slowly along; all these visual, aural and spatial sensations are caught with sensitive exactness and delicacy. As the *Bookman* critic noted, the description of nature is not 'insisted upon' as static passages of writing but is itself part of the narrative, incorporated into it in vivid and often colloquial comments emerging as Patrick responds to one thing after another. He perpetually notices the quick pictures that meet his eyes as he turns, the flashes of feeling that impress themselves upon him with a change of position or a plunge into a valley, the sudden awe-inspiring thunder of a breaking dam or the sharp 'spat' of a bullet against a wall. Everything tends to be movement; as a rule Patrick has no time to stand and take in the splendour of a 'view' since he is too busy pushing his way through a bog or struggling over loose stones up a mountain ridge.

To a great extent the settings of the events directed the events. John MacMillan makes this clear in what he said to Andrew McCormick:

> 'Loch Neldricken and its famous Murder Hole rejoiced Mr Crockett's hert; but when he reached Loch Enoch he was in a rapture. He tellt me efterhin' that he was fairly stuck wi' the plot o' the Raiders until he saw the Murder Hole and Loch Enoch, and then a' was plain sailin' ... He tellt me efterhin' that before he slept that night he had the whole plot o' the Raiders thocht oot.'[84]

The places and the imagined events are tangled in Crockett's mind; once he sees the place he can see what could happen in it. No incident is too ordinary; a tenant of Glentrool Lodge built a small dam to improve the fishing but the first flood swept it away—this became the furious outpouring of waters from Loch Valley when the raiders break down a dam to destroy their enemies. When an event needs a particular setting, he works in the opposite direction and takes liberties with geography to provide the exact environment he wants. Isle Rathan is Heston Island in Auchencairn Bay; he replaces the herd's little cottage by a completely imaginary Tower with many strong stone apartments and a series of cellars (borrowed from Balcary House across the bay on the mainland) for Patrick to be laird of and thus one of the landed gentry. He needs cliffs worn into rocky caves by the sea—caves large enough to be a refuge from the smugglers and gipsies; he borrows them from the Portowarren and Douglas Hall shores of the Solway a little distance away and models the vast cavern on a cave with the necessary two entrances he has visited on the coast of Co Antrim in Northern Ireland.[85]

His most outrageous borrowing is the Murder Hole itself. It is to be found in Nicholson's *Historical and Traditional Tales* linked with the story of a pedlar on a boundless moor benighted in a remote stretch of country in Ayrshire. He knocks on the door of a lonely hut, is alarmed by the reaction this evokes. He peers in a window, and sees an old woman scrubbing the floor and her two sons hastily hiding something in an immense chest. Caught and taken into the hut by these sinister personages, he is virtually imprisoned in a squalid bedroom, and wakes from sleep to see a stream of blood oozing across the floor and hear a conversation about how easy it is to kill a goat compared with the cries and struggles of 'the old gentleman last night'. 'The Murder Hole is the thing for me—that tells no tales—a single scuffle—a single plunge—and the fellow is dead and buried to your hand in a moment.'[86] This gory tale, associated with an area on the borders of Galloway and Ayrshire, between Dalmellington and the Dungeon of Buchan,[87] is exactly to Crockett's taste; he takes it over enthusiastically and makes it one of Patrick's adventures. To do so he has to alter its locality; in *the Raiders* his Murder Hole is not the Ayrshire one known to Joseph Train and by him described to George Chalmers for his *Caledonia*[88] but a curious spring in Loch Neldricken which never freezes but is perpetually black, round and bubbling. Its appearance caught Crockett's fancy; the manuscript of a talk on Crockett by Marion MacMillan shows how it may have grown. She describes how delighted he was with Loch Enoch and all the wonders of the mountains, and

> Loch Neldricken with the wonderful spring in its western arm which bye and bye he created into the Murder Hole. He said the water seemed to have a raised or convex surface like the human eye a most wonderful place. I suppose it needed the eye of the romancer to see it. I know it was the first time I had ever heard of it tho' I had been some years in the Glen at the time.[89]

One can imagine the glee with which he seized upon this splendid horror which he could link so easily with the Ayrshire Murder Hole and its sinister *dramatis personae*, even if it meant perching the hut and its occupants high up near the Wolf's Slock where it was extremely unlikely they would have stray passers-by to prey upon—there was no road. He has had his effect; the 'Murder Hole' is marked on Sheet 77 of the Ordnance Survey of Great Britain in the western part of Loch Neldricken. The romancer has affected the geographer.

The 'Sixteen Drifty Days' in which Patrick and Silver Sand shelter with little Marion in the Aughty are, as far as can be ascertained, unhistorical. Crockett probably found the idea of them in Andrew Lang's story for children, *The Gold of Fairnilee* in which

> for thirteen days the snows drifted and the wind blew. There was nothing for the sheep to eat, and if there had been hay enough, it would have been impossible to carry it to them. The poor beasts bit at the wool on each other's backs, and so many of them died that the shepherds built walls with the dead bodies to keep the wind and snow away from those that were left alive.[90]

Lang may have found the number thirteen in the *Statistical Account of Scotland* relating to the parish of Eskdalemuir in Dumfriesshire, where in 1674 there were thirteen days in the end of February in which the snow killed most of the sheep in the parish;[91] possibly Crockett made the change from thirteen to sixteen because it sounded better, just as he had changed 'Wolf's Slack' to 'Wolf's Slock' and 'Clashdan' to 'Clashdaan'; Buchan thought it good enough to use in *Witch Wood*. But in Lang surely there is the source of the vast and silent pit of snow and dead sheep in which the raiders perished.

But although Crockett's Galloway may not have been exact in either history or geography, his picture is true in atmosphere, tradition and pictured event; it is instantly alive upon the page. He had good precedent for the liberties he was taking; Thomas Hardy, finding his native county of Dorset too small, disinterred the name Wessex from English history and gave it 'fictitious significance as the existing name of the district once included in that ancient kingdom'. Hardy, being of a more serious temperament, is more consistent than Crockett in creating his half-real, half-imaginary Wessex; natural features like hills and rivers retain their proper names; the towns surrounding the area like Plymouth, Bath and Southampton retain their names so as to enclose it in real actual English counties; and only the places where the characters live and work in the deep interior of Wessex are changed, lightly disguised but recognisable—Toneborough is Taunton, the Great Plain is Salisbury Plain, and so on. He brought together a dozen areas of heathland to make up the vast expanse of Egdon Heath and invented the village of Little Hintock so completely in *The Woodlanders* that 'to oblige readers I once spent several hours on a bicycle with a friend in a serious attempt to find the real spot; but the search ended in failure',[92]—a comment that could apply to Crockett's invented localities too, even including the bicycle. Like Hardy, he transposed, shifted and borrowed in order to satisfy the dictates of his narrative without in any way detracting from the essential truth of the scenes and people he was depicting.

Hardy and Crockett, different in so many ways, have much in common— their love of the old ways and customs, their interest in comic country folk with queer names and queerer ideas, their ear for local speech in all its vagaries, and above all their ability to visualise a scene or event so as to bring it flashing before our eyes. *Far From the Madding Crowd*, Hardy's fourth novel and the one in which he adopted Wessex as the name for his locality, is one of melodrama and action with after many vicissitudes a happy ending; it was written before the stark fatalism of his later novels had settled upon the author. In it we can find many phrases and even whole sentences in which Hardy resembles Crockett in *The Raiders*.

Hardy describes a winter morning in brilliant colour:

> ...the frost had hardened and glazed the surface of the snow, till it shone in the red eastern light with the polish of marble; ... in some portions of the slope, withered grass-bents, encased in icicles, bristled through the smooth wan coverlet in the twisted and curved shapes of old Venetian glass ...[93]

Crockett's colouring is more restrained because he is writing of the evening light, but he has noticed the same things and makes us see them in the same way:

> As we went along the pale purple branches of the trees grew fuzzy with rime, which thickened till every tree was a wintry image of itself carved in whitest marble.[94]

They both describe movement through sound and sound through movement, and are attracted by the same onomatopoetic word; Hardy describes Troy's flashing sword-play round Bathsheba's body in the hollow among the ferns:

> ...she could see the hue of Troy's sword-arm, spread in a scarlet haze over the space covered by its motions, like a twanged harpstring, and behind all Troy himself, mostly facing her.[95]

Crockett describes Patrick skating over the ice of Loch Neldricken:

> ...do as I would, I could not hinder the ringing of my ice-runners and the whole loch twanged like a fiddle-string when one hooks it with the forefinger and then lets go.[96]

Both have a delicate eye for colour; Hardy describes

> a fine January morning, when there was just enough blue sky visible to make cheerfully-disposed people wish for more, and an occasional gleam of silvery sunshine.[97]

Crockett's morning is earlier, a quiet dawn on the waters of the Solway:

> what of the sea one could observe was of the colour of the inside of an oyster-shell, pearl grey and changeful.[98]

Both men like sudden changes from darkness to bright light, and can use darkness to intensify the emotional effect of an event; Bathsheba going through the fir plantation catches her dress one night and finds an unknown man going in the opposite direction; he offers to help her if she will let him open her lantern:

> A hand seized the lantern, the door was opened, the rays burst from their prison, and Bathsheda beheld her position with astonishment.
> The man to whom she was hooked was brilliant in brass and scarlet. He was a soldier. His sudden appearance was to darkness what the sound of a trumpet is to silence. Gloom, the *genius loci* at all times hitherto, was now totally overthrown, less by the lantern-light than by what the lantern lighted. The contrast of this revelation with her anticipations of some sinister figure in sombre garb was so great that it had upon her the effect of a fairy transformation.[99]

Patrick is likewise in darkness, lying high on the joists of the byre at Earlstoun above the cattle-stalls watching one of the raiders coming in:

> He walked stealthily, and the dancing lights without glinted on the blade of the long knife which he carried. He glided within with a bowing slouch that was most unwholesome to see. These things I did not distaste so greatly, but I hated the red gleam of the fired stack which shone in the man's eyes through a narrow wicket of the byre as he looked about. A man has been hanged only for showing a face like that in broad day; but in the dark of a cowshed, and with the whites of his eyes flickering red, and his upper lip pulled high over his gleaming teeth, I thought it had been the devil himself looking for me.[100]

Fairy transformation or devil from hell, in both men there is the same enjoyment of strong flashes of colour against surrounding blackness, the same use of exaggeration to splendid effect to convey the exact emotion upon the central character, the same melodramatic painting of the scene in strongly visual terms so that it is imprinted upon our imagination.

They can both convey the very essence of a bog in two or three sentences:

> Bathsheba never forgot that transient little picture of Liddy crossing the swamp to her there in the morning light. Iridescent bubbles of dank subterranean breath rose from the sweating sod beside the waiting-maid's feet as she trod, hissing as they burst and expanded to join the vapoury firmament above.[101]

> As I went the ground became wetter and boggier. My foot sank often to the ankle, and I had to shift my weight suddenly with an effort, drawing my imprisoned foot out of the oozy, clinging sand with a great 'cloop', as if I had begun to decant some mighty bottle. Green, unwholesome scum on the edges of black pools frothed about my brogues, which were soon wet through.[102]

Hardy's description relies on a measure of scientific impersonality, with 'subterranean' air bubbles rising to make their way upward to the 'vapoury firmament', using 'dank', 'sweating' and 'hissing' (the last perhaps with a suggestion of serpents?) to convey the ugliness of the wet surface and showing less concern for Liddy's feet; this is what one would expect, since Liddy is a minor character and the bog is an index to Bathsheba's troubled mind; she has just discovered Troy's relationship to dead Fanny Robin and her dead baby. Crockett is more personal, reminding us that Patrick is an eighteenth-century laird in his simile of a man taking the cork from a huge bottle, the size of it giving a hollow echoing resonance to his 'cloop', and adding the unpleasant details of the bog sucking at Patrick's wet brogues. But both men convey the sound as well as the appearance of their respective quagmires, and without specifically mentioning it add a strong hint of smell in 'breath ... hissing ... burst' and 'oozy ... cloop ... green unwholesome scum ... frothed.'

When it comes to extremes of weather both men write with energy and vigour, summoning the crash and thunder of the elements; the rainstorm which threatens Bathsheba's rickyard and the snowstorm in which Patrick almost loses touch with Silver Sand in the blinding white glare have much in common. Hardy's scene is violent and full of movement and frightening colour;

> A poplar in the immediate foreground was like an ink stroke on burnished tin. Then the picture vanished, leaving the darkness so intense that Gabriel worked entirely by feeling with his hands ...
> At her third ascent the rick suddenly brightened with the brazen glow of shining majolica—every knot in every straw was visible. On the slope in front of him appeared two human figures, black as jet. The rick lost its sheen—the shapes vanished. Gabriel turned his head. It had been the sixth flash which had come from the east behind him, and the two dark forms on the slope has been the shadows of himself and Bathsheba.[103]

> In a moment we were out facing it. In a step we had lost one another. We were blinded, deafened, blown away. I stood and shouted my loudest. When I got my eyes open I saw a fearsome sight. The darkness was white—around, behind, beneath—all was a livid, solid, white darkness. So fierce were the flakes, driven by the wind, that neither the black of the earth nor the dun of the sky shone through. I shouted my best, standing with outstretched arms. My cry was shut in my mouth. It never reached my own ears. So standing, I was neither able to go back or forward. A hand came across me out of the white smother. Stooping low, Silver Sand and I went down the hill, Quharrrie no doubt in front, though it was all impossible to see him.[104]

Hardy and Crockett both stress the way in which the senses are confounded by the ferocity of the storm—Gabriel does not recognise the two shapes thrown on to the slope by the lightning, Patrick is 'blinded, deafened' and to him the darkness is white, a reversal of normal. In Hardy we see 'the brazen glare of shining majolica', in Crockett the 'white smother', vivid pictorial evocations of the unleashed force of the storms dwarfing the puny human beings caught in their elemental buffeting. In both we see clearly in our imaginations a fast-moving picture of sound and fury. One is black shot through with multicoloured flashes; the other is white, blotting out and making one terrifying whiteness both the earth and the sky; the basic colour is the only difference.

Although they are perhaps at their best in these huge panoramas of tempest, both men can use small grotesque touches of description to good effect. Often they remind us in their brief pictures of human beings of the gargoyles created by mediaeval craftsmen. Hardy brings before our eyes a middle-aged man

> with a semi-bald head and one tooth in the left centre of his upper jaw, which made much of itself by standing prominent, like a milestone in a bank.[105]

Crockett gives us Sammle Tamson

> at the door, leaning from the outside to put his head inside, as one might see the bending top of a fishing-rod into an open window.[106]

Hardy gives us the maltster, old and bent:

> This aged man was now sitting opposite the fire, his frosty white hair and beard overgrowing his gnarled figure like the grey moss and lichen upon a leafless apple-tree.[107]

Sammle Tamson is likewise bent and walks

> with a strange forward stoop which approached a right angle. He leaned heavily upon his shepherd's staff as he went—his thin, pallid face with its lack-lustre eyes going before him. He had the air of a man who carries his own head for a hand lantern.[108]

Silver Sand's arms are exceedingly long and

> carried swinging at his sides as if they belonged to somebody else who had hung them there to drip.[109]

These last two comparisons are so like Hardy that one might easily attribute them to him if asked to guess out of context. They are the idiosyncratic narrative of Patrick which counts in a way as direct speech to the reader, whereas Hardy often puts his grotesque comparisons into the mouths of his countrymen.

> 'I believe that if so be that Baily Pennyways heart were put inside a nutshell, he'd rattle', continued Henery.[110]

> 'He got so much better, that he was quite godly in his later years, wasn't he, Jan' said Joseph Poorgrass. 'He got himself confirmed over again in a more serious way, and took to saying "Amen" almost as loud as the clerk, and he liked to copy comforting verses from the tombstones. He used, too, to hold the money-plate at Let Your Light so Shine, and stand godfather to poor little come-by-chance children; and he kept a missionary box upon his table to nab folk unawares when they called; yes, and he would box the charity-boys' ears if they laughed in church, till they could hardly stand upright, and do other deeds of piety natural to the saintly inclined.'[111]

Remove the clerk, the god-father and confirmation from this passage, the phrase from the offertory at the Communion service and the charity-boys, and it would sound exactly like Crockett; Hardy's sense of the ridiculous expressed through Joseph Poorgrass is very like Crockett's—the missionary box kept on the table 'to nab folk unawares' is pure Kailyard, if one finds it worth while to say so. Hardy finds rich comedy in the naive comments of rustics on the religion which is so strong a part of their lives, just as Crockett does with the beadle carrying up the Bible or Patrick proposing to go to church with May behind him on a pillion. In both writers is found the phrase 'a queer Christian'; this small point shows how both men relished the 'queerness' of humanity and particularly of Christians in their attitude to their religion.

But the most significant way in which Crockett resembles Hardy is the power of visualisation which they both possess, the ability to make us see before us in imagination the action they are narrating—the technique of the film director. Even in descriptions which in other writers would have been static, Crockett introduces movement so that landscapes are always alive as they are in a film. The mainland seen from Rathan is not a solid steady mass but a multiplicity of tiny movements blending together;

> Then was to be seen the reek of many farm-towns and villages, besides cot-houses without number,—all blowing the same way when the wind was soft and equal.[112]

When disaster comes to Craigdarroch,

> it grieved me to see the bonny corn that had grown so golden on the braes anent the isle screeing up in fire to the heavens.[113]

The gentle movement of the growing corn slowly and naturally ripening is sharply interrupted by hissing consonants close together that quicken the pace of the sentence and have a flapping effect, to illustrate the flames and their swift destruction 'screeing up in fire to the heavens'; one can hear as well as see them.

Sound often accompanies movement; the sound of water moving in the caves,

> these resounding halls of native rock, with the green water booming solemnly into them, and the sough of their roaring carried far along the coast;[114]

or the tiny sound effects of a group of sheep:

> It was pleasant and cheery to hear them cropping the herbage with short, quick bites, then moving on to another clump.[115]

The sound of the sheep pulling up mouthfuls of short grass can be heard in the simple sharp disyllables equally accented—'pleasant', 'cheery', 'cropping', 'herbage', then we come to their head-movements in a change of rhythm— 'short, quick bites'; after the three monosyllables there is a slight pause, and the next phrase, slower and more irregular, 'moving on to another clump' we feel something of the wandering irresolution of grazing sheep. It is not merely that Crockett describes the sounds and movements; he makes us hear them in the vowels, consonants and varying speeds of the words he uses.

Early in *The Raiders* there comes a highly dramatic account of the smugglers, aided by the hill gipsies, attacking Patrick and the Maxwells in the great cave on Isle Rathan. Crockett plunges us most vividly into this, describing the slow passage of the rowing-boat into the cave, the high cliffs, the tiny plants that grow in the crevices at the entrance, even Quharrie the dog sniffing uncertainly in the prow of the boat because he has never been in a sea cave before. The details build up so convincingly that we are there ourselves, listening to the rock pigeons in the sunshine, quiet and smoothly gliding along, then suddenly surprised when the birds are frightened when the boat grates on the shingle.

> At this the doves took instant alarm, and with a startling whirr and clang they swooped down on us in a perfect cloud, their shining breasts extraordinarily near us, so that the wind came in our faces as the living stream poured out of the narrow and fetid darkness of the cave into the splendid sunshine of the morning.[116]

By the time we are actually in the cave, Crockett has built up so many familiar small details that he can make us believe almost anything; we are convinced of the cave's reality and willing to receive the varying impressions with pleased excitement.

> ...a great round shot came plumping into the mouth of the cavern, breaking away a fragment from the cliff which plunged like thunder into the deep water of the entrance. Myriads of chips flew every way, but not so much as a feather-weight of dust reached the great centre hold called Ossian's Hall, where only the echoes reverberated, and the swells raised by the round shot and the fall of the great fragment came rolling up to our feet in an arching wall of green water crested with white.[117]

Sight and sound are tightly co-ordinated. The force of the 'great round shot' hits our ears in loud monosyllables and goes 'plumping' into the mouth of the cave in one of those homely words which are convincing because they are true to Patrick's type; the cliff fragment falls with a repetition of the same vowel as in 'plumping' but more strongly directed—'plunged like thunder'—until it is swallowed up by the slow quietness of 'the deep water of the entrance'. The flying chips, flying 'every way', not 'everywhere', contrast in their littleness with the hugeness of Ossian's Hall—and how impressive is 'feather-weight' when applied to dust, light and dry and soft in contrast to the sharp brightness of chips—and among the rolling of the echoes the besieged see the 'arching wall' of disturbed and swelling water rolling towards them in words which convey the splash and suck of the disturbance.

When we stop to examine the facts, we are bound to notice the exaggeration with which they are narrated. Any one who has seen the caves of the Solway, or of the Antrim coast, will realise that a cavern of such dimensions is highly unlikely; could a round shot and a fragmented boulder 'plunge like thunder' into the entrance, yet be heard only as distant echoes in the interior? Could their shattering impact send the hard stone flying in chips, yet not disturb the central cave by as much as a movement of dust? Crockett's imagination has been running riot and has conceived a cavern as fantastic as the great underground caverns in Rider Haggard's *She* (1887), a pit about the size of the space beneath the dome of St Paul's in which are piled the dry gleaming skeletons of generations for thousands of years back. Such things may be conceived of in the mysterious city of Kôr in darkest Africa (though even so Haggard had his critics) but cannot be thought of in the common day of the Solway Firth. Yet Crockett's description, has led us so gently and guided us so faithfully in the small things leading up to and surrounding it that we are prepared, momentarily, to believe that tiny Isle Rathan really can accommodate such a vast cave in some subterranean and inexplicable way. As a further aid to our imagination, Crockett devotes three whole paragraphs in the remainder of the chapter to giving us directions about where the cave is to be found, solemnly assuring us that we must not confuse it with another cave nearby, as if it were really possible for us to go and see it. He knows that his invention is in need of corroborative detail.

He plays the same trick of exaggeration in his description of the raiders' breaking down of the dam in Loch Valley in the hope of sweeping the punitive expedition to destruction. The Loch breaks loose with as much force as if one of the Tennessee Valley Authority's monster reservoirs had breached its barrier and poured forth to flood an entire state. In sober fact, Crockett found the idea from John MacMillan's account of the day the weir on Loch Valley had given way.

> One fine day, warm and sunny, our guide tells us that he was working with his sheep high up on the hill, when the roar and rattle of great stones carried along by the water brought him down the 'screes' at a run. Loch Valley had broken loose. The weir was no more, and the Gairlin burn was coming down in a ten-foot breast, creamy foam cresting it like an ocean wave. Down the glen it went ... while the boulders crashed and ground together with the rush of the water.[118]

This was an impressive sight, no doubt, but not as impressive as it becomes when Crockett takes it over.

> We were just at the corner of the burn where, under a great black face of rock it is hemmed in a deep defile, when our scouts on the hillside set up a great crying, the cause of which we could not at the time understand.
> 'Come up!' they cried. 'The water's broken lowse!...'
> Suddenly we heard before and above us a tremendous roaring noise as though the bowels of creation were gushing out as in some great convulsion. The hills gave back the echoes on every side. I found myself climbing the brae with some considerable verve and activity till I was fairly among the higher rocks...
> The great roaring noise still continued ... Suddenly we that were up the side of the Gairy saw a wondrous sight. A great wall of water, glassy black, tinged at the top with brown and crowned with a surging crest of white with many dancing overlapping folds sped down the glen. Our array was pent in the narrow passage—all those, that is, who had not taken the hill at the first alarm. As the wave came down upon them there was the wildest confusion. Men threw away their guns and took blindly to the hillside, running upwards like rabbits that have been feeding in a bottom of old grass. From where we stood the water seemed to travel with great deliberation, but nevertheless not a few of our men

were caught in the wash of it and spun downwards like corks in the inrush of the Solway tide.

The black, white-creasted wave being passed, the great flood ran red again in a moment, with only a creamy froth over it, and we could hear the boulders grinding and plunging at the bottom of the burn.[119]

So much for the Gairlin Burn! One can see very clearly how Crockett has built upon his original (written in the same year as *The Raiders* so that the incident was fresh in his mind) and added the intensifying touches. The central sentence gives him his theme: 'Loch Valley had broken loose'; already an overstatement of a small burn running out of the Loch, it provides the basis for amplification. John MacMillan peacefully on the hillside with his sheep is changed to the watchful scouts whose 'great crying' in its romantic vagueness arouses in the reader expectation of some catastrophe of considerable magnitude. Their cry when heard clearly 'Come up! The water's broken lowse!' adds to this expectation; when followed by the sound appropriate to the catastrophe 'a tremendous roaring noise as though the bowels of creation were gushing out in some great convulsion' we are ready to be appalled; an immense empty resonant landscape opens before our eyes as 'the hills gave back the echoes on every side.'

So far the amplification has been aural, with the scenery implied rather than stated, except for the opening which places the party in a 'deep defile', a vaguely menacing position reminiscent of passes in the foothills of India. Once Patrick climbs higher, Crockett's visual amplification enters into play; he prepares us for something magnificent in 'a wondrous sight' and then provides it. 'A great wall of water' suggests something rather more than the ten-foot breast of the burn, and the two sharp words that follow, 'glassy black', make us feel the height and savage strength of it, poised for a moment to be seen in horror before at the end of the sentence it 'sped down the glen' in terrifying swift simplicity. 'The water seemed to travel with great deliberation' is also intensitive in effect; a rushing river or sea appears to travel slowly only when great distance is involved; by saying that the water seems to move slowly, Crockett places Patrick the observer far removed above it, set in a vast landscape at a point thousands of feet above what he is describing. The mention of rabbits and corks to describe the men flying from or caught by the water is not only in keeping with Patrick's homely experience but adds a hint of man's helplessness in the face of such natural elemental forces of disaster, yet again intensifying the magnitude of the vast calamity. The vividness of the angry spatter of monosyllables tumbling like the water— 'not a few of our men were caught in the wash of it and spun downwards like corks in the inrush of the Solway tide'—not only gives a sense of the ruthless energy of the water's movement but adds the cruel dimension of the Solway tide rushing up its channel, a dimension quite irrelevant to a burn in the hills but splendid in its suggestion of force and majesty; the spreading slower movement of the 'inrush of the Solway tide' confirms our impression of the huge area engulfed by the flood. Crockett makes us see vividly what he wants us to see, and for the moment we forget that he is merely describing the minor incident of a burn breaking down a weir—and that the punitive expedition was not made up of the immense numbers of men he suggests being swept to death and destruction by its force. Everything has been made larger and more terrible by the energy with which his visualisation has worked; we hear and see it so clearly that we are not aware of being cheated, over-excited, manipulated by word-association.

Most of the high points in the narrative occur in passages like this, full of drama and visual touches, full of exaggeration. There is the burning of Craigdarroch:

> The ricks of corn which had been left unthrashed from last year's harvest were in a blaze. Black figures of men ran hither and thither about the house and round the fires. We could see them disappearing into the office-houses with blazing peats and torches. The thatch of the barn was just beginning to show red. Narrow tongues of fire and great sweeps of smoke drove to leeward against the clear west.[120]

There is the defence of the old House of Earlstoun against the outlaws who in the end are driven off, leaving their dead in the courtyard, until the more dextrous creep back to retrieve them and

> each dead man seemed to rise of his own accord and crawl backwards towards the gate. We remained stiff with terror, rooted to the spot with fear, and in a little nothing remained in the courtyard but the red splashes and the broad, shallow pools of blood.[121]

There is the rushing of the maddened cattle at the Bridge of Dee, when the outlaws set fire to the animals' backs with oil and pitch stolen from the ewebuchts at Duchrae, one of the most strenuous pieces of description in *The Raiders*:

> Then suddenly a great fierce light arose in the rear. The outlaws had kindled a fire, and the red light burned up, filtering through the ranks of the cattle, and projecting great horned shadows against the clouds. For a few minutes this picture stood like a painted show, with the Dee Water running cool and dark beneath—a kind of Circe's Inferno where the beasts are tortured forever.
>
> Two half-naked fiends ran alongside the column of cattle, carrying what was apparently a pot of blazing fire, which they threw in great ladlefuls on the backs of the packed beasts that stood frantically heaving their heads up to the sky. Then in a moment from all sides arose deafening yells. Fire lighted and ran along the hides of the rough Highland and black Galloway cattle. Desperate men sprang on their backs, yelling. Dogs drove them forward. With one wild, irresistible universal rush the maddened column of beasts drove at the bridge, and swept us aside like chaff.
>
> Never have I seen anything so passing strange and uncanny as this tide of wild things, frantic with pain and terror, whose billows surged irresistibly to the bridgehead. It was a dance of demons. Between me and the burning backs of the cattle there rose a gigantic Highlander with fiery eyes and matted front. On his back was a black devilkin that waved a torch with his hands, scattering

contagious fire over the furious herd. The rush of the maddened beasts swept us off the bridge as chaff is driven before the wind. There was no question of standing. I shot off my pistols into the mass. I might as well have shot them into the Black Water. I declare some of the devils were laughing as they rode like fiends yammering and girning when Hell wins a soul. It is hard to make any one who did not see it believe in what we saw that night.[122]

Crockett admits in the final sentence that he is straining the reader's credulity and perhaps hopes that the admission will excuse all. There is a remarkable jumble of improbabilities in his details, often contradictory. The sound and magnitude of the herd suggest something like the Calgary Stampede, yet the Black Water of Dee is quite a small river, the bridge therefore a narrow one, whether it be the one called the Raiders' Bridge today or an earlier one, and the number of cattle unlikely to have gone into hundreds. The Maxwells and their men are stationed on the bridge, armed and ready to head the cattle back to their own steadings; guns are blazing and the gipsies have been driven back thrice; it is to charge their way through the opposition and over the bridge that the raiders have to put on their pyrotechnic display with the terrified cattle. They have, the older Patrick explains in a footnote (thus adding a solid feeling of reality to the wild scene), borrowed pitch and oil from Duchrae; their setting fire to the backs of the cattle is their desperate way of forcing the herd over the bridge which lies between them and their headquarters in the mountains.

Yet if they were setting fire to pitch and oil and pouring this liquid flame over the hides of the cattle, why were they also riding on them? The gipsies, especially the two 'half-naked fiends', remind us irresistibly of Red Indians whooping to stampede a herd on the far-off plains of America, yet the dogs suggest something very much more local. The cattle, already terrified by the gunfire from the Maxwells, must have been even more terrified by the burning fire on their back; why should they have suddenly made up their minds to make the universal rush over the bridge? Furthermore, would setting fire to the stolen cattle not have made them wounded and of far less value as booty? For that matter, were the gipsies riding on the burning cattle not risking setting fire to themselves? It is all very confusing, yet this is precisely the effect Crockett is trying to achieve. In some way, in some condition, the cattle charge over the bridge and sweep the Maxwells and their supporters away like chaff before the wind—a Biblical simile which loses some of its aptness by being quite the wrong colour.

The supernatural runs through all three paragraphs, but in different forms. The menacing image of the 'great horned shadows against the clouds' conjures up age-old evil, the folklore image of the devil as a horned beast half-pagan, half-Biblical, brought to mind by the Highland cattle which have somehow found themselves among the black Galloways. It is followed by more sophisticated similes of a 'painted show' and the classical Circe tormenting the men she has turned into beasts, surely not only confusing but irrelevant. The third element builds up in the third paragraph from the 'dance of demons' to the 'devilkin' waving a torch and scattering burning oil or pitch far and near as he rides, and the very Scottish image of the outlaws laughing 'like fiends yammering and girning when hell wins a soul'. This last is perhaps appropriate to the Calvinist setting of Galloway, but, like the Solway intruding into the Gairlin Burn, is over-emphatic, detracting from the reality of the scene by over-writing. Yet in a curious way, when read through quickly the very jumble of images produces the effect of wild clamour and turmoil; Crockett flicks one scene after another so quickly through our minds by means of Patrick's scattered and passing impressions that the confusion of imagery leaves us with a most lively impression of light, darkness, noise and terror; the scene is treated not as plain narrative but as impressionistic flashes of its different parts, so that only later do we realise what has happened—the gipsies have succeeded in forcing the cattle through the Maxwells and over the bridge, the Maxwells themselves are dispersed and are heard of no more, and the mention of a ford enables the animal-lovers among the readers to hope that at least some of the cattle were able to extinguish their burning hides in the river. It is all over in two and a half pages; its energy has carried us along, and only afterwards do we analyse by what means Crockett has produced this exciting and lurid episode of bellowing, yelling and the thunder of hooves—and we conclude that it is mainly through Patrick's muddled and only half-comprehending mind. Patrick, after all, had ended up on the back of a beast himself as a result of trying to slap its back to put out the flames; he is the least likely of all people to have a clear idea of what went on, pitched off the Galloway's back almost on top of a grouse cock.

This habit of exaggeration in Crockett, however, is a fairly innocent one. He becomes caught up in the excitement of his story and can visualise each incident so pictorially that, consciously or unconsciously, he writes wildly to keep up with his imagination. The characters, no matter what happens to them, remain themselves; Patrick is still Patrick after the incredible journey he makes up hill and down dale after May Mischief—a journey impossible in the time allotted to it and owing something to the incredibly long and adventure-packed journeys at mad speed which Porthos, Athos, Aramis and D'Artagnan make in both *The Three Musketeers* and *Twenty Years After*.

Crockett's lens magnifies but it does not distort to any serious degree. Hardy, on the other hand, is prone to a much more dangerous exaggeration; he distorts details, incidents and probabilitites in order to make a philosophical point, the cruel over-riding indifference of Fate. Poor Fanny Robin in *Far From the Madding Crowd* is thwarted by chance over and over again; could so many instances of sheer malign fortune happen to any one person? Sergeant Troy has agreed to marry her. She waits at the wrong church. Troy, waiting at the right church, is so humiliated by a maliciously-ticking clock and the amusement of women bystanders that he casts Fanny off for ever. She makes an incredible three-mile journey on foot, weak, feeble, and we discover later pregnant, to Casterbridge Union Poorhouse, only to die in giving birth to Troy's child, also dead. That journey is so fraught with darkness, gloom and the desolation of Durnover Moor that we recoil in disbelief; the final agonising detail of the stoning away by the poor-house porter of the extraordinarily friendly stray dog which helps her crawl the last half mile is almost too much to bear.

After her death, fate still buffets her coffined body. By chance and the drunkenness of Joseph Poorgrass it reaches the churchyard too late for burial and by perverse circumstance is kept overnight in Bathsheba's house so that first Bathsheba and then Troy discover the existence of the dead child as well as the dead Fanny. Even when safely interred she is not safe from fate; the repentant Troy sentimentally sets in the soil above her grave a selection of plants which are all washed away by the cruel chance of a very wet night and a gutter in the form of a hideous gargoyle, emblem of pitiless fate, which directs the flow of water directly on to her grave. Hardy is here not merely exaggerating, he is manipulating events with careful contrivance in order to make the cosmic conspiracy against Fanny more obvious and thorough. He does the same, often in even cruder terms, in all his novels; he twists characters and events to suit his thesis. 'The characters seem puppets all right; but puppets not in the hands of Fate but of the author.'[123] Crockett is never guilty of this; the lesser author, he is guilty of lesser sins and has no philosophical axe to grind.

One of the sources of Crockett's exaggeration is the material which he uses; all his narrative peaks rising one after the other as *The Raiders* proceeds—the burning of Craigdarroch, the fight in the cave, the cattle thundering over the bridge, the evil house of Craignairny, the Murder Hole, the attack upon Earlstoun, the expedition against the outlaws which is so nearly swept away by Loch Valley, the lonely reconnoitring by Patrick on his skates terrifyingly bearing down upon the outlaws and Silver Sand on Loch Enoch, the bewildering silent blinding of the snowstorm leading to the Cave in the Aughty and the great white pit which is the grave of all the outlaws who have not heeded their leader John Faa—all these lend themselves to treatment which is larger than life; they almost demand it in their originality and their novelty. They are all rooted in violence which asks to be described in terms of violence and heightened reality. And each must exceed the one before.

Ironically, however, the most gruesome of all Crockett's borrowings, the story of the Murder Hole, taken from Nicholson, is in itself so wildly melodramatic that Crockett in re-telling it, with his grip on the visualisation of the actual, makes it less so. The one huge improbability which he creates is the moving of the house of Craignairny up into the wild craggy hills where there is no road and there can be no passers-by for the robbers to rob. Accept that, and every detail thereafter is made more credible, more realistic, more convincingly real. The pedlar boy, in Nicholson's account, is naive enough to advertise his orphan state; not one person will miss him or shed a tear if he dies that very night. This is indeed asking for trouble. Crockett abandons this theatrical melodrama and replaces it with Patrick's naive delight in passing himself off as a pedlar from New Abbey and mentioning his uncle's name which one of the robbers recognises; he is so pleased with himself that—quite in character—he embroiders his story further and says he is carrying 'the siller I got wi' the last pack', thinking himself 'wondrous clever'.[124] This decides the robbers to kill him for his money, achieving the same result as did Nicholson's pedlar boy's lamentations but with a hundred times more likelihood.

The villains too in Crockett's vivid descriptions have a grotesquely wicked reality; the old woman he nicknames Eggface because she has 'a face as smooth as an eggshell and as false as a deal door painted mahogany';[125] the sons cramming something into a chest are transferred into several outlaws in no way related to one another, 'curly-haired, olive-skinned men', obviously gipsies, each with separate and distinct villainous characteristics. The smell of cooking, the warm fire and the bubbling pot contribute homely realism to the bizarre household. The slaughtered goat whose blood escapes under the pedlar's bedroom door in Nicholson and the conversation about 'the old gentleman last night' (who turns out, most improbably, to have been the pedlar boy's long-lost father) are all wisely replaced by much more ordinary grumbling and squabbling among the men; the previous night's visitor is the white corpse whom Patrick sees being stuffed into the black chest; the old woman, in a sentence whose sinister quality derives from its understatement, mentions him carelessly:

> We had a stranger last nicht, nae farther gane, an', indeed, we hae hardly gotten redd up after him yet.[126]

Instead of the goat, we are shown an incident much more horrible because it is so ordinary and domestic.

> I turned down the bedclothes. They were clean sheets that had never been slept in but once or twice. But I turned down the sheet also, for I am particular in these matters. Something black and glutinous was clogged and hardened on the bed. I turned up the bed. The dark red stuff had soaked through and dripped on the earthen floor. It was not dry yet, though some sand had been thrown upon it. I did not need to examine further as to the nature of the substance. I turned sick at heart and gave myself up for lost.[127]

Last night's stranger has indeed not been 'redd up' after; he is present in his congealed blood and some still wet; but Patrick carefully investigating the bed because of his liking for cleanliness derived from his father, is so shocked that he cannot name the blood even after many years; he refers to it obliquely and with a kind of verbal shudder as 'black and glutinous matter' and 'the red stuff'. A further gruesome detail about the body in the black chest 'cut up and piled within, as a winter bullock is pressed into a salt barrel ready for the brine'[128] makes a picture more ghastly than anything in Nicholson because it is such a homely visual simile connected with raw meat. The Murder Hut in the trackless wild, the body packed into a chest when the Murder Hole is near and much more convenient, are wrong, but by the marshalling of lifelike details Crockett brings them much closer to reality than they were when he found them. This time he succeeds by not exaggerating, by translating Nicholson's bloody horrors into daily everyday usages.

In each of his major climaxes, however, there is a flaw; it is his pictorial imagination which enables us to miss improbabilities until we coldly analyse. Even the still white world into which Patrick, Silver Sand and Marion emerge after the storm, though described authoritatively with images from Crockett's Alpine experience, has one small defect. The vast circular snow-crater in which the dead outlaws lie is magnificent, but it contains one major fault.

> So he went upward and I followed him, till we came to the edge. I shall never forget what I saw, though I must hasten to tell it briefly. It was a great pit in the snow, nearly circular, built up high on all sides, but especially towards the south. The lower tiers of it were constructed of the dead bodies of sheep piled one on top of the other, forming frozen fleecy ramparts. But the snow had swept over and blown in, so that there was a way down to the bottom by walking along the side of a wreath. Looking in, we saw protruding from the snow—here the arm of a man and there the horn of a bullock.[129]

It is told in such a plain unemphatic deliberate way, Patrick almost painfully trying to get every detail right, that we can and do believe it—until we come to the bullock-horn. We can accept sheep built up as a barrier but there can be no bullocks high up in the Dungeon of Buchan. The vestigial remains of the Highland cattle at the Bridge of Dee have been Crockett's undoing—or have they? Is it perhaps possible? He has carried off the description so well that even this we are almost anxious to believe.

Patrick's awed simplicity as he looked at the wonder of the great pit of snow is conveyed by his noting of one thing after another, in sentences that are brief in a kind of dazed growing comprehension. He and Silver Sand, without speaking, set about brushing the snow off the faces. They must find out who the dead are.

> I understood at once. We were standing above the white grave of the outlaws of the Dungeon. They had died in their hillside shelter. With our 'kents' we could do little to unbury them, and give them permanent sepulture. It was better that they should lie until the snow melted off the hill. But we uncovered many of the faces, for so much of the work was not difficult. As each white frozen face came into view, Silver Sand said briefly 'Miller!' or 'Macaterick!' or 'Marshall!' as soon as he looked upon them.
> But there were no Faas among them.
> 'The Faas have done my bidding,' he said, 'and they have at least a chance for their lives.'
> Quharrie marked the spots where the dead were to be found by digging with his forepaws, throwing the snow through the wide spaces between his hind legs, and blowing through his nose as a terrier does at a rabbit hole.
> But we found seventeen and no more, all under the great south wall of sheep, which the starving wretches had built to keep them from the icy *bensil* of the snow wind ...
> They looked strangely happy, for the whiteness of the snow set their faces as in a frame. I saw the rascal that would have killed me in the cot of Craignairny. He looked quite a respectable man. Which made me think that some ill devil had, mayhap, long hirsled and harried an innocent body against its will. So may it be. The great God knows. The Day of Judgment is not my business.[130]

The pity which Patrick feels marks a new maturity; compassionately he will not judge; God alone knows the complexity of human motives. The recognition of the man who had held the knife to his throat, and his ordinary respectable appearance, leads to a thought like that of Stevenson's in *Thrawn Janet*; perhaps some devil had 'hirsled and harried' him, just as at the end of that story 'the auld, deid, desecrated corpse o' the witch-wife, so lang keepit frae the grave and hirsled round by deils, lowed up like a brunstane spunk and fell in ashes to the grund'. Patrick's reaction deepens to a quiet Christian forgiveness. 'So be it. The good God knows. The Day of Judgment is not my business'. There may be compassion even for the outlaws in the loving-kindness of God. Universal salvation appears again.

No climax could come after this scene of finality and majesty. The highest peak has been reached. They are brought down literally into the kindlier valley below on an improvised toboggan on which they slide through the Wolf's Slock and over the Cooran Lane to find horses at Clattering Shaws and make their way to the warm wood fires of Earlstoun. Marion is restored to Sammle and Eppie, Lady Grizel welcomes Patrick with a kiss of gladness, Patrick is reunited with May, and *The Raiders* reaches its happy ending. The last word is with Patrick, addressing the reader just as Rosalind does at the end of *As You Like It*, Prospero at the end of *The Tempest* and Puck at the end of *A Midsummer Night's Dream*—reminding us of John Heron's playbooks.

> And now a 'Fair-guid-e'en' to all you that have come so far with us. There is no more that I have to say, and no more that you need to hear. Mistress May Mischief and I love you for your kind courtesy, and we pray you that, like the dear Lady Grizel, you will take the door with you as you go, and leave us thus in the firelight, with only the Earl's great chair for company.[131]

We leave Patrick in the contented comfort that he craved high up in the Dungeon of Buchan. Tidily, he adds a colophon to match his Foreword; his writing of the story was finished on his son John Faa's second birthday, his daughter Grizel Maxwell being 'now in her seventh year, and my dear wife entering her thirty-third—but, as I think, bonnier than ever'. We end as we began with the comfortable satisfied voice of a man who has come through adventure and has no wish to enter into it again.

The style which Crockett uses for Patrick is a blend of the Scots he had heard spoken in Galloway, the Biblical cadences he had experimented with in *Mad Sir Uchtred* and the language of the Covenanting pamphlets with which he was equally familiar; at least once there is a touch of *The Pilgrim's Progress* when Patrick talks of the 'Hill Perilous' in the course of lamenting his having entered into this adventure. George Blake calls it 'an embarrassing pastiche'[132] but at times one suspects that George Blake would say anything; he compared *The Lilac Sunbonnet* unfavourably with the works of Amanda McKittrick Ros, after all,[133] which merely makes one wonder if he had ever read the extraordinary euphuistic creations of that remarkable Larne lady; there is none like her, none. Crockett, a bilingual Scot and a reader of old books, manages the period style, the common practice of that age of historical novelists, rather better than most. For him it was less a conscious literary device than a natural echoing of a flexible old-fashioned Scots with which he was at home.

The speech of the characters is more strongly Scots than the narration. Patrick is Scots in flavour but has been taught by a cultivated and erudite father who introduced him to Latin and English; he writes a good straightforward prose with constructions and phrases that mark his nationality but are not obtrusive. Lady Grizel Maxwell speaks broad Scots as did the old Scottish aristocracy.

> 'But it's a bonny like thing that ye hae to stand here on the steps o' my hoose. I'm an Earl's dochter, ye ken. Didna ye ken? Gin ye dinna, there's Gib Gowdie, that caa's himsel' a butler, he'll sune tell ye—silly auld man, Gib! Will ye come ben, man?' she said to Silver Sand, who stood with his hat in his hand as the gentrice do to a lady. 'It's mony a day since I saw ye ride aff wi'—ye-ken-wha—'[134]

Sammle and Eppie Tamson both speak broadly but much more colloquially with warm lower-class locutions.

> 'Ye mauna think she's sair on me,' he said earnestly. 'I'm aye pleased when she tak's eneuch notice to look after me in the way o' keeping' me to my wark. I ken I wad try a sant. I hae nae memory ava, and the mind that I hae is no worth a buckie. Whiles I think I maun hae hidden my talent in my sleep, and forgotten whaur I put it, for I canna see hilt nor hair o't ... It's an eternal wonder to me how she ever took the like o' me, or how she puts up wi' me when she has me.'[135]

As for Silver Sand, he is polyglot and can move from thundering Biblical prose to plain English and down to many levels of Scots as the occasion demands.

There are careless errors; 'pedlar' and 'peddler' occur in the same chapter; there is a gross error in timing in Chapter XIV, which begins 'Then for some hours we had peace' when the smugglers have sailed away but four pages later declares that 'the sailing away of the smugglers, and the second attack of the gipsies followed within a few minutes of each other'; and, worst of all, Crockett puts the Murder Hole in the wrong part of Loch Neldricken. In early editions it is in 'this eastermost end of the loch', and in later ones is corrected to read 'this western end of the loch', the spacing of the words giving the game away.

But these discrepancies do not damage the story any more than the exuberant heightening of effects in moments of high excitement. Taken as a romance, as it was intended to be taken, *The Raiders* has a great honesty which makes it stand out with lasting freshness. For a romance, its character-drawing is sharp and thorough. For a historical romance, its evocation of the hills and bogs, the mists and storms of Galloway makes the landscape almost another character, interfering, governing and alive. Humour runs through it from start to finish in an original and distinctive way—humour not often found in historical romances—and the personality of its author communicates itself with unself-conscious enjoyment. It is that enjoyment which makes the book a pleasure to read today when we are once more in a period of depression and psychoanalytical 'neurosia'. One can apply to Crockett in *The Raiders* what he wrote in 1893 of Stevenson:

> We seldom find him sitting down to it, as it were, and saying, 'Lo, I will describe a landscape' ... the magic is due not to any very remarkable photographic accuracy of description, certainly not to the cataloguing which sometimes passes for description, but to an author whose personality is never hid from us, and who is conscious of his power to charm us, making himself a part of what he describes, and throwing the limelight of his imagination upon the mad dance of the waters.[136]

CHAPTER 7

The Historical Romancer

I *In Galloway*

Crockett's writing continued without a break after his resignation of his charge. In London he was feted by the Savage Club, the Authors' Club and the Vagabond's Club during February 1895, but was glad to have this over, pleasant though it was. He took a two-month trip to Italy with his wife, but his mother-in-law's death prevented a planned visit to the MacMillans in August to which he had looked forward.

> I am nearly blind and dizzy with overwork & when I shall get away I can't tell ... I declare my dowp is nearly grown to the seat & my fingers had fairly to be pooed frae the keys o' the typewriter.[1]

In January 1896 he spent some time visiting Cassillis, Bargany, Auchendrayne, Maybole and Culzean to see the settings for *The Grey Man* and in March and April went to Holland for the Dutch scenes which open *Lochinvar*, the sequel to *The Men of the Moss Hags*. July and August saw the whole Crockett family on holiday in St Andrews, staying at what is now the Scores Hotel overlooking the Martyrs' Memorial but was then a boarding house, Seaton House, the place for family holidays in many Julys and Augusts to come. Ruth Crockett was not so sure that it was what her husband needed:

> When we go to St Andrews, you know, he gets up at four in the morning and works just as hard as if we were at home, so, although it is a change of scene, it is no holiday as far as work is concerned.[2]

Crockett played energetic golf with Tom Morris and Willie Auchterlonie, the professionals at the Royal and Ancient Club. Willie Auchterlonie had been Open Champion in 1893, the year of *The Stickit Minister*; they were to become good friends. Willie, superb craftsman as well as golfer, made left-handed clubs especially for Crockett, and kept them for him in his shop, since Crockett golfed only at St Andrews.

A hasty note to a friend conveys his enjoyment of this new ploy and delight that the *Glasgow Herald*'s prophecies have been confounded.

> Dear Dan Mowat,
>   I've beat Tom Morris! Two up.
>   *Afternoon.* Tom beat me *four* up. The barometer falls.

> I'll read your cousin's book if in words of one syllable—all I'm capable of at present.
>
> They are printing another 10,000 of *Grey Man* making 45,000 in all before publication.
>
> The Glasgow Herald is believed to be coming out in a mourning border and Marie Corelli is a permanent green.
>
> But MY ambitions are to do the High Hole in 4 and to make Willie Aughterlonie (sic) give me six strokes.[3]

Willie's son, the late Laurie Auchterlonie, himself a fine and famous golfer, reckoned that Crockett must have been good if his father allowed him a six-stroke handicap. He could describe the pattern of his father's games with Crockett. They played two rounds of eighteen holes every day, the first at eight o'clock in the morning, the second in the afternoon. If we take this habit of thirty-six holes day after day alongside the early rising to work at his writing at four o'clock in the morning before the first round and again after the second round, one can understand Ruth Crockett's feeling that it was hardly a holiday for Sam.

Laurie Auchterlonie remembered one of his father's anecdotes. A testy member once asked Crockett why he played with the professionals and not with gentlemen. 'Find me as fine a gentleman as Auchterlonie' said Crockett, 'and I shall be glad to play with him.' During this first St Andrews stay, Crockett was working on *The Black Douglas*, with a trip to Stirling to see the castle, in which he wanted to set some of the non-Galloway scenes. Meanwhile *Cleg Kelly* was running in the *Cornhill* and *Men of the Moss Hags* in *Good Words* during 1895 before reaching book form. *Lads' Love* was serialised in the *Lady's Realm* before publication in 1897 with a sketch of the author by 'FR', probably Frank Richards who also illustrated some of his books. *Lads' Love* introduced the son of Saunders McQuhirr, Alexander McQuhirr, medical student and then doctor, who was to succeed Saunders as the narrator in some of Crockett's later stories, such as those collected in *The Stickit Minister's Wooing* (1900). *The Grey Man of Auchendrayne* ran in the *Graphic* and the *Glasgow Weekly News* before appearing as *The Grey Man* in 1896, as did *The Red Axe* before publication in 1898. *Joan of the Sword* ran in the *Windsor* magazine 1898–9 and came out as *Joan of the Sword Hand* in 1900. *Ione March* was serialised in *Woman at Home* as *The Woman of Fortune* before book form in 1899, and *Kit Kennedy, Country Boy* ran in the *People's Friend* before it became a book in 1899. Clearly Crockett had not given up the ministry for the sake of an easy life. He did not altogether like the serial form, as he wrote to his friends at Glenhead in January 1894, regretting that they were reading *The Lilac Sunbonnet* in instalments in the *Leader*;

> serial publication is rather wearisome, I always think, but it is what makes the siller come in to the author, so it is not to be despised.

'Siller' from books, serial or otherwise, was now the Crocketts' sole income. They lived comfortably with their four children at Bank House—Ruth Mary

Rutherford—Maisie—born in 1888; Philip Hugh Barbour Milner in 1891; George Milner in 1893; and Margaret Douglas in 1896. The children and the middle-class life of dinner-parties and visitors required servants; the Ritchie girls were faithful cooks and nannies and maids for many years, all belonging to Penicuik and almost part of the family. Three generations of Milroys served equally faithfully as gardeners, and sometimes as darkroom assistants, tenders of the stamp collection or dusters of the books in the library annexe. The late Mr James Milroy said it took him and his father six weeks to dust them all, and then they were ready to start again. Astronomy, photography and stamp-collecting were hobbies in which Crockett was able to indulge; he was well enough known as a philatelist to feature as one of the celebrities listed in a chapter 'Who Collects Stamps?' in *All About Stamps* by Fred J Melville, President of the Junior Philatelic Society. (T Werner Laurie, nd)

The children had a remarkable garden to play in; they gradually acquired a dog, a pony and white rats as pets, and their childhood was full of interesting books and hobbies. Crockett enjoyed their company. His first book for children, *Sweetheart Travellers*, collected from sketches in the *Leader* for Christmas 1895, tells of Maisie's five-year-old comments on nature and birds and of journeys through Galloway and Wales when she sat in a basket before him on his Humber Beaston tricycle and continued to comment on what she saw. It was illustrated by Gordon Browne, the son of Dickens' 'Phiz', and published by Wells, Gardner, Darton and Company, pioneers in children's books.

This proved such a success that Crockett followed it in subsequent Christmases with more family stories as the children grew up. They all had devastating, deflating opinions. Crockett grafted on to them adventures he had had, or would like to have had, on the island where stood Threave Castle or on the Solway shore. George could not pronounce the name of their hero Richard Coeur de Lion properly and was nicknamed 'Toady Lion'; *Sir Toady Lion* (1897) and *Sir Toady Crusoe* (1905) feature him as their chief character, an unscrupulous little boy with a childish cunning and an ability to manipulate grown-ups and yet be adored by all the ladies. The robust humour and unsentimentality of these books are in strong contrast to the middle-class comfort in which the children live. In *Sir Toady Lion* they battle with the town toughs, the 'Smoutchy Boys', in a way more reminiscent of Laurieston and Castle Douglas and schoolboy fights than of well-behaved young Victorians. They squabble and throw stones; this amused their father but probably not their mother. In *Sir Toady Crusoe* Toady and his Australian cousin run away from home and worry the life out of a couple of lighthouse-keepers on the Solway. Their 'Farewell' note is a delight: 'Doant grieve for US; we doant for you'.

The children refused to read Scott, alleging that he was boring. *Red Cap Tales* and *Red Cap Adventures* (1904 and 1908) are retellings of Crockett's favourite Scott novels for their benefit, with interspersed chapters filled with the children's derisive comments on the Great Unknown and their ingenious endeavours to re-enact the more exciting incidents, usually ending with cuts, bruises, sticking plaster, the terrified shrieks of Margaret, the youngest and therefore an obvious victim, and at times a walloping.

Seaton House,
St Andrews.

TELEPHONE No. 1123

Oct 2nd (1896)

Dear Ben Mowat

SAM* books!

Ye beat Tom Morris! Run up. Afternoon.

You beat me four up! The barometer falls.

I'll read your cousin's book if one word of one syllable — all I can ejaculate is —

Wiecur

*This is a Scotch word meaning the coutural & climb place of honour at Chimnies; used in the West.

They are printing off the 10,000 of "Say Gran" making 48,000 in all before publication.

The Gazson Herald is believed to be coming out in a mourning border ◪ as thick as that and Marie Corelli is a permanent green.

But My Auditorium

are to do the trip tryst in 4 and to make Willie Anghterlonie give no eye strokes.

You're a grey chap Ben Mowat. There is Sam Whates at the Club.

Yours truly
SR Crockett

4 A reduced copy of Crockett's letter to Mowat (1896). Courtesy of Mrs EF Mowat.

5 Crockett (second from left) golfing at St Andrews with Willie Auchterlonie (second from right) and friends. Courtesy of L and B Auchterlonie.

Mrs Crockett appears in *Sweetheart Travellers* as a shadowy background figure, 'The Lady with the Workbasket', but in the later books is explained away as having died long since. The children (especially Toady) have almost completely forgotten her. Crockett is totally realistic about this and passes over any Victorian sentiment about a loving memory. She probably died at her own request, opting out of being incorporated into her husband's lively but undignified tales. Instead the children's 'father', Mr Picton, is provided with Janet Sheepshanks his housekeeper, Mary Ann a housemaid and a battery of Border gamekeepers and gardeners. They live in a large mansion with an estate attached called Windy Standard, a Scots hill name, and form a kind of semi-English enclave in the midst of Caledonian wilds. The effect is curious but entertaining. In their time, the *Toady Lion* and *Toady Crusoe* books were at the top of their publisher's lists for Christmas; at least one if not two generations must have been brought up on them; beside their voluble arguing and enterprise, Christopher Robin seems effete. They show how eager their author was to try every type of fiction in order to keep his name before the public. Far from being a practitioner of what had come to be called 'Kailyard' fiction, he was almost obsessionally willing to tackle any new fashion that came along. And his own enjoyment runs so breezily through these books for children that, as well as being entertaining in a completely original way, they provide an oblique picture of the author himself.

Crockett had to write to please the public, but he found that he could not go on doing the same thing all the time. He explained his position to a dinner given in his honour in Dalbeattie in 1907.

> Sometimes it is said to me—'Ah, the "Raiders," the "Lilac Sunbonnet,"—this, that and the other—why do you not write us another "Raiders," and another "Stickit Minister?"' Well, it is like this. I do not need to tell a Galloway audience anything about the rotation of crops.
>
> Suppose for a moment that year after year for ten years one of you sowed only one kind of crop. What would be the consequence? The soil would be exhausted. Moreover, before that even, the landlord's patience. (Laughter.) Now, so with books, which are the crops of the mind. You cannot go on producing the same kind of crop.
>
> After each book is finished, the brain becomes something like cold boiled turnips. To recover its elasticity, to strike fresh from that unexhausted soil, one must try a new crop—something as different as possible from the old. There are, besides, for the professional author, not one landlord but many. Editors and publishers who out of their wisdom desire such and such a crop, and will only pay according to their needs.[4]

The number of different publishers' imprints under which he appeared over the years emphasises the precariousness of his position; perhaps he would have been better advised, financially, to stick to the same kind of crop year after year and supply readers with what they expected, but he chose not to. Many a reader must have found the latest Crockett not what they expected—or wanted—at all.

He knew what sort of book he liked and could write. He disliked the slow fastidiously-styled novels of Henry James 'where something is always on the point of happening, but never comes off'.[5] The 'Novel of Purpose' he distrusted.

> The purpose must emerge, not be thrust before the reader's nose, else he will know that he has strayed into a druggist's shop. And all the beauty of the burnished glass, and all the brilliance of the drawer labels will not persuade him that medicine is a good steady diet. He will say, and with some reason, 'I asked you for bread—or at least for cakes and ale—and lo! ye have given me Gregory's Mixture!'[6]

He instanced Shakespeare and Scott in support of these views.

> Scott did not write with any purpose, save with the primitive instinct to tell an entrancing story. And in spite of Gervinus and cartloads of commentators, chiefly Teutonic, I do not believe that Shakespeare did either ... For the 'novel of purpose' developed round some set thesis is not of the essence of story-telling, but of preaching and pamphleteering. These two things are, no doubt, of the world's greatest necessities, but I would not have them trench upon the place of creative imagination ... It will be better if, instead of posing as the religious regenerator of the future, the novelist confines himself to telling a plain tale in the best way he can, simply striving by the thrilling of his own heart to cast a spell over the hearts of others.[7]

Another literary quasi-manifesto on the novel is to be found in *An Adventurer in Spain* (1903), not where one would have expected it. Crockett expresses his belief in the fundamental unexpectedness and improbability of life.

> In a novel you must explain and explain, leading up to how Jane came to know Julius—how the black-hearted murderer Morpher, thinking to rob a church, opens a door and finds himself face to face with his own long-lost daughter, who is the caretaker. Such things must be explained—in a novel.
> But everyone knows that in real life it is not so. The actual connections are never those which you think of. You review an unknown man's book in an obscure periodical, and his daughter becomes your wife through all time. In a house where you never were before and where you are never likely to be again, you notice a girl sitting in a corner. She lifts her eyes—and for the two of you, death itself doth not divide.[8]

Engagingly he uses the example of his meeting with Ruth, his future wife, from a world completely different from his own Galloway one, as an instance of life's unlikeliness, and follows it with references to two recent murder cases, the Ardlamont affair and the trial of Madeleine Smith, as further illustrations. Murder leads him to *Le Petit Parisien* and the French criminal reports:

> of the twenty or thirty cases reported every week, scarcely one runs on 'natural' lines. Hardly one which would be credited if transported wholesale into the pages of a novel. Some are too monstrous—all are too crude. It is the *reductio ad absurdum* of realism. This one and that are unbelievable, because the victim's mother—his wife—his eldest son could not possibly have acted so. But the

strange thing is that they did. The detective and his quarry journeyed together to Le Havre, neither suspecting the other's identity. But, as the local officers had been warned by telegraphs and were on the alert, it was (of course) the detective who was arrested! The criminal got clean away. This is not the plot for a comic opera. It is only a fact. But it would not do for fiction.[9]

Is Crockett here defending himself for increasingly sensational plots? It sounds very like it. He is declaring that life is so full of wild coincidences that storytellers must be allowed the utmost freedom of invention in order to render the full range of Life's rich improbability. He is almost rejecting the sober form of the serious novel and claiming the truth-to-life of the most sensational fiction—*Le Petit Parisien* as a model of the everyday and the actual. This goes far to explain why as his imagination tired and his health deteriorated, Crockett's books grew more and more compact of madness, murder, crime and horror.

In the beginning, however, he met the quest for variety with great success. In *The Lilac Sunbonnet* and *The Raiders* he had opened up his own field— Galloway domestic and Galloway historical—and these served him well. The two were not always distinctly separated; one of the pleasures of his historical fiction is the homespun reality of his heroes and heroines, while a story of contemporary life can suddenly divert into as strange a situation as any Penny Dreadful; *Cleg Kelly* can begin in Edinburgh slums and end with a mad ex-Indian army officer who sleeps every night in a coffin.

The Men of the Moss Hags is prefaced by a declaration that it is based on research among Cameronian and Earlstoun papers in Edinburgh University Library, as well as local records. This is to ward off accusations of plagiarism which had been made against parts of *The Lilac Sunbonnet* and *The Raiders*. Crockett made no secret of his use of historical tradition and folklore; in reply to critics in *The Academy* he stoutly affirmed his intention of continuing to make use of all that he could find.

> I am only sorry that there is so little of this splendid rough popular material extant. It is pure gold to the romancer, and wherever I can lay hold of it and use it, why, I intend to 'do it and do it again'.[10]

'Romancer'—that is the key word. By rejecting Purpose and Probability as literary necessities, Crockett severs himself from the serious writer and declares himself a teller of yarns, which he had a perfect right to do as long as he told them well.

The hero of *Men of the Moss Hags* is, like Patrick Heron, a very ordinary unheroic young lad. He is William Gordon, son of William Gordon of Earlstoun and younger brother of the redoubtable Sandy Gordon, known as the Bull of Earlstoun. These individuals did exist, but Crockett remodels them to suit his purpose, passing them through his imagination and bringing the Covenanters to life with laughter as well as solemnity. William tells the story in his own words; he is no stock figure of Covenanting piety but bored by his brother's endless theological arguments and even more by his sister-in-law's corncrake prayers. Only when he has seen Claverhouse and witnessed the dragoons' cruelties does he range himself with Richard Cameron and fight on his side at Airdsmoss.

William has a cousin, Wat Gordon of Lochinvar, who with his lace ruffles and his amours could have come out of *The Three Musketeers*. He is a protegé of Claverhouse, on the king's side; against his scented affectation William is doubly convincing and down-to-earth. In *The Raiders* Patrick told us that Galloway people were peaceable if not meddled with and that 'chiefly dourness and not fanaticism took them to the hills when Lag came riding with his mandates and letters judicatory'.[11] Through William, Crockett elaborates this, showing with affectionate realism the household at Earlstoun before they were meddled with. Father and eldest son ride off to Bothwell Brig, leaving William envious, Sandy mocking him for having to stay with the women. Then at dead of night come the familiar cough and knocking of boots; when William opens the door to his father, there is only the wind mist-laden round the house. At dawn, Gay Garland, the father's horse, comes home alone.

> He stood and trembled in every limb. He was covered with the lair of the moss-hags, wherein he had sunk to his girths. But on his saddle leather, towards the left side, there was a broad splash of blood which had run down to the stirrup iron; and in the holster on that side, where the great pistol ought to have been, a thing yet more fearsome—a man's bloody forefinger, taken off above the second joint with a clean drawing cut.[12]

The careful precision of this description recreates the shock of William's seeing the frightened horse; a tiny chill at the severed forefinger heralds the terror which is to disrupt the quietness and sunlit roses of the old tower house.

Hope is not given up at once but the next morning as William's mother is baking, Sandy comes home—but only Sandy.

> My mother went to the girdle to turn the wheaten cakes that were my father's favourites, and as she bent over the fire, there was a sound as if rain-drops were falling and birsling upon the hot girdle. But it was only the water running down my mother's cheeks for the love of her youth, because now her last hope was fairly gone.
> Then in the middle of her turning she drew the girdle off the fire, not hastily, but with care and composedness.
> 'I'll bake nae mair,' she cried, 'Sandy has come over the hill his lane.'[13]

These finely observed details, the tears 'birsling' on the girdle, the slow, sad decisive movement, bring the sorrow home to our hearts; there will never be any point in baking for Mary Gordon now. Silence in the kitchen emphasises her acceptance of tragedy. Later she says over and over again 'O thae weary Covenants, thae weary, weary Covenants!', a cry for all women whose men have gone to war and never returned. Yet Crockett does not idealise her; a moment later she querulously brushes aside the comfort Maisie Lennox offers her—Maisie has lost a father and perhaps brothers, but what is her grief compared to the loss of a husband? This unpoetic, unromantic but very real human reaction brings the Earlstoun family immediately before us.

They are much more warmly alive than Wat of Lochinvar whose loss of a father is more theatrical; going down the Canongate with William to a love-tryst in a wind-blown snow-storm he finds that the dark round object which falls from the high Netherbow is his father's head, executed as a rebel.

> ... above us the fitful, flying winds nichered and laughed like mocking fiends. It was true. I that write, saw it plain. I held it in this very hand. It was the head of Sir John of Lochinvar, against whom, in the last fray, his only son had donned the war-gear. Grizzled, black, the snow cleaving ghastly about the empty eyeholes, the thin beard still straggling snow-clogged upon the chin—it was his own father's head that had fallen at Walter Gordon's feet, and which he now held in his hand.[14]

Macabre, grim and gothic as this is, with skilfully-marshalled detail giving a genuine grue, it is less moving than Gordon of Earlstoun's ghostly return; the two elements play off against one another, each contributing to Crockett's total impression.

There is humour too. Tradition made Sandy take refuge at Earlstoun during a lull; William joins him in hiding in the well-house loft. Sandy falls into loud talk, describing with enjoyment a meeting the United Societies had had at Darmead as mentioned in Simpson's *Traditions of the Covenanters*. William listens wearily.

> 'At Darmead, that well-kenned place we had it,' Sandy was saying, his long limbs extended half-way across the floor as he lay on the bare boards and told his story; 'it was a day of glorious witnessing and contesting. No two of us thought the same thing. Each had his own say-away and his own reasons, and never a minister to override us ...'
> Even as he spoke thus, and blattered with the broad of his hand on his knee, the trap-door in the centre of the floor slowly lifted up. And through the aperture came the head of a soldier—even that of the sentry of the night, with whose footfalls I had grown so familiar that I minded them no more than the ticking of the watch in your pocket or the beating of your heart in the daytime.
> The man seemed even more surprised than we, and for a long moment he abode still, looking at Sandy reclining on the floor. And Sandy looked back at him with his jaw dropped, and his mouth open. I could have laughed at any other time, for they were both great red men with beards of that colour, and their faces were very near one another, like those of the yokels that grin at each other emulously out of the horse collars on the turbulent day of the Clachan Fair—which is on the eve of St. John, in the time of midsummer.[15]

Sandy 'blattering with the broad of his hand on his knee' illustrates to comic perfection a Covenanter well pleased with affairs, and we note that to this pious professor of religion 'a day of glorious witnessing and protesting' is one on which everyone is at noisy odds, with 'never a minister to override us'. Crockett is ambivalent about Covenanters; he must admire their bravery but can see the folly of prolonged theological wrangling among these perfervid amateurs. Fanaticism has its touch of the ridiculous.

Men of the Moss Hags is a lively kaleidoscope of events, one following on the other in vivid sharp description, ranging from the gruesome incident of the rotting head to the wide, dignified landscape of figures moving slowly over the moors to the great conventicle at Shalloch-on-Minnoch, seen from afar. William is present not only there and at Airdsmoss but at the drowning of the two Margarets in the Blednoch, perhaps the most famous of Covenanting martyrdoms. He and his brother, in hiding, depend for food on what Maisie Lennox can conceal unseen from family meals, smuggling scraps to them just as the real Grisell Hume had smuggled food to her father in the vault under Polwarth Church. Covenanting character after Covenanting character crowd the narrative,—Mardrochat the Spy, Black Michael, Sir Robert Hamilton, Michael Shields; a minute entry in Wodrow's *History of the Sufferings* recording that Sandy Gordon had become mad in captivity is expanded to a chapter in which he, roaring at the Privy Council, 'lundered them about the broadest of their gowns' with an iron bar torn from its fastenings.[16] Familiar events Crockett treats with care and reverence; less familiar ones he fashions in his own way, adding more than he is given; for good measure he creates horrors of his own devising, like Corplicht Kate and her idiot son Gibbie, more like witches from *Macbeth* than Galloway peasants.

It is unlikely that any one person could have been present at so many great Covenanting occasions as William, but this is romance, not history. To make this clear, Crockett finally places William on the scaffold in the Grassmarket in Edinburgh with the 'Earl of Cantyre', an invented name for the Duke of Argyll; he is making all this up, though with gruesomely convincing detail.

> I heard louder than thunder the horrible crunch as of one that shaws frosty cabbage with a blunt knife. Methought I had fainted away, when I heard the answering splash, and the loud universal 'Ah!' which swept across the multitude of people.[17]

No sooner have we taken in this homely exact comparison, no sooner has William finished the speech which, somewhat to his surprise, he finds himself making, than he hears the crowd shouting and sees it falling back. A girl on a white horse rides through the West Port. It is Maisie Lennox with pardons for William and her father. Grisell Cochrane, daughter of Sir John Cochrane, did precisely what Maisie has done—waylaid the king's messenger carrying her Covenanting father's death warrant.[18] But Crockett, being himself, adds a twist. Maisie has found only one pardon ready and signed; whose name shall she put upon it, her father's or William's? She makes up her mind and writes the name, then finds a second signed pardon to which she affixes the other.

> Maisie Lennox has never told to any—not even to me, who have some right to know her secrets, that name which she first wrote when she had to choose between her father's and her lover's.

She only says, 'Let every maid answer in her own heart which name she would have written, being in my place, that day in the changehouse!'[19]

How wise Crockett was to call himself a romancer.

Unfortunately, by his spendthrift extravagance of event and character, Crockett in *The Men of the Moss Hags* used up the best of his genuine Covenanting material; he had to fall back on his own imagination for the rest. *Lochinvar*, continuing the adventures of the elegant Wat Gordon, is made up of conventional treacheries and romantic misunderstandings. Wat joins Maisie and William, married and in Holland, but offends the heroine, Kate McGhie, another Gallovidian. A villain from Barra carries her off to an imaginary Hebridean island and Wat follows, but the dialogue is stilted and the happy ending contrived to match Scott's 'Lochinvar' poem; the hero comes riding from out of the west on a horse named 'Drumclog' and snatches Kate in her wedding finery from the angry villain, but the atmosphere is wrong; this is not Scott's 'Lochinvar', nor the circumstance, nor even the period.

The Standard Bearer (1898) is much better, set firmly in Galloway and in a definite period. The framework is taken from the life-story of the rebel Balmaghie minister, the Rev John MacMillan, but Crockett changes his hero's name to Quintin MacClellan right off, and refers readers who wish for authentic information to H M B Reid's book *A Cameronian Apostle*; he is going to romanticise freely and indulge in the process which he calls 'leeing at lairge'.[20] Drenched in Galloway speech, it is really very funny.

He fashions a vigorous tale of Galloway men and women, arguing and quarrelling in the familiar settings of Balmaghie, the Black Water of Dee and Crossmichael Kirk across on the other side. We meet old friends from the *Moss Hags*; Sir Alexander Gordon, the Bull of Earlstoun, grown older but still 'a great, strong, kindly hard-driving "nowt" of a man'[21] and his wife Jean, more than ever a 'most melancholious saint'.[22] William is now Sir William, a leader of men, raising a troop to defend the Convention in Edinburgh against Claverhouse.

Quintin's parents are tenants on the Earlstoun estate, moderate sensible Covenanters; his father takes himself off when he sees the persecutors coming. As a boy, Quintin has seen a fleeing Covenanter shot in the back by a laughing dragoon; this turned him into a Covenanter. When he grows up he enlists with Sir William, but his true bent is study; he becomes a student at Edinburgh college, watched over by his invented brother Hob, a device which enables Crockett to have two narratives running parallel, one the idealistic story of events as Quintin sees them, the other the comically despairing account of Hob who deplores Quintin's lack of common sense.

Quintin is licenced and called to the ministry at Balmaghie, where he meets again Mary Gordon, daughter of Sir Alexander; he has loved her when they were children. Her parents have deaved her with the Covenant—

... Have I not broken fast with it, dined with it, taken my four-hours with it, supped with it ever since I was of age to hear knowledgeable words spoken? ...[23]

—and Quintin to her is just another fanatic; she will have nothing to do with him. This is a reasonable point of view but not what one expects from the heroine of a Covenanting novel. Quintin despairs. Pale young Jean Gemmell who knows she is dying asks him to marry her. This bizarre incident could have been cloying but Crockett endows her with dignity as well as pathos. Quintin marries her, the stern silent faces of her family looking on around her bed, and she dies before dawn the next day, Quintin sitting holding her hand.

Quintin continues his ministry, church and state both against him, until the United Societies of Covenanters, the hill men who live in solitude and worship God their own way, invite him to be their first minister. Before he accepts he must cure Sir Alexander of another bout of madness, which he does most valiantly, climbing up into the tower of Earlstoun in spite of cursing and musket-shot and persuading the madman to repeat the prayer he has been taught as a child. Quintin leads him down to his wife and daughter, a human being once more.

Mary is impressed by Quintin's courage and says she will go with him to minister to the hill men in the distant fastnesses; she truly loves him after all. This has been Sir Alexander's purpose all along, his madness a device to bring them together.

Appropriately, Crockett dedicated *The Standard Bearer* to 'the Good and Kindly Folk of my native parish of Balmaghie', and one of the sharp sayings in the book concerns them.

> 'Of one mind?' exclaimed the old man, taking snuff more freely than ever. 'Ye are dootless a maist learned and college-bred young lad, wi' routh o' lear and lashin's o' grace, but ye dinna ken this pairish o' Balmaghie if he think that ye can ever hae the folk o' one mind. Laddie, the thing's no possible. There's as many minds in Balmaghie as there's folk in it. And a mair unruly, camsteerie Pairish there's no between Kirkmaiden and the wild Hieland border'.[24]

The Good and Kindly Folk would appreciate this. As for the lovers, any resemblance to the historical characters they represent has been cheerfully abandoned. MacMillan did marry as his second wife (after three years of marriage to Jean Gemmell) the daughter of Gordon of Earlstoun, but the marriage was 'of affection and perfect religious sympathy' and the lady a widow with several children.

Dark o' the Moon (1902) takes equal liberties. It is a sequel to *The Raiders*; Patrick Heron and May Maxwell, married for twenty years, have a son Maxwell who is carried off by Hector Faa and his gipsies to be married to his daughter Joyce—*The Raiders* a generation later and the other way round. This is the time of the Levellers in Galloway, who were active in 1724 according to Mackie's *History of Scotland*; it is wiser not to inquire too closely how Maxwell Heron had contrived to grow up by this year. The Galloway Levellers (not to be confused with the English thinkers of the same name) are bands of enraged cottars destroying the walls and fences the landowners have erected as enclosures for rearing the profitable black cattle. The Levellers meet by night—the dark o' the moon—and are led by Dick of the Isle, a slim young youth who is really Marion Tamson whom Silver Sand and Patrick rescued from the Murder Hut at Craignairny in *The Raiders*. The landscape is Galloway; we are once more in the high air above the Dungeon of Buchan, looking down on Loch Neldricken and the Murder Hole. Maxwell is a sulky hero; he refuses to marry Joyce by compulsion, though the two are in love and the alternative is death in the Murder Hole—'He prefers *that* to me?' she says very naturally—and has to be rescued by Joyce herself who, in one of those bargains beloved of romantic novelists, pledges herself to Harry Polwart, one of the more cheerless of the gipsies, if he helps her take Maxwell down to safety.

Crockett enlivens this conventional plot with a complex of escapes, captures, escapes and recaptures, everyone always on the move, everyone at odds. There is one splendid storm rolling round the vast landscape in which Harry Polwart, returning to the Dungeon of Buchan with Joyce, is struck by lightning and blinded, trapping Joyce through pity more thoroughly in her bargain. There is Captain Austin Tredennis, crack shot, swordsman, Englishman, sent with his dragoons to put down the Levellers, who, when the plot allows him to realise that his prisoner Dick of the Isle is a girl, falls in love with her. Fortunately, his commanding officer General George FitzGeorge, a lazy Hanoverian by-blow of one of the royal family invented by Crockett as a possible though improbable, ladies' man *par excellence*, sympathetically overlooks this professional misconduct. His complaint about Tredennis is that he is too energetic; he writes to his royal cousin asking that Tredennis be sent to govern some island 'very desolate' so as to bother him no more.

The plot is crowded with characters—Silver Sand in his seventies but still mysterious, Patrick Heron a little out of focus (would Patrick of *The Raiders* have grown into a cultivated gentleman who relishes the Latin authors?), the magistrates of Kirkcudbright, smugglers to a man, who willingly clear their contraband kegs out of Maclellan's Castle to make a comfortable prison if Captain Tredennis will overlook the sheets, chains and false thunderclaps with which they have been promoting the belief that the castle is haunted. Even the Rev John MacMillan is brought in, under his own name, with the best of intentions guiding the blinded villain to the gipsy camp on Hollan Isle in order to marry him to Joyce.

The final scenes are set in Crockett's familiar Duchrae. He manoeuvres his various groups together so that Silver Sand, Hector Faa and the Rev John can contrive a way of freeing Joyce from her foolish promise. Joyce, it appears, is not Hector Faa's daughter at all, which is a help. Harry Polwart, drunk and roistering, turns the Levellers against their leader, but MacMillan and Tredennis (caught as a spy among the gipsies) tumble him into the loch and out of the plot. Both Levellers and gipsies make their escape from the dragoons, saved because Silver Sand, Hector and another gipsy hold off the attack and give their lives, as the snow falls thickly and slowly over the darkening woods—the dark o' the moon—to save the others.

The happy ending is inevitable, though sadness breaks through with the death of Silver Sand, over whose grave the grass grows green as Maxwell writes. Joyce and Maxwell are married; Captain Tredennis marries his Marion and, given a knighthood on the recommendation of General FitzGeorge to get him out of the way, goes out to govern settlements on the east coast of Canada, the Levellers and the gipsies accompanying him and settling down happily.

Dark o' the Moon makes pleasant light reading. It has some of the qualities of *The Raiders* but is much less deeply felt; like most sequels it makes one realise once more the strength and originality of its predecessor. There is one piece of pure mischief. The godly and venerable John MacMillan is made to regret at one point that he cannot come at once

> ... for this is the day of my week-day discourse upon that most comforting text in the Prophet Ezekiel, the thirtieth chapter and the fourteenth verse: 'I will make Pathros desolate, and will set fire in Zoan, and execute judgments in No'.[25]

Crockett is making fun of a certain type of Presbyterian sermon in which a text is wrenched from its chapter and used as the basis of an arbitrary lesson (or lessons) according to the preacher's ingenuity—a man travelling from Dan to Beersheba and tarrying three days, or Ephraim being a cake not turned. John Buchan does the same in the first chapter of *Witch Wood* where the old minister has preached for a year and a half on the twelve wells of water and three score and ten palm trees that are in Elim. John MacMillan's text is a particularly fine example; it is so odd that one searches the Scriptures to make sure it exists. It does, but it is not comforting, whatever MacMillan says.

Crockett's treatment of the Rev John MacMillan, both here and in *The Standard Bearer*, shows how even when historical characters are there for him to use he prefers to push aside the reality and create new personages wandering loosely within it. History is in the background and Crockett shines his light on groups in the foreground. *The Banner of Blue* (1903) deals with two families set melodramatically at odds by the Disruption of 1843. It is so recent as to be not strictly history. Crockett like most Free Churchmen treats it as a continuation of the covenant. But he states again, in Chapter V 'Being a Chapter Editorial', that he is not going to deal with the Disruption itself;

> ... in order that the characters of this history may be seen in their rightful grouping and relations, and that the reader may remark their motives and compulsions, some hint of these graver issues must be supplied in this place.
>
> Yet because this is no chronicle of the events national, no polemic, special pleading cast into narrative form, but only the life-story of certain undistinguished folk at an eventful and stormy period of Scottish history, if any desire to learn further concerning these weightier matters of the law, to range argument, to sift evidence—lo, the books are written. Let him go to them that sell and buy for himself!

> A little sea-washed parish, a few lives writ mostly in water, half a score of green mounds ranged round the Kirk above Gower water—that is all.[26]

He is like Jane Austen politely declining the Prince Regent's secretary's suggestion that she write lofty history; he knows his own scope. And this fifth chapter has another point of interest; it contains two paragraphs describing an elderly Cameronian worthy which W Robertson Nicoll, in his personage as Claudius Clear in the *British Weekly*, lifted and used without acknowledgement in his long article on Crockett after his death, thus conferring upon Crockett on 30 April 1914 the rare privilege of contributing posthumously to his own obituary.

Crockett returned to Covenanting times in *The Cherry Ribband* (1905), serialised as *Peden the Prophet* in the *British Weekly*. It begins at Mayfield farm in Irongray, with blind William Ellison exercising strict discipline over his family. That family is unusually diverse. The youngest son, Raith, is a shy inexperienced youth whom his father sternly turns out into the world for dallying with the owner of the cherry ribband, Ivie Grysland, the daughter of an honourable professional soldier. Beattie, another son, is a smooth plausible tale-bearer who begins by telling his father of Raith's shortcomings and ends by laying evidence against his father and brothers so that they are taken across Scotland and imprisoned on the Bass Rock. Murdoch, another brother, is a stock Covenanting type and is summarily shot by Grierson of Lag. Gib, another brother, says and does little during the narrative; he is there, presumably, to swell the throng of Ellisons. Euphrain, the only daughter, is like her father, all for the Covenant and with his unbending rectitude; she turns away from Raith, who, far from dallying with Ivie, has been tongue-tied, coltish and a source of gentle mocking laughter to her. She is of far wider experience than any of them, having travelled widely with her father, a motherless but beloved child.

The most interesting of all is Marjory Simpson, William Ellison's wife. She rescues Ivie's cherry ribband and surreptitiously gives it to Raith as he goes away, and a mother's blessing along with it. She is attuned to a more compassionate faith and cannot always agree with her husband;

> ...being of the east country I see differently. There is one God, it is true. But we look at Him with other spyglasses here in the east. Smoked they may be, but yet with them we may the better see His brightness revealed.[27]

She does not claim to be as uniquely in the right as her husband and Peden do, but Crockett gives her a vivid yet simple metaphor; one looks at the sun through smoked lenses so as to see it clearly, and so it may be with God. She does not pray as her husband and Peden do, but like the repentant publican in the Temple may be more pleasing to God than assertive Pharisees.

> Her husband and Mr Peden would wear away a flat stone in their closets with their knees. They would spend whole nights in crying. And in this they were deeply earnest. It was of their kind and country. But in Marjory's 'cauldrife

east,' as her husband called it, where most of the ministers had long ago 'conformed' and where there were no 'blowings of the trumpet on the mountains,' nor any slaughtering of the saints on dykeback—there was yet a true and real type of piety—Marjory Simpson's kind.[28]

She rebukes Euphrain for her hostility to Ivie who for all her frivolity and laughter, for all her innocent ignorance of religion, is loving and true, eager to learn what she lacks through no fault of her own.

> She seeks the light—perhaps not your Light, or mine, but *a* light! Perhaps not our way, but *a* way. Shall I trip up her feet and send her headlong? ... Do you your duty, daughter Euphrain, and leave me to do mine![29]

This is an interesting development in Crockett's slightly critical attitude towards Covenanters. He does not condemn the zealots outright—'it was of their kind and country' and 'there had been no slaughtering of the saints on dykeback' in the east of Scotland, but he does not agree with William Ellison that the east is therefore 'cauldrife', lacking in religious fervour. Marjory's more tolerant, kindly faith prevails in the end and William Ellison is the better and happier for it. And since the Covenanting mood gradually relaxes as the story proceeds, we are not surprised that this is Crockett's most wildly adventurous Covenanting novel. *The Cherry Ribband* is by far the apter title.

Raith, for one thing, enlists as a dragoon, and no one except his father and brothers thinks the less of him for it. He serves under Grif Rysland, and is one of the garrison on the Bass Rock when to his horror he sees his father, his brothers and Alexander Peden brought to imprisonment there. Much could have been made of the sufferings they endure but Crockett is more interested in the Bass Rock itself, that high volcanic mass rising sharply and sheer out of the sea off the Lothian coast, the haunt of gulls, cormorants, gannets and guillemots. First of all Ivie is swept off the rock by a gust of high wind; this derives from a piece of Peden folklore. While a prisoner on the Bass, Peden is said to have been mocked by a serving-maid and to have prophesied her destruction;

> shortly thereafter, she was walking upon the rock, and there came a blast of wind, and swept her off the rock into the sea where she was lost.[30]

Ivie is not mocking; she tries to bring comfort to the prisoners, seeing Raith's unhappiness; and she is not lost, she is picked up by a fisherman who takes her to Canty Bay where Marjory and Euphrain are living to be near their menfolk. Later Raith to escape a mutiny jumps off the rock. He is almost sucked into the tide as it rolls into the cavern which perforates the rock and pulls back again—most vividly described—and is rescued by the same fisherman. Later still the prisoners escape, helped by Simpson cousins and fishermen; Grif, sympathising and in any case dismissed from his post sets the guards drunk and helps the Covenanters down with a complicated system of barrels and a crane. One barrel—a brandy-keg—is set on fire and almost gives the game away.

The next day a government ship arrives to inspect the fortress. Grif, wounded by burns, dresses up the guards and shuts them up as Covenanters. After their drunken debauch the night before, they are most convincingly miserable and whining. The dapper little Captain, moaning over the difficulty of climbing up to the prison and chattering about his friend Mr Samuel Pepys, is quite taken in.

Ivie and the two Ellison women are captured by Lag and taken to a gloomy mansion called Houston-in-the-Hollow. Lag insists that they dine with him and insults Ivie by admiring her beauty and declaring that he must take her to court and make her the king's mistress. She whips him twice across the face, and Lord Liddesdale (Crockett for Lauderdale) makes Lag answer the challenge. Ivie is not a soldier's daughter for nothing; accepting a rapier from Liddesdale she fights with dexterity and runs Lag through just where the shoulder joins the body. Lord Liddesdale prudently removes her and the Ellisons to his house of Kingsberry.

Raith, following the trail, comes to Houston-in-the-Hollow on a night of lightning and storm. He climbs the great staircase, sword drawn. As he pushes open a door, he finds himself caught in a wolf-trap with an old woman tightening a rope round him so that he is trapped indeed. Stephen Houston sits drunk and half-mad at the table, taking potshots with several pistols at the walls, making patterns like Sherlock Holmes in Baker Street with his 'V R'. Now he turns to Raith (he is in love with Ivie and madly jealous) and outlines his body with shots, boasting that the last bullet will be for his heart. Ralph loses consciousness and floats into a blue region of cloud which is eternity.

But Ivie has had a presentiment. She and Lady Liddesdale return and are in time to see the old woman Sue Fairfoul turn against her master and shoot him dead, running off into the darkness for ever. Ivie calls on Raith over and over again as they take his body down; he hears her voice in the blue of eternity and returns to life and love. Ivie is well worth returning to; she rides with Lord Liddesdale to Morton Castle in the nick of time; Grierson of Lag is about to shoot all the Ellisons out of hand, and her father also. The final tableau is of the Ellisons safely back at Mayfield, Ivie and Raith and their children around them and Euphrain, who has learned the warmth of human love, married to Grif Rysland.

This is a rattling good yarn, full of event and adventure; the cast of minor characters, fishermen, dragoons, guards, grumbling, arguing, commenting and plotting, carries one along irresistibly with energy and gusto, making the incredible seem probable and the impossible almost normal. Crockett's lively Scots dialogue brings even the oddest figures to life, and through it all flickers his humour and his vivid pictorial presentation of the small details which hold the narrative firmly in his own kind of reality. It is easy to see how readers looking for a sombre picture of Covenanting saints may have been disappointed so that his stature as a serious historical novelist gradually diminished, but he never claimed to be that; we must judge him by what he set out to do. And he told his readers so often exactly what he intended that it would be ungenerous to ignore it. Take him for all in all, he spins a good tale and entertains us, at his best, with a lively panorama set against the scenes he knew and could describe with affectionate exactness.

II *Elsewhere*

Ayrshire is not far from Galloway, especially its southern division Carrick whose landscape merges imperceptibly into that of Galloway, few roads traversing its moors, mountains and bogs. It provided two new elements for Crockett—the sea, not a sandy estuary-like Solway Firth but a wide expanse to the west, and the traditions of the Kennedy families at feud with each other and any other family that offered. In the old verse, the two areas shared the same outlook:

> Frae Wigtown to the toun o' Ayr,
> An' laigh doon by the cruives o' Cree,
> Nae man may howp a lodging there
> Unless he coort wi' Kennedy.

The feud between the Kennedies of Cassillis and the Kennedies of Bargany had already been used in 1890 by William Robertson, an authority on Ayrshire folklore, in his novel *The Kennedys*, reshaped as *The Kings of Carrick*. Crockett had read Robertson's worthy but pedestrian account and borrows episodes from it, but passes them through his transforming imagination to emerge fresh and new—and, above all, pictorial. He adds items of his own contriving, incorporates Ayrshire traditions drawn from his reading, and presents a colourful crowded landscape of interlocked feuds with an excursion into Galloway and a legendary cannibal for good measure.

His treatment of the borrowed passages show his creative reworking at its best. His 'Grey Man' is built up from Robertson's statement that John Mure was a man of great villainy.

> He was cruel and vindictive; he never forgot an insult or an enemy; and he was tenacious as a sleuthound (sic) in following up the track of his vengeance. Still, he preferred, whenever he could, to work behind the scenes. It was for him to plot, for others to execute; and many a blow that was struck at the Earl of Cassillis was directed by a hand that itself remained invisible.[1]

Robertson tells us this; Crockett shows it happening. The unknown silent form appears in the first chapter, looking on as the Cassillis Kennedies burn the Tower of Ardstinchar, belonging to Bargany,

> a tall man who sat on a grey horse, and was clad from head to foot in grey, having his face shaded with a high-crowned, broadbrimmed hat of the ancient fashion,[2]

a secretive menacing figure. When the Bargany Kennedies swear revenge on a blood-stained Bible from a dead Kennedy's pocket, he contemptuously throws it into the fire, shocking even them by his treatment of God's word. The hero's father, a peaceful farmer from Galloway, a Kennedy too but of Cassillis, cannot allow this evil; he leaps impulsively down from where he and his young son are hiding and snatches the Bible from the flames, risking his own life. Gilbert Kennedy of Bargany holds up his hand when his men move to seize the intruder:

> '... because ye stopped devil's work and, it may be, kept away a curse from us for the burning of the Holy Book, ye shall not die in my house. Take your life and your son's life as a gift from Gilbert Kennedy of Bargany ... Put the Bible as a keepsake in your winnock sole ... and come no more to Ballantrae in time of feud, lest a worse thing befall you!' So said he, and waved us away, as I thought grandly ...
> But from a knoll of the left of the entrance the man of the grey habit, he who had thrown the Bible, sat silent upon his horse and watched. Him my father took to have been the devil, as he said to me many times that night ere we got to Minnochside.[3]

The grey man is a power of evil, suggested rather than described, always watching on the edge of events, bribing, manipulating, plotting, sending men to their deaths without scruple, with his identity as John Mure of Auchendrayne gradually becoming clearer as his appearances grow more frequent, until he and his son stand to be executed at the Mercat Cross of Edinburgh. Robertson had made James Mure worse than his father, but Crockett represents him as a cowardly weak shivering catspaw; when King James offers clemency in return for a confession, the grey man agrees if only his son be executed first. Once the son is silenced and dead, his father laughs at clemency and opts for death—a situation Crockett may have found in Stevenson's 'Heather Ale' (*Ballads* 1890) when the aged Pictish chieftain, fearing his son's weakness, made sure that the secret of the ale was kept by having his son killed first.

Asked in what religion he dies, John Mure answers smilingly.

> 'Of the ancientest persuasion,' he said, 'for I am ready to believe in any well-disposed god whom I may chance to meet in my pilgriming. But in none do I believe till I do meet him.'[4]

This to the sixteenth century (and to the nineteenth) would have an added grue, since he was going in a few moments to meet a God not in the least likely to be well-disposed, with all his sins piled high upon him.

The first-person narrator is taken from Robertson too, but how enlarged and made human! Robertson described how, as Sir Thomas Kennedy of Culzean rode unwittingly to his death, he was

> in high spirits, and as he rode along he chatted familiarly to his servant, Lancelot Kennedy, an humble member of his family—far-removed, but still a Kennedy.[5]

This dim personage under Crockett's pen becomes Launcelot Kennedy, the eighteen-year-old squire to Sir Thomas, a young man with a good conceit of himself, vain of his appearance, full of adolescent self-importance but proud of his honour and devoted to his master. 'Chatted familiarly' is developed into a most warm and touching relationship between the young lad and his master the elderly man, loving and protecting on the part of Launcelot who, though knowing that he is sharper than Sir Thomas, recognises that the noble unsuspecting trustfulness of his master towards all men derives from the goodness of his nature.

> He had ever, indeed, been kindly and generous, forgiving and unsuspicious. But during these spring months ... he seemed to ripen like a winter apple when it is laid by, till there was no more sourness in him anywhere ...
> Indeed, to talk with him and watch his life was better than any sermon. I declare that before I understood his character and thought, I knew not that religion was aught more than the colour of a faction—a thing to fight about, like the blood feuds of Cassillis and Bargany, considering the wrong and right of which not one in a thousand knows anything, and still fewer care.
> Yet for all his increasing gentleness there was naught unmanly about my lord, but ever the bearing and speech of a most courteous knight. He had a great love for noble and sweet music, and often diverted himself on the viol, upon which he played most masterly. The scurril jest, indeed, he would sharply reprove; but his heart still inclined to wit and mirth, and his countenance was constantly cheerful.[6]

This is a new note in Crockett after his Covenanting *Men of the Moss Hags*, that of the innate courtesy and goodness of a civilised gentleman of good birth. Religion appears mainly through this element in Sir Thomas, not an obsession but a quality of mind which distinguishes him from the traitors who destroy him; he is a man of peace, as Christ was.

Launcelot, learning all this fresh for the first time from his own experience, comes to respect and love this goodness in Sir Thomas, though he knows he is too acute and knowing to lay claim to it himself. Likewise, being young and impressionable, he can see nobility and honour in Gilbert of Bargany; when he comes upon him at the Holyrood guard-house, he feels impelled to salute him with grave respect, although he is the enemy,

> For a more kingly-looking man did I never see—far beyond our Earl (shame be to me for saying such a thing!), and indeed, before any man that ever I saw. But Gilbert Kennedy of Bargany was the bravest man that was to be gotten in any land, as all men that saw him in his flower do to this day admit. And hearts were like water before him.[7]

Launce's directness enables him to see the nobility of both men, and scorn in comparison the meanness of spirit shown by the Earl of Cassillis. Through the young untarnished vision of the squire, Crockett can give a more fresh robust and exuberant picture of late sixteenth-century Scotland than if he had written as an older experienced man; Launce, without realising it, is describing a watershed in the country's history and classifying the characters according to the allegiance to a vanished past or a strange sinister future. Sir Thomas and Gilbert, in their courtesy and fairness, belong to the times that are past. Sir Thomas trusts the lying words of John Mure of Auchendrayne and weds his daughter Marjorie to James Mure to seal what he thinks is a bond of peace, since he is too noble to doubt it. Gilbert despises guns and bullets as weapons not fit for gentlemen, and he too is destroyed by lies and deception which he is too noble to suspect. The Earl, greedy, ungenerous, cowardly, married to an old woman for the sake of her money, is a symbol of the money-grubbing commercialism which is the present, boding ill for the days to come.

Launce is a squire to Sir Thomas, being trained in the household of Culzean like Chaucer's Squire so that he will become a man of courtesy and honour himself. He is inclined to be a prig, full of his own glory, at first, but he is comically human in his vanity; in his verbal duelling with Nell Kennedy, Sir Thomas's younger daughter, who sees through him and mocks him without mercy; in his kindly playing at children's games with the younger boys of the Culzean household. He grows in warmth as the book progresses and as his juvenile airs are swept away by hard experience and he finds his values in this age of transition. Crockett gives him an educated Scots style which marks him out as gentle. There are only three occasions where he breaks into lower-class speech, two of them in the castle kitchen when the cook sets about her useless husband and abuses idle hangers-on, and once at the farm of Chapeldonnan when the farmer's wife speaks uncivilly. Launcelot comments that he is merely reproducing what others lower in station than himself are saying. The cook

> broke into the vulgar speech of the country, which, because I learned to write English as those at the Queen's Court do, I have used but seldom in this chronicle—though, of course, not for lack of knowledge.[8]

Crockett is using Galt's method of letting a character give himself away. Launcelot has had to write coarsely, but the reader must understand that this is not his habit—though of course he knows all about coarseness. The tiny point so insisted upon brings it to our notice, and we smile at something we might not have noticed if Launcelot had not been so anxious to free himself from any lower-class taint.

In the matter of religion, Sir Thomas and his friend Maister Robert Bruce, minister of the kirk at Edinburgh, St Giles, represent the best. Bruce is 'Maister of Arts' at St Andrews University and has studied law at Louvain before entering the church; he marks a point half-way between John Knox in the past and the Covenanters that are to come, and is better than both. He appears now and again, always quietly assured as a man of birth; he preaches regularly before King James VI and his court and is not afraid to chide them when he thinks it necessary; when, for example, the King talks and whispers during a sermon, Bruce stops until good manners prevail, saying that the Lion of the Tribes of Judah is now roaring in the voice of his Gospel and it behoves all the petty kings of the earth to be silent.[9]

Bruce was a powerful figure in his day; he has been largely forgotten since he lacked the fiery rebelliousness of both his predecessors and his successors; it was skilful of Crockett to introduce this calm, quiet man of moderation and wisdom, shaking his head sadly as he sees how poorly religion fares in Ayrshire—'the word of God is indeed made of none effect in Kyle and Carrick'[10]—and expressing forebodings of what will come if the King persists in his favouring of Catholics and his interference in the Scottish Church. He can foresee the bigotry of the unlearned Covenanters but can condemn the foolishness of the policies which will make them rise against the throne. He is a background figure in the story, always there when he is wanted, providing a balance among the more prominent characters; his comments are quiet but to the point.

The bad old ways are illustrated by the Earl's cook's husband Sir Thomas Tode, virtually a lunatic. He has been a monk, part of the old world which the Reformation rejected, and was present on the grim occasion when the Earl's forefather, as greedy as the present Earl, roasted the Abbot of Crossraguel on a gridiron to make him yield up the secret of his money-bags, a familiar Ayrshire tradition. Sir Thomas had helped to baste the unfortunate Abbot, and this had so crazed his wits that he is forever garrulous about his part in the gruesome affair, unable to stop talking about it. He is the present Earl's chaplain and his wife the cook hauls him about by the long yellow hair which has grown from his head where his tonsure used to be, a grotesque visual touch which, whether possible or not, may be taken to symbolise the twisted inheritance the Church of Rome has left, and is shut up in a cupboard whenever he grows too much of a nuisance.

Through Launcelot's eyes we see and experience passing events, all clearly brought before us. His narrative moves on in stylised period fashion like a chronicle from one to another, interspersing moments of violence with quiet interludes, walking in the gardens of Culzean and enjoying its civilised beauty. But quiet interludes are brief in comparison with the vigour of the more violent. Kelwood Tower is besieged and taken by the Cassillis Kennedies largely through Launce's strategy, and the Cassillis treasure, stolen from the Earl's father and now in the hands of Kelwood, is regained, to the Earl's delight; 'it was ever the bitterest draught to the Earl to lose siller or gear'.[11] The touch of amused contempt conveys Launce's attitude to such avarice and is repeated frequently through the story; the Earl was far indeed from generous chivalry.

As the Kennedies rejoice in their success at the Inn on the Red Moss, the treasure once more disappears, being left unguarded; and the only clues as to the thieves are small sinister naked footprints on the mud outside the inn. These mark the introduction into an Ayrshire story of Sawny Bean the cannibal, moved up a little to the north to provide a fearsome thread in the narrative. Crockett had known him from Galloway hearsay and from

Nicholson's *Tales Connected with the South of Scotland* (Kirkcudbright 1843) and put him firmly into his plot as an additional horror.

Next, a very foolish enterprise is undertaken, borrowed this time from Ayrshire traditional folklore. The Earl of Cassillis has a feud with Crauford of Kerse, and to show contempt, the Earl orders his men to tether a sow on the Kerse lands and keep it there for a day. Crockett devoted five chapters to the narration of this incident which may seen an inordinate amount of space for so trivial and tedious an activity; it is a digression from the main plot and in itself is too trifling to arouse much interest. But Crockett ties it in firmly with his characters—the insulting tethering of the sow is because Crauford is sheltering Kelwood of the stolen treasure chest—and is so leisurely and specific in his retelling of the old tale as to make it fresh and new. Through it moreover he provides a panorama of late sixteenth-century Ayrshire which fixes many characters firmly and pictorially in the reader's mind and shows the fragments of ancient chivalry which remain in the midst of brutality and folly.

Launcelot is by now so well respected that it is he who is sent under safe-conduct to announce to Crauford of Kerse that such an insult is intended. He is proud to have been chosen, though not of the purpose of his message. As he goes he meets a quiet elderly gentleman riding and reading a religious book; he reveals himself as John Mure of Auchendrayne and tries by sly insinuations to make Launce change sides for his worldly advantage. Launce in scorn rides on his way but notices men lying in wait by the bridge as if in ambush. He crosses the river at a deep place where there is no ford to elude them, and is met by David Crauford of Kerse who courteously escorts him to his father's presence.

In the hall crammed with angry Craufords Launce delivers the taunting message formally but without fear, though he is aware of his solitary figure in the midst of enemies; there is courage under his vanity, and he thinks that, if he is killed, Marjorie and Nell will realise that he is a hero in spite of their mockery. He is a picturesque figure, a mediaeval herald standing calmly while his enemies roar around him. Even Crauford of Kerse is impressed. He sends back by Launce a strong defiance but compliments him on his bearing, and the young Craufords accompany him as a guard of honour.

It is in the journeying here and there, the coming and going of men of all kinds, the waiting for orders, the delivering of news, the receiving of messsages, the arrival of friends, that Crockett builds up the picture of the bustle and life of Culzean and at Cassillis. Maister Robert Bruce, Minister of Edinburgh, arrives and is greeted with honour and made welcome; at the other extreme, a young blade tries to quarrel with Launce, and Robert Harburgh, seeing what is happening, intervenes and tells Launce that he should not trouble with such a brawler; Harburgh deals with him as he deserves. The hot kitchen is a common meeting-place, with Thomas Tode perpetually babbling about the roasted Abbot. The Earl comes to thank Launce for his skilful carrying out of his duties as messenger; he wants to reward Launce with a sword, yet is so greedy, so sweir to part with anything, that he holds it longingly in his hands, looking at it, before he can bring himself to hand it over. Launce stands waiting, relishing every moment and knowing what is passing in his master's mind, amused, a little contemptuous—and quick to take the sword and go away before the Earl has time to regret his intention. He is not too taken up with his own achievement; he is observant and objective in his attitude to his feudal superior; he knows he deserves the reward, yet while wishing his Earl had been more generous in character can feel not a boy's eagerness but a man's calm acceptance of the conflict in the giver's mind.

The affair of the Tethering of the Sow is carried out in all its foolish grotesqueness, with much noise and disarray, to emphasise how crude and brutal even the nobility of Ayrshire are when old feuds fester and lead to more violence. The unfortunate animal is dumped on the Crauford land and prodded into 'snorking and yellyhooing' to make sure old Crauford of Kerse hears it and knows the insult has been carried out. The men on both sides abuse each other, cursing, shouting filthy names, behaving like brutes. Maister Bruce turns away with distaste and goes to reason with Kerse, taking Launce with him—Launce gladly turns his back on the ugliness of this silly scrimmage. They find the old man swearing and blaspheming because he is too old to take part in avenging the insult; he is waiting for news that the Sow has been 'flitted'. News comes that one of his sons has been killed in the affair but this is nothing to him—the death of many men are nothing to him as long as the Sow is flitted; this is the only question in which he can take any interest. After the chivalry of the herald delivering the message and being courteously received and despatched, there is shown the brutality of the times in this vulgar blasphemous brawling over a trifle—brutality in the insult and in its avenging. Launce respects the chivalry but is disgusted by the grossness of its opposite. 'God be thanked for His ill-deserved mercy' he comments, 'in the quarrel that had been so evilly settled, there was no loss to Culzean'.[12] He is gradually maturing.

To show how he has gained confidence, Launce is made to suspect danger when Sir Thomas, trusting and brave, goes to Maybole to spend New Year with his friend the Provost. He follows his master in the snowy darkness and sees the enemies gather in the shadows, sinister against the walls and hedges, waiting for the portly knight to emerge, genial, alone and in all probability a little unsteady from the good cheer. Launcelot persuades the Provost to keep Sir Thomas overnight and himself dons the heavy armour the Provost lends him, takes the Provost's pistol ('Gin ye live ye can keep the pistol,' the Provost says most kindly) and impersonates Sir Thomas. He successfully dodges the sharpshooters who spatter him with their bullets and makes his way home to Culzean, not without having to defend himself in a small summer-house where he is joined by Robert Harburgh with whom he eludes his enemies, helped by the good people of Maybole who come to the aid of Sir Thomas whom they love.

These adventures fill in vividly the wildness of the times, as well as the character of Launcelot; they are carefully linked together and we learn not only of the events but of the people who are involved. No one is there without a purpose. Even Robert Harburgh, an apparently casual acquaintance, has his part to play in Launce's development; he marries the grieve's daughter with whom Launce has had an affair, about which Nell Kennedy teases him unmercifully, revealing something of her own feelings as well as Launce's vanity. Crockett without seeming to do so builds up clear character-studies merely by dialogue and the manner in which actions take place. In one incident he draws on a memory of his own youth in *A Galloway Herd*; in a time of heavy snow Walter Anderson was as a joke terrified by his uncle wrapped in the hide and horns of a newly killed bullock appearing before him in the dark of early night.[13] In Chapters XVIII and XIX of *The Grey Man* a similar joke plays itself out in the snow-filled courtyard of the castle among the young Kennedy sons, one pretending to be the fearsome 'Something'. Launce puts an end to this, then goes himself to investigate what one of the lads has said about a figure with a drawn sword and a wild beast standing by the barn. He finds Marjorie Kennedy talking to a tall figure—the Grey Man—then slipping away. When Launce challenges the intruder, he wounds the man but is himself mauled by the beast-like creature—Sawny Bean; the key to the treasure-chest of Kelwood is found clutched in Launce's hand when he is found unconscious after the alarm is raised. Two mysteries are left with us, both to be solved. The first is the sadder; Marjorie Kennedy has been talking with the Grey Man because she knows her father wishes her to marry his son and bring peace to Ayrshire through this alliance, and she must make clear that this marriage will be one in name alone. The second one, the Kelwood treasure, forms an enduring thread running through the plot until it is finally discovered by Launce, Nell Kennedy and the Dominie in Sawny Bean's hideous cave, knit into a complex and winding plot of feud, of hopeless love and of the Grey Man. In the beginning Launce is foolishly proud of his part in the Kennedy feud; they are declared a danger to the King's peace with their brawling in Edinburgh. All cock-a-hoop at being declared a criminal,

> I rade forth from Edinburgh town with infinite glee and assurance of spirit. No longer would I be slighted as a boy, for that day I, even I, Launcelot Kennedy, had been put to the horn—that is, I had been proclaimed rebel and outlaw at the Cross of Edinburgh with three blasts of the King's horn, 'Against John, Earl of Cassillis, Sir Thomas Kennedy, Tutor of Cassillis, and Launcelot Kennedy, his esquire!' So had run the proclamation. I wondered what that unkempt, ill-tongued lassie, Nell Kennedy, would say to this. But the honour itself she could not gainsay.[14]

The brash pride of the lad, the formal ceremony of the proclamation, the wild nature of the times when such things are made little of among the nobility, and above all Launce's joyful conclusion that Nell Kennedy will have to think much of him now—giving away his own feelings about Nell that he does not himself understand for what they are—are all economically conveyed in the space of one paragraph. This is Crockett at his best.

Nell Kennedy is a torment to Launce; he writes of her with lofty scorn. It is with the elder sister Marjorie that he imagines he is in love, a fact which

Nell laughs maliciously over, being human and a little jealous. Marjorie is quite different; she is a heroine of old romance, a 'princesse lointaine' who is beautiful, cold and apart, but to bring her to life Crockett lets Launce describe the effect she has upon him.

> For myself, I declare that when she came down and walked in the garden, I became like a little waggling puppy dog, so great was my desire to attract her attention. Yet she spoke to me but seldom, being of a nature as noble as it was reserved. Silent and grave Marjorie Kennedy mostly was, with the lustre of her eyes more often on the far sea edges, than on the desirable young men who rode their horses so gallantly over the greensward to the landward gate of Culzean castle.[15]

Crockett can have seen Culzean Castle only after Robert Adam had enclosed the old tower house within the finest example of his later castle style, but he speaks of it carefully and only in terms of its older form, taken perhaps from old prints—the greensward at the landward gate, as here; the towers 'builded upon a cliff, steep and perilous, overlooking the sea'[16] (with an echo of Keats); the sea spread wide 'clattering pleasantly on the rocks, and with the birds blithely swirling and diving about it all the year round'[17]; and 'the dule-tree, or tree of execution, which stands by the great gate and bears medlars at any season, but only for an hour at a time.'[18] Round the courtyard are gathered the outhouses, the byres, the barn with its threshing floor and the stables, with a little higher the armoury where Launce works over the weapons and, in the White Tower with its jutting turret, his own room to which he climbs by means of a rope past Nell and Marjorie's room after his excursion to Maybole fair. Marjorie belongs to this mediaeval Culzean, a figure from an old tapestry, remote and still; Launce, the waggling pet dog of a lover, is part of the new, undignified in comparison. When she once did talk to him, holding his hand and making him so happy that he slept with his precious right hand in a silk glove for a long time afterwards, Launce is emulating the lover from an old romance in a time that is long past.

Marjorie is in love with Gilbert Kennedy of Bargany, the enemy of her branch of the Kennedies; her interest in Launce is because he admires Gilbert and can give her news of him. She knows that their love is doomed; Bargany will never acknowledge the overlordship of Cassillis, and a marriage has been arranged between him and one of the Queen's ladies. They meet by the caves under Culzean and part in anger (Launce by accident and to his grief overhears their last harsh words to one another, close in under the walls of Culzean). She sends him away and agrees to marry James Mure of Auchendrayne to please her father, who believes the marriage will bring peace to Carrick and Kyle. Instead, because the greedy, wavering Earl of Cassillis once more breaks his word, fighting erupts again and Gilbert Kennedy is killed by one of Auchendrayne's men, a spy among the Cassillis Kennedies.

> The poised lance struck young Bargany full in the neck and stayed. So in the midst of his foes, and striking at them to the last, he fell, who was the bravest

man of his age. And at his overthrow there fell a silence for a space, and the battle smother cleared. Only the snow fell and scarce melted off the face that was already white and set in death.

We crossed our spears and made a bier with our cloaks, whereon we laid him. Then very gently I drew away the deadly lance, though the wound bled not much, but inwardly, which was worse. We thought to bear him to some castle of his own folk, as it might be to the house of Auchendrayne. But the Earl John came and looked at his foe and kinsman as he lay on the ground with his eyes closed.

'Carry him to my castle at the town end of Maybole,' said he, 'for that is near by.'

Now I thought that not the best place in the world for the young man's recovery, but, being bidden, it was not mine to reply but only to obey.

We came to the portcullis gate of Maybole, and were bearing him in upon our shoulders, when from the road to the town there came, riding like the wind, first a lady and then a man that followed hotly in pursuit. When they came nearer, I saw that the lady was she who had been Marjorie Kennedy, and that the man riding after was her husband, James Mure. At sight of us who bore the soldier's bier slowly on our spears, Marjorie leaped from her horse, and left it to wander, bridle free. But a page seized and held it . . .

Then she that had been so proud and haughty to young Bargany when he was alive, took the fair, wounded head in her arms, crouching beside him in the dun, trampled snow, while the flakes blew in upon her unbound hair. She crooned and hushed him like a bairn, while we that had borne him stood wide from her, some turning away altogether. But, because I knew all and loved her, I stood near.[19]

This, the most romantic episode in *The Grey Man*, has been quoted at length because in its slow detailed simplicity it is almost poetic; in the sad elegiac words Marjorie says to her dead love in the paragraphs that follow, it is wholly so. One can hear Malory behind the sadness of the prose and in the clauses linked by co-ordinating conjunctions or simple 'then' and 'so' and 'when'. One can also hear, perhaps more accurately, Tennyson in *Morte D'Arthur*.

> So all day long the noise of battle rolled
> Among the mountains by the winter sea;
> Until King Arthur's table, man by man,
> Had fall'n in Lyonesse about their Lord,
> King Arthur; then, because his wound was deep,
> The bold Sir Bedivere uplifted him,
> Sir Bedivere, the last of all his knights,
> And bore him to a chapel nigh the field,
> A broken chancel with a broken cross,
> That stood on a dark strait of barren land.

The cadences, allowing for the more varied rhythm of the prose, are similar in the inevitability with which they fall on the ear, tolling sadly and solemnly; both passages mourn the passing of an age—with Bargany as with King Arthur, chivalry died. Crockett's details are built up effortlessly and yet with cumulative effect; the silence which even enemies feel at Bargany's death, the snow continuing its relentless falling, the improvised bier of spears and cloaks, the dull command of the Earl to whom this is merely another enemy wiped out, the irony with which they think to take him to a house of his own people—Auchendrayne's, not yet known to be the greatest enemy, the slow movement towards Maybole suddenly interrupted by the hurrying riders frantically riding. Then comes a great stillness as Marjorie, heedless of the snow and her dishevelled hair expressing so classically her sorrow, holding in grief Bargany's cold head as she had never done in life. It lasts only for a moment; real life breaks in; Launce who, in a tiny detail observed almost silently, had stood by the two lovers 'because I knew all and loved her', runs to ask Marjorie if she will come back with them to Culzean. She refuses and rides off again, and as the news spreads Nell stops her young brothers from playing tennis. Life goes on, but something has been lost forever.

The next episode is gentle and ordinary in comparison; Launce accompanies Sir Thomas to visit Sheriff Agnew of Lochnaw, another daughter's father-in-law, after Launce has seen his old love the grieve's lass married to Robert Harburgh, with only a slight pang. On the journey back to Culzean, he and Sir Thomas visit Launce's father and mother at their farm of Kirrieoch. Launce is more than delighted when Sir Thomas, sitting at the table spread with the best damask and silver to honour him, takes up a spoon and remarks with surprise that the crest on it is the same as that of his great-grandfather. He was also the great-grandfather of Kennedy of Kirrieoch, Launce's father, and for the rest of their visit Sir Thomas calls him 'Cousin', with the exquisite old-fashioned courtesy of the truly noble.

The next incident is Sir Thomas's murder. In Robertson's account, this is narrated in a heavy style which makes even the central event sound laboured.

> The Knight of Culzean realised the situation. It flashed on him in an instant. He put his hand to his belt, where he carried a heavy pistol, and was in the very act of drawing it when Cloncaird sprang upon him, thrusting at him with his lance, and inflicting a wound which made him reel in his seat. Turning to face his assailant he was met, not by Cloncaird, but by Bargany, who, thrusting his associate aside, waved his naked sword on high, and, with eyes flashing fire, stood for a moment face to face with his victim. Bargany spake never a word; he was in too stern and grim a mood for that; but attacked Culzean so impetuously that with the first blow he fell from his saddle.[20]

There is another half-page of this plodding, Latinate commentary before Sir Thomas is 'despatched' and Bargany, dead Gilbert's brother and heir, feels 'the necessity for instant flight'.

Crockett vitalises the murder to instant reality by natural, seemingly trivial detail, which contrasts in its ordinariness with the central savagery of the killing and throws it into strong relief. Launce and Sir Thomas, having, they think, unfortunately missed meeting John Mure, pass Greenan Castle and reach the sandy links above the bay at Ayr.

'Launcelot, ride a little way in front. It approaches the hour of noon, and I would do my devotion and meditate a little alone,' said Sir Thomas. So I drew myself a bowshot before him, riding upon Dom Nicholas, and taking my hat in my hand. I rode easily, enjoying the sea breeze that cooled my brow and tossed my hair. I wondered if ever the time would come, when I also would be thinking about my religion at noon of a fine heartsome day. It seemed a strange time enough for a hale, well-to-do gentleman to set to his prayers.

Presently I saw a man standing upon my right hand somewhat above me upon the crown of a sandhill. And he raised his hand as one that cried to clear the course in the game, so I thought no more of the matter. But I looked round, thinking perchance that he cried to my master, who was riding with bared head and holding his little red Testament in his hand.

Suddenly, even as I looked at him, I heard the sound of shots behind me, and, turning Dom Nicholas, I saw my master reel in his saddle, with white blowing puffs of gunpowder rising all about him, from behind the desolate sandhills among which the murderers had hidden themselves. Drawing my sword, I set spurs to the side of Dom Nicholas and galloped towards them. I was aware, as I rode, of my master lying on his back on the sand, and his palfrey galloping away with streaming mane. A little black crowd of men stood and knelt about him, and I saw the flash of steel again and again as one and another of them lifted a knife and struck.

I yelled aloud to them in my agony and bade them wait till I came. So they hasted to make front against me, some of them leaping on their horses and others biding a little to put as it had been booty into their saddle wallets.[21]

Launce engages the murderers in fight before they can all get away, and as he crosses blades with James Mure of Auchendrayne notes with a sideways glance that the man who had made the warning sign from the sandhill was the Grey Man, watching and then riding off, as of old. Launce cries for help from golfers, and they come in answer to his cry of murder but only when they have finished their hole, by which time it is too late. Sir Thomas is on the point of death; he does not care for his purse but gropes for his red Testament, which Launce gives him, shedding tears of grief. Sir Thomas forgives and even sorrows for his murderers and bids Launce be a good brave lad—'and be kind to Nelly', which provokes a smile even in this tragic moment; Sir Thomas has noticed what has been going on between Launce and Nell. Then without anger or struggle he dies and there is only his body on the sands.

The varying moods make for life—the quietness of Sir Thomas as he says his noontide prayers, the careless enjoyment of Launce in the pleasant day, the surprise he feels that so healthy a man should wish to say prayers which, Launce implies, are suitable for those near death, the irony of death coming so quickly and unforeseen in such bright happy weather, the spurt of gunfire into the sandhills, the futile helpless shout to the enemies to wait for him— and the grey man once again in the background.

The remainder of *The Grey Man* is Launcelot's search for the murderers, all the more keen because he knows that the treasure of Kelwood, the killing of Sir Thomas and his own future with Nell Kennedy are linked together. He and the Dominie of Maybole question the boy Dalrymple who took a message from Sir Thomas to John Mure but did not deliver it, told lies about it, and later disappeared. The name Dalrymple comes from Robertson, who had described the messenger as a poor scholar who earned a living by writing letters for the poor people of Ayr,[22] but by changing him to a schoolboy Crockett not only adds a dimension of cruelty to the grey man's crimes but enlists the Dominie as a companion in Launce's search. Nell, Launce and the Dominie visit Auchendrayne and find the Laird at his prayers with his household, smooth, sinister and plausible. He allows Nell to see her sister Marjorie, who, weary and pale, talks of her father's death with sorrow but says significantly that she will clear the matter to the roots; 'my work is not yet done at Auchendrayne'.[23]

For her own safety, Launce and the Dominie send Nell to Kirrieoch and Launce's mother, and follow clues from place to place, pretending to be merchants, talking to the people in the farmhouses, the Dominie being a skilled cross-questioner (because of his profession) and occasionally entertaining the company with his bagpipes, like Nicholson, the Galloway poet. At Chapeldonnan, the good man of which, Bannatyne, was on Ailsa Craig supposedly gathering solan geese, they are warned not to take the road south to Stranraer by Benane because 'ye wad mak' braw pickin' for the teeth o' Sawny Bean's bairns'.[24]

At this point the plot makes what seems an unnecessary detour and takes Launce and the Dominie to Ailsa Craig; this is because Robertson's Dalrymple is sent to Arran to be out of the way. The three threads of Dalrymple, Sawny Bean and the search for the murderer are neatly combined; Launce and the Dominie camp out on Ailsa Craig in the ruined castle and are attacked by Bargany Kennedies in a manner suggested by some of Crockett's boyhood games at Threave. They defeat the enemy but their boat is stolen so that they are marooned which gives the Dominie the chance to tell of his lost love who had disappeared many years before, leaving only a rosary, a stain of blood on the seashore grass, and the prints of many naked feet with great birds' claws.

Not surprisingly, when they hear a voice calling from the sea that night and see a white figure moving towards them, they are transfixed with terror, but it is not a spectre; it is Nell Kennedy, come with a boat to take them back to the mainland—Marjorie is missing from Auchendrayne and has sent a letter which declares she knows the truth about the Mures' villainy.

They row towards Ayrshire, and when the wind catches their boat set up the sail. Soon they are in under the cliffs and steering by a moving light which they see high above them. Suddenly a familiar voice cries out from the heights and a white form flashes down into the water near them like a seagull diving. It is Marjorie, escaping from the Mures. Hastily Launce throws himself into the water towards her and finds that her hands are tied behind her back so that she is helpless to save herself. He grasps the cords and pulls her towards the boat, into which they are both hauled not without difficulty, and Marjorie is laid in the arms of her sister.

Now Crockett gives us another cave, a dark sinister cavern as large as the one on Isle Rathan but for the moment less lively, except for echoes, the melancholy sound of breaking waves, and a sense of much air and great space above them. They leave the boat and make their way further into the cave, finding a flight of rough steps in the darkness which leads them up to warmer, drier air which should have been pleasanter than the dripping sea-cave but is not. The floor is hard, as if it had been tramped; there is a pungent smell which fills them with loathing; and Launce stumbles in the darkness against tubs and feels soft cold objects brushing his face.

He also finds the treasure-chest of Kelwood, but this is of little good; they are in Sawny Bean's cave, and soon hear sounds and see torchlight approaching. They hide in a small chamber high up in the rocky wall.

> Then the horrid brabblement filled all the cave, and seemed louder and more outrageous, being heard in darkness. Suddenly, however, the murky gloom was shot through with beams of light, and a rout of savages, wild and bloody, filled the wide cave beneath us. Some of them carried rude torches, and others had various sorts of back-burdens, which they cast down in the corners. I gat a gliff of one of these, and though in battle I had often seen things grim and butcherly, my heart now sprang to my mouth, so that I had well-nigh fainted with loathing. But I commanded myself, and thrust me before Nell, who from where she sat could only see the flickering skarrow of the torches upon the roof and walls—for the place seemed now, after the former darkness of Egypt, fairly bursting with light ...
>
> The cavern was very high in the midst, but at the sides not so high—rather like the sloping roof of an attic which slants quickly down from the roof tree. But that which took my eye amid the smoke were certain vague shapes, as it had been the limbs of human beings, shrunk and blackened, which hung in rows on either side of the cave. At first it seemed that my eyes must certainly deceive me, for the reek drifted hither and thither, and made the rheum flow from them with its bitterness. But after a little study of these wall adornments, I could make nothing else of it, than that these poor relics, which hung in rows from the roof of the cave like hams and black puddings set to dry in the smoke were indeed no other than the parched arms and legs of men and women who had once walked the upper earth—but who by misfortune had fallen into the power of this hideous, inconceivable gang of monstrous man-eaters. Then the true interpretation of all the tales that went floating about the countryside, and which I had hitherto deemed wholly vain and fantastical, burst upon me.[25]

In 1896 this must have seemed indeed the acme of horror; to us, after the worse horrors of Belsen and Auchschwitz it must necessarily seem less appalling; but Crockett builds up his details with careful variety and intensity, making his revelation slowly and with growing ugliness, all the more ghastly for Launce's comparisons with hams and black puddings. Nothing seems left but merciful death for all; the two men agree to kill the women, and the women accept their offer; anything is better than to fall into the hands of these savages.

We are startled and delighted with the simplicity used to free the characters from their hopeless predicament. The Dominie suddenly has the idea of playing his bagpipes. In that confined and echoing space, with caves honeycombed around and no apparent exit, the sound of the pibroch must have been earsplitting and terrible. Crockett borrowed the idea from a story which Harper quotes from *Blackwood's Magazine*; two Highland pipers sheltered from the weather in a cave 'of incredible dimensions' in the side of Cairnsmore-of-Fleet which unknown to them was the headquarters and store-room of Billy Marshall and his band of gipsy outlaws, and were still there when the outlaws returned. They expected nothing but death, but had the idea of playing their pipes, and the yelling noise issuing as it seemed from the bowels of the earth sent Billy and all his band flying, never again to go near that terrible place.[26] Sawny Bean and his crew react as did Billy Marshall: Launce and his three companions march triumphantly forth to the sound of the pipes and are saved. Once more Galloway has moved up to Ayrshire and solved the problem.

After this escape comes the trial of the Mures, father and son, at the Bailzie Court of Carrick held at Girvan, for the murder of Sir Thomas and the strangling of young Dalrymple, which Marjorie has witnessed. She tells her story well; Crockett extracts an additional grue from her account of how Dalrymple's body refused to be disposed of in the sea but was always driven by the wind and the tide back to the shore—once more a hint borrowed from Robertson, and improved upon. Even when they took him far out to sea in a boat and cast him overboard, their doom was still with them, as Marjorie testifies,

> For there, not thirty yards behind the boat, and following strongly in our wake, as a stark swimmer might do, now tumbling and leaping in the wash of the seas and now lunging forward like a boat that is towed, was the murdered boy himself. And thus he followed with a smile on his face, or what looked like it in the uncertain light of the morning.[27]

Her evidence seems conclusive, but Auchendrayne has a dramatic trump card; he produces King James VI himself, baggy breeches and shambling walk, who declares in lengthy learned words that Auchendrayne, a trusted councillor and a good historian, cannot possibly be guilty. Their accusers instead are under suspicion, but as they are led off to prison, the crowd accompanying them is faced with the drowned body of William Dalrymple, washed up on the road by the seashore to confront them in all its ugliness. Auchendrayne's kerchief is still round his swollen neck and Bannatyne's rope drags by his side. There is still a final test, the ancient mediaeval one for a murderer; when James Mure is forced to touch the body, blood comes welling from it; no doubt can remain.

John Mure under cover of the horror and excitement has quietly ridden off, but Launce seizes the King's horse and pursues him. Unfortunately he is too venturesome and is once more caught in Sawny Bean's cave, but Marjorie and Nell lead the rescuers and all is soon well. Sawny and his loathsome mob are herded together as prisoners, John and James Mure are taken for formal trial in Edinburgh, and Launce is in possession of the treasure of Kelwood.

All the savages and both the Mures are executed. Marjorie feels a pang of compassion for the man she had married without any intention of ever being his wife; he is weak and stupid compared with his father and less guilty; she talks quietly with him and moves him to repentance before his execution, mounting the scaffold with him to lend him courage. Then, her work accomplished, she herself dies with visions at the end not of Victorian angels, but more cheerfully, of Gilbert Kennedy of Bargany.

Launce is in favour with the Earl because he has kept quiet about the treasure and the King has not heard about it; it will remain with the Earl and not be confiscated. He is in favour with the King, and goes to London to be made one of the new knights on the King's accession to the throne as James I of England. And he is in due course married to his Nell at Cassillis, the ceremony being performed by Maister Robert Bruce, who for the moment is banished and out of Edinburgh, living quietly and safely with the Earl.

Crockett has managed the diverse turns and twists well. After *The Men of the Moss Hags*, the turning away from fanatics and rebels to the kindly religion of Sir Thomas and the strict but courteous Maister Bruce is in line with his own development and is both different and pleasing. Launce, a careless youth, is moved by Sir Thomas's example, not by preaching. It is significant that the only scene of household prayers is that at Auchendrayne, when Launce, Nell and the Dominie are witnesses of the Grey Man himself conducting prayers at an assemblage of his servants, and doing so in a most professional and learned manner like a minister, choosing to expound a passage of Holy Writ which prophesies damnation of hell to all those who spill the blood of the righteous. The chapter is entitled, appropriately, 'The Devil is a Gentleman'. Religion at the level of superstition appears when even the marauders draw back in horror when the Bible is thrown to the flames at Ardstinchar; true religion is shown by Sir Thomas and by Maister Robert Bruce, the one kindly, trusting, serving God and the cause of peace, the other sad, fearing for the future of Scotland, commenting with sorrow on the savagery he sees in Ayrshire.

The threads of the narrative run strongly through the complexity of the story, holding its widely varying moods and incidents firmly together. Even what appears at first to be a needless digression, the Flitting of the Sow, adds characters and reality to what might without such a digression have been too Tennysonian and romantic, like *The Lady of Shalott*. In its small specific details it is vitally relevant, adding bulk and density. The treasure of Kelwood is always present in the background, interesting the reader—he knows it must be found or at any rate explained. The tiny naked footprints, first found at the Inn on the Red Moss, appear again and again, particularly in the tale of the Dominie's lost love, until their final exposure in the ghastly cave. The relationship between Nell and Launce ebbs and flows throughout, beginning in teasing and taunting but gradually changing and growing deeper as troubles gather; she knows all about the grieve's daughter whom he has flirted with thoughtlessly in the past, but in her heart she knows that true affection lies between them and that in time he, the slower because he is a man, will come to know it too. The love of Marjorie for Bargany seems to be broken by her sharp renunciation and the two are necessarily estranged in this world; but his death allows her to express it without shame to all who hear, and her own death is a bringing of the lovers together again in eternity.

No one is unexpectedly or suddenly introduced so as to jar the plot—there is no sense of shock, as there is in *The Raiders*, when the mysterious strange glamorous Silver Sand astonishes Patrick by announcing that he has been anything so homespun as a Covenanter; King James VI appears unbidden at the Court of the Lord Bailzie at Carrick, but he has been present distantly in the background as King all the time and behaves quite in character. Launce's clear running style, mannered and period as was the fashion with most historical novels in the 1890s, holds each episode in its place, pleasantly flavouring the narrative with Scots words—eame, ettercap, tairge, ell-wand, castle-toun, break-tryst, remead, feckless, blate, whinger, paddock—and slipping effortlessly from rough jesting in the castle kitchen to noble and tragic romance, containing each mood with the consistency and sincerity of an educated and serious man and recording the different levels of speech from the lowest to the highest with a keen ear for idiosyncrasies and speech-habits.

There are flaws. It is difficult to believe that Sawny Bean, no matter how much given to incest, could have begotten such a diverse and populous tribe of cannibals and have them all living hale and hearty at the same time; there is perhaps a touch of H Rider Haggard's Zulus behind their remarkable multitude. It is difficult to accept that Nell, winsome and pleasant lass though she be, could have persuaded the woman at Chapeldonnan into confidences or even how she could have found that Launce and the Dominie had been at Chapeldonnan at all; her appearance with a boat at Ailsa Craig is as marvellous and incredible to the reader as it was to the two who welcomed her so gladly once they were sure she was not a ghost. It is even more difficult to accept that the three of them in their little boat could contrive by chance to be under the shadow of the cliffs just when Marjorie was thrown, hands tied behind her back, over into the dark waters by the two Mures, ready to be rescued by Launce and helped into the boat and the arms of her sister.

It is hardest of all to believe that Marjorie Kennedy, proud and fastidious, should be hob-nobbing with John Mure and Sawny Bean on that dark and snowy night by the barn. One can understand that the reader must for Marjorie's sake be assured that the hateful marriage will never be consummated, but it says little for the defences of Culzean Castle that they could be breached so easily. Why in any case should the Grey Man wish to discuss the marriage with Marjorie at all? He was not given to delicate considerations in his plotting. And why should he bring Sawny Bean along with him? The whole incident is well buttressed with excitement, pictorial distraction and vigorous movement in the eerie shadows; perhaps we should not be too nice in our examination of it but put it down to the Grey Man's ability to come and go as he pleases without means being given; he is a mystery. Sawny Bean must be there so that Launce may be found with the key to the Kelwood treasure chest inexplicably clutched in his hand, and his wounds provide the opportunity for him to be immobilised while he recuperates in the grieve's house so that Nell and the grieve's daughter may give him lessons in the nature of women.

On the whole, for a writer so inclined to run away with credibility, Crockett has taken more care than usual with his coincidences and used them thriftily to tie up his plot. They all are necessary. His control over the varied scenes and events is remarkable. They are not merely narrated one after the other like a series of short stories loosely strung together but linked firmly into the progressing story, so that if one does not lead logically to the next, at least each adds something vital, novel and relevant to the whole. He does not allow himself to ramble, but knits his material thoroughly into a seamless fabric; through Launce's robust energy, wry comment and sharp anger at all that is mean and despicable he carries the reader along to an ending which is firm and satisfactory, all threads woven in and everyone accounted for.

Peace appears to have come to Carrick with the downfall of Auchendrayne, and the Union of the Crowns promises new wealth and new ideas spreading through Scotland. Only Maister Bruce's forebodings remind us of the religious persecution which is to come. Crockett has chosen this moment in time as one from which one can look nostalgically back to the days of chivalry and forward to an age of money-grubbing and greed; King James has climbed to a peak in history from which after a pause his successor was to plunge into the valley of dark shadow. Not all historians will agree but Crockett uses his personages and his descriptions to build a convincing picture. And Launce, youthful adventures over and now Sir Launcelot, with land given by the Earl on which to build his new house of Palgowan, rides home to Kirrieoch with Nell on Dom Nicholas, the horse given him by his beloved master, assured that the Dominie will come and educate his family in due course, and that he has the good wishes of the Earl and his elderly Countess, Maister Robert Bruce, Robert Harburgh and his wife, formerly the grieve's daughter. It is into Galloway that he goes, to be welcomed by his mother at Kirrieoch and carry out what for Crockett is a truly classical ending; in the convenient absence of his father who is 'from home', Launce reads the evening's portion of Scripture from the scorched and bloodstained Bible which had been rescued from the flames at Ardstinchar in the first chapter.

The Grey Man is a more assured and better written book than any which Crockett had written before or was to write after it. It unites history and romance without offending probability excessively, and when it verges on doing so, he remembers to include as plausible a 'cover-up' as he can devise and diverts attention quickly elsewhere. He is in the seventeenth century, a period in which his imagination can move freely among traditions which can be adapted to fit into one another, even if he has to alter geography. *The Grey Man* was serialised but shows little sign of being divided into instalments or into a series of parts. Its characters are in the heart of the action, not merely appended to it in the foreground. The two doomed lovers might have been operatic like Tristan and Isolde, but while Marjorie is a sad remote high-born lady and Gilbert is heading towards being 'a verray parfit gentil knight' in Launce's hero-worshipping eyes, they remain realistic. Their parting under the walls of Culzean is one of anger and harshness. Marjorie forces Gilbert to face facts; he is to marry 'a soiled bower-maiden of the King's court and an earldom with her' and the woman he really loves will not deceive herself. It is a 'black, black world' but they will not improve it by breaking promises they had made to others.[28]

Gallovidians, clutching *The Raiders*, may not all agree, but *The Grey Man* is the best-shaped, best-controlled, best-written of all Crockett's books, and the one for which critics have to make least apology. Galloway, however, comes a close second with *The Black Douglas* (1899) and *Maid Margaret* (1905), both of which receive the same picturesque and imaginative treatment. They belong to history, but in such a shadowy and distant way that Crockett is not trammelled by too much documentation. Their characters come from a period two centuries before the Covenanters and their well-pamphleted sufferings, in a landscape familiar to Crockett from his boyhood in which he can move freely with noble figures traditional, legendary and belonging to folklore. Threave Castle is rich and splendid and the Black Douglases walk proudly in possession of it, the red heart on their banners challenging the Stewart kings.

The Black Douglas begins with all the colour and pageantry of a mediaeval tournament; the sixth Earl of Douglas is the host, and twelve thousand knights and their ladies have come to take part in and view the contests, their tents and fluttering pennants filling all the green fields from Threave Castle to the kirk hill of Balmaghie. Earl William rides his horse Black Darnaway to Carlinwark so that the loose shoe may be made firm by his armourer Malise MacKim, whose two sons Sholto and Laurence are growing up to serve their father's lord.

Earl William rides slowly back to Threave in an 'hour of mystery and glamour';[29] Crockett is here using 'glamour' in its original sense of 'gramarye', deluding false enchantment. He encounters the Lady Sybilla de Thouars and is caught in the spell of her beauty and her rose-coloured silken tent—an illusion too. She is a sorceress, the servant of the wicked Gilles de Retz, French ambassador to Scotland, and at his behest lures Earl William and his young brother David to Edinburgh, to be slain at the infamous 'Black Dinner' by the King's advisers. She has in the meantime come to love William sincerely and his death is softened by the knowledge that she is proud to tell him so before all the assembled courtiers.

Successful in one villainy, de Retz embarks on another. He carries off young Margaret Douglas, the Maid of Galloway, to his hideous fortress of Machecoul in La Vendée. The children of the countryside are disappearing one by one; their blood is drunk by de Retz in order, he hopes, to make him eternally young and their bodies tumbled into the base of one of his ghastly towers. Margaret and her maid Maud Lindsay are to suffer the same fate. Malise and his sons travel to France in search of them; they defy de Retz and his god Barran-Sathanas and snatch the victims as they are about to be sacrificed, de Retz's knife raised above them. Lady Sybilla with a crucifix and calling upon God shakes the castle like an earthquake and brings its towers rocking to destruction. Once again Crockett is following fashion and following it well; *Dracula* had appeared in 1897.

The continuation, *Maid Margaret*, is a longer slower, more finely conceived book; the psychology of Margaret is worked out with delicacy. She, petulant and spoiled, tells the story herself; she is the Countess of Douglas, the lady of noble lineage trapped in the political and warlike intrigues of her day, shut up in Threave while events play themselves out inexorably at a distance. She is married to two Earls of Douglas, her cousin William, noble but cold and ambitious, and then to his brother James, courtly and charming but utterly untrustworthy, after William is murdered at Stirling. James is faithless; he seduces the daughter of Malise MacKim the smith, flies in dishonour, and is defeated at the battle of Arkinholm, near Langholm, which marks the final fall of the Black Douglases. He takes up with a lady whom he calls 'poor Jack Neville's Anne'[30] and Margaret is freed from him by a specious argument in canon law and marries Laurence MacKim, the Abbot of Dulce Cor, whom she has loved all along, ever since she was a child and he made water-mills for her in the River Dee. He is able, in the manner of those far-off days when

> we of the Southern House did much as we liked, in the Church as in the state, our yea being yea and our nay, nay[31]

to disentangle himself from his Abbacy, never having been fully a priest.

Crockett gives us some splendid glimpses of quiet days at Threave; by day

> the plunging splash of the cattle wading clumsily in the shallows of the ford, the iterated calling of a cuckoo far away in the woods of Glenlochar, belated and forlorn, and above all the dark flashings of the swifts' wings athwart the blue oblong of my open window ... the oft-repeated *whish* they made as they crossed before the sill, like the hissing rending of fine silk, and then, seen but all unheard, the same black wings half a mile away, beating the stir as they went.[32]

and by night

> the twilight darkened early into the solid blackness of Egypt. Wrapped in shawls, Maud and I sat about the fire, after we had supped, the candles feeble behind us, and the tapestries on the walls moving in long, regular waves, that seemed to go from one end of the room to the other, giving boars and hunters and steeds a wonderful appearance of life.[33]

Margaret dismisses the murder of the Tutor of Bombie as 'Highland lies sired by the Stewarts and damed by their lick-spittle clerks'[34] and sweeps aside scornfully the country saying that the gallows-knob of Threave seldom lacking its tassel:

> Were not the Douglases noble gentlemen, dukes of the realm of France, as well as the greatest lords in Scotland? ... Would they then, think you, have come home to set so much carrion swinging under their own nostrils and those of their ladies in their mansion of Thrieve?[35]

Crockett moves familiarly within these mediaeval Galloway traditions, bringing his characters in petulance or anger most convincingly to life. The minor characters, shadows in the legends, become fully in the round; we watch the building of Malise's second cannon, the 'Royal Stewart', intended to kill the King yet built under his very eyes and with his interested approval; we see the wedges steeping in their pails of oil, 'black, dripping, polished like glass',[36] ready to slip from their places so that the cannon explodes and kills the King and all his Stewart sycophants—destroying Malise too as he knew it would but avenging the five Black Douglas Earls he had served so loyally. The proud doomed Douglases caught Crockett's imagination more than the Covenanters, over whose squabbling beliefs he was in two minds even while he paid tribute to their courage. And the Douglases were in the heart of the action, not merely touched by it at a distance.

What happens when his characters are illuminated by Crockett's limelight while important events go on in the background is illustrated by *The White Plumes of Navarre* (1906), depicting the wars between Huguenots and Catholics in the sixteenth century—a situation not too far from his Cameronians and Royalists. It starts with the Massacre of St Bartholomew's Eve in Paris; Claire Agnew's father, a Scottish spy, is killed in the street near the Sorbonne leaving her friendless. Three companions come to her aid—an elderly Professor, one of his students, Jean d'Albert, a well-born Catholic, and a strange half-mad Calvinist fanatic called Cabbage Jock. They travel adventurously and picaresquely through a France torn by political rivalries—the Duke de Guise, Henry of Navarre, Henry III, Catherine de Medici, Philip of Spain, crowding in and out of the scene, all at odds with one another. It could have been a rich panorama, but his attention is taken up with the affairs of Claire and Jean.

The Professor takes Claire to the south of France where she will be safe with his mother. But the Spanish Inquisition is on her track; Jean dresses himself in a mantilla and cloak and is taken prisoner instead of her. He is tortured, not with the usual rack and red-hot irons, but with curiously modern devices—a totally silent walled room painted with ghastly eyes which almost drive him mad, and a perpetually burning lamp which deprives him of sleep. Completely disorientated, he is released deliberately and stumbles out into the sunshine where fair-haired Valentine de Niña has been brought to ensnare him. She is a legitimate but unacknowledged daughter of Philip II of Spain. Even in his weakness, Jean resists her wiles, and she, liking him, lets him escape.

Captured once more, Jean finds himself a galley slave, sharing an oar and a bench with none other than Claire's father. Francis Agnew had not been killed; the two servitors sent by the Professor to bury him had thought to sell his body to the doctors for dissection—shades of Burke and Hare—and had thrown a pailful of cold water over him so that the body would 'keep' in the hot weather. This revived him. They had then sold him, much more lucratively, as a galley slave. Agnew and Jean talk much together, of Claire and religion and politics, and Jean gradually is moved to become a Protestant, though not perhaps a Presbyterian.

By chance Valentine de Niña boards the ship. She sees them and has them freed. She has grown to know Claire and finds that she is worthy of Jean's love. Her father the King of Spain has long wished for her to take the Black Veil of the Carmelites and so vanish forever, ceasing to be a dynastic inconvenience. Although she loves Jean, she agrees to do this if he and Claire are spared. A most peculiar marriage takes place outside the convent at Madrid at a special altar and in the presence of King Philip. Agnew gives Claire's hand to Valentine, who in turn gives it to Jean as Claire's bridegroom. Then, knowing that they will never forget her sacrifice, Valentine goes to the convent of the Carmelites; her new name is pronounced, Sister Maria of the Renunciation, and she passes, with one last look at Jean, into the dark shadows and the heavy door clangs sullenly behind her for ever.

We try to take seriously this extraordinarily Protestant view of the religious life, but it is difficult. *The White Plumes of Navarre* is lively and colourful, but its defects as a historical novel are gross. Today that form of fiction has become a much more serious creation than the loves of a Principal Girl and a Principal Boy. *The White Plumes* will not stand comparison with the novels of Sigrid Undset or Mary Prescott or Mary Renault or even Alfred Duggan; in Crockett's time it could not be thought of alongside *The Cloister and the Hearth* or *A Tale of Two Cities*; the Manettes and Sidney Carton were minor figures but the French Revolution raging around them was taken from Thomas Carlyle. The change in taste has made Crockett's Continental-Historical books virtually unreadable except by the devoted student.

An exception is a shorter novel *The Silver Skull* (1901) which, as well as being a good story illustrates exactly how Crockett treated genuine historical sources. It is set in nineteenth-century Apulia, where the different companies of brigands terrorised the neighbourhood. He says he had heard of them first in Brindisi but later found articles in *Blackwood's Magazine* by a Mrs E M Church, wife of a canon of Wells Cathedral; the Rev Canon Church's uncle had been General Richard Church who had served between 1810 and 1820 in the army of the King of Naples against these brigands. Mrs Church had also written a book about her husband's illustrious relative, *Memoirs of an Adventurous Life: Sir Richard Church in Italy and Greece* (1895).

Her story must be summarised briefly. The Vardarelli, she says, were brigands who harassed the two provinces of Apulia but never killed in cold blood; they had a certain glamour, like Robin Hood. They were led by five brothers, the eldest, Gaetano, being their leader, and had a sister who rode out and fought by their side. One day she was badly wounded, and Gaetano shot her to save her from the hands of the enemy.

General Church, alone one day in an inn with only an aide-de-camp, was told that the Vardarelli were nearby—five hundred of them. He summoned Gaetano and asked to be allowed to review them. He stood alone, on a night of storm and rain, while the whole troop rode past him, saluting him. Only Gaetano guessed that he had none of his own troops to support him.

Another much more blood-thirsty and evil band, the Decisi, was led by a priest, Ciro Annicharico, whose eyes had a red tinge. Their practice was to disguise themselves as Punchinellos, mingle with carnival merrymakers, and slaughter them at a given signal. Their sign was a silver skull. They infiltrated a hill castle, Montano, and killed everyone there but one small boy.

The Vardarelli in the end were all wiped out by an angry mob. Ciro in due course was captured, along with his twelve officers; all were condemned to death. At Ciro's execution the crowd muttered and shouted threats; his nerve failed and he allowed himself to be blindfolded before being shot. His head was placed in an iron cage over the gate of Grottaglia, where Canon Church had seen it as a boy visiting his military uncle.

This sounds wild enough to be a fabrication of Crockett's own mind, but he makes it even wilder. The little boy who survived the massacre at Montano becomes a little girl, Isabella, who alone survives a similar massacre at the fictional castle of Monte Leone. It is she who tells the story. Hidden under a table she has seen the dreaded silver skull and witnessed the wild merriment and the killings that follow. Next morning she is found among the corpses by the five Vardarelli brothers; Gaetano takes her up on his horse.

Riding home, they encounter the priest Ciro—known only as a priest—who laments the deaths and reproves them for their violent lives. Only Isabella notices his eyes with the red tinge, and feels fear. She is taken back to their mountain fortress and brought up by their mother; she becomes the sister who goes out riding with the band.

When General Church summons Gaetano, Isabella, disguised as a boy Pietro, goes with him—she goes everywhere with Gaetano who is in love with her—and meets General Church and his aide-de-camp; in the *Pall Mall* serialisation he is called Campbell, in the book Cameron. The review takes place as Mrs Church describes it, only with the storm of wind and rain very much improved upon.

Thereafter Isabella becomes more feminine, performing women's tasks like tending the animals and gathering firewood, only not very well. She is remembering the attractive aide-de-camp. But old habits die hard; when the Vardarelli ride out to destroy the Decisi, she rides with them. They are ambushed, caught between the white-coated soldiers and Ciro's murdering band, and almost completely wiped out.

Gaetano rescues the wounded Isabella; he throws his pistol to his wounded brother Giovanni, wounded beyond remedy, so that he can kill himself; wounded himself, he tries to kill Isabella and then himself, but is too weak. Cameron, unexpectedly in the battle without his men, takes them to refuge in a stone hut. Gaetano who recognises that Isabella loves Cameron, prevails on him to take her to safety and leave him to die in a last heroic stand.

The Vardarelli are destroyed. In a slow dramatic scene, bearers from Cameron's Neapolitan men carry the five dead brothers to their mother and lay them before her. She and another woman harness a cart and take them two by two to a vast cavern in the throat of the mountain in which a massive surge of water rises and falls perpetually, carrying away whatever is laid before it on the smooth wet limestone floor. This is how the Vardarelli dispose of their dead. The mother intends that she and Isabella will follow, but General Church, there outside the cavern, dissuades her by promising revenge.

After a deceptive lull, the General acts. Ciro and his twelve Punchinellos are captured and tried; all (like Deacon Brodie) are respected citizens under their masks. They confess their sins to a priest. Ciro refuses; he cannot make his confession to one lower than himself in priestly rank. Airily he smokes a cigarette as he faces the firing squad, going nonchalantly to his death. As soon as his body falls, the mother of the Vardarelli rushes with a sword and hacks off his head, holding it up dripping blood. It is placed in the cage above the gate.

Isabella in the meantime has been discovered to be the legitimate heiress of the murdered Duke and Duchess of Monte Leone. This means nothing to her. She marries Cameron and as they ride out together on a military errand for General Church, they see the mother of the Vardarelli sitting by the gate, cold and stiff in death, but still looking up with a fixed ghastly smile at Ciro's white bloodless head.

Crockett has added much that is his own to the source from which he drew—the descriptions of the Vardarelli stronghold through the pass in the mountains, the complex crumbling passages of Castle Rotondo where the Decisi met, the dignity of the five brothers as they are borne dead back to their mother, the vast mysterious cavern where the rising water pulls the bodies erect as they pass down into the unknown depths. He has also invented the narrator and her quick dramatic style, a little too foreign and emotional to be everyday English, yet natural for a girl to whom English is a second language, with more exclamatory constructions than usual; Isabella may have married a Scotsman (who does not altogether approve of what she is writing, as she says) but she has remained an excitable Italian. She has told her story well and it is a gripping story, but he has departed so much from the truth that one wonders what Mrs Church thought of his creation erected around her authentic historical narrative.

There is another area of 'historical romance' in which Crockett is both entertaining and original. In *The Red Axe* (1898) and *Joan of the Sword Hand* (1900) he could let his imagination range and soar as he liked because like Anthony Hope in *The Prisoner of Zenda* he was inventing his own reality, and setting his plots in imaginary European duchies, Wolfsberg and Hohenstein, in the fifteenth century when gunpowder was a novelty and printing had just been invented. Wolfsberg was ruled tyrannically and bloodily by Duke Casimir, Hohenstein charmingly but equally autocratically by the Duchess Joan, and the author can play what tricks he likes with landscape and topography so long as the tricks are vivid and unexpected.

A letter to an inquirer, Egan Mew, Esq, of Gray's Inn Place, declares rather loftily in 1897 that

> ...it may interest you to know that 'The Red Axe'; a story of the Baltic lands on which I have been engaged for the past year, is founded upon the annals of the hereditary executioners of these provinces, and reflects as faithfully as possible the period when feudalism was breaking up before the new movements for freedom, as the light of the Renaissance travelled slowly Northward.[37]

Again in 1898 we find him writing to James Thin, his friend the Edinburgh bookseller, asking for a selection of Roman Catholic books—the Douai New Testament, the History of the Popes, Lord Bute's translation of the Breviary and a Roman Catholic dictionary, explaining

I am busy with a book for the *Windsor* which involves Cardinal-Archbishops & other kittle cattle. Is there any history of mediaeval Germany i.e. before the Reformation, and could you get it?[38]

He adds that Smith, Elder sold 25,000 copies of *The Red Axe* in ten days 'which is decent'. Obviously he 'read around' the remote and distant periods in which he had decided to set these two stories, but after what he had done to the source from which he borrowed *The Silver Skull*, we must take this show of historical research with a grain of scepticism.

Both stories are pleasant entertainment in a period manner if the reader is willing to be surprised and amused. Hugo Gottfried, the hero of *The Red Axe*, is the son of the hereditary executioner and will in due course succeed his father. They are both shunned by everyone because of the cruelty and blood with which their figures are seen; they live in the Red Tower along with the sharp gleaming axe, looking down on the city spread out below. On Hugo's clothes are sewn red patches to denote who he is, and the other children shout oaths and curses at him; even the old cleaner crosses herself whenever she passes his father in the courtyard.

As a lonely small boy, Hugo begs from the cruel Duke the life of a small girl whose father is going to be thrown to the ravening dogs as food. Through many incidents and adventures, in spite of the wiles of an enchantress who can see the future in dark pools of ink, he remains true to his youthful playmate. When she is about to suffer cruel death as a witch, Hugo, now Executioner, exercises his hereditary right to save one prisoner during his life by making her his wife. He discovers that she is the long-lost Princess of Plassenberg, and he, therefore, its new-found Prince.

Joan of the Sword Hand is the Duchess of Hohenstein who delights to dress as a man and try her hand as a duellist; her skill is formidable. By her father's will it has been decreed in fairy-tale fashion that she marry the ruler of the neighbouring state of Courtland, on the Baltic. Not unnaturally having considerable curiosity about this person, she travels to Courtland in disguise to see him secretly. Unfortunately she sees his younger brother and falls happily in love with him. He is a Prince-Bishop. A year later she approaches the altar confidently expecting to be married to him; instead he is there in full vestments to marry her to his dismal brother. The marriage goes on, but the wilful bride immediately rides home again to Kernsberg with her four hundred men at arms. War ensues, fanned by the ambitious Prince of Muscovy who is determined to marry Margaret, Princess of Courtland. She, however, has seen and fallen in love with Joan in her disguise as a man and flouts her hateful suitor.

By chance there is a young man in Joan's entourage who bears a great resemblance to her; Joan is taken for safety to a lonely castle by the northern sea and the young man goes to Courtland as the Duchess, still in disguise, which solves the Princess Margaret's problem but leads to magnificent complications.

Events explain themselves. Maurice de Lynar, the mysterious young man, is Joan's half-brother by her father's secret marriage to a noble lady still alive, who in a splendid climax blows up the Prince of Muscovy with his own gunpowder. Maurice is married to Margaret and inherits both the Princedom of Courtland and the Duchy of Hohenstein; Joan counts her rank well lost in marriage to Prince Conrad, who has contrived to buy his freedom from his Prince-Bishopric by a generous contribution to the Vatican coffers of Pope Sixtus. Jorian and Boris, the tall thin man-at-arms and his short fat comrade, slow-minded but stout-hearted, ride, argue, fight and manage to make their loyal way through both tales, and in both there is a wise old councillor who would have been played magnificently by the late C Aubrey Smith.

It is all delightful nonsense, comedy mingling with the drama so as to make easy the reader's momentary suspension of disbelief; and as one would expect of Crockett, the imaginary duchies and principalities have plains and cities, rivers and mountains, villages and byways, described with folklore grimness or fairy-tale delicacy, whichever is appropriate. All the mediaeval trappings are there ready to be made into the old-fashioned kind of colour film or ballet—the snow-covered city of Thorn spread out

> like a painted picture, with its white and red roofs bright in the moonlight[39]

waiting for the brooding Duke Casimir to ride home with his marauders and their victims; he

> loved to come home amid the red flame of torches, the train of bituminous reek, and with a dashing train of riders clattering up to the Wolfsberg behind him, through the streets of Thorn lying black and cowed under the shadows of its thousand gables.[40]

In contrast, the morning of Duchess Joan's bridal day dawns

> cool and grey. A sunshade of misty cloud overspread the city and tempered the heat. It had come up with the morning mist from the Baltic, and by eight the ships at the quays and the tall beflagged festal masts in the streets through which the procession was to pass, ran clear up into it and were lost, so that the standards and pennons on their top could not be seen any more than if they had been among the stars.[41]

In this kind of adventurous colourful romance, whether half-historical or wholly invented, Crockett could write in a mannered style with aristocratic settings, in Ayrshire, Galloway or the Baltic. In them he was free of Covenanters whom, with all the will in the world, it was hard to make fresh and new. Even their deaths, however meritorious, were necessarily monotonously alike, as the many identical tombstones in Galloway and Ayrshire, all in the same lettering, mutely demonstrate. One shooting by a dragoon or dragoons is very like another.

Crockett did his best to invent variety, to enliven the personages of Covenanting times; when he did, his Presbyterian critics were not pleased. It is tempting to think that Marjory Simpson of *The Cherry Ribband* with her expressly more liberal religious sentiments represents a mild rebellion on

Crockett's part, and that *The Grey Man, The Black Douglas, The Silver Skull* and the others were Crockett putting that rebellion into practice by turning his back on the Suffering Remnant and enjoying himself in free creation among vastly different values and characters.

CHAPTER 8

Cleg Kelly Arab of the City

The Play-Actress was the first of many books in which Crockett ventured into areas of contemporary life far from those of his Cameronian and Free Church boyhood. Whatever the setting, there is usually at least one statutory minister, to keep the promise he made in his resignation speech that he would continue in his fiction the Christian beliefs he had preached in his sermons. These beliefs, of course, had broadened and changed since his ordination, and his ministers—those he approves of—tend to be distinctly unorthodox, and in *Cleg Kelly Arab of the City* there is no minister at all. In it he is making a direct onslaught on luke-warm Christians and misguided Sunday School amateurs, and his setting is the Edinburgh slum in which he had worked as a student missionary—the Pleasance.

Cleg Kelly, the slum urchin whose name means 'Horse-fly', appeared first in two stories in *The Stickit Minster*. He proved so popular that a full-length treatment was given to him, serialised first in *The Sunday School*[1] and the prestigious *Cornhill Magazine* before being published as a book in 1896. It shows both Crockett's strength and his weakness. His strength is the unsentimental harsh realism with which he depicts Cleg against the squalid Edinburgh slums in which he was born; Crockett's years as a slum worker had remained alive in his memory since the 1880s, and Cleg afforded a chance to reiterate the Christian Socialism he had expressed in *Vox Clamantium*. His weakness is the rambling narrative made up of 'Adventures' instead of chapters; his memories provided material but it was random and disorganised; the narrative straggles like a series of anecdotes. He uses incidents one after another by fits and starts as he thinks of new items to work into the whole. It is not until he uses an evangelical article about Manchester waifs written by his wife that *Cleg Kelly* makes progress forward directly, from Edinburgh to Galloway.

Cleg himself is so original a creation that he must have been based on some boy, or been the composite of several boys, who had caught Crockett's imagination. Though by 1896 many of the worst conditions had been remedied and the Deaconess Hospital stood on the site which Cleg gave—falsely— as his address in 1893, the Pleasance was still a violent and ugly place; a New College student writing to a friend in 1906 describes the street fighting and drunken brawls with which missionaries still had to contend, and in which his prowess as a Rugby player helped him to manhandle drunks up common stairs to their six-storey homes.[2] The conditions Crockett describes as existing twenty years earlier were not exaggerated.

Liveliness is the core of Cleg's being. He is by no means what the hymn-writer would have called a little candle burning in the night. He is more like a fire-cracker. The good works he performs are startling rather than edifying, undertaken for his own satisfaction, and often accompanied by activities of very dubious merit. Readers expecting the normal Sunday School stereotype must have been jerked into astonishment by the opening sentence, Cleg's declaration to the teachers and pupils of Hunker Court Mission School that

> It's all a dumb lie!—God's dead!

For 'dumb' read 'damn'; which is what Cleg undoubtedly said.

There is a deathly silence as the pupils wait for justice to fall, from man, if not immediately from God. The 'bare-legged loon of twelve' has rejected the platitudes with which the superintendent has been admonishing him, saying that

> ...if you do not repent, God will take you in your iniquity—and cast you into hell. For, remember, God sees everything and punishes the bad people and rewards the good.

This, comments Crockett drily, is 'the most ancient of heresies—that which Job refuted'; he is on the side of the rebel. The outraged superintendent, nicknamed derisively 'Pund o' Cannles' since he is well known for giving short weight in his grocer's shop, castigates Cleg as a blasphemer and an atheist (terms not likely to be familiar to Cleg or his fellow pupils) and expels him as a disgrace to any respectable mission school, unfit to associate with the 'innocent lambs'. But as Cleg is forcibly ejected, he 'explained his position' (a sly hit at theological argument) in terms bitterly true.

> 'It's all gammon, that about prayin',' he cried; 'I've tried it heaps of times — never fetched it once! An' look at my mother. She just prays lashings, and all the time. An' me father, he's never a bit the better—no, nor her neither. For he thrashes us black and blue when he comes hame just the same. Ye canna gammon me, Pund o' Cannles, with your lang pray-prayin' and your short weight. I tell you God's dead, and it's all a dumb lie!'[3]

Cleg takes himself off to the open spaces of Holyrood Park where, having a box of matches in his ragged pocket, he sets fire to the whins to relieve his feelings. As he watches with fearsome fascination the progress of the blaze, two agitated hedge-sparrows flutter above their nest of fledglings in the path of the flames.

> 'Guid life,' cried Cleg, who kept kindness for birds and beasts as the softest spot of his outlaw heart, 'Guid life, I never thocht the birds wad be biggin' already!'[4]

He sacrifices his coat and his ragged waistcoat (all cast-offs given to him by pitying slum-dwellers like himself) to beating out the fire, scorching his hands but saving the nest. The park ranger, roused from his Sunday nap, comes panting up; he assumes, rightly, that Cleg started the fire, but makes no allowance for his having put it out. Cleg's father's jailbird reputation is enough to condemn the son without trial. But the ranger is heavy and torpid; Cleg slips from his grasp leaving the scraps of a ragged shirt behind. He climbs to the top of a high wall, from which he shouts cheeky abuse until this palls and he jumps down and runs off.

This neatly establishes the theme. Cleg is poor, neglected, an outcast, but kind to creatures weaker than himself. For authority he has little respect; it tells him what his experience knows to be lies when it preaches and judges unfairly when awarding punishment. The only exception is Miss Celie, a Sunday School teacher who cares enough for her unruly boys to try kindness and put herself out to help them. The story of the book is how the small flame of kindness and honesty in Cleg, fanned by Miss Celie, combines with his hatred of dirt and love of fair play to make him, without his realising it, a Christian.

Cleg's mother had been a country girl who listened to the wheedling tongue of the Irishman Timothy Kelly and married him, coming with him to the lanes and alleys where he lived and practised his trade, burglary. He beat her when he was drunk, and when he was sober stole the few shillings she earned from scrubbing and cleaning for others, in order to make himself drunk again. Her life was wretched, her only comfort her small son. It is a typical tract scenario, but Cleg, unlike the tearful hero of a tract, fought back.

When he is seven, he falls ill with small-pox, and his father steals the money and wine left for the sick child by the slum minister and doctor, knocking his wife unconscious when she pleads with him. Immediately he is attacked by a small hitting kicking figure from the bed who dashes himself again and again against the man who has hurt his mother. Cleg conveys the infection to his father, but the excitement, says the doctor, is probably what pulls the child through. 'So this adventure' comments Crockett

> tells the reason of three things very important to be known in this history—why, six months after, Isbel Kelly was glad to die; why Cleg Kelly hated his father; and why smooth-faced Tim, who had once deceived the servant-girls, was ever after a deeply pockmarked man. What it does not tell is, why God permitted it at all.[5]

His mind is still running on the problem of evil, which no amount of pious tracts can explain, and which so often seems to make God favour the ill-doer.

In order to make Cleg live, Crockett disciplines his visual imagination, abandoning all exuberance of natural richness and narrowing it down to look through the eyes of the street urchin and describe what he sees. Even Arthur's Seat, that green eminence among parkland rising suddenly with its lochs and romantic crags from among the city streets, becomes merely a refuge from pursuit, without softness, without refreshment. Cleg's district in Edinburgh, the parish of St Leonards, is a rabbit-warren of closes and evil-smelling alleys, a hard indifferent jumble of decaying tall tenements or 'lands', with, farther south, rows of square stone houses all alike in their neat gardens, all middle-class and all hostile to the poor. The landscape is a grim utility one of timberyards and brickfields, coal depots, printing works, railway sidings, public houses, breweries and engineering works. For Cleg, the tenements have walls which his sturdy bare feet can climb; their back yards are hiding-places; the alleys between them easy to dodge through, their chimney-pots and roofs places to which he can clamber and hide.

Cleg's colourless spatial perception of Edinburgh is gradually built up by brief descriptions embedded in the narrative so that we see him perpetually on the move among ash-buckets, common stairs, streets which in their ugliness, static, indifferent, hard, emphasise his optimistic energy. Cleg has known nothing else and regards these places as home because he can survive in them. When he reaches Galloway, he finds its quietness unfamiliar and worrying at first.

> He grew distracted with the silence and the wide spaces of air and sunshine about him. He longed to hear the thundering rattle of the coalcarts coming out of the station of St Leonards. He missed the long wolf's howl of the seasoned south side coalman ... [6]

Only when he comes to the railway lines cutting through this alarming silent landscape does he find comfort:

> Cleg knew himself on sure ground again, so soon as he came to something as familiar as the four-foot way. He felt as if he had a friend in each telegraph post, and that the shining perspective of the parallel metals stretched on and on, into direct communication with Princes Street Station and the North Bridge tram lines, which in turn ran almost to the Canongate Head. He was, as it were, at home.[7]

This same reaction was to be felt by evacuees in World War II when they were taken to the country for safety and found it intolerable. Crockett foresaw it in 1896.

Cleg has learned the necessity of cunning. When his father looks over his jemmies and lock-picking tools, Cleg purposely plays near the police station to show that he is no part of his father's activities. Perhaps his innate honesty derives from hatred of his father. He follows Tim one night as he sets out— a wild Edinburgh night on Arthur's Seat which illustrates vividly Cleg's vision of his native city,

> Tim Kelly bored his way into the eye of a rousing south wind that 'reesled' among the bare bones of Samson's Ribs, and hurled itself upon Edinburgh as if fully determined to drive the city off its long, irregular ridge into the North Sea. Bending sharply to the right, the burglar came among buildings again. He crossed the marshy end of Duddingstone (sic) Loch. It was tinder-dry with the drought. At the end of a long avenue was to be seen the loom of houses, and the gleam of lights, as burgess's wife and burgess moved in this order to their bedrooms and disarrayed themselves for the night.[8]

Tim lays down his bag of tools at a back door and reconnoitres the front. Cleg whips up the bag, runs gleefully back through yards and waste ground to the Loch and hurls it out into the black waters where it sinks forever. He has outwitted his father with satisfying thoroughness and his own thieving method.

When Tim is sentenced to yet another year in prison (Cleg at the back of the court calling out joyfully to the magistrate to make it three years and being summarily ejected, still joyful) Cleg loses his home, a hovel by a brick-yard rented to the Kellys by an avaricious Jew. No Timothy, no rent, so Nathan clears out the sticks of furniture and throws them in the street. Cleg takes his revenge:

> ...that very night, with the root of a candle which he borrowed from a cellar window to which he had access (owing to his size and agility) he went and ransacked his late home. He prised up the boards of the floor. He tore aside the lathes where the plaster had given way. He removed the plaster itself with a tenpenny nail where it had been recently mended. He tore down the entire system of accumulated papers from the ceiling, disturbing myriads of insects both active and sluggish, which do not need to be further particularised ... [9]

This calm precise description of a vermin-ridden hole makes it easy to understand why the police, when summoned by an angry Nathan to uphold his rights, do nothing more than send for the sanitary inspector and leave him to deal with it. In any case, Cleg's thorough search has revealed his father's hiding-places; he puts in a wicker basket a collection of silver spoons, ormolu clocks, forks with the initials broken off, silver teapots, a presentation toddy bowl and nearly a score of watches and takes it all to the police station. From this time on he is 'in' with the police, who in any case are kindly disposed towards the young scamp.

In search of a new abode, Cleg remembers a timber-yard where he knows of a disused construction hut. This he cleans up to his satisfaction, even planting a few drooping daisies in the soil around it. Mr Callendar, the owner of the yard, is astonished at the transformation. Cleg is quick to forestall suspicion. He has whitewashed the interior of the hut: 'I didna steal the whitewash ... I got it frae Andrew Heslop for helpin' him wi' his lime-mixing.' He has tarred the outside: 'I gat the tar frae a watchman at the end o' the Lothian road, where they are laying a new kind o' pavement wi' an awesome smell.' He has installed a mattress: 'It was the Pleasance student missionary got it in, for my mither to lie on afore she died.'[10]

Mr Callendar accepts the explanations and comments sympathetically

> 'Aye, and your mither is awa'' said the builder; 'It's a release.'
> 'Aye, it is that,' said Cleg, from whose young heart sorrow of his mother's death had wholly passed away. He was not callous, but he was old-fashioned and world-experienced enough to recognise facts frankly. It was a release indeed for Isbel Kelly.[11]

There is no sentimentality in Cleg; he has had to develop toughness to match his circumstances. He is not callous, but when Mr Callendar can remark so casually, apparently knowing the details, that Isbel Kelly was better off dead, with no sense of Christian responsibility, he shows that it is in him that the callousness lies, pillar of the Seceder Kirk though he be.

Crockett has unobtrusively surrounded Cleg with adults who are of dubious quality in their business dealings. The Sunday School superintendent gives short weight. The landlord Nathan is a receiver of stolen goods, to be melted down in the back of his jeweller's shop, though the Police cannot prove it. Mr Callendar has men working in his yard planing deal boards so that they can be made to look like mahogany. When Cleg, through Miss Celie's courageous interest, is employed at a papershop, the owner's husband urges him to steal from the till whenever he gets the chance; this is one of the perquisites of the job—he does so himself. The papershop itself is a shebeen where illicit liquor is sold in the back shop. It is also filthy, rustling and crawling with cockroaches under the dirty papers with which the floor is covered. Cleg immediately, without being asked or rewarded, sets to with a brush and clears the infestation away. He stands out brightly against all this accepted corruption, moral and physical; even Mrs Roy grudgingly admits that he is the only boy she has been able to trust with the paper money. It may seem unlikely—even sentimental—that a lad in this environment with so little encouragement could react against it so instinctively. Yet Timothy Kelly is so ugly, so vicious, so filthy in mind and person, that a boy of Cleg's intelligence and with Cleg's reasons for hating him must be turned in the opposite direction. He has seen so much evil that he must immediately see and cleave to the good, in his own way.

The hovel in the brickfield was at least surrounded by clean bright new bricks. The home he has made for himself in the timberyard is as clean as he can contrive. The home of his friend Vara Kavanagh is so much worse that it stands out all the more clearly in its evil-smelling damp horror.

Vara Kavanagh and her two young brothers are not Crockett's own invention. He borrowed them from an article which his wife had written for the *Christian Leader* of 2 July 1892 entitled 'Child Greatheart and her Pilgrims. A True Story of Today', based probably on some experience of mission work in Manchester with her philanthropic father.

'Child Greatheart' in the article is Maggie Sullivan, and her pilgrims are her two young sisters. Deserted by their father who has gone to Glasgow seeking work, they are at the mercy of their drunken Irish mother who alternately neglects and beats them. Maggie runs away with her small charges to look for their father. They meet various kindly and some unkind people on the way, but when they reach Carlisle, railway workers, knowing their quest is hopeless, raise money to send them back to Manchester, where mission workers settle them in homes. Maggie is found a steady job at a mill, where she works happily until her drunken mother appears and shames her. She changes lodgings but lives in fear, and it is decided that all three sisters should be sent out to Canada to make a new life for themselves.

The article, as one would expect from its title, is couched in conventionally sorrowful terms. The mother is a 'sad character', seldom sober unless after a night in the 'lock-up'. She comes home one night 'in her usual state, utterly useless and senseless with drink', hardly managing to 'crawl to the old wooden bedstead and fling herself upon it without a word or a look for her starving children, but this was merciful compared with some evenings, the story of which I shall spare you'. It is no different from dozens of similar articles in evangelical magazines, competent but lifeless.

Crockett takes the framework of the story and builds it into the adventures of Cleg. He alters very little but adds the searing graphic detail which makes everything come to life. He spares the reader nothing. Vara Kavanagh is his 'Maggie' and as real as Cleg; the relationship between them is carefully and delicately portrayed—delicately in that each detail, each look and phrase is exactly suited to the pair of city waifs. Instead of sisters, Vara has two brothers, one a toddler Hugh, the other a baby, and for them Cleg feels the same protective instinct as he had for the sparrows threatened by his fire among the whins.

Once he has settled in his timberyard hut, Cleg sets off to visit the Kavanaghs. They live in a cellar below ground level in 'Tinkler's Land', one of the worst tenements in an area of very bad tenements; their home is one dark insanitary room.

> Cleg ran down into the area and bent over the grating.
> 'Vara!' he cried, making a trumpet of the bars and his hands.
> 'Aye, Cleg, is that you?' said Vara. '*She's* oot; ye can come in'.
> So Cleg trotted briskly down the slimy black steps, from which the top handrail had long since vanished. The stumpy palings themselves would also have disappeared, if they had been anything else than cast iron, a material which can neither be burned or profitably disposed of to the old junk man.
> Vara met him at the foot. She was a pleasant round-faced merry-eyed girl of ten—or rather, she would have been round-faced but for the pitiful drawing about the mouth, and the frightened furtive look with which she seemed to shrink back at any sudden movement near her. As Cleg arrived at the mouth of the cellar, a foul, dank smell rose from the depths to meet him; and he, fresh from the air and cleanliness of his new abode among the shavings and the chips, noticed it as he would not have done had he come directly from the house by the brickfield.
> 'She gaed awa' last night wi' an ill man,' said Vara, 'and I hae seen nocht o' her since.'[12]

The listlessness of Vara's greeting and her weary acceptance that her mother is a prostitute contrast sharply with Cleg's briskness. She is accustomed to be afraid. Moreover, she has a rough bandage on her brow.

> Cleg looked at the bandage with the quick comprehension which comes from a kindred bitterness.
> 'Her?' he queried, as much with this thumb and eyebrow as with his voice.
> 'Aye,' said Vara, looking down at the floor (for in the Lands such things are not spoken of outside the family), 'yestreen'.

This nutshell economy of three words and a gesture shows how often this happens, how much it is taken for granted by the victims, and how close Cleg is to Vara in friendship. But she is not the only sufferer; her little brother Hugh comes towards the voices on his thin uncertain legs. He has one hand bandaged and whimpers over it when he remembers about it, making a sorry dirty unpretty picture; he is whining for sympathy. Crockett is honest enough to show how irritating this could be, refusing to stir the hearts of his readers by depicting a sweet little darling.

> Cleg again looked his query at Vara.
> 'Aye,' said the girl, her eyes lighting this time with a glint of anger; 'the bairn toddled to her when she cam' hame, and he asked for a bit piece. And wi' that she took him and gied him a fling across the floor, and he hurt his airm on the corner of the bed.'
> And Cleg, though he had given up swearing, swore.[13]

Swearing would not be approved of by Hunker Court Mission School but it is a clear measure of Cleg's anger. He has genuinely tried to give up foul language, but this is too much for him, and we like him for it.

The baby is a poor thing of skin and bone with the face of an ancient mummy, but Vara thinks he is 'bonny'. The voices almost wake him up, and Vara hastily hushes him; she wants to keep him asleep because she has no food to give him—she has no food at all.

> 'God!' said Cleg. 'I canna stand this.'

In these words the boy Cleg speaks like a man. He runs off to Mrs Roy of the papershop and by threats and arguments gets her to give him half a week's pay in advance.

> Then, with two intact silver shillings in his hand, Cleg went and bought twopence worth of meat from the neck and a penny bone for boiling, a pennyworth of carrots, a halfpenny cabbage, a large four-pound loaf, and twopence worth of the best milk ...
> Vara met him at the door. She raised her hands in amaze, but mechanically she checked the cry of gladness and admiration on her lips, as Cleg came scrambling down, without ever minding his feet on the slippery stairs.
> 'Cleg Kelly!' said she, speaking under her breath, 'what are ye doin' wi' a' that meat?'[14]

The significant 'a' that meat' applied to twopence worth of mutton scrag and a penny bone hammers home real poverty. But she will not take these riches until she makes sure he does not need them himself. He lies casually but convincingly—'juist some things that I hae nae use for this week'—and she sets about giving the baby its milk and water, happily. Cleg watches for a while, then departs well satisfied. But in case this incident should be too affecting and Cleg appear an angel of mercy, Crockett makes him express his pleasure in a characteristically mischievous act.

> So altogether happy did he feel that as soon as he found himself in a respectable street, he went and cuffed the ears of two well-dressed boys only for looking at him. Then he threw their new bonnets in the gutter and departed in a perfect glow of happiness and philanthropy.[15]

This is so true to Cleg, and so funny, that we share his enjoyment, noting that it is a 'respectable' street, that there are two boys against the valiant one, that they are well-dressed and that their bonnets are new. The contrast with what has gone before is so pointed that we delight in Cleg's cheekiness.

The next day he returns. The door of the cellar is locked and all is silent.

> 'They're a' killed,' said Cleg, who had been at the opening of just such a door, and had seen that which was waiting within.[16]

Here the sobering grim vagueness of 'that which was waiting within' effectively shows Cleg's bitter knowledge. Crockett knows when lack of detail is sinister. Cleg can hear Vara sobbing within, but she tells him to go away.

> 'Vara,' said Cleg, 'What's wrong? What for will ye no open the door?'

The hurt boyishness of the question reminds us that he is only twelve years old, in spite of his adult knowledge. Vara explains that she is tied to the bed; her mother is sleeping off a drunken debauch. Cleg understands immediately 'with his sad unchildish wisdom' and begins to pick the lock, a skill he has learned from his father. The lock-picking is so minutely described that we feel that we too could manage it—fish the key from the inside of the door with string and a hooked wire until he can bring it under the door and use it to open the lock—'a very pretty trick' as Crockett comments.

Cleg frees Vara, and looks for a moment at the sodden heap in the corner with its heavy black hair straggled over its face. He wishes it had been his father so that he could have killed it. Instead he turns to the others.

> 'Come awa' oot o' this, Vara, and I'll bring the bairn and Hugh,' he said to the girl, when she was somewhat recovered.
> 'But Cleg, where are we to gang?' said Vara, starting back.

This almost frightened reaction emphasises the helplessness of children belonging to sluts and drunkards. It is an authoritative Cleg who answers.

> Never you heed, Vara; there maun be nae mair o' this frae this time o'it.[17]

He establishes the sorry little trio in his own hut in the timberyard, their only possession the baby's feeding bottle, and runs off to make all right with Mr Callendar. He is eating his solid delicious dinner when Cleg arrives, having managed to talk his way past the affronted servant-girl. It would have been easy and popular to make Mr Callendar sympathetic at this point, eager to help. Cleg tells Vara's story plainly, working up to a climax:

> 'Will ye turn them away to gang back to a' that?' ...
> The builder, good man, was troubled. The tale had spoiled the relish of his new potatoes, and it was the first time he had had them that year. He turned with some little asperity upon Cleg.
> 'But I dinna see what I can do,' he said; 'I canna tak' them here into my house. The mistress wadna alloo it.'[18]

We can all recognise this; the middle-class conscience of a 'good' man resenting the disturber of its peace. Cleg has the answer. He who has nothing but a rickety old hut will give it to the homeless waifs if only Mr Callendar will let him. This he agrees to do, reluctantly, as long as there is no trouble. Cleg is overjoyed.

> 'I kenned ye wadna turn them awa'—I juist kenned it, man.' Then Cleg realised where he was, and his enthusiasm subsided as suddenly as it rose.
> 'I shouldna behave like this on a carpet,' he said, looking apologetically at the dusty pads his bare feet had left on the good Kidderminster.[19]

The thick carpet, the new potatoes, the servant-girl, the grudging permission which costs nothing, the solid comfort—these all divide Mr Callendar from the poor. He is not a bad man, merely an unimaginative one who is willing to be kindly as long as he is not put to any inconvenience. He even offers Cleg a cubby-hole at his other yard at Echo Bank where he could sleep if he had a blanket. It never occurs to Mr Callendar to give Cleg a blanket himself.

Thereafter the story takes on the lines of Ruth Crockett's article, with Cleg and his hut replacing the children's home. Cleg by skilful blackmail of the Junior Partner in a papermaking firm who he knows is enamoured of Miss Celie finds employment for Vara. Crockett calls the firm the Hillside Works but is probably thinking of Nelson's Parkside Works which occupied the site of the present Scottish Widows Insurance Company. For the whole summer things go well. Vara grows brighter and happier, Cleg delivers his papers and sleeps in Mr Callendar's cubby-hole at Echo Bank, an area at the foot of Dalkeith Road near Newington Cemetery. Then disaster strikes. Sal Kavanagh, swearing and drunk, appears at the factory and shames her daughter so that she cannot go back.

That night Cleg, trying to think of what to do, sees the sky above Callendar's yard glowing red; the yard is on fire. He rushes to save the children but they are not there; instead he stumbles across the soft heavy inert body of their mother, sound in a drunken sleep after setting the fire going.

> Cleg stood a moment wondering whether he would not do better to leave Sal Kavanagh where she was; and more than once since that night has the same thought crossed his mind. He still fears that in dragging her away by the feet from the burning hut, he interfered unduly with the designs of an all-wise Providence.[20]

That brief vignette of Cleg's hesitation before he drags the woman out by the feet—no dignity or compassion here—reveals the hard edge of Crockett's realism. For drunkenness he had no pity, especially when it caused the weak and helpless to suffer. In falling for a moment into the present tense, he seems to suggest that Cleg is a personality outwith the present story whom he knows and with whom he has talked of just such a dilemma.

We lose sight of Vara and her brothers. Cleg can hear no news of her from the police, the milkmen or the scavengers. He has to go through twelve more 'Adventures'—advising a soft Sunday School teacher to give more 'lickings', taking Miss Celie to a 'penny gaff', seeing Big Smith the missionary, following the love affairs of the butcher's boy—before in Adventure XXXVIII he meets Duncan Urquhart, an engine-driver. The worthy Carlisle railway workers of 'Child Greatheart' have suggested a series of railway incidents to unite Cleg and Vara.

Duncan, among other anecdotes—including one about Muckle Alick, the Cameronian railway porter at Netherby Junction, a figure based on Crockett's Uncle Bob[21] tells of a little ragged boy carrying a baby, 'tinkler weans gaun the country' and their agitated elder sister, a 'lassie rinnin' wi' a loaf in her airms'.[22] Cleg recognises Vara and her brothers, and travels down to Galloway with Duncan the next morning.

The story backtracks to pick up the trail of the fugitives. Their long journey on foot follows the 'Child Greatheart' pattern, but with each incident made alive by graphic and unexpected details. Other incidents are added; a stalwart young minister with a stick and a soft hat and a strong resemblance to Crockett prevents their being robbed by a sturdy beggar. Little Hugh wanders off one night and meets a little girl who offers him a kiss: 'What is a kiss?' inquires Hugh, repeating the Walter Anderson incident from *A Galloway Herd* and pointing forward to Peter Pan eight years later. *Cleg Kelly* was dedicated to J M Barrie; he must surely have taken from it Peter's much better known query, along with other traits which Peter shares with Cleg—solitariness, boasting, skill in swimming, a tendency to crow and show off, a great pride in his own cleverness.

One morning the three are found asleep under a haystack; this gives another chance to mock the respectable. Mary Bell the byre lass finds them but her mistress, like Mr Callendar, will not take them into the house (the master would not allow it) but sighs sentimentally about how bonny they are, calling to her mind what she imagines is a Biblical text, 'I will both lay me down and sleep, in the land of the leal'.

> 'Aye,' said Mary Bell, '"In the land of the leal". Ye had better gang ben and look up the text, mistress. I'll attend to the bairns.'[23]

When the children reach Galloway, they are met with kindness and pity, expressed in help and comfort. The tone of the writing changes, the warm-hearted simple humour of the country people is mellow in contrast to the sharpness with which the city characters are treated. Hugh and the baby remain with the childless Alick and Mirren at Sandyknowes (Uncle Bob being supplied with a wife for the sake of the plot) while Vara goes out to service with the sister of a neighbour, a Mrs Walter MacWalter, who will train her well, though she is known to rule her husband and household with rough vulgar scolding—the country is not all ideal; it has its shrews as sharptongued as those in the city. Among the MacWalter household is a lad Kit Kennedy whom readers may perhaps have met already in a sketch in *Bog-Myrtle and Peat* (1896) and would meet again later in a full-length novel. His main function here is to love Vara and arouse savage jealousy in Cleg; as Vara leaves the MacWalters to go back to Mirren, Kit asks only for one kiss, recognising that it is Cleg who has and deserves her love because he has served her so well.

Cleg's association with railwaymen—for example 'Poet Jock' who sings one of the railway verses of 'Surfaceman', Alexander Anderson, one of Crockett's 'Laureates of Labour', enables Crockett to slow his narrative and digress for several pages on the virtues and hard lives of railway workers.

> A railway never sleeps. A thousand watching eyes are at this moment glancing through the bull's-eyes of the driver's cab. A thousand strong hands are on the driving lever. Aloft, in wind-beaten rain-battered signal-boxes, stand solitary men who, with every faculty on the alert, keep ten thousand from instant destruction.[24]

Crockett, fascinated by railways since his uncles went to be porters at Castle Douglas, never lost his interest. They crop up over and over again in his books. He himself had, according to tradition, worked as a booking clerk at Castle Douglas during vacations. At Bank House, in the days of his prosperity, he entertained to dinner occasionally Mr David Deuchars, Superintendent of the Line, and Mr Paton, Stationmaster at Waverley. Humbler members of railway staff ran to carry his bags when he was seen alighting from a train.[25] Here he sings their praises in gratitude; two and a half pages are devoted to these unknown heroes, little regarded and poorly paid, taken for granted by the travelling public and by holders of railway shares. In this he included himself; he held shares in the railway.

In order to stress his theme, he uses Muckle Alick as one heroic railwayman who, because of a wild night and a series of accidental errors and miscalculations made by overtired, overworked men, gave his own life to save the passengers of the express from London to Stranraer connecting with the steamer to Larne.

> With a hoarse roar and a leaping volcano of fire-lighted smoke the express leaped by, the glow from the engine illuminating for a moment the strong man bending with tense arms and set face over the bar beneath the overturned waggon.
> 'Thank God! Thank God! Thank God!' muttered Muckle Alick between his set teeth as each winking carriageful tore past, the travellers within reading their papers or settling themselves to sleep, alike unconscious of their deadly peril and their brave deliverer.
> But something, it was thought the iron framework of the catcher on the postal car next the guard's van, suddenly caught Muckle Alick and jerked him thirty feet from where he had been standing. And then, without so much as a

quiver, the express flew past the Junction and out again into the darkness, the black tempest hurtling behind her and the engine whistle screaming a true man's death-knell.[26]

Crockett knew his trains. It was the postal car that did the damage, the one which in the days of steam trains had a projecting arm to pick up packets and letters in their bag from where they hung ready, so that an express did not need to stop to collect the mail. The wording of 'it was thought' suggests that Crockett had been present at an inquiry into just such an accident, and used it for his fictional hero.

Alick himself it is who comforts his fellow-workers as he lies in the left-luggage office, dying, surrounded by his colleagues stricken with shame. His strong Cameronian faith makes him calm in the face of death, his concern all for others. He reflects that Mirren his wife will find his death hard to bear since there are no children to comfort her, then says

> more brightly, 'There's three comed noo, though. Maybe they'll be a blessin' to her. The Lord sent them to her, I'm thinkin'. He wad ken o' this aforehand, nae doot.'[27]

Vara and her brothers, outcasts without a place in the city, are in Galloway part of the great unfolding purpose of God.

Up to this point, Crockett has been drawing on his own experience in the slums and among railwaymen, leaning on his wife's article for the backbone of his story. Cleg's travelling to Galloway with Duncan and cheating over a train ticket he has no money to buy towards the end of his journey are convincing and credible, true to every detail. After this, Crockett's imagination goes wild, as it often did when he was left to devise his own plots, although in this case the narrative remains calm and serene, visualising everything precisely, with a quiet explanation of how everything has come about, though the events themselves are beyond belief.

Cleg through his cheating meets General Theophilus Ruff, retired from the Indian Army, and enters his service as cook, servant and handy-man-factotum. General Theophilus is monstrously contrived. He has survived the Indian Mutiny but been driven mad, it seems, by his love for a lady who played him false. Once he led a brilliant social life at Barnbogle House, his splendid mansion, but now, since his Indian servant died, he lives there alone, guarded by a multiplicity of locked gates and doors, surrounded by art treasures but allowing no woman to come near. He sleeps in a strong-room under the mansion dug from the adamantine rock, the door of which opens and closes by hydraulic time-locks answering to a combination he sets and resets himself. His bed is an open coffin, with one closed coffin on each side of it. He settles himself to sleep each night by smoking Indian hemp, with a mechanical contrivance to raise his head and shoulders at regular intervals lest he accidentally brings on apoplexy or asthma.

One can usually find a source for Crockett's sensational touches—even the minister singing Handel to the cows—but this one defies explanation. The only ordinary fact stated about the General is that the Junior Partner who is in love with Cleg's Miss Celie is his nephew.

Cleg, with his inimitable capacity for taking things as they come, without wonder or fear, becomes a contented and efficient servant, carrying out all his peculiar master's commands as long as he has mornings or evenings off to help Mirren with her house and small-holding. For her he chops sticks and carries water, then returns composedly to cook herring and bacon for his master after changing his clothes (by the General's command) as if there were nothing strange about Barnbogle House at all.

> 'And how do ye get on wi' the daft General?' asked Mirren, with great interest in her tone.
> Cleg was amused at her question. He had become quite accustomed to the wonder on people's faces, usually shading into awe, when they asked him concerning his position in the household of the redoubtable General Theophilus Ruff.
> 'Fine,' said Cleg, 'him and me 'gree fine. I hae nae fault to the General.'[28]

He remains discreet about his master's sleeping arrangements but is quite willing to describe the vaulted passages, the iron-barred casements, and the little lean-to kitchen and bedroom for himself built on to the mansion. He sleeps and works there, cooking herring and bacon, but never using any of the corned beef in tins on the shelves which he has been ordered not to touch.

He is kept busy, and this suits him. Besides, he has changed since he came to Galloway. Not only has he grown up, but he has developed under the influence of the kindly God-fearing people among whom he has found a place who never try to hector him into religion by texts or threats but show a quiet unselfconscious example. For the first time he belongs to a community and is respected. He has thought of a way of earning a living for himself—setting up as a grower of rare wild flowers, which there are in abundance in Galloway. He will be a market gardener with a difference, cultivating species otherwise unobtainable or dying out and sending them by mail to his customers—a remarkably modern idea for 1896. He has even thought of 'speaking' to Vara, but cannot quite think of how to do this without becoming 'soft'.

Then Timothy Kelly and Sal Kavanagh stagger back drunkenly into the story. On the very night when the General tells Cleg that he has the premonition of death for which he has been waiting, they break into Cleg's kitchen, lured by the General's fabled riches. Cleg has just time to shout to the General to go to the strong-room before he is knocked unconscious.

He lies thus for twelve days, tended by Vara and Mirren and the local doctor. When he comes to himself, he tells where the search for the General should be made, but the combination hydraulic lock is too much even for its manufacturers when they do not know the word at which it is set to open. Dynamite must be used. The General is found peacefully dead in his coffin, Tim Kelly with a bullet in his head, Sal dead out of sheer terror, and the two other coffins now open. On one side of the General there lies a beautiful young lady's embalmed body, with the label 'False Love', and on the other side, a similarly embalmed young man, with the label 'False Friend'.

This splendidly sensational array of bodies is no problem to the Galloway lawyers who are men of experience. The bodies are all buried 'as privately as possible, the two embalmed bodies being laid within the private mausoleum at the foot of the garden. For in noble families a private burying-place is a great convenience in such emergencies'.[29] Sal Kavanagh and Timothy Kelly lie there too, the Procurator Fiscal making no difficulty since he was a friend of the Dumfries solicitors who acted for the General and revealed the contents of his will. His nephew the Junior Partner inherits the mansion and land, and £30,000 'lying money' is bequeathed to Cleg in return for his faithful four years' service. Unfortunately, not a penny of this fortune can be found.

Crockett is so quiet and persuasive about all this sensational nonsense that we almost suspend disbelief. He has tied up every end neatly, and above all he has maintained Cleg and Vara exactly as they have always been, inarticulate city waifs grown up into better times, in spite of the Grand Guignol circumstances in which they find themselves. Cleg is still a shy 'rough diamond' whose first expression of affection for Vara is the remark that

> ye are takkin' your meat well to a' appearance.

Vara is well content.

> It was more to her than all Kit Kennedy's sweet speeches ... 'He maun think an awfu' deal o' me to say that!' she told herself.[30]

And this is only right. To launch them into romance would have been false and sentimental; they plight their troth in terms of milk and butter, the leasing of Springfield Farm as well as Mirren's small-holding, and Vara coming to help Cleg run it.

> Do you think that ye could—(Cleg paused for a word dry enough to express his meaning)—come over by and help me to tak' care o't? I hae aye likit ye, Vara, ye ken.[31]

Even when Vara discovers through curiosity the hiding-place of the vast fortune stowed away by the General, she takes it in a very matter-of-fact manner. Miss Celie comes rushing with excitement to tell the others, but

> Vara was standing at the table at which Cleg used to cut the bacon for the General's breakfast and his own. She was calmly opening tin after tin of Chicago corned beef, cans of which stood round the walls. Each was filled to the brim with bright, newly-minted sovereigns.[32]

It is all too much. The reader is stunned to laughter at the wild inconsequence of it all—which is probably what Crockett intended. He had said what he wanted to say about the wickedness and harshness of the slums and the courage of the individual in the face of apparent hopelessness. He had castigated the hypocrisy of middle-class Christians who take no notice of poverty and cruelty, just as they ignore the heroism of railwaymen. Then, having preached both directly and indirectly to his readers, he rewards them for their patience with a rattling good tall story. He had said several times that he did not like the Novel of Purpose; it is quite conceivable that the mad ending and the astonishing General were his apology for having inadvertently written one. There was much of the spirit of sheer mischief in S R Crockett.

CHAPTER 9

Kit Kennedy: Country Boy

It would be difficult to put a date to the events chronicled in Crockett's comedy *Lads' Love*, serialised before publication in *Lady's Realm* and appearing as a book in 1897. It is set in Galloway, but like many of his Galloway domestic love stories it has no internal references by which it can be fixed exactly in time. *Strong Mac* (1904), for example, begins with a ploughing-match between older 'man-muckle' boys playing truant from school. The school is run by a dominie and a daughter whose situation is similar to that of Duncan Duncanson; poachers are mentioned, gamekeepers, lairds, smiddy arguments, an alleged murder and much lively talk which could be late nineteenth century, and it is with some surprise that one finds the heroine setting out for Spain to bring back Sidney Latimer as the strongest possible proof that he has not been murdered. He is an officer serving with Wellington in the Peninsular War.

Changes in agricultural methods and farm practice came slowly in Galloway and the farmers, dairymaids and ploughmen of Crockett's childhood may have differed little from their counterparts at the beginning of the century, but credibility is a little strained by the discovery how early in the century the story is set. However, *Lads' Love* has no such hidden surprises. It is called 'an Idyll of the Lands of Heather', one suspects with tongue in cheek. Idylls Scottish, Irish and Welsh were proliferating at the time, and Barrie's *Auld Licht Idylls* were in no way comparable to Tennyson's *Idylls of the King*. He called his tales of strong rough weavers *Idylls* because they are totally unidyllic. So with Crockett. There is more rough-and-tumble love-making and bucolic trickery than could possibly be called idyllic.

The narrator is Alec McQuhirr, the son of Saunders of *The Stickit Minister*; he is a student at Edinburgh University but in the Faculty of Medicine, not of Divinity. He is not going to be a minister. He comes home for long vacations and enters fully into the light-hearted daffing of the girls at the farm of Nether Neuk, most of it thriftily taken from *A Galloway Herd*. Crockett weaves into it the tragic love of Rab Anderson's daughter Lizbeth for the cheating packman Nathan Murdoch, whose flashy watch chain and breast-pin were not enough to warn the inexperienced girl of his lying tongue. Her father almost kills Murdoch for seducing his only child, but the packman does not die. He recovers, but only just; he is left childlike and dependent, bereft of understanding, but a greater joy to Lizbeth his wife than he would have been as his full evil-hearted self. She shows him infinite love and care, and he cannot be without her.

The minister puts his hand on the man's head.

'Perhaps,' he says to comfort her, 'he is being tried in the furnace here below and will come out, hereafter, as gold that is seven times refined. Though now he be dead while he lives, yet may his true life be hid with Christ in God!'

For which doctrine, though doubtless it comforted the woman, his Presbytery, had they known it, would have entered into judgment with him.[1]

Crockett again declares himself a rebel through his minister—who plays no other part in the story. The drop into the present tense is unusual; one could imagine him using this kindly and imaginative theology to console a woman like Lizbeth himself. Here he does it by proxy.

In *Kit Kennedy: Country Boy* there is no fretting about dates. In it he returns to the familiar landscape and personages of his boyhood and depicts himself growing up in Galloway through Kit, his chief character. The book was serialised in the *People's Friend*, a much more serious and literary publication than it has since become, before appearing as a book in 1899, and the publishers, James Clarke and Company, knew that it followed a path so much like Crockett's own that they advertised it as 'Mr Crockett's *David Copperfield*', though hastening to add that the events are not to be identified with those of the author's own life.

In fact, Crockett's childhood had been so happy and uneventful—so ordinary—that it was necessary to add a great deal of spice to make a story out of it. The habit of nostalgia for vanished childhood *per se* had not yet arrived. It took two world wars and the disruption of the accepted social structure and beliefs to make childhood, plainly and delicately described in all its small pleasures and sunlit gardens, something to be thirsted after like a lost paradise, though Stevenson came near to it in *A Child's Garden of Verses*—perhaps because he brought about the disruption himself.

Crockett had to build on to his memories some sort of plot to hold the attention of readers in the 1890s and 1900s. For good measure, he took several and tangled them together, with his familiar fields and lanes as the setting. His illegitimacy was a good point at which to start, though it had to be doctored a little and made acceptable. On to it he grafted stock Victorian melodramatic themes—the woman betrayed and left to bear her shame alone, the girl persuaded if not forced into a loveless marriage by the villain who holds the parents' debt over her head, the plausible charming lover who proves false and flies from debt and denunciation, the lad of promise who goes astray in the wicked city, the aged parents turned out of their home by the villain, the blustering redfaced rich well-dressed man who is recognisably the one Victorian audiences loved to hiss. They are all familiar clichés but given a strong Scots flavour they lose their triteness in the originality with which they are made flesh.

The geographical setting of young Kit's boyhood is exactly the same as that of *The Lilac Sunbonnet*, Loch Grenoch, the Crae Hill, the little stream where the horses are watered, the gate, the lane and all, but instead of prosperous Craig Ronald there stands a long, low, one-storied white-washed farmhouse called Black Dornal (an anagram of Ronald), recognisably Little Duchrae.

Matthew Armour, ruling elder of the Cameronian Kirk on the Hill in nearby Cairn Edward (Castle Douglas), farms there with the help of his wife Margaret, his son Rob, and Betty Landsborough the faithful if frivolous servant-girl. Matthew is a portrait of Crockett's grandfather, just as the sharp-tongued Margaret is his grandmother, but their daughter Lilias, Kit's mother, is—like her name—too airy-fairy to pass as a true picture of Crockett's mother poor Annie. Kit's circumstances, a boy in a household of adults, are those of Crockett himself, and to him Crockett gives many of the experiences of his own boyhood. Yet the total impression left by the book is much darker and more sombre than that left by the *Sunbonnet*. It depicts merely the ordinary familiar workaday background of a small farm, seen as a realistic peasant would see it. Ralph Peden in the *Sunbonnet* finds country life a radiant source of life, drenched in sunlight. Kit takes it completely for granted and pays little attention to it. The narrative is full of the dark days of winter, the snowy mornings at five o'clock when the neaps have to be sliced for the sheep, hands blue and aching, storms over the hills, the harsh treatment landlords could mete out to tenants at their whim, the poor food, the bitter greed and inhumanity of farmers—some farmers—to their workers. The Armour family stands out in piety and kindliness against the kind of social structure described by Robert Burns, where farming is a hard killing struggle and the factor's 'snash' can make or mar a farmer's life. Even Edinburgh, when Kit reaches it, seems to consist of haar during the day and cold foggy nights on the Meadows or windy streets with snow in the air. There are sunlit passages if one looks for them, but the total impression is grey and bleak.

Crockett invents for Kit an educated father Christopher Kennedy, MA, classics master at Cairn Edward Academy. There is a tradition in Galloway that Crockett knew who his father was, that his mother one day lifted up her young Sam so that her son could see the man who had wronged her, and that he was well-to-do and prosperous. If this be true, it may well be the genesis of the fictional Christopher Kennedy whose fine words and charming manners win the heart of Lilias Armour. The opening chapter where Lilias keeps tryst with Kennedy at five o'clock on a summer morning, she letting out the cows, he ostensibly botanising, is the sunniest part of the book. Yet there is a hint of sorrow to come; Lilias is inexpressibly happy to hear that she is so beloved that Kennedy wishes to marry her, but shows alarm and fear when he says that he has already spoken to Bell Kirkpatrick about acting as a witness.

> There came a quick, leaping terror into the girl's face.[2]

She knows that she is pregnant, but has not told him.

They go through the old-fashioned Scots form of marriage in which the acknowledging of one another as man and wife is sufficient to satisfy the law, as long as there are two witnesses. There has to be such a form of marriage to save Lilias's reputation with the readers of the *People's Friend*; the secrecy is necessary because Kennedy is a gambler and a drunkard, and Lilias's father has sternly set his face against him as a profligate.

And not without reason. Kennedy suddenly disappears, without warning or farewell to Lilias; he has been dismissed from his post in disgrace, penniless and leaving many debts behind him. In due course Kit is born, to all the world (except the readers of the *People's Friend*) a shameful bastard. True, Lilias has the marriage certificate given her by Kennedy, but when she shows it to her father, he scorns it as worthless, being unsanctified by God's blessing, and burns it before her horrified eyes. This part of the action Crockett has borrowed, along with the name Armour, from the father-in-law of Robert Burns, who cut the names out of Jean Armour's similar certificate thinking this the best way of invalidating it. At least Crockett's character has the sense to be more thoroughgoing about the matter.

Matthew Armour, as well as regarding the certificate as worthless, has been told by Walter MacWalter, an incomer to the district from the same northern fishing village, Sandhaven, as Kennedy, that Kennedy is already married to a local fisherman's daughter, Mary Bisset—he can produce the documents. His interest in the matter is that he wishes to marry Lilias himself. We are not shown the 'courtship'; the book jumps from Chapters II to III with the marriage in between, so that both author and readers are spared the embarrassment of events that must inevitably have been painful and distasteful. MacWalter is

> a well-attired, well-groomed figure, leather-breeched, riding-whipped, blatantly aggressive, floridly prosperous,[3]

so stereotyped a stage villain that no ruling elder would have let him under his roof. He never comes to life for a moment, but strides through the book with his riding-whip looking out for some further villainy to commit. Wisely, Crockett leaves the marriage a *fait accompli*, leaving us to note how Lilias has become a sad, weary, ill woman, while Kit is now a lively youngster of six or seven about to enter upon his schooldays. From other parts of the book we learn that MacWalter has held over Lilias's head the bond he holds for a debt of six hundred pounds incurred by Matthew's father (it would not have been seemly or in character for him to have incurred it himself); for her parents' sake she has yielded, without any pretence of love for or to him, going to live with her husband in the fine new red standstone house of Kirkoswald and leaving her son to be brought up, a happy mischievous boy, by his grandparents. She visits him when she can, when her surly husband is away at market. He is no pleasant companion; sitting in the mansion raging at his wife for loving her 'nameless loon' he

> grunted, thrust his fingers into the bowl of his pipe and turned the red-hot contents out upon the polished mahogany of the dining-room table.[4]

He is coarse and brutal in every word he says to her, and it is little wonder that she has gradually lost her beauty, her spirits and her health. One wonders why she remains with him, but the religious code in which she has been brought up declares that a wife must stay with her husband at whatever cost and keep the promises she has made.

Crockett has thus provided us with two villains at which to hiss, one a bully, the other a cad. It is later that we see which of the two engages his imagination.

At first, MacWalter is in the ascendant. He persuades the factor to wheedle the local Lord, always in need of money for his 'ladies', into letting him sell Black Dornal to MacWalter in order that he may have the pleasure of evicting his father-in-law. This affords the chance of describing a country 'roup' such as Crockett must have seen at first hand when his grandfather retired from farming and moved into Castle Douglas.

The neighbours buy the stock and plenishings at good prices, out of sympathy with the Armours, but they are not idealised as Ian Maclaren idealises the Drumtochty folk in 'The Replenishing of Burnbrae' in *The Days of Auld Lang Syne*; there the purchasers buy the plenishings and present them back to the tenant as a gift when the eviction order is rescinded. Not so in Galloway, where peasants are neither so wealthy nor so willing as to give away with swelling bosoms goods for which they have paid. They are indignant, but cannot afford expensive operatic gestures. But the sorrow of the old couple is brought out movingly, contrasting with Kit's cheerful excitement; boylike he does not fully understand what is going on but runs to and fro, insisting that his toys be auctioned so that his granny will stop crying. As he brings his pet lamb Donald to be sold, the frightened animal knocks against MacWalter, already in a bad temper because Matthew Armour is not sufficiently cast down and has paid, in full view of all, the whole amount of the six hundred pound debt. MacWalter kicks the helpless animal. Kit leaps up to his throat, seizes his beard and bites him, holding on in fury until he is pulled away. The sympathies of the onlookers are with the child, despite his outrageous behaviour.

They are shown in other actions, less unlikely than those of Drumtochty. A kindly landowner, disliking MacWalter and admiring Matthew Armour, gives him one of his cottar houses in which to live. Betty Landsborough insists on moving with them and staying, even without wages.

> Service in a countryside so primitive as Whinnyliggate argued nothing of social inequality. And Betty Landsborough, the daughter of the cooper in the village, a man with a good business connection, took her place not as servant but as helper, almost as daughter, in the house of Black Dornal.[5]

The signs are that in the end she will marry Rob Armour. And old Matthew is not too proud to learn a new trade. He becomes a breaker of stones for the road, helped by the advice of a kindly roadmender who teaches him the right way to tackle the stones so that they split or break easily. His minister comes out to see his elder at work, sitting on the wall beside the heap of stones he is in the process of breaking and sharing humble bread and cheese while they talk of their beloved Kirk and theology. Armour has lost no respect by MacWalter's action; it is MacWalter who, thinking to crow over the old man's degradation, is quietly put in his place when he rides out to show himself superior. Armour will give him no satisfaction.

> The evil as well as the good is in God's hand, not in yours, Walter MacWalter. I pray that these threatenings come not home to your own door.[6]

The sombre colouring of the story is by no means due to the Cameronian household, although in other hands it might have been. Crockett has grown up in an atmosphere which, although pious and devout, is warmly human. The stern duty of the father is so handled as to keep him both dignified and kindly; he has feeling for his daughter even when he must seem to punish her most. When she has fled in despair after her marriage certificate, her all, has been burned,

> He stood a long while thus praying, his face softening strangely as he did so with a kind of inner light shining out from it.
> 'Perhaps *I* have done wrong,' he said, 'as well as that poor young lassie.'
> And as he shut the book he said again yet more gently than before, 'My poor, poor lassie!'[7]

It is a curiously moving picture of a father carrying out his duty according to his lights, working against the expectations of post-Shelleyan romanticism, Crockett insists that we respect the father even while we sympathise with the daughter.

There is a warm loving relationship between Kit and his grandfather; Kit is a favourite, to his grandmother's half-scolding, half-laughing despair.

> 'A bonny like thing,' she went on shrilly, among her milk pails, 'that after bringing up his ain in the fear o' God and a guid hazel stick, Matthew should be turned aboot the wee finger o' a bairn like that. It's easy seen that some folks are growin' early doited.'[8]

This is obviously a reflection of the situation when Crockett was a child at Little Duchrae; his aunts have disappeared and of his uncles only one is retained, but what we know of William and Mary Crocket fits this mellow picture of the small boy stealing cream and running to his grandfather's knees for protection. The grandmother's exasperation is not altogether harsh, either.

> 'No that he's sic an ill bairn either,' she said, relentingly, 'but only that mischieevious and worritin'. Ye'll meet the loon wi' a face on him like a thanksgiving service, an' ye think what a grand wiselike bairn. But a' the same ye are safe in giein' him a daud on the side o' the head, for I'se warrant ye that he's either on the road to some ill-doin', or coming direct frae a mischief.'[9]

There is affectionate comedy behind this outburst, with long slow vowels taking away the sharpness. Mrs MacWalter of Loch Spellanderie farm, MacWalter's sister-in-law, invariably scolding Kit when he is her farmboy, is given speech which shows her meanness and spite, rattling with consonants colliding with one another.

> 'Shake yoursel' weel, na', an' knock your great clamperin' feet on the doorstep,' cried the voice of Mrs MacWalter, as Kit laid his fingers on the latch of the kitchen door. 'Whaur hae ye been a' this time? D'ye think I pay ye good siller and feed ye up wi' the best o' meat for you to gallivant aboot the countryside? ... Gang and sit by the door, and be thankfu' that ye hae a meal o' meat to eat in a decent God-fearin' hoose, which is mair nor a nameless kinless loon like you has ony richt to expect. And no a word oot o' the head o' ye, pervertin' the minds o' my innocent bairns and bringing disgrace on your maister, that may be an elder o' the parish in twa-three year, gin he keeps in wi' the minister and the factor.'[10]

Crockett's ear for speech differentiates between the speed and even the pitch of the two voices. Margaret Armour is a peppery old lady who enjoys sharpening her tongue on those she loves without for a moment meaning a word of it. Mrs MacWalter is a spiteful scold whose sharp phrases are meant to hurt. She taunts Kit with his fatherless state and does not hesitate to call her household 'decent' and 'God-fearing', a claim which Matthew Armour even in his dealings with his daughter had not presumed to make. The cheap boast that her husband may be an elder some day in the Established Church 'if he keeps in wi' the minister and the factor' is far indeed from the humility with which Matthew Armour walks before his God. And we know about the 'best o' meat'; Kit has to eat the left-over porridge which he shares with the dogs and have recourse to his own cleverness in taking milk from the cows secretly as he fodders them. The two households of the Crae and Loch Spellanderie are shown as two extremes in a countryside in which the norm is probably somewhere between the two.

Kit's schooling at Whinnyliggate is described in detail; Kit is quick and clever, bilingual in that he can use English as well as Scots speech; the other scholars are dull and oafish in comparison.

> Presently the hum of the school droned lower and lower. The arithmetic pupils along the wall communed as to results in subdued tones. The writing classes joggled each other's arms and elbows with cautious circumspection. Dominie Duncanson leaned back in his chair and bethought him of his new pupil.
> 'New boy, what's your name?'
> 'Kit Kennedy, sir,' said Kit, the polite son of his father, rising to his feet.
> The action instantly roused the deepest resentment in the breast of every boy in Whinnyliggate School. They gazed at him in amazed horror.
> 'Did ye hear him?'—the whisper ran swiftly as ill news athwart the school—'he said "Sir!" And he stood up to answer the maister.' And then heads were shaken, and resolves were taken that betokened no good to Kit Kennedy. Such a disgrace had not been heard of in Whinnyliggate School within the memory of boy. Who was this upstart that had come off the heather to take away their good name?[11]

Worse is to come. Kit when tested reads Macaulay at first sight, without effort,

> while the master gaped, and the school paused in its scufflings to listen in an amazed contempt, which slowly sank into a kind of dull uncomprehending disgust.[12]

Kit had to 'fecht', and fecht hard, to restore his schoolfellows' respect after this extraordinary lapse. He has shown that he is eager to learn, and must pay for being so different from the other country clods. Fortunately, he can hold his own—as Crockett did in his time. The school itself, governed by the tawse and with pupils uninterested and bullying, gives no very complimentary picture of Scottish rural education, the master very different from Ian Maclaren's venerated Domsie of Drumtochty.

Kit learns in spite of rather than because of his schooling; his education, says Crockett,

> was easily gotten. He had the natural faculty for letters which makes nothing difficult. He was possessed of a good general idea of the next day's lessons before the other scholars had done marking the place.[13]

He does not bother to take his schoolbooks home with him but hides them under the hearthstone of an old mill halfway along his road home—the mill that was used in connection with Leeb M'Lurg. He can catch out the master in finding Newfoundland on the map.

Crockett may here be innocently giving himself away. So much of Kit can be shown to be based on himself that this easy facility in learning may likewise apply to him. It would explain many of the defects which mar his later fiction. If he had this happy knack of picking up information without effort, and 'never remembered the time when he could not read any book which came in his way', Crockett would inevitably fall into habits of carelessness, inaccuracy, lack of thoroughness, and it is these which emerge in much of what he wrote, defects in so much that is otherwise strong, vivid and lively, especially in description. He wrote quickly; mistakes crept in; and he was too impatient by temperament to consolidate and make sound.

In order to carry out the plot, Kit has to run away from his kindly home and easy-going school to enter the bitter harsh service of Mrs John MacWalter of Loch Spellanderie. This at first consideration is not the sort of thing he was likely to do. It is unnatural, incredible even. Crockett surrounds it with small details, none of them improbable, but all of them together carrying the story over the hump and suspending our disbelief. We know how much importance his mother and grandparents placed on his education. By a skilful arrangement of simple events, Crockett makes Kit appear to have told a lie about attending school one day when he has played truant only in the morning. Hurt at their not taking his word, he refuses his tea and strays out, feeling justifiably wronged in the way that small boys do. MacWalter is lying in wait for him. He suggests to the boy, now twelve, that his keep is a burden to his grandparents in their reduced circumstances. Kit thinks this over and finds truth in it. MacWalter offers him employment at Loch Spellanderie because he is sure that his sister-in-law's vicious domineering will break Kit's spirit and turn him to evil ways, which in turn will break his mother's heart. Kit, however, having accepted the offer, is healthy and philosophical enough to put up with the harsh treatment, the unfairness, the constant abuse, reflecting that 'After all, she keeps me' and taking his wages proudly home to his grandparents every quarter day.

It is at this point that the second villain, Christopher Kennedy, MA, comes back to the scene, no longer a charmer but a drunken tramp whom Lilias finds lying asleep by the quarry. She gives him money to go away—she does not wish him to find out that he has a son—but the banknotes are marked and enable MacWalter to have him arrested for theft. Three months in prison and six months in the poor-house hospital give him back his health; his hand no longer trembles. On the day of the fatal truancy, Kit's mother has found him swimming in the loch; for the first time she tells him of his father (without naming him), how she had loved him but he had been weak and forgotten his duty and his promises. She is afraid that Kit, by playing truant, will be like his father; she warns him and sends him on his way to school. By chance, Kennedy is among bushes nearby; he hears the whole conversation. It completes his return to manhood. From this time on he is always in the background watching over Kit. His son has given him a purpose in life.

This could have been as melodramatic and stagey as MacWalter's villainy, but again Crockett overcomes the improbability by building up the small convincing details. Kennedy had thought that Lilias was dead—someone had told him so. This is the weakest link (apart from Kennedy's being in the bushes in the first place) but he was just the sort of man who would accept this hearsay as truth and take it on trust out of laziness. As they talk, a faint ghost of the old feeling between Lilias and Kennedy emerges. Kennedy in self-mockery uses a Latin tag: '*Vive memor amoris nostri—et vale*'.[14] Lilias immediately, automatically, instinctively, asks 'What does that mean?', as she had done often before, and in that flash we can see the relationship that had existed between them and know that it is not entirely dead.

Kennedy takes a job as an Orra Man—a general labourer—at a farm near Loch Spellanderie to be close to Kit. Again Crockett makes this credible by details; the farmer has a useless poisoned hand, labour is scarce, the 'tramp' would not ask high wages. The kindly farmhands and ploughmen at Cairnharrow respect him as a 'weel learnit' man fallen on bad times, and goodnaturedly help him learn his work at the stables and in the fields. Kennedy learns quickly. He gets to know Kit naturally when they meet at the smiddy; the Orra Man offers Kit a lift home, and on the way offers to teach him Latin and Greek, if he likes.

Kit does like; had he not sworn to his mother that one day he would be a Great Man and settle her in a big house? On his next visit to Dumfries, Kennedy seeks for the textbooks he will need. He looks for them in a junkshop in Friar's Vennel, a place highly unlikely to stock the classics—immediately improbability, incredibility raise their heads—but there, row upon row in a glass cupboard, he finds his own old books.

'There,' cried the old man, laughing senilely, 'if ye set up for a learned man, there's something to bite on. She bocht them at the sale o' a dominie that ran awa' frae Cairn Edward a lang while since—made a munelicht flittin', that is. You'll see his name on the boards. He was just desperate for debt, they say!'[15]

This rings very true. Kennedy explains that he cannot afford to buy them all at once but will do so in twos and threes as he can manage. The man assures him that there is no hurry; there's not much learning in Dumfries and even Bibles and Shakespeare are a drug on the market. The Stewartry man cannot resist a dig at the neighbouring county town; this type of 'in' joke is simple enough for anyone to appreciate but especially welcome to Gallovidians.

Kennedy and Kit arrange to meet every evening when their day's work is done and enter upon three years' hard study. The situation is so well embedded in homespun detail that we are convinced that Kit can enter for the Galloway Bursary and win it.

> Both the 'Orra Man' and Kit lived for these stolen hours, when by the light of a stable lantern they read together the solemn-sounding, grave-thoughted Latins, and after a while, with infinite stammering, the nimble-witted Greeks.
>
> During all that first winter Kit met his teacher every night in the Black Sheds—certain ramshackle erections of wood on the boundary line of both farms. Here, wrapped in old sacks, and by the feeble shine of a tallow dip set in a stable lantern, Kit mastered his verbs regular and irregular and so macadamised his way to the Latin version which he hoped one day to write.[16]

As he did his work on the farm, Kit had lists of vocabulary on the barn door, irregular verbs affixed to the harness in the stable, and rules and inflections pinned above his candlestick. His learning went on during the day's work as well as by the teaching at night. Crockett's magpie mind may have borrowed this touch from the story of David Livingstone, who had educated himself by night classes and learned by day from books propped up before him as he worked at the cotton-mill in Lanarkshire. The story would be familiar to Scots readers and to many readers abroad, and the parallel, though never made explicitly, makes Kit's success all the more possible.

The examination time comes on, it too being surrounded by solid Castle Douglas detail—Crockett had gone through the ordeal himself. He adds the additional joy of Mrs MacWalter's rage when she discovers that Kit is a candidate, competing against her clod of a son John. Kennedy waits anxiously for Kit to come out from each paper, interrogating him about his answers and calculating his possible marks with a short pencil stub in the margins. As for Kit, he

> had never sat in an examination hall before, and the rustling of so much printed paper, and the scratching of so many pens—all moving rapidly forward, foundered him for a little. But soon the wits came back to him, and he remembered the classical master's advice—the easy questions first, and keep cool.[17]

When, a fortnight later, the results are announced, Kit has won. Rob Grier from Garlieston, the friend he has made from among the candidates, has done so well that he is given a second subsidiary bursary. When Crockett sat and won in 1876, the same had happened; the one who came second and was similarly rewarded was Bob Blair, who went on to become a prominent educationalist, Sir Robert Blair, Director of Education for the London County Council.[18]

Mrs MacWalter's raucous outbursts can be imagined. The Orra Man is so carried away with joy that he goes on a glorious celebration in the Black Boar and has to be driven home dead drunk in the Cairnharrow cart by a sorrowful Kit, who reproaches himself for having reduced his friend to this sorry state—a touch both comic and unexpected.

Thereafter comes Edinburgh, lodgings, matriculation and new friends. The most important of these last are a family who live on the same stair as Kit's landlady and are called Bisset. Daniel Bisset is a free-thinking educationalist—Crockett calls him an Infidel Lecturer—who combines social work with teaching. He has a daughter Mary, also a teacher, a pleasant young girl with firm ideas of her own; Kit falls in love with her. He has a son Dick who introduces Kit to questionable companions and steals his Bursary money. But just as Kit is escorting Mary from Dick's flashy supper party in St James's Square to the equally flashy Elysium Theatre (the Theatre of Varieties, opened at the east end of Chambers Street in 1875), Christopher Kennedy appears at the doorway as a kind of avenging angel, no longer the Orra Man but an authoritative figure who forbids Kit to enter such a den of iniquity. For reason, he reveals that he is Kit's father.

Many revelations follow. Daniel Bisset is Kennedy's old friend of Sandhaven days, the brother of the Mary Bisset MacWalter alleged that Kennedy had married. Kit fears that his father has stolen his Bursary money; the quick-witted Mary guesses that the thief was her brother Dick, forces him to disgorge as much of it as he has left, persuades the jeweller to take back a brooch he had bought and refund its price, and makes up the rest of the stolen money out of what she had intended for a winter coat. Through Bisset, Kit is introduced to a kindly Free Church minister Dr Strong who works with Bisset in the slums; this is a portrait of Dr Alexander Whyte. Dr Strong has been a college contemporary of both Bisset and Kennedy, and acts as *deus ex machina* in unwinding the tangle; miraculously he can produce both Nick French, the second witness at the irregular marriage, and a copy of the certificate. Along with Bisset, he interests himself in the further reformation of Christopher Kennedy.

Letters come from Galloway telling how oddly MacWalter is behaving, shutting Lilias up a prisoner from all contact with the outer world and talking of taking her to Sandhaven at Christmas. Bisset, Kennedy, Kit and Mary set off to rescue her, which they do on a sunny snowy Christmas morning when the now insane MacWalter is on the point of pushing Lilias over Baxter's Heuchs to her death on the rocks far below, just as twenty years before he had pushed his first wife—Mary Bisset. His tale had been lies, the documents forged. Lilias wakes from a faint to find herself in the arms of her true husband,

Christopher Kennedy, and MacWalter, trying to escape, is so terrified by the resemblance of young Mary Bisset to his dead wife that he starts back, stumbles, and falls to his death over the cliff crying 'Mary Bisset! Mary Bisset!'[19]

Lilias and Kennedy are thus united, Kennedy having found a teaching post in Edinburgh. Kit returns to Edinburgh University and wins two medals, Mary's scoldings having had their effect. Unfortunately she is now a rich woman; Walter MacWalter 'with one of the curious freaks of violent and passion-driven men' (convenient for novelists hurrying to end their book since they are of their nature inexplicable) had left his possessions to Mary, 'the only daughter of his dead wife'.[20] This is all very well, but how had he known of her existence? Is Daniel Bisset whom she normally calls father really her uncle? Her worthless brother has called her 'a foundling picked out of a hedge root',[21] information which he says he has gleaned from his father's papers. But surely Walter MacWalter cannot be her father, although he was her mother's husband? Was she born before the first Mary Bisset was pushed over Baxter's Heuchs—she must have been if Walter MacWalter knows of her; she certainly cannot have been born after this sad fatality. It seems as if Crockett had intended a further twist to his narrative, but either had not time to work it out or in the end found there was not room in his allotted instalments but carelessly left its vestigial remains to irritate anyone who has been trying to make sense of the story.

The reason for the riches is clear; Kit must be cast down by the vast difference between the rich young lady Mary has become and his own humble station, even if he has won two medals. On the advice of Betty Landsborough, he shyly approaches her; she lets him see that she loves him and wants nothing more than to be his wife.

In contrast with the sensational but carefully detailed ending of *Cleg Kelly*— in contrast with the careful detail of the first three-quarters of the book— this ending is sheer nonsense. It frays away into ragged edges. Kit's University career is dealt with in a slack and slipshod way, without the stiffening details that could make it alive. It takes a poor second place to his friendship with the Bissets, perhaps because Crockett's own University career, dominated by journalism, was so far from normal that he could not visualise the life of an ordinary student. There is a brief flash of vividness in the ending, in the white Christmas landscape and the grumbling Hoggie Heuch the ostler, but Crockett was writing carelessly, without editing or checking. Alastair French of the early chapter is Nick French at the end. Bisset's wife on one occasion addresses her husband as William instead of Daniel. And worst of all, Crockett leaves us without any definite information on what Kit's future is to be. He and Mary plight their troth, but will he return to his University life and become a minister as his mother had hoped, or will he settle down to manage the estate of his rich wife? One can see that Crockett might find difficulty in consigning him to the ministry since he himself had made that decision and changed it later. Yet the *People's Friend* readers might have disapproved of their hero's being lured from that sacred calling by his wife's wealth. He had created a dilemma for himself, and we are left cross because he did not solve it; Kit has been such a real and lively character that he deserved more thoughtful treatment.

It is interesting, however, that the theme of the story is not, as in 1894 and *The Lilac Sunbonnet*, the liberating influence of nature and the countryside on a personality too much dominated by dry learning, but in 1899 the liberating influence of education which frees Kit from the ploughman drudgery of the land. Crockett knows how a clever mind can be choked by hard realistic circumstance; had it not been for John Cowper and the Bursary in 1876, he himself would have remained a country lad or become perhaps a railway porter. The trend of the book is towards education. The Armours want Kit to do well at school. Lilias has set her heart on his becoming a Great Man, preferably a minister. All are sadly concerned when he plays truant and seems to be neglecting his school-work. Yet Crockett is by no means sympathetic towards the village school or its schoolmaster; he is critical of the rule of the tawse and the sluggish stupidity of Kit's classmates. Uncle Rob, when he goes to Loch Spellanderie to find out how Kit is faring, reports

> ...the man is an honest man, though the woman is an ill-tongued tairger. But I wad let him bide a while. The boy wasna learnin' muckle at the schule onyway![22]

It was Christopher Kennedy who educated Kit—the equivalent of John Cowper of Cowper's School in Cotton Street, Castle Douglas, whom Crockett revered. Yet there is no hint that Crockett ever questioned the merit of a system which makes Latin and Greek the only escape routes for clever boys—and for girls no escape at all. Crockett is no rebel in this; he accepts what he has known. There is no suggestion that country children should be given an education more suited to country life. Future farmers, future ploughmen and future wives are all subjected to the same mechanical unimaginative educational grind not at all adapted to their lives on the land. It is because of this, perhaps that Scottish literature is so full of mothers longing for their sons to be ministers. It was the easiest way out—easier than medicine or the law.

The Bisset family in Edinburgh continue the educational theme. Bisset is a lecturer though we are not told on what or where, and Mary is a capable teacher, good enough not to be handicapped by her father's free-thinking reputation, and well able to take Kit to task for laziness. Dick is the shifty character on whom education has made no impression; he is sent off to the army as a last resort.

The Edinburgh chapters introduce Dr Strong with some care. He is a minor character in the plot, merely a friend who in an unexplained way is able to sort out the tangle, but the fact that Dr Strong is based on Dr Alexander Whyte forces Crockett to elaborate the portrait he gives; he cannot pass over his revered old master without doing him justice. By using him, too, he can express some of the ideas which are still working in his mind. Daniel Bisset works among the slums, trusted by the police, an influence for good in spite of his free-thinking. Kit accompanies him to the bedside of a poor cobbler in the Grassmarket who is dying, and he sees the cobbler's wife angry with Bisset, blaming him for leading her husband away from Christianity.

> 'You are very ill, Bartholomew!' said Mr Bisset, touching the man's wrist lightly, and as it seemed mechanically, in search for his pulse.
> 'I am going, sir—going to find out!' He smiled as he said it.
> 'Ah, Bartholomew, I envy you to-night if that be so,' said the Lecturer sadly, 'that is the best thing after all. They have called us Agnostics so long—Know Nothings. You have your chance now to prove them wrong.'[23]

Bartholomew is worried because of his wife and children, left without the provider by his death. Bisset comforts him in quiet talk, then says that his family will be cared for by a man he knows.

> 'What, not a minister?' cried the voice of the cobbler, 'No minister would trouble himself with the wife of a dead unbeliever.'

If this be true, it says little for ministers, but Bisset knows at least one who is prepared to work in harmony with agnostics, those whom people call atheists though Bisset denies that they are so empty a thing.

> You are no unbeliever, Bartholomew. Only fools are unbelievers. And, at any rate, Alexander Strong would not care what you were. I promise you that your wife and bairns shall not want.[24]

Bisset and Kit go from the Grassmarket to rouse Dr Strong at a tall house, Number 52, in a fashionable quarter. Dr Whyte lived at 52 Melville Street before moving to 7 Charlotte Square in 1889. Crockett is a little out of date, but he is describing the man as and where he knew him.

> Then the minister came out, a tall squarely built figure with a leonine head and a countenance grave and kindly, capable, too of kindling into an Isaiah fire upon occasion—a man affectionate in private, tender of heart above most, but dangerous to cross when charged with his message and when the decks were cleared for action.[25]

The three walk together to the Grassmarket, and in the snowy darkness

> the Agnostic Lecturer and the Christian Teacher conjointly laid their plans for the helping of poor human creatures.[26].

Whether or not such close co-operation did take place—and it in all probability did—it is clear that Crockett wanted it to. We would be glad to hear more of it, but it is mentioned only in passing, though in its unexpectedness and its precision of articulation it remains in the mind much longer than the shadowy Dr Strong producing solutions out of thin air. Crockett is still on the side of the goodness that is strong enough to be unorthodox, unbound by the dogmas of any one church.

He shows us the Preacher of the Gospel standing looking down on the serene face of the dead Bartholomew and saying gently

> Fear not! It is written, 'to his own Lord he standeth or falleth. Yes, he shall be made to stand, for the Lord hath power to make him stand.'
> And his hand was upraised over the dead face as if in benediction.[27]

If this be not the doctrine of universal salvation put into the mouth of a real identifiable Free Church minister of status and authority by his friend and disciple S R Crockett, it is very like it.

CHAPTER 10

Scenes of Contemporary Life

I City and Country

We have seen how in historical romances, Crockett is happiest when he has a framework on which to build, even although he departs from it. When he writes of his own times, he usually has no such framework. In *Cleg Kelly* he could write of a Pleasance urchin in a string of anecdotes but without his wife's 'Little Greatheart' article the book would have lacked the movement to Galloway which is its backbone. *Kit Kennedy* contained so much of his Galloway boyhood that it ran on fairly convincingly for the first half of the book, but to end it he used so much intractable material borrowed from melodrama that it shuddered to a halt and fell to pieces. In *Ione March* (1899) he is writing on his own, putting together scenes and occurrences as they came to him, and for all their variety the reader is disappointed.

Ione March is a young well-educated American woman determined to earn her living as a typist (eleven years before Barrie's *The Twelve Pound Look* in 1910); her story ran in *Woman at Home* as *The Woman of Fortune* before it came out as a book with three chapters added. Crockett never visited the United States but had met in Switzerland two pleasant Americans to whom *Ione March* was dedicated; possibly on their account the heroine was American. She has lived a life of relative luxury—her father is the Governor of Callibraska—but longs to be independent, one of the New Women. After a leisurely holiday in the Alps, during which she meets two friendly Englishmen and breaks off her engagement to Kearney Judd, a brash American who cannot climb but blames his honest guides, she goes to London, with her father's permission, to find employment through her own ability. She works in a typewriting agency but finds herself favoured and leaves, regretfully, when she discovers she has been employed through her father's influence. She becomes secretary to a very odd business tycoon but leaves when he falls in love with her and proposes marriage. She meets once more Keith Harford whom she has known and liked in Switzerland; he has just been appointed teacher in a College of Dramatic Art; remembering her success in amateur theatricals, she signs on as a student. The School is shabby and dusty, on the verge of bankruptcy, and reaches it within a few days, throwing both Ione and Keith into unemployment again.

Her situation is now desperate. Her father, unknown to her, is facing financial ruin in New York; she learns of his death through over-hearing the spiteful comments of Kearney Judd who, with his father's shady business deals, has contributed to Governor March's ruin. She continues—of necessity now—as a flower-arranger at a group of hotels but is deeply unhappy. Discovering that Keith Harford is ill—with that favourite vague illness 'brain fever'—she rescues him from a grasping landlady and sees that he is looked after by her own kindly Scottish one, never letting him know that she is near, though his 'ravings' show that he is in love with her.

The sister of Kearney Judd, a lively chattering American beauty who has no time for her father or brother, sweeps back into the plot with Marcus Hardy, Keith's friend in Switzerland, whom she has married against her parents' wishes. Together she and Marcus take Ione and Keith (now convalescent) to Rayleigh Abbey, where Marcus's mother presides over a motley household of spiritualists, faith healers, ritualistic followers of something called 'The Power'. Mrs Hardy imagines herself in love with Keith and is enraged when he favours Ione. With some difficulty they get free of the strange house but not before a clairvoyant has told Ione that, since she prayed to God that her life be taken in place of Keith's, she will in truth die before long. Weary and ill after all this (and little wonder) she goes to a famous consultant who tells her that she has only a year and a half to live. In spite of this, without telling Keith, she marries him for the sake of the happiness they will have while they can.

They are marvellously, idyllically happy. Ione manages Keith and his work as a writer, correcting faults in his manuscripts and making editors pay him what they promise. He becomes more and more successful but Ione is haunted by the spectre of death. She returns to the same consultant and when he examines her he is surprised; the shadow of illness, whatever it was, has passed from her, she is healthy and well and she is expecting a child. The story ends on this high note of joy and hope.

The book has no recognisable 'plot'. It meanders rather than progresses from one episode to another, sometimes hiccuping badly in the transition. The scenes are sketched in adequately but not brilliantly; even the Alps are merely a slight unemphatic background. Crockett can add touches which light up a scene—the roomful of girls at the agency typing with their machines each chattering with its distinctive note, the 'masher' who accosts Ione and is knocked over by a girl friend's young man, the dim cold rehearsal rooms at the dramatic college, the knowing professional talk of the disillusioned students, the unhealthy drugged swaying of the groups at the Abbey chanting meaningless incantatory words in subdued light or flaring torches—but his mind is not engaged. He is writing for the readers of *Woman at Home*, combining the clever independent woman who was in the public eye at the time with the loving mother-figure whose career is with her husband and her home. He has made up for his lack of description by multiplicity of scenes, but this does not constitute a unified story; *Ione March* is not even as good as *The Play-Actress*; it is a competent pot-boiler and is of interest mainly because Crockett has realised the social changes brought about by the typewriter.

Two books may be considered as rooted in Galloway in a time roughly contemporary with Crockett's own, though there is little indication of the date of their settings—*Cinderella* (1901), serialised in the *People's Friend*, and *The Loves of Miss Anne* (1904). *Cinderella* retells with a Galloway and London flavour the story of the disregarded girl who marries the prince, and this keeps ingeniously to the plot—more or less. *The Loves of Miss Anne* has such a simple theme—the shepherd lad who makes good and marries the heiress—that Crockett has to fill the chapters between beginning and end with whimsical diversions of his own creation. The second story is loose and uncontrolled because of this structural difficulty; the first holds together better.

The Cinderella is Hester Stirling, the fairy godmother is the Duchess of Niddisdale, the two ugly sisters are cousins Ethel and Claudia, Prince Charming is Carus, Master of Darroch, the Duchess's grandson. Hester has been brought up by her grandmother Mrs Stirling at the prosperous Galloway farm of Arioland; her mother died when she was born and her father, outcast by his father for marrying far beneath him, has sworn he will never again enter Arioland and gone to Burma to make his fortune at the ruby mines.

He appears briefly (but only in the garden) when Hester is a little girl and gives her a ruby necklace to play with; it is rescued and put away safely by the Stirling's old family retainer Megsy Tipperlin. He also brings a large mysterious leather bag which he asks his mother to deposit with the family lawyers in Drumfern; it is put away in the store cupboard and forgotten about, pushed year after year farther to the back out of sight behind the jars of jelly and jam on the top shelf.

When old Mrs Stirling dies, her daughter and son-in-law the Torphichans come quickly up from London to claim Arioland and all it contains for themselves, except for the £2,000 left to Hester in her grandmother's will; they would claim that too if they could. Sylvanus Torphichan, Hester's uncle, is a doctor eager to make his way in society. He finds the leather bag of rubies but says nothing about them, even to his wife; they will be a good foundation for his career. Hester is an unwanted poor relation; the Torphichans are relieved when Megsy offers to take Hester herself and bring her up on her own savings.

Megsy goes to Mr Borrowman the minister for advice. He has just dismissed his thirty-ninth housekeeper for dusting his books and tidying up his room. Megsy, invited to be the fortieth, is scornful until the minister proposes a working arrangement.

> '... suppose we agree to meet each other half way. I will not observe that you have been dusting, if you will refrain from moving one single book out of its appointed place.'
> 'D'ye ca' this the appointed place o' that buik, minister?' said Megsy, pointing to the top volume of a pile on which the master of the house was leaning. 'There, what did I tell ye——'
> The pile slipped sideways on its unstable foundations, broke in the middle, and distributed itself over the floor with a slithering clatter, disengaging clouds of dust on its way.
> 'I'm making you an offer, Margaret!' said Mr Borrowman, quite impervious to so slight an event as that.
> 'And I'm answerin',' said Megsy, 'if ye will gie a bit quiet hour to the bairn's learnin' when ye hae nocht better to do, I'm willin' to bear wi' your temper

as far as is in mortal woman, and also to leave your buiks in their appointed places—savin' always those that may be as it were accidentally disturbit!'[1]

So the matter is settled, in a way which gives a pleasant Galloway flavour to Hester's happy childhood. She is brought up by Megsy and 'Revvie' with a great deal of love and an education both sound and Presbyterian, spoiled by both her guardians without losing her sweetness of temper.

The trials come when the Torphichan-Stirlings (as they now call themselves, having risen in the world) remember the £2,000 legacy when Hester is nearly twenty-one and demand that she come down to London to be governess to their younger children. They are a spoiled rowdy lot who have terrified former unfortunates but by her fairness, her honesty and her refusal to be bullied she wins their respect, though the two eldest sisters resent her as a rival. Victoria and Tom, the middle range, take her side, and Hester is by no means unhappy with her London company; when an Anglican clergyman, shocked by her Presbyterian allegiance, proposes to 'instruct' her into the finer truth, she sends up to Scotland for books to confound him—

> ... please, dear Ursa Major, send me Pearson on the Creed, and Doctor Whyte's book on the Shorter Catechism, and Rutherford's Lex Rex—and anything else you can think of, and oh, Principal Rainy's Reply to Stanley, and everything. I will read them all, so that I may be quite ready to be instructed. There is not much fun here, but I think that will be funny.[2]

Crockett, like many Scots, found Anglicans, especially Anglo-Catholics, much more irritating than the Church of Rome.

To the rage of Ethel and Claudia, Hester delights the heart of the Duchess of Niddisdale; the Duchess gives a ball for her and insists on dressing her in rustling silken attire and dainty shoes; the Master of Darroch sends to Scotland to have heather especially for her—he has known her as a child. Like Cinderella, she startles everyone with her beauty. She startles Sylvanus, too, by wearing the ruby necklace with delicate gold chains which her father had given her and Megsy kept safe. He immediately accuses her of theft, saying that the necklace is one of his, and has her charged and taken into custody. The Master of Darroch bails her out and takes her to where she will be safe, with an elderly French dancing master and his wife, aristocrats both, refugees from the Revolution.

An Old Bailey trial follows, described in detail with witnesses for and against Hester. Carus Darroch has a friend who is a clever barrister; he calls as witness an expert from the Burmese Embassy who interprets the words carved on the stones. They belong to David Stirling, Hester's father, as do the other rubies in the possession of her uncle—by now Sir Sylvanus Torphichan-Stirling, a Member of Parliament and a prominent philanthropist. Cast down publicly and disgraced, he commits suicide. Hester, acquitted but still under a shadow, takes refuge with Megsy in Galloway, where after a long search Carus, Master of Darroch, finds her and tells her of his love. They are married in the Manse garden, Hester wearing her mother's wedding-dress instead of the superb creation made for her by Madame Celine—Megsy has treasured the simple plain dress and the Duchess understands. As a final joy, Hester's father, long thought dead, escapes from prison in Burma in time to come to the wedding—and faint with the happy shock of seeing Hester so like her dead mother.

The Cinderella theme, given a twist here and there, adapts neatly to the Scottish touches, and the London sisters and their father provide suitable heartless effects. The Duchess of Niddisdale is a delightfully outspoken and eccentric old lady, enjoying outwitting the Torphichan-Stirlings who court her for her title's sake; she cheerfully devours yellow-covered French novels which lie alongside the *Gardeners' Chronicle* in her boudoir, and gardens energetically, bullying her old Scotch gardener. The sympathetic Torphichan-Stirlings are lively romps, and the reader is human enough to rejoice that Victoria is to marry the ineffectual but kindly Lord Kipford. The London localities are firmly worked out; the Torphichan-Stirlings live in Empress Gate, the Duchess in Scotstarvit House, SW and the police station to which Hester is taken is Ebury Street.

The most wildly Scottish of the characters is old Megsy Tipperlin, whose tongue would clip clouts but whose softer side is for Hester. She is at her best in invective, which she justifies by comparison with David in his denunciatory Psalms, such as the one Mr Borrowman had read the previous Sunday:

> ... whatna precious and comfortin' psalm o' Davvid's was that! Ah, he was the graund man, Davvid. Ye speak aboot puir Megsy Tipperlin, but ye canna blame her aboot her tongue, as lang as yon is within the leds o' the Bible. Hearken to Davvid. 'Let them be confounded and put to shame ... let them be turned back and put to confusion.' 'I'm wi' ye, Davvid' says I, 'and when ye are at it dinna forget that their name is Torpheechan.' 'Chaff before the wind let them be. Let their way be dark and slippery, and let the Angel o' the Lord chase them'. (Torpheechans hear ye that—I'll hae Gawbriel himsel' hard on your tail afore I hae dune wi' ye!)[3]

This is not altogether caricature; the older generation knew their Bible and like the Covenanters were grounded in the Old Testament.

> Oh, Davvid, Davvid, though ye were a terrible chiel amang the lasses, ye had the root o' the matter in ye, and wi' a fu' heart and a willin' tongue auld Megsy will pray your prayer: 'Rescue my soul from their destructions, and my darling from the power o' the lions'!
>
> It was indeed small wonder that Megsy Tipperlin preferred the Old Testament for her private reading.[4]

The same Megsy can be tender as she guards Hester and prays that she may be happier than her mother whose life was brief and clouded with sorrow. Yet when Hester's happiness dawns, Megsy knows with flashing clarity that she has given up most of *her* life's joy.

> 'Megsy, Megsy,' she said, 'ye hae lost your bairn for ever and a day. She is her mither's ain dochter. Frae this day forth she will never cast mair nor a

> kindly thocht ower her shooder to auld Margaret Tipperlin that happit the baby clouts aboot her, and wha's heart has yearned ower her ever since, night and day, dark or shine. Oh, Megsy, Megsy, verily ye are a weedow and a woman without bairns this day.'
> And with her apron to her eyes she lamented bitterly, because that for which she had besought the Lord with tears in the night watches had been given to her.
> For the cup of the Lord's brewing is ever a mixed chalice when He chooses to set it to our lips.[5]

This is the ironic truth, but few writers of romance would be honest enough to point it out so sharply.

The Galloway background is full of Crockett's affectionate remembrance, from Dalveen Castle where the Duchess in tacketty boots digs fertiliser into the roots of her rosebushes with a spud and a graip to the graveyard where Anders MacQuaker has bought a plot next to the Tipperlins' one; Megsy has refused to marry him but he will be buried near

> so that at the judgment-day her and me will sit up in oor shrouds thegither, and I will juist nod to Marget, and she will nod back, weel pleased-like to see a kenned face at sic a time. For we will no be able to hear yin anither speak for Gawbriel and his trumpet![6]

He enjoys like Carus the smell of the store-cupboard at Arioland with its rows of bright jars of jam and jelly, jewel-like in their colours, the white pots of redcurrant jelly, the marmalade with long amber straws lying across it cut into lengths, the scent of the honey as it is strained through gauze nets into the clear glass jars. The cottage high in the hills above the Clachan of St John's which belongs to Anders but is lent to Megsy and Hester to give them privacy is most vividly brought before us.

> Megsy lit the lamp and went from room to room with her nose in the air. Of these there were but three—the kitchen, wide and blue-flagged, its beams rough and hung with hams, and with shining utensils on the wall. A tiered and many-plattered dresser climbed to the eaves, gay with blue willow-pattern. Strings of onions and dried herbs wavered in the dusky V of the roof where the wood-smoke hung. Then there was the 'room,' where a white bed, turned down to show pillows and white linen sheets like the drifted snow, waited their pleasure. A new 'register' grate in the fireplace, told that Anders had been at Cairn Edward, and had left some of his hard-earned 'siller' with the local ironmonger.
> There was even a carpet in lurid hue on the floor, and pictures on the walls representing incidents of the chase in scarlet and grass-green. A great family Bible, bound in what must indeed have been 'whole calf' (if not cow), lay on a worked wool-mat on the chest of drawers, to represent the outlook upon the spiritual, and on the table general literature was represented by a fishing-book of wonderfully dressed flies.
> At the back a little room opened off, just affording space for a bed, a round table, an oaken chest, and one chair. In this Megsy without a word bestowed

her chattels. After she had finished her inspection, during which she had said no word of praise or blame, she turned to Anders, who had followed her from room to room with anxious brows of suspense.

'It'll do,' she said, generously, 'it's nane sae ill—for a man.'[7]

It is neither romantic nor idyllic; it is a Galloway cottage with homely furniture, a smoky fire, onions and herbs among the beams, a splash of colour in the willow-pattern plates (the commonest pattern), a new grate and a 'worked wool-mat' which suggests clumsy country fingers working in clumsy materials. The carpet is not beautiful but 'lurid' and the hunting scenes cheap and commonplace. This is what Crockett knew as a boy and shows us honestly without pretence. This is where he came from and he describes it lovingly.

But country life is not all clean and bright like this. He describes why Megsy had to take Hester away from the village. Grumphy Guddlestane, the newly-appointed game-keeper to Lord Darroch, Carus's father, has found Hester sitting reading in the sunshine by the ruined 'Auld Castle' of Darroch. He sets upon her with a torrent of filthy abuse, calling her the 'madam that stole the necklace' and ordering her off his master's land; she'll be sent back to jail if she is found here again. White-faced and ashamed, Hester goes away. Megsy finds her crying and soon discovers why.

The next week she comes upon Grumphy on the eve of Market Monday when the village is busy; she speaks her mind, calling him a 'pasty-faced, dottel-nosed vaigabond' and wonders why the Almighty permitted

> sic a thing as ye are to crawl on the face o' this bonny earth, blackening the verra licht o' the sun, and fylin' the clean mools as ye walk the fields.[8]

Later still, when Carus has just found out that Hester has left the Manse, he walks down the street and hears Grumphy Guddlestane, turned out of the Cross Keys, relating once more how he had sent the 'besom' about her business. Carus takes him by the collar, propels him to the farm at bottom of the village and pitches him over the low dyke into the midden, at that season rich with a shallow sea of liquid top-dressing. When Grumphy rises like a dripping scarecrow, his two-pound Tobermory suit ruined, spluttering and threatening to kill this man, the bystanders joyfully tell him that the man is his master's heir and beg him to spare them the smell of the dung. Carus departs, wishing he had had his Alpine boots on. Incidents like this made the squeamish reader complain that Crockett was coarse, and there is a crude bucolic humour in Grumphy's fate which might offend if read in a drawing-room. But village life in Galloway was not compounded entirely of roses and honeysuckle; there are stinking middens and unsavoury louts as well; he describes it as he remembers it; with a mild apology to all good game-keepers, he ducks Grumphy in the top-dressing with relish.

The Loves of Miss Anne is a much slighter creation built around Dan Weir, a herd laddie who wants to go to college in Edinburgh to learn surveying and land measurement so as to become a factor. He tends his sheep and lambs on the hillside with a Latin Grammar in his pocket, and thinks of Anne Kilpatrick, the daughter of his employer Sir Tempest Kilpatrick, with estates in Lothian and Galloway. He has seen her once and fallen in love. One evening, instead of Daft Davie bringing up the provisions to him, Anne comes, having a whim to see what a herd is like. It is a threatening evening with a storm brewing, but Dan is so taken up with Miss Anne that his dogs have to look after the sheep and lambs that he is neglecting. The storm of rain and lightning breaks upon them and both dogs are struck by lightning. Miss Anne for once finds herself ignored as he tries to revive one with whisky and leaves her alone as he goes with the other to bury its body in the woods. She tries to go home but her pony has disappeared and the paths are streaming water.

He puts her in his hut with the living dog and lights a fire for her, telling her she must look after herself, sitting down himself outside the hut in his plaid. Dried, she joins him and asks about his family; he tells her about his ambition to go to college (at which she feels uneasy; she does not want him in her world) and about his father, but she falls asleep with her head on his shoulder. In the morning a search-party finds them and take Miss Anne home, but Dan never forgets her nor she him—the lad whose dogs and sheep were of more importance to him than she was. He goes off to college when he has saved enough, and the reader is left with the narrator, Clemmy McTaggart, Anne's servant and companion, who has been taken up to the Big House to share Anne's life, as Katie Stewart was in Mrs Oliphant's story, when a little girl.

Clemmy is writing in her old age, looking back on her life with Miss Anne. She is a tart, astringent Galloway girl, daughter of the wood-forester, more a friend than a servant to Miss Anne, but seeing her with a loving but critical eye. Without Clemmy, the book would be insipid. Dan we hear nothing of until he comes back as Sir Tempest's factor, planning and supervising the building of a new mains farm. Just as Sir Tempest is showing off his new building to a party of friends, he collapses and dies. John Barnaby Kilpatrick, his worthless son, comes back to claim his inheritance; his mother and sister—and Clemmy—keep to one small part of the mansion while he and his rowdy cronies carouse in the remaining rooms. One of his friends is a prize fighter, another Jim Scudamore, a solicitor known to all as the 'Drucken WS'—Writer to the Signet. All the old servants, including Dan, are dismissed. John Barnaby wants Anne to marry Jim Scudamore but he, knowing that he is not worthy of her, in Sydney Carton manner drowns himself and John Barnaby in a dark loch so that she may be free of them both.

Miss Anne is now the heiress. Dan, for all his learning once more a herd, is on the hilltop on Beltane Night and lights a bonfire to match the others blazing on Tinto and Minchmuir and all the hills around. Miss Anne appears through the light of the leaping flames; she asks him to be her new factor as he was her father's, but there is to be one condition—he is to take her as his wife. When the fire has died down she tells the tenantry who have straggled up to join them that she and Dan are to be married and that Dan will be their master. For all that, Dan stays with his sheep for the rest of the night. He is not going to neglect them twice, even for Miss Anne.

Thus the book has a beginning and an end. What it lacks is a satisfactory middle. Crockett has to fill his book with the pranks and whimsies of wilful Miss Anne, and even when narrated by Clemmy his story cannot convey the charm which he seems to think she possesses. Clemmy is a deliberate foil;

> Alongside of her I was but a spiky thorn-bush that bore sour sloes. A few people liked me, but mostly my quick temper set folks teeth on edge. Now, my Anne was a lily among the daughters, as the Bible says in the part girls read in church, glancing between the leaves when the sermon is over-long—as, indeed it often is in Scotland.[9]

She has to take part in all Miss Anne's amusing diversions—organising a mock elopement in old Lady Bombie's old-fashioned coach to tease a romantic young artist; changing clothes and places with Anne to fool a procession of suitors of all ages who come wooing, in love with Anne's money, not Anne, and quickly scuttle off when they discover their mistaken courting of her maid; encouraging a silly poet who writes a poem in praise of a dark-haired lady, Clemmy, but changes his rhyme quickly to suit a fair-haired one, Anne, and is well laughed at. Without Clemmy, these antics would be arch and silly; with her, they benefit from her sarcastic commentary but are still tiresome. The funniest prank is when the minister, the Rev Physgill McMachar, fancies himself in love with Clemmy; Anne arranges for her to be spring-cleaning the library, banging, thumping and throwing the books about, stuffing them back into the shelves pell-mell from a confused heap in the middle of the floor mixed up with candlesticks, old boots and pieces of dirty carpet. This is too much for the minister; he goes off exclaiming at Clemmy's awful behaviour so that she feels she is lucky to have escaped being put under the greater excommunication of the church. Clemmy, we understand from frequent references in the text to the Captain, is safely married to an elderly sea-faring man who has never met Miss Anne and would be immune to her. He sounds dull, kindly and faithful, which Clemmy finds very satisfactory. Anne annexes all the men but she will not annexe the Captain. These things are all very well—as is the name of the minister involved in the mock elopement, the Rev Mr Heatherbrod of Drunts,—but they are hardly subtle.

Perversely, now and again the book rises to a different tone. The woods, the trees, the pines and beeches and lines of woodland, are described with affectionate exactness. Clemmy's father, the wood-forester, is a deeply religious Calvinist contemptuous of the failings of feckless Whinnyliggate and all its inhabitants, yet caring most deeply for his trees, going about with a billhook in the manner of a Thomas Hardy character to cut away poor growth or a cankered branch. His belief in 'Yelection' is stark, with no time for watery evangelists. He rounds in fury upon one such preacher:

> Salvation is not sugar-candy ... Gang hame, laddie, gang hame and pray the Lord to have mercy on your feckless sowl![10]

Yet he has a touch of George MacDonald too. He talks of his trees as if they were part of the eternal mind. He sits on Sabbath afternoons with Thomas Boston's *Fourfold State* open on his knees but not reading, yet

> taking in the Eternities for all that—the warmth of the sun, the caller grip of the air which made it a pleasure only to breathe, the scent of the pines, the stir and scuffle of the young rabbits in and out of their holes down on the wood-edges, the singing of the blackbirds, mellow as so many heavenly lutes, the clean-cut repeated bursts of the mavises, the robins making melody deeper in the coppice, and the tits shrilling their silver saws as they grated down the pine cones high above his head.
> One day I sat beside him and he listened a long time, saying nothing. I also waited silent. At last he closed the book writ by good Thomas of Ettrick, took off his broad blue bonnet, and said with a fine large wave of his hand that I can never forget: *'This IS God!'*[11]

What is so deeply felt a character as this doing in the midst of Miss Anne's foolishness? Is he a remembrance of Crockett's grandfather suddenly demanding expression? And if so, why did Crockett make him take part in the nonsense of the mock elopement and drive old Lady Bombie's coach?

Even the melodrama of John Barnaby's drowning is described with some care. Clemmy is there, sitting un-noticed by the loch while the laughing crowd dare John Barnaby to row out in the rotting old boat. Before Scudamore dives in to 'save' his friend when the boat founders, he has time to whisper to Clemmy 'Tell Miss Anne that I kept my word. I did what I could for her sake. I can at least clear her way!'

> Scudamore had reached John Barnaby. He was clasping him. There appeared to be something of a struggle. The fat black water broke in oily waves on the peaty margin of the loch. The dark green lily leaves, not yet tipped with yellow or white, dragged at their submerged cables. The popular theory afterwards, supported by a cloud of witnesses, was that John Barnaby, losing his presence of mind by the sudden immersion, clasped his benefactor too tightly about the neck, and that Scudamore had to strike his friend in order to release himself. It may be so. All I know is that with my own eyes I saw Scudamore raise his hand to strike—once, twice, three times. Then both went down together, and though the water bubbled oozily for some moments, neither ever came up again alive.
> Two hours afterwards the bodies were recovered, still clasped tightly together. But the foresters declared that they had to cut away the lily stems, so firmly had Jim Scudamore's right hand grasped them close to the roots in his dying agony.
> I saw both young men lie side by side on the bank. I could not tear myself away. The features of John Barnaby were distorted by a great anger, but on the face of James Scudamore abode only peace, and (if I did not deceive myself) a slight ironical smile, as if at the vanity of all things worldly.[12]

Clemmy hears her father say, as if puzzled, that the water at that place was no more than four feet and a half deep. She too is puzzled. She does not believe that Jim Scudamore had grasped the roots in his dying agony, yet her short sentences and hesitations are effective. She knows what she has seen. Fascinated she stays to look at the dead faces. Melodramatic it is, but such real feeling does not accord with Miss Anne's light frivolity any more than does the religious thinking of Donald McTaggart. She is not worth it.

The Loves of Miss Anne therefore can be said to have moments of worth. Unexpected comments startle the reader. Dan Weir has improved himself, been to college, become a land-steward, but seeing Jim Scudamore move off in the evening shadows, clean-limbed, graceful, slightly stooping, he suddenly not with jealousy but with a pang of something like anger realises that he, Dan Weir of Venturefair, can never be quite what Scudamore is; he can never be a gentleman. But it is an untidy unsatisfactory book. It is a mixture—or more uncharitably a ragbag—of girlish wilfulness, crude melodrama, natural description, religious sentiment, shrewd comments on human nature, vivid descriptions of Whinnyligate, things coming at random into Cockett's mind and finding a place for themselves wherever they could. Not even the original and likable Clemmy can hold them all together.

In these three books, *Ione March, Cinderella* and *The Loves of Miss Anne* Crockett was trying to entertain without instructing. They are a condemnation of his decision to tell yarns without moralising. Yet they are not boring. His personality flickers through them, especially in the Galloway pair, and makes them different from the works of Annie S Swan and the two Hockings. In *Cinderella*, the best of the three, he uses comedy most freely. Sir Sylvanus is a comic figure as well as a villain; when Sir Sylvanus summons Hester to face the police he adopts what he thinks a suitable pose.

> He was holding his head a little more erect than usual. It was, in fact, the manner he cultivated for addressing his constituents. This, as it were, released another fold of chin, and was accompanied by that haughty throwing forward of the left knee which one sees in political statues, in company with a togaesque frockcoat and a roll of papers held in the left hand.[13]

Just before he is confronted by his wife's brother, come back apparently from the dead, he is buttressed with dignity.

> Sir Sylvanus sat in his writing-chair at a great desk with a roller-top. He was banked in with an array of serried pigeon-holes that rose above his head and extended on either side of him, as if the distinguished philanthropist were about to soar to tracts unknown on French-polished mahogany pinions, carrying all his correspondence with him, as documents of importance even to the recording angel.[14]

These mischievous Victorian social comments are Crockett enjoying the ridiculous side of his contemporaries, especially the prosperous ones. He can be sharp as well. David Stirling, having seen Sylvanus reduced to a crushed ruin, tells the lawyer that he has let him down too lightly. The lawyer disagrees but David holds to his opinion.

> 'You have not had fourteen years in prison as I have, Mr Chetwynd,' he said.

"'Vengeance is Mine, I will repay, saith the Lord." But that is because He wants to keep all the pleasure of it to Himself!'[15]

But Crockett himself has pity for Sir Sylvanus.

> Sir Sylvanus was never the same after the great collapse of his 'speculations.' He remained a rich man still, but somehow to himself the savour had gone out of his life. So one day he measured out carefully a triple quantity of the same white powder into a glass of water, tranquilly took it, and came in to where his wife was sitting.
> 'Have I been a good husband to you, Sarah?' he said, quietly sitting down beside her.
> 'Why, Sylvanus, dear, what is the matter?' she cried, startled; 'of course you have—never a better!'
> 'Ah, then there is one person on earth who will regret me. Give me your hand, Sarah!'
> And he shut his eyes and slept—never to wake again on earth.[16]

This suicide was oddly underplayed; it was perhaps his admission of guilt and a plea for forgiveness. Mr Molesay, the slum missionary of *Kid McGhie A Nugget of Dim Gold*, serialised in the *Christian World* before appearing as a book in 1906, would certainly have seen it as that; a wife's affection is a sign that a man is not wholly bad but can hope for mercy and redemption.

The multiplicity of plots in *Kid McGhie* appears on first reading to be tangled and straggling, but they are all held together by the theme, the grace of God even in the most ugly circumstances. The kindly bachelor Archbold Molesay moves through them with unquenchable love for humanity. He has spent twenty years working among the outcasts of the Edinburgh Cowgate, men and women who have sunk so low that the Christian churches cannot reach them and have given up trying. Mr Molesay is a college friend of the Rev Harry Rodgers of the Peden Memorial Church in the Cowgate, but since he is not an ordained minister but only a missionary, what Crockett calls 'mere labourer in hope',[17] he has greater freedom and a more unorthodox theology. Rodgers cannot accept that a barman can be a Christian. Molesay smilingly but firmly disagrees, knowing Billy Earsman, one particular barman, who is putting up a brave fight to be just that. Molesay's people, he says, are 'a feeble folk—like Peter we follow afar off'.[18] He brushes aside Rodgers' harsh comment on what Peter did after following afar off—deny his Master three times—and persuades the sceptical minister to come and talk to his 'folk' the next week, promising that he will see not only a barman but 'a kid of the flock'. After Molesay has gone, the phrase 'kid of the flock' remains in Rodgers' mind. He has heard it before. He tracks it down in a minor sonnet by Matthew Arnold in the green cloth Golden Treasury series, 'The Good Shepherd with the Kid'. An austerely intolerant second century sect of Christians, commended by Tertullian, believe that only the sheep can be saved; Christ has no pity on the goats and the Chuch no power to forgive them. Arnold's sonnet personifies the church as a woman smiling through tears of compassion and drawing on the wall of the Catacombs a picture of Christ—one that actually exists;

> She her Good Shepherd's hasty image drew
> And on his shoulders—not a lamb—*a kid!*[19]

The nickname Kid holds a deeper significance than one expects; Crockett through Molesay and Arnold, is again propounding the belief in universal salvation which he found in Whittier and George MacDonald.

The story begins harshly enough in Kirkmessan in Galloway. Kid McGhie's father David, by inheritance the chief of the clan McGhie, has been dragged down to shame by his wife Mag, the Kid's mother, a drunken brutal swearing harridan seldom out of jail. She is due out now but Davie cannot face life with her any longer. He proposes first to shoot the Kid, then himself. They discuss this quietly but with mounting horror in the Kid's heart. He is on the side of life and runs away, hearing as he goes the shot which cuts short his father's life. He is only nine years old.

Mag emerges from prison in a torrent of foul language. There is no husband waiting for her. Enraged, she pushes her cursing way through the ministers, priests, members of Prisoners' Aid societies, goes for a drink to a low lodging-house, then staggers to the Back Mill Lands where she hammers on her peeling broken door, so that the neighbours put out indifferent heads and say that Mad Mag's out again. The Kid has followed her, keeping out of sight. When she turns and sees him, she picks up a heavy spanner left lying by a man mending a wheel and strikes the Kid on the head. He is knocked unconscious. Within an hour she is in jail again, but this is normal and there is little interest once it has been made sure that the Kid is not dead.

He has crawled away to safety, which happens to be the nearby garden belonging to a pretentious suburban villa 'Balmaghie', the residence of P Brydson McGhie, Esq, JP, who has come up in the world from being a mere packman and hopes to prove that he is the head of the clan McGhie. Archie Craw, the little hunchback lawyer and local historian, knows better; David McGhie was the chief, and the Kid, Alexander McGhie, is his successor. But Crockett warns the reader not to expect riches and rank for the Kid in the final chapters; this is not that sort of a book and the Kid's ancient name will do him little good. It will do little good to P Brydson McGhie either; he may mean the world to recognise his importance and substance but the world is not taken in, although no one has a word to say against his three daughters. Their father is not their fault.

Patricia, the middle sister of the three, finds the Kid lying unconscious; she and her sisters—principally she, being used to doctoring wounded dogs—care for him secretly without telling their father. She cuts away the blood-stained hair and washes the wound clean. Half-conscious, he seems to be saying something; the spanner had struck a jingle out of his head:

> I'm wee Kid McGhie, I'm wee Kid McGhie!
> My father killed himsel'
> And my mither killed me![20]

When the Kid is well enough to know where he is, he leaves without thanks or explanation. He must find his mother. By inquiring at police stations he finds out that she is in Edinburgh and goes there. She has married a new husband, Knifer Jackson, a very different proposition from the despairing David McGhie. Mag is afraid of him. She has seen him kill a man and knows he has killed others. When the Kid says who he is, Knifer takes a fancy to him, liking his spirit. He will not let Mag ill-use him.

> And then the boy wondered at the man before him, thinking him to be a kind of god, who had wrought this marvellous change in his mother. Ministers, Salvationists, temperance folk, preachers unattached, elders, mission workers—all had had a try at Mag down in Kirkmessan, and she had chased them one and all from the door, and gone on worse than ever. Whence had this man this power and authority? *Even the devils obeyed him, trembling.*[21]

The General Epistle of James II; 19 reads

> Thou believest that there is one God, thou doest well; the devils also believe and tremble.

Crockett here is intensifying his idea that Knifer seemed like a god to the Kid and pointing out that fear and fear alone will subjugate such as Mag, and that Knifer was given his power by the one God. Pious exhortations are of no avail. He seems here to be contradicting Mr Molesay but the question is debated once more later. It is true that Knifer has killed men; the police know this, and Knifer knows that they know, but that he is in no danger. He kills only those who deserve to be killed but whom the police cannot touch. They turn a blind eye to his burglaries because he is doing their job for them. Henderland, the Chief of Police, has been known to let him go free when he has been caught in a police net, nodding to his subordinates. Yet Knifer is no 'nark', no 'split', no 'sawny plant'—no 'grass' as we would say. He is in his way the vengeance of God. It is a strong hard concept but not that of a sentimentalist.

The Kid is introduced to what is to be his trade, the tricks and devices of burglary, in a 'school' for criminals, 'Blind Jacob's', based explicitly on that of Fagin in *Oliver Twist*; all the youngsters know Dickens' story and scorn the 'softs' in it who do no more than steal handkerchiefs. They in Edinburgh are taught greater skills like picking locks of all types, opening safes, breaking into houses by every variety of method. When the Kid is 'trained' sufficiently, he goes with Knifer and his mate Joe to burgle a Big House where the rent money collected by the owner will be ready in a safe, ripe for burglary. At the end of a rail journey, the Kid realises that the Big House is in Kirkmessan and the owner P B McGhie whose daughters had befriended him. Feeling disloyal to Knifer but determined to pay his debt of gratitude, he sends a message by the baker's boy: take the money to the bank at once.

Patricia, in the house alone, does this, and when Knifer and Joe enter the study they find her waiting for them with her father's revolver. Not by so much as a flicker does she reveal that she knows the Kid.

Patricia McGhie is teasing, fearless and kind, but a sorry fate awaits her. Her father plans to have her adopted by his wife's rich childless brother and his wife, the Boreham-Eghams, who live in Egham Castle near Edinburgh, both of them senile, washed, dressed, taken out and put back by their butler Algernon Hammer who is in league with P B McGhie. Once adopted, Patricia is to be married to Lord Athabasca, an elderly colonial peer who has made a huge fortune in Canada and has had for his first wife an Indian squaw. Hammer is to be paid £10,000 on the day the marriage takes place. Patricia herself is willing to marry in order to help her sisters to happiness; she knows her father's determination to be rich and powerful; she has always known the burden would fall on her.

The Kid is entrusted with getting into Egham Castle and stealing a box of documents which prove that P Brydson McGhie is descended from a cattle-dealer, two pig drovers and a tinsmith; they must be destroyed. He succeeds, but the blame falls on Patricia; immediately he gives himself up. He is sent to the Hearne Mackenzie Reformatory for five years. Hearne Mackenzie is the son of Lord Athabasca and his Red Indian wife who is estranged from his father because he will not live in idleness; a man must earn his way. He has invested money inherited from his grandmother in the Reformatory which bears his name but has appointed another, better man to be superintendent, earning his keep as assistant. Despite these odd arrangements, the Hearne Mackenzie Reformatory is based directly on the Wellington Reformatory Farm School on the moors near Penicuik; Crockett took particular interest in it, he and his wife visiting it for social occasions. The activities he describes are taken from what he saw there under the superintendence of his friend John Craster; he approved of the hard work and discipline which turned young criminals into good soldiers, brave sailors and splendid colonists. The talk of the boys in the Hearne Mackenzie suggests that he has listened tolerantly to the young offenders; it is doubtful however whether modern lads would be well enough versed in Scripture to nickname the Kid the 'Beast' from Revelations because his number is 666.

The Reformatory not only reforms the Kid, it brings together three of the principal characters for the first time. Patricia, anxious, walks over the moors from Castle Egham and meets Hearne Mackenzie. She meets him several times. Hearne knows that she is to marry his father and accepts this calmly; he knows his father is a good and kindly man. Inevitably they fall in love as they talk together but Patricia feels herself bound by her promise and Hearne will not ask her to break it, even when he begins to feel that she is selling herself. Mr Molesay, also anxious about the Kid, makes his way across the moors and comes upon Patricia in tears. Appalled by the loveless marriage, he takes her away on the early morning of the wedding day, chaperoned by Kate Earsman, the barman's wife. Hammer is travelling into Edinburgh on the same train—to cash his £10,000 cheque—but can do nothing when he sees Patricia; Billy Earsman calls on his friends the railway workers to manhandle Hammer down to their engineering works at St Margaret's and make him work there with pick and shovel for several hours. By the time he reaches the Bank of Scotland on the Mound, Lord Athabasca has prudently stopped the cheque—no bride. Hammer collapses fainting, and later a body, identified as his, is fished out of the sea near the Isle of May. Patricia is safe, staying with Mr Molesay's friends the Rodgers at the Peden Memorial Church Manse.

More plots begin. A master at the Reformatory, jealous of the superintendent and of Hearne, induces one of the boys to set the school on fire. Hearne, seeing the conflagration, goes to his father's mansion Three Ridings to get help and fire fighting equipment. He finds his father dead, murdered, with a knife in his throat. He is arrested for the murder because he was there, alone. Patricia rushes to the police-station, admitting her love for him without hesitation. Mr Molesay finds himself cheerless and forgotten, in love with Patricia himself, but he reminds himself of his greater family in the Cowgate and puts his sad thoughts aside.

Hearne of course has to be set free, the evidence being wholly circumstantial and a better suspect being found—Knifer Jackson who with two friends were burgling Three Ridings that same night, knowing that it would be empty of servants. He is tried and convicted, the Kid to his anguish having to identify the knife belonging to his step-father; Knifer is sentenced to death. Mag struggles out to the Reformatory to kill the Kid in revenge, but she is weak and half-paralysed; when the Kid bends over her in concern, her knife fails and cuts only the collar of his regulation jacket. Mr Molesay is with her as she dies and hears her confession—she killed the man, not Knifer. This is not true, but he finds in it a flash of goodness; even Mag can take another's sin upon her out of love.

The Boreham-Eghams die of fright at all this violence, leaving their fortune to Pat, who will not accept it. Marthe her sister, now married to a minister, rejects it also. The third sister Atalanta falls heiress and, secretly, donates £10,000 to Mr Molesay for his mission. Such an amount enables him to buy the public house which has been the disgrace of the district, Ogg's British Imperial Palace, and without changing its name turn it into a centre for meetings, functions, the sale of soft drinks and nourishing meals, religious services and lantern lectures—a community centre, if the name had been thought of.

> It would not be 'Christian Institution' or Christian anything. For Mr Molesay had observed that that word, the noblest adjective in the world, affected even the circulation of journals, and kept the average man away from the doors of halls over which it was carved or gilded.[22]

Crockett is bitterly aware of how the behaviour of his own generation has brought the very name of Christian into disrepute—he may even be admitting wryly that the *Christian World* was not the best market for his stories.

On the night of the opening of the establishment under its new management—the last night of Knifer's life in the Calton Jail—a lantern lecture on 'The Prodigal Son' so moves a woman in the audience that she rises up crying in anguish. It is Marigh Hammer, Algernon's wife; the body found near the Isle of May was not his. He, driven mad by the loss of the £10,000, is the one who murdered Lord Athabasca and still insanely haunts Egham Castle, driving the country people to terror by strange lights and movements. The police find him, by the Boreham-Egham mausoleum dead.

Knifer, who has been listening to the hammering of the men putting up the scaffold for him, breaks down when Mr Molesay tells him that he has been cleared. When he is released, on Mr Molesay's advice he goes with the Kid to the backwoods of Canada. Between them they work the 'Patricia' mine, the Kid the master, Knifer the foreman, and produce a good yield. Pat and Hearne marry and live in contentment. Only Atalanta guesses what Mr Molesay has sacrificed.

The tale is preposterous. Only the shrewd details and the lively talk of the characters carry it off—just and no more. It was greeted with a slashing review in the *Scottish Review and Christian Leader*, 'The Decline of Mr S R Crockett'. It spoke well of Mr Molesay but accused Crockett of having ransacked the Newgate Calendar for characters of the utmost ugliness and squalor;

> out of such a tangled skein of criminality his essentially country must can make nothing.[23]

This is more than a little ironic. Nelson's had bought the *Leader* in 1905 and when John Buchan joined the firm he was made its editor. He wanted to raise its standards with *Scottish Review* in its title and turn it into a Scottish *Spectator*, outward-looking, literary and political, dropping its parochialism and substituting articles on the Balkans and German foreign policy. The change was not to the taste of those who had read the old *Leader*. The *Scottish Review* perished with its last issue in 1908.[24] In 1895 the young Buchan had slated Crockett for being too boisterous, jolly and wholesome; in 1906 a reviewer, writing presumably with his editor's blessing, is taking him to task for being unwholesome, squalid and sensational, bidding him go back to his healthy rural scenes—to the Kailyard. It is little wonder that Crockett at times felt discouraged.

The charges are unfounded. The plots are wild and based on lurid situations, but underneath the sensational lies serious comment. Crockett had no need to go to the Newgate Calender for his *dramatis personae*; he had heard of them, read about them in the papers, perhaps had met them. Henderland, his Chief of Police, is based on William Henderson the real Edinburgh Chief of Police; others may have been identifiable in their day. Later, after the 1914 war, the public accepted with enthusiasm the sensational escapist plots of 'Sapper'; after the Second World War we were prepared to enjoy Ian Fleming and Len Deighton. Crockett is not romanticising urban crime; he may be showing it as part of unlikely combinations of incidents, but he is honestly showing readers the violence and ugliness of slums. There is no Bulldog Drummond, no James Bond or Goldfinger, just Mr Molesay moving with his dulled silver head, his shabby neat clothes, his greening hat, among the most unkempt, unlovely of sinners.

In *Kid McGhie* the slums emerge more harshly than in *Cleg Kelly*. Cleg was a survivor; the Kid a victim. The huge tenements sit sullenly in their unredeemed evil, introduced by bitter phrases without verbs as if they are so distasteful that Crockett cannot bear to put them into sentences.

> A cliff-like face of grimy grey stone, broken by rows upon rows of small windows with small panes, many of them broken, stuffed with rags, and mended with paper. Seven and eight stories the rule, ten and eleven the exception. Four families, sometimes eight, on each landing. These landings lit by day through one narrow slit in the tower of the turnpike stair—by night not lit at all. Thirty to sixty families in all, exclusive of lodgers and casuals, lived in that grimy barrack, all going to and fro upon occasions up and down that winding staircase, indescribable in its filth. A faint, keen odour of packed humanity grew more and more insupportable as you mounted higher, which you did, holding on to a greasy rope, stanchioned to the wall. Children swarmed underfoot at all stages of the ascent, and it was a constant miracle how more of them did not tumble over, and so achieve (which was the best thing for them) Nirvana at the earliest possible age.
> Some did, and were happy ever after. The others survived and were both sorry for it themselves and made others sorry also.[25]

There are few 'lands' like this in Edinburgh at the time of writing, he admits; thirty years earlier they were the rule; and the disgrace is that the 'few' remain at all. There is no sentimentality here, merely a cold revulsion of disgust. Death is the happiest way out for children in such crowded animal deprivation.

Yet out of this mood of darkness there are—there have to be—some gleams of laughter. Mag's brother Alf Craigton, is in the 'historical' line—forging genealogies and pedigrees for aspirants like P Brydson McGhie—and the Kid may be useful to him.

> For this McGhie pedigree I have need of a smart boy to open the doors of church vestries where books are kept, to lose documents writ by me, where they will be found in the nick of time—churchyards, too, where there are little alterations in the lettering of tombstones to be made—I attend to that myself at special terms. But I need a boy to look out and hold the lantern so as to suit the chisel.[26]

The brisk pomposity of this pushing young person comes as a brief respite from gloom; it is to Knifer's credit that he dislikes his brother-in-law, who looks like a cross between a groom and an undertaker.

Algernon Hammer's being whirled down to St Margaret's (now no more but once near where Meadowbank Stadium stands) is both sardonic and sharp. Billy Earsman hands him over to the short-distance driver who says that it is clean against regulations but

> doon yonder they'll rivet a man up in a biler for twa gallon o' Usher's best.

Crockett cannot resist a chance to describe those parts of the railway system which passengers never see but which he, popular friend, has been shown.

They took him down in that intractable grey of the morning, which is darker than the dark of midnight, through a murk of tunnels, past the yellow wink of many gas lamps, the brassy reek of naptha flares, to where there were digging operations going on for the new station. They left the electrics far behind, the high-bunched kaleidoscopes of the signals standing long aloft in the west. They delivered Algernon Hammer, shaking and much afraid, in a darksome place, to a gang of brawny giants who worked under a naked arc light which changes its 'pitch' every quarter of a minute. These men ran little waggons into a black hole, a wet, greasy, unsatisfactory hole in the ground ... They gave him a pick and told him to dig. When he indignantly refused, Mr Hammer became aware that the makers of the new tunnel wore No 12 tacketty boots and, desiring no more knowledge, he grasped the pick and struck his first stroke of decent manual labour.[27]

And underneath the ebb and flow of incident after incident, there goes on the continual argument at the heart of the story, an argument which in an odd way reminds one of Graham Greene's faith in the good that is to be found even in burnt-out cases, arguments with the Rev Harry Rodgers and with policemen, maintained with quiet faith by Mr Molesay. Over and over again he has to defend his position:

'Well, well—I haven't much time to think of my wretched self,' said Molesay. 'I have been so long in the front fighting line. This constant forlorn-hope business gives a fellow little time to think of drill—though, doubtless, drill helps to carry him through. Man, Rodgers, I declare I don't even pray very much now. Shocking, isn't it? I haven't time. But for all that I can understand that fellow who sends his electricity into space, on the chance that some one will hear his cry for help. So when I get quite heartsick with the squalor and the misery and the crime, which none regards (not even, to all appearance, God Himself), I send my cry up between the darkening roofs toward the sky and the stars. Let Him answer—*if He will*. He is far away, and, with the press of universes, has doubtless many claims.'[28]

Science supplies Crockett with a vivid metaphor for the discouragement which makes the missionary pray despairingly into the void like someone sending messages without knowing whether there is any answering intelligence to respond. Molesay's honesty is complete; there is little indication that God cares at all for the misery in the world which He has created; a note struck here and there in *Cleg Kelly* now resounds like direct accusation. God may be too busy; Molesay admits this without losing faith, without complaining, and even excusing the apparent indifference of his Maker.

He has none of George MacDonald's faith in the divine in nature; there is no nature, no green tree or bright flower in the Cowgate. He has humour. When the Irish Ashbacket Moll, reeking of gin, demands his blessing, saying 'I'll not touch a drop this day',

'This calling of mine brings me precious near lying sometimes!' he murmured. And lifting up his right hand—for he knew that Moll would hold his best blessings of no account whatever without that—he mumbled hurriedly, and with a straying eye, the Lord's prayer in Greek, a relic of Professor Blackie's class room.[29]

That 'straying eye', hoping that no one will catch him at this dubious concession to a Papist sinner, is well and comically observed.

Molesay believes that imprisoning, transporting, penal servitude and hanging are not the answer to crime. Crockett probably does not agree with him altogether—fear was what held Mad Mag in check; Cleg was possibly wrong to rescue Sal Kavanagh—but he portrays with sympathy a man more good and patient than he could be himself. He lets Henderland and Molesay argue the matter out.

> 'Stuff!' said the Chief with excusable vehemence, 'great stuff! Where's your Bible with its "Eye for an eye, and a tooth for a tooth"?'
> 'Oh!' said Mr Molesay, gently, 'that was before HE came to teach us any better. That's about as out of date as the giants that were before the flood. HE said "Love your enemies, do good to—— "'
> 'Hut!' cried the chief, impatiently, 'Look here, Molesay, do you mean to say that you *love* Knifer Jackson and your friend Mad Mag—— ?'
> 'Yes, I do,' said the little missionary stoutly.
> 'And will you swear that you have hope of doing them any real good?'
> 'Yes, I have—I, at least, had such hopes. I have seen worse cases—more hopeless, I mean.'

This is to much for the Chief, though we notice the tiny hesitation of honesty which makes Molesay correct himself and put his hopes in the past tense.

> 'You are an impossible fellow, Molesay,' he cried; 'the Cowgate is too good for you—too calm and holy. You should be missionary down below—in a fireproof suit—among the subjects of the black gentleman with the forked tail!'
> 'I should like that very well,' said Mr Molesay, simply. 'it's been tried before.'
> 'How so?' queried Henderland, looking up to see if the little man were not joking.
> 'Well,' said the city missionary, 'one Peter, a fisherman, who ought to have known what he was talking about, says that HE went and preached to the spirits in prison, *"which sometimes had been disobedient!"* If HE could, I don't see why it should be impossible for me ... '[30]

This is carrying universal salvation to its exact Biblical source; Molesay is no watery evangelist but has the root of the matter in I Peter 3: 19–20, and he speaks with authority.

The Chief may argue with him, but, speaking to the Fiscal, admits his value to the community.

> What we are doing is just repression ... Molesay cures. We scorch the nettle tops. He digs out the roots.[31]

But the Fiscal thinks that the Chief of Police is sometimes too sentimental.

In case we should think Molesay a man so dedicated to his calling that he has no doubts, no regrets, no sacrifices, Crockett at the end of the final chapter shows us how human he is. He is not a good speaker—even in his arguments he is not eloquent but mostly quiet and almost inarticulate—and seldom preaches, knowing that his people will distrust him if he behaves like conventional ministers. He is reading from the Gospel according to Matthew; Patricia and Atalanta, disguised in borrowed shabby clothing, creep quietly in to join the subdued audience.

> He was reciting his text a second time before 'speaking a few words upon it'—Mr Molesay's words were always few and excellently ordered.
> 'And everyone' (he began slowly, spacing the words) 'that hath forsaken ... houses, or brethren, or sisters, ... or father, or mother ... '
> He lifted his eyes and, under the plain dress and poor woman's disguise, he knew Patricia at the first glance. But his voice, though it checked, did not falter. He went on:
> 'Or wife, or children ... or lands, for My name's sake, shall receive an hundredfold ... '
> Then the voice of the speaker broke away into a kind of gust, or gale of the spirit.
> 'An hundredfold they shall receive!' he cried. 'Ah, it would need to be—it would need to be! For how hard is that giving up—O Lord, Thou alone knowest!'[32]

Then in a moment he is himself again, smiling silver-haired Archbold Molesay coming down from the platform to welcome his friends. In that anguished flash we have seen how very dearly his necessary solitude has cost him, his composure suddenly broken by the sight of Patricia whom he loves but has never tried to come near except as a kindly friend. There is a depth of sorrow in that momentary cry to God 'It would need to be!' and the appeal to Christ who gave up earthly love when he gave Himself to take away the sins of the world that shows a strong compassionate understanding in Crockett, so different himself, so unable to rise to heights of sacrifice, but humbly eager to pay tribute to a man better—infinitely better—than himself.

Any suspicion that Crockett took religion lightly must be dispelled by his admiration of the little city missionary, not clever, not rich, but going always alone among officials and ordained ministers and mission workers, unromantic, defending lost causes, never entirely despairing of his fellowmen. It is difficult to depict in fiction or on the stage a truly good character because erring mortals and authors and playwrights do not often have the quality of goodness strongly enough in themselves to draw on. In 'Accepted of the Beasts' Crockett had tried, and failed; in Mr Molesay he succeeded so well that it seems likely that he had one particular missionary in his mind as a model. At any rate he succeeded, and even the *Scottish Review* had the grace to say so.

II *Industrialism and the Day's Work*

In 1909, Crockett obeyed the voice of the *Scottish Review* and returned to his healthy country scene in *Rose of the Wilderness*. It might have been better if he had not. Rose the heroine relates the story in a thin girlish style which does nothing to recreate the beauty of the Galloway landscapes in which she lives. She is a silly girl and silly things happen to her and she does silly things. We catch an occasional glimpse of the hills but they do not save the story from sickly improbability; good strong improbability we can tolerate but not this. Crockett makes a joke about himself:

> 'A man wrote a lee-buik aboot [Galloway], and the rate thae raider-folk o' his nippit aboot the country wi' their nowt-beasts was something remarkable —'[1]

which shows that he can take criticism without being unduly perturbed, just as, after J H Millar's diatribe against *The Lilac Sunbonnet*, he could remark, in the Preface to *Lads' Love*, 'To my Unanswered Correspondents'

> You have informed me that your great-aunts cannot be expected to approve of certain passages in my books[2]

which puts his alleged salaciousness in a new light.

But these later years of Crockett's life produced books far better than *Rose of the Wilderness*. *Vida, or the Iron Lord of Kirktown*, serialised in the *People's Friend* before publication in 1907, has a beginning worthy of Sapper's Carl Peterson; a wealthy mine-owner and iron-master, tired of his tearful wife, sends her off with his daughter for a cruise round Scotland in one of his ships, instructing the captain to scuttle the ship and escape with his crew before it sinks. The wife dies, mercifully in her sleep, but Vida is rescued by two eccentric lighthouse keepers first introduced to us in *Sir Toady Crusoe*. One is a red-headed Irishman, Billy Bryan, the other Dick Finnan, elder of the Kirk. They decide to 'adopt' Vida, and in order to look after her Dick takes on the position of store-keeper at the Incubus pits owned by Jacob Romer, Vida's father. She does not tell Dick or Billy her name; she grows up as Vida Bryan, living in the lodge beside Romer's mansion, a stubborn attractive young lady with strong views on the value of work.

The setting for the novel which creates the working community of Kirktown is the same as the one used in *Vox Clamantium*, the Incubus Coal and Iron Company, owned by Romer and run by Hector McKill and Walter Grindling. The town houses the workers, in long streets of back-to-back houses named by letters of the alphabet from A to Q; such streets exist in Co Durham to this day, showing the little care the old mine-owners had for their workers. Crockett now has time to expand the scenes he had used in the short story. He has watched miners coming up from their work at Mauricewood, tired and dirty; he has been in their homes and knows their habits; and he has realised and resented on their behalf the cramped unnatural lives they lead. Their accustomed place is among

> great piles of debris which rose a hundred feet into the air, rusty waggons full of iron ore waiting to be taken to the smelting bank during the night. It was the hour of changing shifts. The miners passed up, silent and exhausted from

> their labour, as the great engine swung them into the fading light of a day they
> had spent in darkness. For a moment they gazed about with a bewildered air,
> as if scarce sure of their bearings. Then they plodded off through the warm dust
> of the summer evening like so many tired animals, their feet falling strangely
> on the kindly round of the earth. Those arriving had lamps in their caps ready
> to descend. They looked blanched and weary. The only difference was that the
> relieving shift muttered a little the one to the other in groups of two or three,
> while those returning from underground kept wholly silent.[3]

They are like H G Wells' Morlocks in *The Time Machine*, without the energy of those sinister dwellers in darkness. And for a miner's family there is no escape; the children too are slaves of the pits.

> Thus it was in Kirktown, thus also in a thousand mining towns. Even the
> children there are taught not to shout and scream across the street like other
> children. The very babes learn not to cry—because the breadwinner is taking
> his rest for the next shift, and must on no account be disturbed. There are times
> in the hot noonday when the windows are darkened, when the doctor goes on
> tiptoe, when not even the minister calls. The sleep of the labouring man is a
> sacred thing. So it ought to be always. The men go to work. The women stay
> at home. They work. They wait. As soon as the laddies leave school they follow
> their fathers down the mine. That is their vocation. They have never thought
> of doing anything else. The wide airy world is not for them—except that straight
> piece of dusty road between two dustier hedges which conducts them from the
> little red kitchen in Block C to the hole in the ground down which a great cage
> of iron dives incessantly.[4]

The Biblical phrase begins, then turns in an unexpected direction, showing Crockett's quiet anger. 'The sleep of the labouring man ... is sweet' is what we expect, but what we are told about are the unnatural silences in which a miner's family lives when he comes home worn out and exhausted; no happy laughter, no noisy play, but an imposed silence so that the miner may sleep heavily without disturbance. And that sleep is not sweet; it is the sheer animal exhaustion which must be overcome so that he can face going down the pit again the next weary shift.

Round the grimness of the mines there is a varied community of interests and professions. *Vida* is a well-populated book; the people from the villas overlooking the rows of red-brick houses meet one another socially, running their lives as they choose—the doctor's easy ill-behaved family running wild, the little music teacher Rose Munby caring for her selfish English father, Vida living with Dick in the lodge. Hector McKill, the hypocritical manager, remains from the earlier story but Grindlay has become Walter Grindling, more fair-minded since a longer story gives more room to manoeuvre.

At Rose Munby's cottage several individuals meet to argue and discuss. Vida is Rose's friend and favourite; Phil Calmont, son of the doctor, a literary lad given to dreaming because there is no reason for him to earn his living, is often there. So is Vic Morris, the mining engineer, honest and arrogant, who is a fiery agitator for the rights of the workers—a socialist in all but name. Even after he is dismissed for demanding better conditions for miners, he continues to agitate secretly for a Government inspection; there should be a second exit for every mine shaft but this has not been provided. Both Phil and Vic are in love with Vida; they quarrel when they meet for the first time in the Lodge, Vic accusing Phil of sponging on his father, easy and idle. Vida sends them both about their business, but Vic's accusation has taken effect. Phil acknowledges to Vic that his charge is true, and when Vic offers him the place of office assistant, working under and being trained by him, Phil eagerly accepts.

There are three kirks in the town, the Auld Kirk—the Established—whose minister preaches vague dry sermons and does not come into the story; the Valley Kirk—the Free Kirk,—founded after the Disruption, whose minister is a learned man Mr Fowler with a plain hard-working daughter Janet, his housekeeper; and the Cameronian Kirk—the Kirk on the Hill—whose minister is a kindly man, the Rev Benjamin Irongray, who has had to deny Rose Munby's father communion because of his behaviour but grieves over this necessity.

The villain of the piece is Kahn, the foreign—Serbian—confidential secretary to Jacob Romer, a swarthy sinister figure who drives a Mercedes and has guessed that Vida is Romer's daughter. He too loves Vida in a greedy passionate frightening way. She rejects him firmly. The humiliation works in his mind; on the day when Dick Finnan proudly takes Vida down the pit, Kahn lets them go down with suave compliments, then sets the pit on fire. The flames are deep down in the mine; Vic goes down on a steel ladder to bring up Vida and show that it is possible to climb to safety, but a group is cut off in the East Workings by water when fire stops the pump—this, with the exception of the plot, comes from the Mauricewood disaster. The trapped men die and their bodies have to be left until it is safe to bring them up—this too is Mauricewood.

> And so they were found after seven months under water, their bodies almost perfectly preserved by the iron which the water held in solution. They made two great circles, dark, indistinct shapes worshipping God. Some had fallen forward. Some had simply sunk down, but all were still kneeling, and one of the little boys who had 'run to warn the men' was found with his head on the parental knees. He at least had found his father! Who shall say that the others had not also?[5]

Vic Morris and Phil had continued working together over plans and calculations, Vic living in Mr Fowler's Manse since his landlady had been too much afraid of Romer to let him stay in his lodgings. After the disaster, Vic leaves Kirktown and goes to the Rio Tinto mines in Bilbao. Janet knows that she cannot compete with Vida's beauty but writes to him in letters so full of her personality that when he returns it is Janet he loves, not Vida. Phil in the meantime has profited by what he has learned from Vic. Financed by Vida's 'guardians' Billy and Dick, he has found seams of coal at Portogarten (Portowarren on the Solway) and is mining there, showing so much initiative and skill that old Jacob Romer is so impressed that he lends his own Incubus workers. This idea was probably suggested to Crockett by the coal and iron deposits worked during the eighteenth and early nineteenth century in the Auchencairn area.[6] It forms a neat device for bringing Phil and Vida happily together; he is working for his living now. The two guardians build themselves a lighthouse on Rough Island to make them feel at home and Vida keeps house for them in a little green cottage at Portogarten.

Kahn, however, must not be forgotten. He robs Romer of his entire fortune in banknotes, share certificates and documents of monetary value and drives off by car. Casimir, another Serbian employed by Romer, takes the Mercedes and follows. There is a long mad car chase in which the police join over the hills from Dalmellington to Carsphairn, New Galloway and Creetown, Phil helping the police track the cars by their distinctive tyre tracks. Kahn does not escape to the waiting ship; Casimir has all this time been seeking revenge for the slaughter of his entire family in a Balkan uprising for which Kahn was responsible (this is told in a long letter sent to Jacob Romer in due course). The police car breaks down and 'nobody but Penman can put this right, and for him you must go to Dumfries'[7] a graceful tribute to Crockett's old schoolfriend.

The Mercedes is found, driven over the edge of a cliff and burned to a metal skeleton by the exploding petrol. Nearby on the soft mossy peat hag Phil finds footprints which lead to Kahn's body, a bullet shot from behind in his head. Casimir, revenged, has escaped completely.

The shock of Kahn's duplicity—which included his leaving Vida's birth certificate proving she is Romer's daughter—literally paralyses the old man, though since he had lent Phil £10,000 in shares to help his mining activities and the Portogarten mine is now yielding a profit, all is not lost. Romer is brought, helpless and ill, to be cared for by Vida at the little house near Rough Island; all past iniquities are forgiven and forgotten. Vic has returned and married his Janet. Rose, through the good offices of her maid Leeby, becomes engaged to the Rev Benjamin Irongray, and her sinful father goes off to live with his sister in Wigan.

Vida is a pleasant exciting romance with sociological overtones. It makes over again in very much longer detail points which Crockett has made in 'In the Matter of Incubus and Company' but with stronger description. The chapters dealing with the mine disaster are carefully, slowly and vividly written; Kahn the villain is just part of the plot but the burning of the mine, the water in the East Workings of No 2 pit, the women gathering waiting for the bodies to come up and the carts rumbling along the dusty lane taking them to their homes are authentic in detailed vocabulary and Vic Morris's gradual, planned heroism—not a sudden impulse but a decision based on knowledge of the steam pipes and his experience as a manager. Crockett has remembered Mauricewood well.

He makes another point in writing almost like a conservationist of our own time when he considers the scars and ugliness that result from the mere existence of a mine,

> the dreary mounds of refuse and shale spread out everywhere, the complexity

of level crossings and multi-coloured railway signals, the tall stagings of the pits, with swiftly spinning wheels, whirling and reversing as they wound and unwound the endless steel cords. Phil had the gift of imagination, and he could see beneath him the braes of Kirktown before all this came to pass—the quiet old-fashioned white-washed hamlet, the serried rows of the corn stooks, the shy questing bairns with their mouths stained with blackberry juice in the autumn—all now passed away to give place to rows on rows of brick-built houses, each exactly the pattern of all the others, in which lived the 'employees' of the Incubus Company—gardenless, pleasureless, almost crushed out of the sight of heaven by the vast mounds of *debris* which represented the tailings of the Romer millions.

But beyond these the woods still stood up untainted all about; except, that is, for a dingy skirting of pines and larches straggling about the smelting banks. The lower branches of these had been burnt brown by the furnace fumes, whereupon one of the neighbouring landlords having threatened proceedings, Jacob Romer had bought up his property, lock, stock and barrel. This, however, was a mere fringe. It seemed as if the smell of vernal woodlands, of the unwinding crosiers of the ferns, of the glades where shy rabbits played and leaped and pattered, were able to form a barrier against the encroachment of the desecrated lower valley, which at the bidding of Incubus and Co had been given up to smoke and flame and rubbish heaps.[8]

Moral questions—the need of a man to work in order to fulfil his manhood, the greed which sacrifices fellow-creatures in order to make more and more money, the irresponsibility of mine-owners and managers—and government inspectors—in not making mines well-planned, the nemesis of Romer who had thought too little of these things, the forgiving spirit of Vida—wind in and out of a plot which is basically sensational but the peak of the book, the mine disaster, is quiet, grim, detailed but controlled, not in the least sensational. The moral questions do not come from the narrative but from the characters' comments as events move on; the message comes from the people in the story and does not dominate it or preach. It is the formula Crockett set out in his remarks on the Novel of Purpose.

There is one interesting theological point; Jacob Romer attends the Cameronian Kirk, not because of deep spiritual devotion but because he approves of its grim theology.

> 'If a man is saved, he *is* saved, and there is no more to be said,' so Mr Romer argued in his rare theological moods, 'if he is lost—well, it was so arranged in the Councils of Eternity. Either way, the man has no responsibility in the matter. An Excellent doctrine! I conduct my business of these principles, and I expect you, Kahn, to do the same, Promote a man or discharge him. But never give him a reason. Every going concern ought to have but one head, stern, infallible, irresponsible—the Incubus Pit is just the same as the Universe.'[9]

Crockett has grown so far from Calvinism that he makes Romer set himself up as all-powerful, approving the manner in which a Calvinist's God awards damnation or salvation without any given reason beyond the doctrine of Election. This system is good for business; if Calvinist doctrine is true, then the Calvinist God is no better than Romer. But Romer repents, Vida forgives, and the shy Irongray is hardly a bigoted Calvinist. Is Crockett still in two minds? When one remembers the kindly happiness of Little Duchrae, perhaps this is inevitable in the man who was young Sam so many years ago.

Princess Penniless, serialised in the *British Weekly* as *The World Well Lost*, came out in 1908 and made similar points, using as its setting the northern industrial town Thorsby in Crockett's imaginary country Cheviotshire, where Pritchard Engineering and Shipbuilding Works provide a background of underpaid, hardworked, rough men and women who are working-class. Hubert Salvesen the hero is deliberately the opposite; he is the son of a retired Army Surgeon-General devoting his retirement to working out the vials and horns, the prophecies and signs of the Book of Revelations with a view to finding where and when the Wrath to Come may be expected. Hubert has qualified as a doctor, his brother as a barrister, but their father refuses to allow them to follow their professions; they are gentlemen and must be of leisure.

Hubert is in love with Edith Dillingham, whom he has known from the time when they were both children watching the trains pass at Green Lane station high on the moors above Thorsby. Edith is a working-class girl living with her family in a row of brick houses all built exactly the same by the Moon Washington Building Society.

> A little house, 109 Bourne Street, Cheviot Road, in the Moon Washington Building Society district, in its reddest, red brickiest unpaid-upest depths, stood or rather was propped up between two others, the cottage of the Dillinghams. You knew it easily as you came along the street, passing the grocer's shop at the corner (with its aggressive biscuit-tin advertisements) by an oval glass shade with waxen fruit underneath, and a couple of books laid corner-ways so as to show the gilt on the edges. Edith Dillingham knew better than that as to decoration, but she would not vex her mother by any change. Besides, the oval glass cover was a difference. All the others were round. And none had books.[10]

They are ugly, but the devastated moors, once green and pleasant but now blackened by smoke, scored by railway lines, made barren by fumes and smoke, are much more ugly.

Edith Dillingham is a working woman who has kept house for her father and ineffectual mother, her brother and her sister all her life. She has more education than others but knows the reality of work. When Hubert asks her to marry him, she is forced to criticise and hurt him.

> ...I have a pride too. And the man I marry (if I ever do) shall be a worker, a breadearner. Even now I do all the work of a house—I have done it for years. See how my fingers are drawn and puckered with a fortnight's washing. Tonight I shall have the ironing. It will take me till midnight. I shall be up at five again on Monday morning to get my father and brother off. I could earn my living any day, even as I do now, but more easily. I could be a maid, a laundress, anything. But I would not live a day on the bounty of another—no, not if it

were my own father, least of all perhaps if it were my own father, and I a young man!'[11]

Hubert has an idea. He approaches Mr Pritchard of the Engineering Works and offers to set up medical care for all the workers for £2 a week—less than Ned Dillingham earns. This may have been suggested to Crockett by the Lloyd George proposals for social security and national insurance which must have been current topics at the time; Old Age Pensions came in 1908, the year of this book, and the National Insurance Act followed in 1911. Hubert is allowed to commandeer the second young Mr Pritchard's room as a surgery and young Mr Pritchard is persuaded to drive up to the Manor House for Hubert's medical and surgical equipment. Splints, bandages, carron oil, cotton wool, lint will all be needed; young Mr Pritchard's room has a sink and running water. His shirts are torn up to make bandages for the first patient, Ned Dillingham himself, thrown from the railway delivery lorry he is driving when the horses bolt because a malicious workman throws red-hot cinders at their legs.

Ned Dillingham is an 'out-and-outer', an atheist with a heart of gold. Because of his being the first patient, Hubert enters Edith's home for the first time. Edith makes up a bed for him overnight in case Ned's injuries are internal, but he is up and off at six in the morning like the others—he has seen a man working with white lead mixture without gloves and has ordered him to come to his office. He establishes himself as a familiar figure in the works, happier than he has ever been before; a life of skill and usefulness and service is before him. He and Edith plan to be married; Mr Pritchard offers them at a low rent a little house in the Old Quay looking over the wide glittering river. Edith, scenting some defect, asks why the rent is so low; Mr Pritchard explains that he and his first wife began their simple married life in this house; he would like Hubert and Edith to find the same happiness there.

Melodrama rears its head. Jo Challoner, the weak scrounger next door to the Dillinghams, hates Ned because Ned has lent him money. He is also madly, insanely in love with Edith, and has poisoned his wife in order to be free to marry her. Hubert blocks his way. After several attempts to kill him by 'accident', Challoner puts poison in a Lancashire hot-pot he has prepared for the doctor. Mr Pritchard sees the stew and fancies some of it himself. He is of course poisoned, and Hubert is arrested on a charge of murder. Diaries kept up to date by Mr Pritchard and left in the Old Quay house reveal that he had noted Challoner's attempts on Hubert's life; Ned Dillingham finds them—just in time to prevent Challoner from blowing up the house, himself and Edith.

Hubert is no longer to be employed by Pritchards. Edith now his wife finds a house suitable for a surgery and establishes Hubert with her father's help in making alterations; he is to be a doctor to working-class patients who will pay on a turnstile system, a shilling for a consultation, only sixpence for men from the yard—paid as they come in. This is so successful that a second doctor has to be brought in to cope with the flood of patients. Hubert's pretty cousin May Heathcote, fresh from a famous new school at Oxford, comes to see what is happening, full of admiration. But Edith's strength has been taxed too strongly—she is in any case pregnant—and the old family doctor orders her up to a quiet cottage near Green Line station for rest and recuperation. Hubert cycles up from the surgery when he has been kept too late for the last train, and Edith sets a candle in the cottage window to show that she is waiting.

One evening villainy strikes. A syndicate wishes to buy the Old Quay buildings but Hubert and Edith, acting on legal advice, refuse to sell. Hubert is ambushed one night on his way home, chloroformed, his pockets ripped open and his papers taken. Edith rushes out to find him; the pair are carried home by Geordie pitmen, and that night Edith's baby is born, to everyone's joy, including Hubert's father who is completely reconciled by being made a grandfather. All, one would think, should be well now, but Edith, lonely and far from the bustle of the surgery and the rapidly growing practice, suffers from what we would call post-natal depression. She is jealous of May and sits up reading books in order to be better educated. She wearies herself with architectural history and Sir Thomas More, the kings of England, Froude, Carlyle and Governor Eyre. It will not do, she despairs; and taking the baby goes to destroy them both under the wheels of the express. It is May who sees and stops them, removing Edith's jealousy by confessing that she is about to elope with Dr Larkins, Hubert's assistant.

All is well. Edith gives up Sir Thomas More and Hubert is relieved for as he tells her he finds the books rather boring. It is he who has married above his station, not she. Once more she is in control and they return to the surgery in town, giving the deeds of the Old Quay property to the Pritchards and living above the surgery in their old happy ways.

Once more Crockett has produced a competent if not brilliant book, with sensational elements but interesting characters. The necessity of work to make a man or a woman's life worth respecting comes out strongly once more—the Protestant work ethic, deriving in Crockett's case perhaps from Carlyle—and linked with it an examination of the class structure in society, tailored for the predominantly middle-class readers of the *British Weekly*, since if it comes to any conclusion at all, it is that the middle class is the best. The noise and harshness of life in the industrial north of England are a constant background; even the moors have the trains and are scarred by industrial pollution.

The title *Princess Penniless* states the situation in an extreme form; a princess, normally expected to be rich, who is penniless. The *British Weekly*'s original title, *The World Well Lost*, seems to have no meaning at all related to the story. Hubert is the gentleman of leisure, uneasy in his situation since he has a profession which he wishes to practise, jerked out of his acquiescence in his father's snobbery by Edith, the strong-minded working woman, perhaps even the New Woman. He knows the working-class types—the Geordies, the workers in the engineering works—Thorsby and East Dene appear to represent Newcastle with Gateshead on the other side of the river.

> They laid bets, though many had never seen a race-horse in their lives. He had

seen the rush for the sporting editions of the evening papers. They 'spotted winners.' They had their favourite jockeys whom they would follow through an entire season—in the betting columns.

But still they acted squarely and honestly, worked hard, earned their money, and in the main spent it well. A little drink, a sparring match, a row of horny knuckles shoved in another man's face; but good husbands, good fathers— even fair-to-middling brothers.[12]

It is a patronising picture, perhaps, but recognises that the working man has no money or time to go to race-courses and has to find his excitement from a distance. It is a meditation in which Hubert indulges the night Edith has said she will marry him; he lies listening to the tugs on the river and the paddles on the ferries, thanking God for Edith, for Ned Dillingham, for her mother and even Sue, but reflecting that after they are married they need not see much of Edith's vulgar brother Will and his raucous ill-mannered cronies. The chapter is called 'The Crumple in the Rose Leaf'—the inconveniences brought by marrying 'out of one's class'. He does not know it, but Edith is lying awake that night too, worrying about that same problem, beginning halting little notes breaking off their engagement. This shared anxiety is not snobbish but realistic; it is only because Edith has had more education, thanks to her father, than the working-class girls around her that she is able to be Hubert's wife; she is thought 'stuck up' and 'above herself' by her peers in Bourne Street because she does not go to dances or care to be walked home from church by anyone who offers. She has, metaphorically as well as literally, an umbrella of her own. There are books in the Dillingham's house.

Others make a chorus of comments on the marriage. Hubert's father writes a letter of protest to Mr Pritchard deploring Hubert's engagement to the daughter of 'one of your employees—an infamous and well-known atheist'[13] and demands if Mr Pritchard would like one of his sons to marry the Salvesen cook; Mr Pritchard replies that he would be delighted to have either of his sons marry such an honest hard-working woman—or any of the same kind. Hubert's aunt and her circle of gossips concoct a letter to Mr Pritchard's second wife, a lady of title, warning her that her husband is associating with the undesirable low-class Dillinghams. 'Lady Etheldreda Conquest mariée Pritchard' pays a Lady-Catherine-de-Bourgh visit to Edith, dressed severely and mannishly in plain tweeds and high-laced boots like a gamekeeper; she recognises immediately that Edith is ladylike and educated, with gentle manners; she apologises for troubling them and retires in a most friendly frame of mind, hoping that their acquaintance will prosper so that they know one another better—and forgets all about them in a week. This is probably Crockett's own view—it is really of no importance what social class one belongs to as long as one is a human being—a man's a man for a' that.

Love in Pernicketty Town (1911) does not bode well as a title; one is fearful of arch girls and crotchetty old ladies. The town in question is Longtown in the imaginary Cheviotshire, which in this book seems to be in Scotland, and the subject-matter is surprising; it is the damage that can be done by a clever evangelist who is also a charlatan. The hero-narrator is Adrian Ross, classics master at the High School whose dreamy scholarly lazy headmaster leaves him to do most of the educational organisation. Dr Cassells has three daughters, May, June and January, abbreviated mercifully to Jan, but his wife is dead. Adrian is on the warmest terms of friendship with all three, but he and June are in love. The town also has its gossips, principally Adrian's outspoken landlady. Dr Cassells and his daughters have a comic maid Persilla; and there is a friendly group of ministers who meet once a week (except for the Episcopal one who holds to the Apostolic Succession and does not mingle). They all have nicknames, but the one of importance is the one nicknamed the Bairnly Minister who keeps preaching about a tiresome little boy called Tommy; his colleagues tease him for his sentimentality. Adrian is an honorary member of the group.

Upon this little market town there descends a high-powered evangelist Reston Rigg. The ministers regard him with amusement as a kind of circus, but the gentle Bairnly Minister startles them by declaring that he is the work of the devil. He explains his vehemence apologetically by saying that his only daughter Ella had fallen under the influence of just such a man and had run away from home with him, leaving her widower father desolate. He has not heard from her since.

Reston Rigg, the 'Mesmeric Evangelist', is very different from the normal travelling evangelists and even from Moody and Sankey. He is almost American in his approach. Dark, handsome, with an exotic Oriental power that is almost hypnotic, he employs every kind of sophisticated publicity to draw the crowds. His first appearance in Longtown is memorable. After a 'Forerunner' has proclaimed his arrival with a silver trumpet, he is driven into the market square by a chauffeur in a blue and silver limousine gifted by a rich lady admirer. Alighting, he announces in ringing tones

> The Word of the Lord is among you! Peace be on this city, on the men thereof, on the women, and on the little children![14]

If this has an echo of Mr Chadband this is unfortunate; Crockett did not intend it. At his first meeting, in a large marquee erected by his staff, the townspeople are confronted by footlights, dazzling overhead lighting, a choir, a concealed orchestra and a First Soloist, Hester Vane, singing to throbbing languorous music part of the Song of Solomon. These all combine in richness of effect to throw into contrast Reston Rigg's sudden appearance clad gravely in black, commanding all sinners to show repentance.

> 'Come,' murmured Reston Rigg, stretching out his right hand, and his eyes wandered here and there over the meeting of folk whom he now felt himself able to move at his will.
> His hands described curves, as though to draw the wounded birds into his net. The lights darkened till the vast tent was in shadow, and all that stood out of the gloom was the scarlet Altar of the Penitents and the forceful figure of Reston Rigg, Mesmeric Evangelist.[15]

His appeal is totally to the emotions, not the judgement, and he wields it deliberately with a sexual undertone so as to influence women. Mrs Jimson, the publican's wife, is one of his ready victims. When the lights go up after a session and the tentflaps open, letting reality and the winking gaslights replace the magic, Adrian notices how the crowds shuffle out dazed, looking back into the tent as if wishing to be there still

> and it seemed to me certain that the next night would find them back again to taste the perilous pleasure of that wizardry which they mistook for the Kingdom of God within them.[16]

He notices too that Hester Vane, the First Soloist, is not part of this quasi-sorcery. She helps in the manipulation, controls the lights, the choir, the volume of the music, so that Rigg times his appearances by her, but she watches the 'penitents' come forward with her lip slightly curled; she has seen it too often before. She has been behind the scenes. Rigg's hands raised in blessing before he disappears into the carefully contrived darkness have no power or mystery for her.

Jan Cassells, the middle daughter, becomes a victim, going forward in a burst of hysteria to kneel. Adrian persuades her to come away but she is hostile, and in spite of the vigilance of her sisters she contrives by smuggled notes to remain in contact with Rigg. She agrees to go with him when he moves on.

Hester Vane, the First Soloist, asks Adrian to meet her. She reveals that she is Reston Rigg's wife, kept a secret because it would diminish his power over women—a touch of Hollywood again. She and Adrian foil the elopement by sending Jan to the wrong rendezvous; when Rigg drives off, it is his wife whom he has abducted, his wife who was his first victim, Ella, the daughter of the Bairnly Minister. Jan is heart-broken, unbelieving, desolate. She transfers the feelings she had for Rigg to Adrian and becomes dependent on him for her sanity—an eminent psychiatrist when consulted diagnoses this. Adrian and June must sacrifice their love for Jan's sake, they see no other remedy for her diminished hold on life.

Reston Rigg meantime is at Forelands, his uncle's house overlooking the Clyde, a pleasant light architect-designed villa with a touch of Charles Rennie Mackintosh; Rigg falls ill, with our old friend brain fever, but with it comes terror at his own defiling of the Gospel. He has preached not Christ but Reston Rigg, and made money by it. He must go back to the towns where he has practised his unclean charlatanism and confess his sin.

When he returns to Longtown his sincerity moves the ministers to give their friendship and lend the Bairnly Minister's church. As he brings his confession to an end, genuinely repentant, he is almost radiant with a sense of forgiveness. As he leaves the church, his hearers crowd round but a woman with rough tangled hair, the publican's wife, aims a pistol at Hester. Rigg shields her with his body and is killed immediately. Meanwhile Jan at home has known nothing of this or even of Rigg's presence in Longtown. She behaves strangely and seems to be listening for something. In the silence, she hears and answers that she is coming. It is Rigg whom she hears calling her, and in answering him she dies. June and Adrian are free, but they have peace of mind; they were willing to give one another up for Jan's sake.

A little market town very like those in Galloway, plenty of ministers, religion in the forefront of the story—but very far from the Kailyard! Crockett describes, analyses and makes very clear the dangers of emotional personal magnetism on crowds willing to be stirred—wanting excitement. The natural mysticism which he has been proclaiming is very different from this unclean trickery for the sake of money. Yet he suggests that in Rigg's repentance there may be forgiveness, and that in the heart of the trickery there may be a core of truth, as Browning did with *Mr Sludge the Medium*. Jan, innocent, loving, pure, goes to join him in whatever eternity has been granted to him, responding to his dead influence. This is one of the few occasions in which Crockett makes use of the supernatural in a modern setting. He will use madness with careless frequency but is wary of the supernatural, though he does use it in one short story 'The Cry across the Black Water'[17] which suggests that he could have been a master of the form.

Other slighter books are taken from varying contemporary backgrounds. *Little Esson*, (1907) serialised in the *Windsor* before publication, is an ordinary romantic tale based on the artists and studios with which his friendship with William MacGeorge and E A Hornel had made him familiar. *The Lady of a Hundred Dresses* (1911) takes us into diamond dealing and stealing; the story is moving towards the modern thriller, though with very odd Scottish touches. *Deep Moat Grange* is perhaps his worst book (1908); it is hard to see for what audience he was writing—possibly for juveniles. The book begins with a pointless macabre murder and proceeds into realms of fantasy so wild that it is hard not to lose patience. Everyone in the book is mad except the few characters in the foreground, from the household of indeterminate nuns who inhabit the Grange to Jeremy their servant who plays the fiddle madly in his insane enjoyment of evil. *Me and Myn* (1907), being written for Stanley Gibbons' Stamp Magazine, has limited appeal even to stamp collectors, and is written in racy colloquial schoolboy slang which makes it more of a linguistic curiosity than a readable book.

In *Sandy's Love Affair* (1913) we see the mingled dangers and delights of Crockett's improvisation when his imagination was tired and his strength wearying. Sandy is a Galloway lad hoping for literary fame in London. He makes his first success in a carriers' business which he runs until it is so successful that his brothers have to join him. He also meets in his lodgings a music-hall actress with whom he falls in love. The story wanders from a Presbyterian church in London to which he takes his actress 'VV' (he is black-balled later by the elders who think her unsuitable) to the music-hall in which she performs and to which he becomes 'chucker-out'; from a tour with her in a real play, a cut above music-hall, which visits Edinburgh and acquires a young lady from Leith, McComie, as an addition to the cast, to Ferniehill in Galloway where we recognise in the Prydes, his parents, portraits of William and Mary Crocket once more. They welcome VV for all that she is an actress and think she will make a bonnie wife for Sandy. The factor insults her; Sandy throws him and his guffawing friend out of the hotel window to the approval of a local dignitary whose name if not anything else leads us to recognise Lord Ardwall.

The company proceeds to Ireland, which is in the grip of Home Rule agitation. They play golf at Portrush, and VV and McComie sing 'The Wearin' of the Green' with such innocent emotion that hardened Ulster Unionists join in and brush away a tear. But the injured factor has turned the Prydes out of Ferniehill, and we are in for another roup, and Crockett this time *does* borrow from Ian Maclaren. The roup, having caused its quota of sorrow, is halted by the arrival of the new Lord Balmaghie whose father has died in the Channel Isles and who has married McComie.

In all this activity, Sandy has somehow found time to write two successful novels, *Cold Steel* and *Greying Gold*. In the middle of a third, *Sword Bayonets*, he succumbs to the dreaded brain fever. It has all been too much for him. Serialisation of the story has begun but it has not been completed. What is to be done for the remaining instalments?

A young woman from the Galloway gentry exerts herself on his behalf; we have met her early in the book when she has fallen in love with the very homespun Sandy but her passion, being unrequited, has made her throw herself into a dark deep Galloway pool. Sandy has fished her out, but has had the tact to disappear once she is in safe hands. She bears him no grudge, and persuades one of her society friends, Dean Forfar, the famous novelist, to take Sandy's notes and by imitating his style complete the book. It becomes a success and no one is any the wiser; as a reward, the Galloway lady tidies up her part in the plot by marrying Dean Forfar.

Leaving aside the Galloway lady, the finishing of a novel by another author so as to leave no trace and make it a success seems the most improbable, impossible part of this rambling book. In fact, it is taken from actuality. William Black, a successful Scottish author of the time, noted for *Macleod of Dare*, *A Princess of Thule* and *A Daughter of Heth* to name only three, did precisely this for his friend Charles Gibbon when he was stricken by illness halfway through a novel.[18] One is never sure with Crockett whether he is making it all up or borrowing from real life; his misfortune is that it is always the most bizarre events that he borrows.

Two books are difficult to classify as either historical novels or novels verging on the contemporary, *Anne of the Barricades* (1912) and *A Tatter of Scarlet* (1913). They deal with events in 1871 when Paris was in the grip of the Commune after the Franco-Prussian war, and a rising of the same political kind took place in Marseilles. Crockett had been interested in these times early in his career; the Commune appears towards the end of *A Galloway Herd*. *Anne of the Barricades* is a picture of a city under attack and in the hands of rebels, its streets unsafe and its buildings demolished by explosives. Anne is the daughter of an old Colonel of the Scots Guards whose house is a meeting place for conspirators. Jean Larzac is an aristocrat who has shortened his name and serves in the government army. Anne is his friend but not in love with him; she introduces him to Nini Auroy, an actress at the Opera, a woman of elegance. Authentic figures enter—de Rochefort the pamphleteer, two generals who are shot (in the garden of the house in the Rue des Rosiers where Anne and her father live, for the benefit of the story), M. Thiers who befriends Jean and Nini, and is to lead the government after the fighting. Nini plays the same part as did Sarah Bernhardt—organises a hospital for the wounded and the sick. When it becomes obvious that the Commune is to fall, Anne and her father man a barricade as a final gesture and are shot, as they know they will be. Jean and Nini marry and are happy, remembering Anne with sadness and love. *A Tatter of Scarlet* tries to present a picture of rebellious unions rising to free themselves with socialist, Marxist fervour from the bosses. It is less successful than *Anne* because it is hampered by two schoolboy heroes. Gambetta, Garibaldi and others make brief appearances and the beautiful Eastern daughter of a rebel has to be protected; the owner of an armaments factory is the father of one of the heroes. Interestingly Crockett comes down against the rebels who are not understood even by their supporters. One of the leaders sadly declares this to the narrator, saying

> I have dreamed my dream. I thought (as thought Carl Marx) that these working men were ready for an ideal reform, for government over themselves. I saw other cities joining themselves to us, the good seed sown over the country from department to department, till all should work for all and no man only for himself. Now I see that the nature of man cannot be changed by a theory of a form of government.[19]

Crockett is a realist; like Mr Molesay he knows that man is not able to rise above his own weaknesses but must be accepted for what he is, an imperfect being struggling but always failing, and at times not even struggling.

These many books—and others—differing in style, setting and quality of writing, are contributions to Crockett's picture of his own times. He was acutely conscious of social conditions. He condemned drunkards, bullies, thieves, the greedy and the uncaring. Perhaps if he had remained a minister and written about Galloway, he would have had a less up-hill struggle to place his books; if he had been content to be 'Kailyard' he would have been more secure. Lord Guthrie remarked confidently of Ian Maclaren in 1906 'I don't suppose he's made so much money as Barrie, but more than Crockett'.[20] He was the least financially successful of the triumvirate of Barrie, Maclaren and himself, and with his gentle-born wife, his large house, his servants and gardeners, his four children growing up and seeking careers, and his poor health, he was the one most in need of a settled income.

If he had lived longer, the outbreak of war in 1914 might have given him new impetus; he might have joined 'Sapper', Buchan and Dornford Yates. On the other hand, the horror of war might have been too much. Creating horrors on paper is different from their reality. He had written about a world that was to disappear a few months after his death at the age of fifty-four in April 1914. In one thing he would have been different. Peter Usborne in *Clubland Heroes* has pointed out how the womenfolk of the main characters tend to be helpless and fragile in the background, either suffering anxiety about what their men are doing or else, still worse, liable to be abducted, drugged, scared into immobility by giant spiders or held in dark cellars with the water rising. Crockett's would have played a more positive role. From his earliest writings—Mrs McQuhirr, Leeb M'Lurg, May Mischief, Winsome Charteris, Maisie Lennox—Crockett's women show more initiative and sense than his men. *Ione March* is a portrait of the New Woman; she may have dwindled into a wife, but she still has a career—managing her husband. Vida can hold her own with anyone. Hester Vane can outwit Reston Rigg. Edith Dillingham, the most outspoken of them all, defines the conditions on which she will marry Hubert, makes sure he is carrying them out and creates a practice for him when he is at a loss. Even the tiresome Miss Anne gets her own way, and Clemmy too, in her particular manner.

It is not because he is writing for a female audience that Crockett writes about strong women. This comes from his peasant background, where the women ruled the household and the men went out to the open-air work of the farm. Moreover, he had a remarkable grandmother in Mary Crocket. She is depicted most fully, most warmly, in the pleasant eighteenth-century Edinburgh story *The Dew of their Youth* (1909) in which she dominates the hero's youth and when he marries and settles near the Meadows in Edinburgh, turns up once more, box and all, ready to take over when his first son is born and a woman is needed.

They would have had their gentle side; they would have been soft-hearted under their strength; but they would have scorned to be tied up by Peterson or left at home worrying. They would have been there in the thick of things, managing very well, with or without masculine help.

CHAPTER 11

'Climbing on the Steep Stairs'

The first flurry of Crockett's success as a popular writer was lively while it lasted, and it lasted until the turn of the century and a little beyond. Postcards, some issued by local stationers like Adam Rae and John Low of Castle Douglas and 'Brown's Series', as well as by larger firms like Valentine of Dundee and Ritchie of Edinburgh (the 'Reliable' series) represented among other Galloway scenes 'The Duchrae, Birthplace of S R Crockett', whitewashed, humble, rather muddy in its surroundings, sometimes with, sometimes without a homely farm cart beside the door. 'The Murder Hole, Loch Neldricken' must have been inspired by Crockett, since he was the first to bestow that name upon a harmless spring. 'Threave Castle, Crockett's Black Douglas' is clearly another Crockett tribute, as is 'U F Church, Queen Street, Castle Douglas, Crockett's Kirk on the Hill'. 'Earlstoun Castle', 'The Dungeon of Buchan' and 'The Raiders' Bridge'—a perfectly ordinary stone bridge over the Black Water of Dee until Crockett transformed it—are all part of what was becoming a local legend. Tourists were making their way to the scenes of which they had read with so much enjoyment and local inns and hotels were taking travellers in hired conveyances over roads from which they could view the Merrick, the River Ken and the Kells Range.

The *Dumfries and Galloway Standard* of 30 May 1896 reported the interest shown in the circular tours promoted by the Glasgow and South Western Railway Company in conjunction with the Port Patrick Railway, Mr Milligan of the Lochinvar Hotel, Dalry, and Mr Brown of the Black Bull, Dalmellington, who provided transport by arrangement over the thirty-three miles of the route not covered by railway line. Tickets were issued at Dumfries, Glasgow and Ayr, as well as at stations through which the trains passed. Burns, Bruce and the Covenanters were the attraction while the tour was passing through Ayrshire, but

> Another name of power in these parts is the name of Crockett. The latest of Galloway's literary sons has drawn abundantly from the Glenkens material for his vivid character and scenic sketches. As we look across the rock-hewn channel of the Ken to Earlstoun and its giant oak we feel ourselves among the company of 'The Men of the Moss Hags', the coach in which we ride borrows its name 'Gay Garland', from the pages of that work. The district too is redolent of association with 'The Raiders' and 'The Lilac Sunbonnet'.

The tours were into their second year and showing no diminution of demand

Little Duchrae, The Birthplace of S. R. Crockett.

6   Little Duchrae, the Birthplace of S R Crockett. The illustrations on this and the opposite page are from postcards of the time.

Raiders Bridge, New Galloway Station

7   Raiders Bridge, New Galloway Station.

'CLIMBING ON THE STEEP STAIRS' 255

8   The Murder Hole and the Merrick.

9   U F Church, Castle Douglas. (Crockett's 'Kirk on the Hill').

or popularity. Gay Garland, appropriately for a coach, was the name of the elder William Gordon's horse.

Articles on the new popular author appeared in magazines ranging from the *Windsor*, the *Idler* and the *Westminster Budget* to the more homely *Weekly News*, the *Christian Commonwealth* and the *People's Friend*; interviews were printed describing his house, his method of work, his books, his typewriter and his Galloway upbringing. The author's residence, Bank House, his study, his drawing-room, his children, he himself sitting sideways at the typewriter so that the machine could be seen clearly, or playing golf at St Andrews with Willie Auchterlonie, were reproduced for the benefit of readers who were interested—and they were many. Crockett was read and admired in Canada and the United States, the Far East and Australia, as well as in the British Isles; some of his books were included among those specially printed 'For India and the Colonies only' by George Bell and Sons, London and Bombay. A copy of *The Men of the Moss Hags* stamped and with an accession number proclaiming that it was part of the Library of the Hong Kong Club made its way back to the tenpenny shelves of an Edinburgh bookshop in the 1980s, battered, dirty, worm-eaten, with several pages missing, but having been read so thoroughly that it had had to be rebound at least once.

The *Christian Leader* had its own meed of praise to offer. Along with its Christmas and New Year Extra for the turn of the year 1894–95, it presented its readers with a large one-page Calendar on stiff paper for the whole of the New Year. Featured on it were the photographs of five Eminent Divines; four of them were ministers or DDs; one of them was a Rev Professor, and the fifth, in the place of honour right in the middle, was the author of *The Raiders*. This production must have caused Crockett some mild embarrassment; if it hung, as it was meant to hang, in the kitchens or parlours of families who took the *Leader*, it would be a mute reminder throughout the entire year that in the very first month of 1895 one Eminent Divine, the Rev S R Crockett, had left the fold, had laid lown his ministry, had taken to writing story-books and had of his own free will cast aside the honour of being an Eminent Divine at all.

The lecture on *Scottish National Humour* which Crockett delivered so often, sent as an article to the *Contemporary Review* and reprinted himself, with minor variations, in *Raiderland* in 1904, is of particular importance to his practice as a writer. It was repeated not because of dearth of material but because he attached such weight to what he said in it. It was about humour, and Crockett's impish humour and delight in the ridiculous, often warmly teasing, at other times grimly sardonic, were each individual qualities in his writing. It contained, as we have seen in Chapter 7 his theories about the writing of fiction; rightly or wrongly he defined the writer's art as one of entertaining his readers without preaching or trying to thrust moral lessons upon them. He must be 'purposeful, but conceal his purpose and write with his heart'.[1] To this he remained faithful.

Another valuable part of the article is its discussion of vernacular Scots. There had arisen in the last quarter of the century a fashion for Scottish stories by William Alexander (*Johnny Gibb of Gushetneuk*), Gabriel Setoun

(*Barncraig*), Barrie, Stevenson and Ian Maclaren, and Crockett's fear was that localisation of Scots would be the result. If Alexander wrote in strong Aberdeenshire Scots, Gabriel Setoun in Fifeshire, Barrie in the accents of Kirriemuir which was Thrums, Stevenson in Midlothian and Ian Maclaren in the Logiealmond speech of Drumtochty, there would come about a breaking up of the Scots language into dialects, each differing according to the author and his locality. Scots was not, as so many imagined, a corrupt kind of English but a national tongue which had served the whole country before James VI and I had moved his court and culture south to London; if each man, now that interest in it was reviving, wrote strictly and pedantically in his own local accent, the Scots language would be lost even more completely than it had been already.

> Now, what I understand to be the duty of the Scottish romancer is that he shall not attempt to represent phonetically the peculiarities of pronunciation of his chosen district, but that he shall content himself with giving the local colour, incident, character, in the noble historical, well-authenticated Scots language which was found sufficient for the needs of Knox, of Scott and of Burns, to name no other names. Leave to the grim grammarian his 'fous' and 'fats' and 'fars'. Let the local vocabulary-maker, excellent and indispensable man, construct cunning accents and pronunciation marks. Leave even Great Jamieson alone, save for amusement in your hours of ease.[2]

What he favoured was a renewal, or attempt to renew, a kind of standard Scots belonging to the whole country, eclectic and understood in all districts and regions, the Scots of Barbour, Dunbar, Henryson and Douglas which Ramsay, Burns, Scott, Hogg, Galt and Stevenson had already been using for serious writing.

Crockett wanted Scots words that were still in use when Scots people were speaking, words that could be picked up by keen-eared writers when heard about them in daily affairs. One of the Bank House maids, Elizabeth Shanks, described to her daughter how Crockett used to pounce upon unfamiliar words when they caught his ear, especially among ordinary working people who preserved old forms.

> Crockett often stopped and talked to the servants. He was interested in their childhood, their families, their hopes and aspirations. If they uttered a strange word or phrase, particularly a Scottish one, he would immediately ask them to repeat it and ask them what they meant by it. Sometimes if, in the course of his writing, my mother chanced to be in the room he would look up and ask her for the Scottish word for something, eg a door–yett; a turkey–a bubblyJock; or he would ask her what 'dreich' meant, or 'wairsh', etc. One day he heard my mother say to one of the children 'Yer een are waur to fill than yer wame', and she had to explain the meaning word by word.

The speech of Midlothian could have been slightly different from that of Galloway, and if so he was keen to find out exactly in what way and extend his knowledge of Scots. He would have been happy writing entirely in Scots for Scots, if that had been financially possible. He would have written in a broader Scots than he did, but he explained at the Dalbeattie dinner in his honour that editors do not like what they call 'dialect' and made him cut it down for the sake of the non-Scots public. He regretted this. Yet he never wrote the book he promised to write at that dinner in 1907, a book in the Scots of Nithsdale and Galloway so individual that only those of Nithsdale and Galloway would understand it. He would like to have but admitted that he did not know who would publish it as it would not pay.[3] Scottish writers were dependent for their living upon English publishers

Elsewhere, in his introduction to *Annals of the Parish*, Crockett makes another interesting distinction. Galt, he says, writes the Scots of Burns, another Ayrshireman, learned at his mother's knee and around the hearth and family circle. He was brought up among people who spoke nothing else.

> Galt's variety of his Scottish tongue is full of fine old grandmotherly words, marrowy with pith and sap. Scott, like Stevenson, wrote his vernacular a little from the heights. He had learned it, as it were, for love and adventurousness, as men in these days learn Romany. But Galt writes Scots like one who had been cradled in it, who lisped it in the doorways and cried it to other loons across the street. He lived among men and women who habitually spoke it. In some ways, the Doric of Scott may be finer, more literary, a 'clear metropolitan utterance', indeed. But, though I reverence Sir Walter above all the sons of men, yet do I say that the Scots, even of Caleb Balderstone and Andrew Fairservice, has hardly the rich tang of the mother-earth which I find in the 'Annals' and the best books of John Galt. But that may be because I am Westland born, and of the Whigs, Whiggish.[4]

It is also because they both grew up in Scots-speaking homes, and came to English as a second language, handling it well but knowing that it was to be used at school, in the kirk, for formal occasions and when writing serious prose.

The final paragraphs of 'Scottish National Humour' sum up in a flourish of pride Crockett's affection for the Scots language. He regrets that music hall comedians can use it vulgarly for the sake of a cheap laugh and call their rubbish Scottish dialect; he himself harks back to the genuine flavour of old Scots, the Scots of knee-breeches and buckled shoes that is just a little old-fashioned in modern days, and can be sometimes coarse but never vulgar. This reminds us at once of Henry Cockburn's account of the old Edinburgh ladies of his time who 'all dressed, and spoke, and did, exactly as they chose; their language, like their habits, entirely Scotch, but without any vulgarity other than what perfect naturalness is sometimes mistaken for'.[5]

> There never was a nobler or more expressive language than the tongue of the dear old ladies who were our grandmothers and great-grandmothers in these southern and western counties of Scotland. Let us try to keep it equally free from Anglicisms which come by rail, Irishisms which arrive by the short sea-route, from the innuendo of the music-hall comic, and the refinements of the boarding-school—in fact, from all additions, subtractions, multiplications

and divisions, by whomsoever introduced or advocated. There is an idea abroad that in order to write Scottish dialect, it is enough to leave out all final g's and to write *dae* for do—which last, I beg leave to say, is the mark of the bungler.

Now the honest Doric is a sonsy quean, snod, and well put on. Her acquaintance is not to be picked up on the streets, or at any close-mouth. The day has been when Peg was a lady, and so she shall be again, and her standard of manners and speech shall be at least as high as that of her sister of the South.

The result will not show in the reports of the Board of Trade; neither will it make Glasgow flourish yet more abundantly, or the ships crowd thicker about the Tail of the Bank. But it will give broad Scotland a right to speak once more of a Scottish language, and not merely of a Dundee, a Gallowa', or a 'Doon-the-watter' accent. And it will give her again a literature frankly natural, written in her ancient language, according to the finest and most uncorrupted models.[6]

This is a manifesto which the Scottish Renaissance writers of the twenties could have agreed with whole-heartedly, if they had known that it existed. By their time, Crockett's waning popularity and the cheap sneer of the 'Kailyard' nickname had placed him far below their interest or even knowledge.

So much for lectures. By this time Crockett had had enough of them, and the *Dumfries and Galloway Standard* reported his intention to make no more public speeches.

Mr Crockett is not an ideal lecturer. He has a fine presence, a tall, well-proportioned form, a massive head crowned with wavy brown-black hair, a ruddy complexion partly clothed with reddish-fair whiskers and moustache. His manner is perfectly self-possessed, and his voice is powerful and resonant; but is strongly marked with a somewhat harsh, unsympathetic Galloway accent, which amounts at times to a decided lisp.[7]

Such a strongly local personality was all right for a minister, conducting a service of which he was only a part. If he were alone on a platform, the entire show, as it were, the mannerisms of speech would be too intrusive for easy listening.

Another commentator, in the *Scots Pictorial* in October 1894, commends Crockett for having refused the offer of £6,000 made to him for a lecture-tour in America by the indefatigable Major Pond who spent his time luring celebrities to make such tours of talks and readings.

I have heard Mr Crockett lecture, and, frankly, I am not greatly enamoured of him on the platform. This, however, has nothing to do with my congratulations. These are simply due to my gratification at finding that the author of 'The Raiders' evidently means to adhere to the rule which he made some time ago to eschew the public platform. I am old-fashioned enough to hold that the author's place is *not* the platform; and to dislike the self-advertisement practised by certain well-known novelists.[8]

As well as continuing with the writing of the major books for which he had contracted, Crockett continued assiduously—with the help of his agent

A P Watt, the man who invented the profession of literary agent and was serving nearly every writer at this time—to contribute short stories to many magazines—the *Pall Mall*, the *People's Friend*, the *Young Man* and its companion the *Young Woman, Leisure Hour*, the *Graphic, Woman at Home*, the *Windsor*, the *Idler*; most of these were collected later and republished in one or other of his books of short stories, *Bog-Myrtle and Peat* (1895) which contains several of his *Christian Leader* contributions, chapters from *A Galloway Herd* which could stand on their own, his best ghost story, 'A cry Across the Black Water', a short novella set in Italy, and a poem by Andrew Lang; *The Stickit Minister's Wooing and Other Galloway Stories* (1900), *Love Idylls* (1901); *The Bloom of the Heather* (1908) and *Young Nick and Old Nick. Yarns for the Year's End* (1910).

A further indication of Crockett's success in England came when Edmund Gosse took note of him. Morton Cohen in his book on Rider Haggard explains the significance of this.

> The Gosses, from the earliest days of their marriage, gave Sunday afternoon tea parties at their home at 29 Delamore Terrace, across from Paddington Canal. For forty-five years, these Sunday gatherings were a London institution, particularly among literary people. Edmund Gosse, a very orderly person, kept a record of each of these parties in a thick, narrow book known now as the 'Book of Gosse'. Here are recorded the dates of each occasion and lists of all the guests present ... Some of the entries are underscored, Gosse's way of indicating those who stayed on for supper ... Haggard had dinner at the Gosse's with S R Crockett and Frances Hodgson Burnett, author of *Little Lord Fauntleroy*, among others.[9]

Further investigation of the Book of Gosse, now in Cambridge University Library, shows that Crockett's name appears on three other occasions. On 1 April 1894, he was present at Sunday tea at the Gosses', with Mr and Mrs Joseph Pennell, Mr and Mrs Rider Haggard, Mr and Mrs Arthur Waugh (the parents of Alec and Evelyn) and Mr Robert Ross—Oscar Wilde's 'Robbie'—among others, and Crockett, the Pennells, the Rider Haggards and the Waughs have their names underscored; they stayed on in the evening. During February 1895 Crockett again appears. On the seventeenth he was entertained along with several others, and on the nineteenth he was one of a party who lunched with Gosse as his guests at the National Club. This latter group included Aubrey Beardsley, Robert Ross again, George Moore, David Hannay, Sydney Pawling and Sidney Colvin.

It is exasperating that the very orderly person Edmund Gosse listed only names and did not think to give a hint of conversations. It would have been interesting to know how Crockett got on with the Pennells and whether this was their first friendly encounter; Joseph Pennell was one of the artists who contributed illustrations to the eighth Illustrated Edition of *The Stickit Minister*, choosing their own particular subject-matter; Pennell's illustrations of the Edinburgh slums and rainy city nights are exceptionally striking. One can also imagine Crockett's pleasure in meeting H Rider Haggard; the vast caverns which feature from time to time in his stories are so like those in *King Solomon's Mines* and *She* that Crockett must have been familiar with and an admirer of those and other Haggard stories. He would have been glad to talk with Sidney Colvin about R L Stevenson. When Colvin published the Skerryvore edition of Stevenson's letters in 1926, several which had been written to Crockett were included; perhaps it was on this occasion that Colvin heard of their existence. On the other hand, it is difficult to imagine what the massive country-bred Crockett would have had to say to the aesthete Aubrey Beardsley; they probably gazed on one another with interest and astonishment rather than any warm fellow-feeling. And it is an unexpected juxtaposition to find Crockett sharing Sunday supper with Arthur and Kate Waugh.

In comparison with other literary figures who appear frequently in Gosse's lists over the years, Crockett is mentioned only four times. Had he been invited because for the moment he was in the news, and dropped because he was not especially interesting or congenial? Did Crockett himself find Gosse and his gatherings not altogether to his liking and decline future invitations? Or else was he simply not available because he was so seldom in London for any pre-arranged length of time?

This last reason seems at least possible. Catherine Robertson Nicoll, who married Robertson Nicoll as his second wife in 1897, wrote in 1934 'for private circulation only' a detailed record of her life with her busy literary husband and their friends in Bay Tree Lodge, Hampstead; she called it *Under the Bay Tree* because one of Crockett's letters began 'Dear good friends Under the Bay Tree' and the phrase caught her fancy. She writes of Crockett with warm affection but never as a long-term visitor; he often visited them on his way to somewhere else:

> We often had a visit ... from S R Crockett on his way through London to or from Spain or France.[10]

Annie S Swan mentions in *My Life* that she and her husband often met Ian Maclaren and J M Barrie at Bay Tree Lodge

> and that stormy petrel Crockett who was always dashing up from Penicuik on some pretext or other ... he was a queer mixture, with something most lovable about him ...[11]

which would confirm the picture of Crockett always on the move, turning up unexpectedly, and not in a position to accept invitations offered formally and in advance. One feels that people did not just 'drop in' to see that very orderly Edmund Gosse.

Crockett would in any case feel more at home among the Robertson Nicolls, the Barries and the Burnett-Smiths, less sophisticated and warmer-hearted to his mind than the favoured literati of the London and southern counties scene. Scots readers will recognise the significance of Annie S Swan's familiar comment 'a queer mixture'. Catherine Robertson Nicoll, English herself, found him entertaining and generous.

> He used to talk of his early days on his parents' farm near Clatteringshaws and Lauriston (sic); his mother had taught him his letters, tracing them for him on her baking board while she made the oatcakes. One autumn, after a visit of his when he had sung the praises of Galloway heather honey, a great box arrived for me containing twelve sections packed with heather. Such a Scottish gift I have never had before or since. He was publishing a novel almost every year and he sent me one always at Christmas.[12]

She had met the Crocketts for the first time at Bank House; she was made most cordially welcome and liked the Crockett way with books.

> It was a nice house, and round the dining room and drawing room were bookcases about five feet high on the top of which stood photographs and ornaments. I was much struck with this arrangement and reproduced it later at Bay Tree Lodge, making the shelves rather lower. Mr Crockett was a fine, fair man with very good almond-shaped eyes. Mrs Crockett I found very charming. There were four jolly children.[13]

The books formed a friendly bone of contention between Crockett and Robertson Nicoll.

> Crockett was heart and soul a bookman. He delighted in accumulating rare editions, and in binding them finely ... could not endure any approach to disorder, and this was irksome to an enquiring reader, who was apt to find that the books he had taken out had been carefully replaced in their original homes if he absented himself for five minutes.[14]

Mrs Robertson Nicoll prints in her book of reminiscences the whole of the 'Dear good Friend under the Bay Tree' letter; it suggests that Crockett was happiest at home, about his own pursuits and not eager for society.

> I have taken to photography and like it much. It keeps me out in the open air and makes me walk 'with an object'. I have built me a lordly library 40 feet by 18, and now sit at ease up away from the house and the maid answers 'Not at home!' and does not lie ... I send you one or two rough home products including one of my place where I live, sleep, work when I am busy—or desire quiet. It consists of a complete establishment—observatory, bedroom, library, studio. Some day you and the good man will come again and see it—and us.[15]

This was, of course, the stout wooden annexe which he had had built while at Bank House and which went with the Crocketts when they later moved to Peebles and was re-erected there.

He received, however, one tribute from London society. The fashionable weekly *Vanity Fair* was a periodical which summarised and commented upon political and artistic events, not always with respect. It was the magazine of the 'Smart Set', written by and for the Victorian and Edwardian establishments. One of its most popular features was the coloured lithographic caricature in which week by week it caught and exaggerated the foibles and mannerisms of personages who were in the news—the nobility, bishops, judges, politicians, journalists, writers, sportsmen, actors, artists, foreign diplomats, landed gentry, masters of fox hounds, generals, admirals and leaders of society. It became a mark of distinction to have appeared as a caricature in *Vanity Fair*. Many artists took turns in producing the drawings, Ape (Carlo Pellegrini) and Spy (Leslie Ward) being the most famous. On 5 August 1897, Samuel Rutherford Crockett was *Man of the Day* Number 686, with the caption 'The Stickit Minister'. He did not achieve the highest distinction of being drawn by Ape or Spy; his caricature is signed 'FR', probably Frank Richards who was his favourite illustrator and had drawn a crayon sketch of him as a frontispiece to *Lads' love* in the same year.

Along with the caricature went a brief biography written by the founder T G Bowles himself and signed 'Jehu Junior', Jehu being and Old Testament warrior and prophet who first of all called doom down upon his victims and then destroyed them. Crockett was treated with comparative geniality.

> Eight and thirty years ago he became the son of a farmer at Duchrae, New Galloway; who sent him to the Free Church Institution at Castle Douglas, where in the fullness of time he rose to the rank of a pupil-teacher. At Edinburgh he got a bursary, and wrote verse; which he published in a book called 'Dulce Cor' and improved himself into a Minister of Penicuik. Very naturally, 'The Stickit Minister' followed; and its success assured him that he had a mission. So he gave up the Ministry to make much money and many books: some of which have achieved quite unusual success. He is now one of the most popular and (probably) one of the best paid of our novelists: and even publishers run after him.
>
> He is a very shrewd fellow who came in on the top of the Kailyard boom; and though some think he has not deserved success there is no denying that he has commanded it. One leader of public opinion is, indeed, said to have gone so far as to compare his 'Sweetheart Travellers' with the New Testament; and he can certainly write broad enough Scotch to satisfy most, and bore some, of us. He is a great big boy who is quite above dress; yet he wears his ulster which is fearfully and wonderfully made, with the manners of a minister. He is a keen observer of birds; whose habits he finds inspiring. He has played cricket; he is said to have climbed a mountain; he cycles; he is not above golf; and he likes dining at the Savoy.
>
> Though he is no beauty he was once painted by Whistler. But the summit of his success is achieved to-day.

There is enough truth mixed with the inaccuracies in this commentary to make it bite. The comparison of 'Sweetheart Travellers' with the Old Testament sums up the foolish over-enthusiasm of Crockett's first readers. To say that the success of 'The Stickit Minister' made him sure he had a mission, so he gave up the ministry to make money, is a cruelly epigrammatic statement of what some Presbyterians thought of him. The sarcasm about the broad Scots is, of course, standard.

The caricature shows Crockett as an immense figure, his head at the top

10   The Vanity Fair Cartoon: 'The Stickit Minister'.

and his boots down below breaking the neat line which marks the margin of the picture. He is gazing soulfully aloft with a thick mop of dark chestnut hair, holding in his right hand a copy of *The Lilac Sunbonnet*; his own bonnet or cap lies on a cane-bottomed chair beside him. His left hand holds brown gloves clumsily against his pocket, and the whole massive form is enveloped in a blue-grey Inverness coat and cape, the coat almost reaching his ankles. His boots are square-toed and black, solidly planted on the ground, and his red tie is just showing.

One part of Jehu Junior's biography arouses immediate interest; was Crockett ever painted by Whistler, and if so, when? The definitive work *The Paintings of James McNeill Whistler*, published in 1980 for the Paul Mellon Center for Studies in British Art by Yale University,[16] confirms that he was, in 1896, but that the whereabouts of the portrait are unknown. The publisher T Fisher Unwin had arranged for Whistler to make a lithograph of Crockett, but in addition Whistler in 1896 began a small portrait in oils. This was interrupted by the death of Whistler's wife. It was to have been called 'The Grey Man', and Whistler had told the Pennells that he was rather pleased with it.

The Pennells, in 1908, published *The Life of James McNeill Whistler* in two volumes. In the new and revised edition of 1921, there is a full account of Crockett's dealings with Whistler, contributed to the Pennells by Crockett himself in a letter. The studio at 8 Fitzroy Street was a huge place at the back of the house, one flight up, reached by a ramshackle glass-roofed passage; Crockett went there to give his sittings, rather nervously.

> I don't think he liked me at first. Someone had told him I was a Philistine of Askelon ... He told me lots about his early times in London and Paris, but all in fragments, just as the thing occurred to him. Like an idiot, I took no notes. Lots, too, about Carlyle and his sittings, as likely to interest a Scot. He had got on unexpectedly well with True Thomas, chiefly by letting him do the talking, and never opening his mouth, except when Carlyle wanted him to talk. Carlyle asked him about Paris, and was unexpectedly interested in the *cafés*, and so forth. Whistler told him the names of some—Riche, Anglais, Vefour, and Foyot and Lavenue on the south side. Carlyle seemed to be mentally taking notes. Then he suddenly raised his head and demanded, 'Can a man get a chop there?'
>
> Concerning my own sittings, he was very particular that I should always be in good form—'trampling' as he had said otherwise he would tell me to go away and play ... Mr Fisher Unwin had arranged for a lithograph, but Whistler said he would make a picture like a postage stamp, and next year all the exhibitions would be as busy as anthills with similar 'postage stamp' portraits. 'Some folk think life-size means six foot by three—I'll show them!' he said more than once. I wanted to shell out as he went on, and once, being flush (new book or something), I said I had fifty pounds which was annoying me, and I wished he would take it. He was very sweet about it, and said he understood. Money burnt a hole in his pocket, too, but he could not take any money, as he might never finish the work. Any day his brush might drop, and he could not do another stroke.
>
> It was a bad omen! His wife grew worse. He sent me word not to come. She died, and I never saw him again. I wish you could tell me what became of that picture. He called it *The Grey Man*.[17]

It is a pleasant vignette; Whistler, who had been nervous of painting the irascible Carlyle, telling the story to Crockett, who was nervous of being painted by the irascible Whistler. And the thought of that grey sombre head in Whistler's portrait of Carlyle turning to inquire whether he could get a chop in the best Paris restaurants adds a comic dimension to the painting.

Later, in 1898, Crockett himself wrote to Whistler in France to ask about his portrait. Whistler's reply shows that he had found Crockett likeable and was prepared to joke with him.

> Why not further astonish me now that you venture to remind me of the picture at all, by coming on to Paris and presenting yourself!
> That, by the way, will really be your only chance of ever getting your portrait for I could not possibly go back to black London!
> So if you want the little painting after all you will have to make your pilgrimage and your peace—to say nothing of proving to me that you have not too completely put yourself out of drawing for me to touch again!
> I doubt if you had any right to experiment with bicycles while still as who should say under an engagement as model to
> Whistler![18]

Since no more is heard of the portrait, one must assume that it was never completed.

There was one social occasion in Scotland at which Crockett must have been pleased to be present. Lord Kitchener of Khartoum came to Edinburgh in 1899 to be given the freedom of the city and an honorary degree from the University. He was entertained at Dalmeny House by Lord Rosebery. Among the company assembled by invitation to meet the guest of honour were many titled names, many legal figures, many soldiers of high rank, many Members of Parliament—and Mr S R Crockett. Crockett sat next to Kitchener who, when he was told his name, turned to him and said 'Good heavens! are you the fellow who wrote *The Grey Man?* Let me shake your hand. Why, the night before the battle of Omdurman, when I was ready to the last button, and lay in my tent, I read *The Grey Man* from cover to cover and how that fine book steadied me'[19] Kitchener was inclined to be brusque and difficult, and was not a keen reader; the tribute was all the more hearty, coming from such an unlikely admirer. The story may not be precise in all details, but it came from Maisie Crockett, who had heard it from her father himself.

Unfortunately such happy encounters were becoming fewer as time went on. Critics were either cursory in their references to Crockett's books or else positively hostile. In 1905 *Maid Margaret* received harsh treatment from the *Scottish Review*: 'One is inclined to say that, if people like this sort of book, this is the sort of book they will like.'[20] *Kid McGhie* as we have seen was greeted with scorn in 1906. Even local newspapers were less than enthusiastic; *The Cherry Ribband* in 1905 was dealt with by the *Midlothian Journal* in sadly indifferent words:

> This book reflects Mr Crockett's well-known style and will be welcomed by many readers.[21]

The *Academy* headed its review of *Me and Myn* in 1907 with the contemptuous words 'Stamps and Stickiness'[22] and declared that, for all his vitality and exuberance, Crockett

> may go on pouring forth words in endless profusion for the rest of his life but neither nature nor art will ever make of him anything but a third-rate novelist.

Me and Myn is the book that was written as a serial for Stanley Gibbons Stamp Monthly. The fact that such a slight work for a specialised audience should have been allowed to come out as a novel for the general public shows how much Crockett was anxious to publish as much as possible and gain an income from every literary source. He could not please the critics, whatever he did; if he wrote of slums and sordid reality, he was told to go back to his healthy country ways; if he wrote of country ways, he was dismissed as a mere Kailyarder; and the *Academy's* review concluded its tirade of scorn with the cutting remark that

> There is one point, however, in which 'Me and Myn' marks a distinct advance upon Mr Crockett's previous works. It is not written in dialect.

It is little wonder that Crockett grew discouraged.

His health, too, had been giving trouble. By 1902, and probably before this date, he had been finding the cold Scottish winters too harsh for him and spent them abroad. In July 1902, he wrote to a friend saying that he had been having no visitors because of his wife's illness, and had taken refuge in his chalet-library, trying to settle

> on the hill ahint the house along with some thousands of books when in this country and write—yes write—to keep from thinking. A curious life—about a third here, and the rest in the wild places of the earth.[23]

For most of the year, this home-loving man was forced to take leave of his books and his beloved gadgets and live abroad; in this letter he says he has had Maisie with him, now a girl of fifteen, and a good companion, but the homesickness is felt in how he writes.

In December 1903 he writes to Sir John Hammerton thanking him for the article about his work in the *Black and White* magazine—'clear, square, right, tho' too kind'—adds philosophically

> Many people have got to like me against themselves. I don't go to London anymore, (sic) or at least but seldom, and I am as like the image they make a Kailyard cockshy of in the leeetary papers as John Keats was like the Holy Ghost.[24]

and says that he is about to set off again for Spain and North Africa.

It must have been a lonely and anxious life for Ruth Crockett as well; she would know of his anxieties and his worries about his health, yet she had her own problems—four lively children to bring up to a large extent on her own. Even the comfort of a fine house and affectionate servants may not have compensated for a husband who was always hard at work when he was at home, and so often was abroad for long periods, in search of sunshine and wellbeing. She occasionally accompanied him, and the whole family at times joined him on the continent for holidays and were united for spells of travelling and staying in pleasant foreign places, but the winters must have been long for Ruth, especially after Maisie had gone off to St Andrews to board at St Leonard's School and George had entered Osborne as a naval cadet.

In 1904, Hodder and Stoughton published a curious compilation which Crockett called *Raiderland All About Grey Galloway*, a book which gathered together articles on the Galloway hills and essays on different towns and villages like Castle Douglas, Colvend, Auchencairn, Borgue, Kirkcudbright, Dalbeattie, Balmaghie, Loch Ken and Wigtown, all places which he had written of in his Galloway novels. It included in the relevant places long extracts if not entire chapters from these books, as if he were trying to advertise himself and bring them to the reader's attention. *Raiderland* is partly autobiographical, describing the farms which had been the background to his boyhood, Little Duchrae, Drumbreck, Airieland and adding as the fourth Glenhead of Trool, with a tribute to the oaten farles and kindly welcome he received from the 'dear and worthy friends' who still live there. It is half a guide-book to Galloway, half a guide-book to Crockett's already published work, providing names and dates and publishers in footnotes, the whole made more attractive and interesting by Joseph Pennell's pen and ink illustrations. Negotiations for the publication of this book as recorded in the contracts relating to it between Hodder and Stoughton and A P Watt[25] were extremely protracted, beginning apparently in January 1901 and not finally concluded until May 1905 with agreements about the overseas and American editions. Ominously, a letter from Watt to Robertson Nicoll in April 1905 contains the information that the delay in finally establishing Crockett's publishing terms was 'owing partly I expect to the fact that he has been unwell and out of the reach of letters'.

The intelligent housemaid Elizabeth Shanks had her comment to make in respect of Crockett's writing. After he had left the ministry in order to free himself for literary work,

> he missed the personal contacts with members of his congregation, whose problems usually became his problems, so that he exercised himself in helping them to overcome their difficulties. Moreover such contacts inspired his writing.[26]

Ironically, Crockett himself had been of this opinion. The unidentified newspaper which reported his resignation from the ministry and is preserved in the Penicuik Cuttings added to its report what must have been an earlier interview with 'the special commissioner of a popular religious weekly', so that immediately after his announcement of his resignation the voice of Crockett is heard declaring how much his writing depended upon his moving among his people.

'CLIMBING ON THE STEEP STAIRS' 269

11 The Crockett Family on holiday abroad. *c* 1908.

> I think I reap a distinct advantage by going among the people freely. There is all the difference in the world between an author who practically lives in his club and gets his material perhaps from talking to his fellow-authors, and then goes home to try to realise a situation out of his consciousness, and one who comes daily into touch with some of the deepest realities and tragedies of life. After seeing some poor old body pass away, or giving someone a friend's hand, I can write a chapter with infinitely greater grip upon the realities of life than if I imagined something, and said 'I will write this, because it is picturesque'. A minister has plenty of material always before him; it is part of his life.[27]

In order to free himself from the time-consuming duties of the ministry (which he felt he was not carrying out satisfactorily in any case) Crockett gave up his contact with the ordinary members of the congregation, the source of much of his inspiration. The freedom to write and travel was some compensation for he was still in contact with scenes and characters on which his imagination could work directly; but gradually increasing ill-health began to sever him from even these. It is hard not to think that Crockett was dogged by bad luck. He meant all for the best, but all worked together to defeat him.

In 1901, he resigned from the eldership of the Free Church at Penicuik; his long stays abroad made it impossible for him to continue to hold the office of elder with any conscience. In 1906, the link with Penicuik was severed entirely. The lease of Bank House terminated, the Clerk family wanted the house for their own use, and the Crocketts had to find other quarters. They decided on Torwood House, Peebles, a large mansion on the Bonnington Road, standing a little above the town. Their servants and gardeners, the Ritchies and the Milroys, moved with them, with a faithfulness almost feudal in its loyalty; the Crocketts were well served and loved by their retainers. They left Penicuik with much regret but in some style; the long wooden building which housed the library, the studio and the observatory went with the rest of the furniture and was set up again in the grounds of the new house, and the books themselves, estimated to be in number between thirty-five and forty thousand,

> were conveyed by steam traction, to the wonder and delight of the neighbouring population.[28]

While Crockett and presumably his family were taking refuge in the Tontine Hotel, Peebles, from the upset and misery of moving, Crockett received the invitation for the dinner in his honour to be held at Dalbeattie. It must have cheered his heart. It came from the Hon Sec of the Dalbeattie General Improvement Committee; Crockett remarked in his reply that he was glad to be regarded as a General Improvement. He acepted with pleasure; the date finally arrived at was 28 September 1906.

In his letter of acceptance and thanks, Crockett made a typically kind request in regard to the guests who might be invited to do him honour.

> If Castle Douglas is to be considered, I would like the following to be present—

if not to be on the Committee. I would like them to be in a manner my guests and would be your debtor to the amount of their expenses.
 1. John Payne, Esq, Douglas Arms, Castle Douglas
 2. Major Malcolm Harper, British Linen Bank
 3. Rev George Laurie, Queen Street Manse
 4. Henry Maclellan, Late manager, Bank of Scotland
 5. W S MacGeorge, ARSA, Artist, 11 Melville Place, Edinburgh
 6. Andrew S Penman, Esq, Carriage Works, Dumfries
 7. William Sproat, Esq, Barend, Laurieston, Castle Douglas
These were the props and friends of my boyhood and if it is agreeable to the commitee I should like to have them now—at least at the banquet.
 I wish it to be understood that the Committee will allow me to pay (privately) for the dining expenses of these gentlemen, or as many of them as accept.[29]

All these gentlemen but one accepted their invitation and attended the banquet, none of them realising that it was at Crockett's request and expense. Some of the names are familiar—William MacGeorge and Andrew Penman, Crockett's cronies at Cowper's School; William Sproat, auctioneer, who had married Ruth Crockett's sister Alice and prospered as a factor and property manager; the Rev George Laurie, the minister who had been Crockett's home minister and sponsor in the New College Matriculation forms and had presided at his licensing; John Payne of the Douglas Arms because of the friendliness Crockett had received when staying there on visits. Malcolm McL Harper was a prominent local amateur antiquarian, author of *Rambles in Galloway* and *The Bards of Galloway*; much older than Crockett, he had been a familiar figure setting out on exploratory walks, and had himself provided much of the splendid traditional material for Crockett's plots.

Inevitably, and as a tribute to Crockett's popularity in his own part of the world, Sir Herbert Maxwell was in the chair and proposed in glowing terms the health of the author; if he had left the ministry for the life of a writer of fiction, did not Our Lord himself use parables to illustrate his truths, and were not parables fiction? It is interesting that this old knotty criticism more than ten years old should have roused Sir Herbert to refute it yet again. If Crockett had not taught those present to love Galloway, because they loved it long before they had heard of him, he had shown the inner meaning of common things,

> thrown over all our landscapes a web and glamour of romance, and it will be long before that will passs away. He has done, in short, for Galloway—and it is a grand thing to say of any man—what Sir Walter Scott did for Tweedale.

Other speakers followed in much the same terms, with toasts followed by replies to toasts, rather like a Burns supper, even to playing in of a haggis by Piper Robertson of Dalbeattie. Crockett stood up to it well; his chief anxiety was that out of the banquet arose the suggestion that Malcolm McL Harper write a life of Crockett. He was understandably alarmed by this thought, not so much for himself as for the reception any book about himself might receive; he knew his own position in the literary field much more accurately and realistically than all these enthusiastic Gallovidians, out for a good night at ten and six a ticket, making hyperbolic and largely irrelevant speeches. Galloway was like a knight in armour, its lochs flashing like burnished steel; Galloway was never subjugated by the Romans like Dumfries but jagged the enemies' thumbs with its thistles; Galloway through St Ninian at Whithorn sent the light of Christianity north and south through all the land and Crockett was a worthy descendant of these monks, keeping the light burning through their ruined fanes. Three kings—Banquo, Allan Fitzallan and Robert the Bruce—came from Galloway (a dubious statement) to say nothing of Paul Jones. It is evident that these worthy gentlemen were growing a little intoxicated, and not with their own eloquence entirely.

Crockett's well-thought-out, canny amusing, deprecating, modest reply to Sir Herbert's toast was the speech most in touch with reality; he talked of the dilemma of writers as it was, not of any noble fantasies. He could keep his head and accept compliments for what they were worth, gratefully but without illusions. He knew he was not the giant they made him out to be.

On 10 November 1907 he wrote from Peebles to his friend John Geddie of the *Scotsman*, asking him to look out for Harper's book about the 'Galloway banquet an' me';

> it will be a sore day for decent Harper if it is no dune justice to in the *Scotsman*. Review it yourself, I wish ye could. When it arrives grab it. Personally I don't know what he has said, whether truth or myth, praise or slating. But he is always Malcolm Harper to me, and I see him still rising solemn in the midst of the CD Cameronian Kirk when the 'Union' with the 'Frees' was given out, taking hat and Bible and marching out, murmuring 'Na, Na, I couldna' stan' *that*!' I was a boy at the time and held in by the authority of mine own seniors, but I always thought of that as *fine*. For this, and because he is a good writer, never slovenly, always with the artistic faculty, and because he has left fifty years of generous kindness behind him, I want you to see he gets decent treatment ... I don't *like* the idea of the book a bit, but I wouldn't hurt him or the kind folk down there by saying so.[30]

Crockett need not have worried. *Crockett and Grey Galloway* is a book written by an old man, uncritical, unexciting, but packed with facts. Harper notes the sharp-tongued energy of Mary Crocket, adds to our knowledge that William Crocket was lame because of a fall from a horse, tells the reader that *Dulce Cor* was commended by Lord Tennyson (as well it might be, since it was a pale faded copy of his own poetry) and reveals that Crockett had had a long talk with Mr Gladstone on a Sunday evening at Sir John Cowan's house Beeslack when he was still an unknown country minister.

> Mr Gladstone had read 'The Stickit Minister', and questioned Crockett closely on the conditions of clerical life in Scotland. He congratulated him on his settlement in the quiet rural charge of Penicuik, and said his own ideal would be to end his life in such a place, but ... circumstances, not his desire, had thrown him into politics. Mr Crockett recalled his first sight of Pio Nono in the Vatican, and thought the veteran premier was not unlike him. The young

minister was questioned on the waning prospects of Disestablishement, on the Church-going of the peasantry, and on the prevalence of family worship.[31]

Pope Pio Nono died in 1878; did Crockett, during his six months keeping himself by journalism in London in the summer of that year, make a journey to Rome and see His Holiness? There is no record of such a foreign trip, but it would have been easy to make and characteristic of the young man curious about all things to make it.

The latter part of *Crockett and Grey Galloway* reproduces the 'full and exhaustive account' of the banquet provided by the *Dumfries and Galloway Courier and Herald*, which lists the names of the provosts, councillors, editors of local papers, ministers, earls and baronets and landed gentry who attended it, along with their photographs. Young Philip Crockett was present to see his father receive praise and admiration from his own native county and its neighbours. It also reproduces the elaborately illustrated menu card, with a photograph of Crockett looking young and eager, set into a Galloway scene and a large letter 'C' holding a quotation from Scott and another from Crockett (exact place unknown), the whole romantically executed by Crockett's old Laurieston schoolmate John Copland who also provided the many water-colour illustrations reproduced in grey and black throughout the book.

As was to be expected, Harper's book contained nothing about Crockett in Peebles, beyond saying that he and his family had moved there. Peebles is only twelve miles away from Penicuik, but it might be in another country; its ambience is quite different. Penicuik was homely, warm, busy, workaday, in Crockett's time dominated by its paper-mills, its coal and shale mines, its iron foundry and its saw-mills. Peebles is an old-established grey town in the valley of the Tweed, with ruined ecclesiastical sites testifying to its romantic past. Tweed-making was its industry, but it was kept out of sight; the town was rapidly developing a fashionable reputation as a genteel and pleasant place for retirement or summer visitors. New villas were going up on the other side of the river from the old town; and on the slopes of the wooded Ven Law above the town a Hydropathic Establishment had been built in the French Renaissance style by 1881. To say that Peebles is the Priorsford of O Douglas's popular novels perhaps sets it in perspective. Crockett was never a familiar or important figure there; probably Mrs Crockett liked it better than her husband did, but that was only fair; she was to live there. He, because of his health, came only on visits.

He returned to Scotland usually in the summer and stayed until the autumn months, either at Torwood or at Auchencairn, a small village on the Solway Firth to which his uncles had retired. Uncle Willie was the last of them to survive, and lived until his death in a two-storey granite semi-detached house called Castle Daffin (or Dauphin); its garden ran by the side of the garden belonging to the Free Church Manse, and the Rev William Thomson, Free Church minister in Auchencairn, grew to know Crockett well during these visits. The Manse looked over the Solway to Heston Island—the Isle Rathan of *The Raiders*. He talked of this with vivid pleasure to the Sanquhar Literary Society in 1935.

On a full moon night in full tide, the swiftly flowing Solway becomes a sea of silver with the island set in its bosom like a big black diamond.

Through the orchard you reach the garden at the back of the Manse and alongside was Crockett's garden and the cottage, Castle Daffin ... in which his Uncle Wm Crockett lived—a real old godly Cameronian. He was for many years a porter at Castle Douglas Station. The novelist came every year from 1895 when I began my ministry till the year before the Great War and stayed each time from one month to three. After his uncle's death he kept on the cottage and the housekeeper, so for eight years I knew him—often at his place and he, jumping the dyke between his place and mine, often in the Manse.

He got up each day about 5.30. Mary had a big bowl of coffee for him and a 'piece' as she called it. Then at 6 he was at typewriter and desk, his big curved pipe or cigar never out of his mouth, on until 12, and then—so far as writing goes—done for the day. After that rambling, reading and Lady Nicotine mistress of all!

The last year he was with us he was far from well, and ere he left to go to Spain to seek more pabulum for his pen, in the Manse, depressed in spirit he said 'I'm going off and somehow I have a feeling I'll never be back again.' I tried to minister to that need of his—beseeched him to throw it off, believing that seeing Spain would set him right.

But that gipsy mind of his had its ain thochts. I had letters from various places in France, now saying he was feeling better and then—not so well. Then there was a bit of a break, and one day a message came to us from Avignon, from a hospital, that he had passed away ... I can claim to have been his last minister on earth, and big though he was and once a minister himself, I think I can truly say he loved me and was grateful for any little thing I did.[32]

The exact nature of Crockett's illness is difficult to discover. His height and bulk, his enthusiasm, his delight in travelling and his tirelessness as a golfer created the impression that he was a strong healthy man with no weakness. As early as 1895, however, a newspaper report recorded that he had been so ill in London, at Morley's Hotel, that his wife had had to come down from Penicuik and nurse him; this illness lasted over two months. The next year the *Athenaeum* reported that he was in an impaired state of health brought on by overwork; this was at once denied, but similar reports crept into newspapers from time to time. These were always denied, but the pattern became familiar. His journeys abroad, once joyful explorations, became quests for warmth and sunshine because of necessity.

In November 1907, he wrote to his friend John Geddie from Peebles in his old breezy way, but there is a touch of worry and anxiety behind what he says.

> Your last letter cheered my day, as yours always do. Peebles, or rather a mile and a half up the hills towards Hundleshope is my stance and whaur ye'll find me—or *no* find me for I'm a terrible wanderer. I was in Palestine and N Arabia in June and July of this year—also in Tunisia with the poor devils of the 26th French regiment who wouldn't fight against their own folk at Narbonne. Very wrong of them, but when you see these laddies of 21, ye think of your ain and say, Politics be damned! Particularly French politics.
>
> I write about one foreign (i.e. Spanish or French-of-the-Midi) buik between

each Scottish one if I can manage it. But whiles it doesna juist fit. A man that has bairns canna juist aye choose his wark.

I am glad to hear of your scattering and well-doing brood. Oh, it's fine, fine! I wish I juist saw my four as far forrit. It's hard for the mither, and maybe whiles for the faither, but there's naething like guid reports aboot the bairns for garrin' the heart sing kindly within.

My eldest (daughter) keep her looks of 'the Sweetheart' of old days and I fear we won't keep her long in the nest by all appearances. My elder boy is still at school but more brilliant at 'Rugger' than at his lessons where he is 'slow'. Only he is 'a fighter' having early learned 'the gloves' at home (against his mother's wish but I knew what I was doing). So he is 'much respected' at school, is six foot high, and the Head finds him very useful, reliable, and *'a strict disciplinarian'*—which makes me grin.

My second and impish son, prototype of Sir Toady Lion, is well into his last year at Osborne for the Navy. He is clever at Exams and laughs himself through life. Margaret the tomboy is at school here and wins 'open' foot-race events, preferably with the boys. That's my stock and the Lord be good to them,

> to you and your hoose
> Me an' ma hoose
>   Amen.

Thank you for what you say of the kind Harper, I daresay I should have tried to 'save me from my friends'. But I let him juist say and do what he liked. My only motto which I commended to him being 'No flowers by request!' and I don't think he will have erred in that way.[33]

At the same time the quality of his writing began to vary widely, as if the writer were both physically and mentally weary, the imagination at times as exhausted as the body and whipped into life only by the determination of will. It would not be true to say, as has been said, that he had written himself out; there are always flashes of his old originality and his old vigour and humour, however diminished; occasionally he can pull off a book which is almost as good as ever; but the need for continuous production told upon him. He was himself aware that his writing was losing its freshness. When his New College class held their 25th Anniversary Dinner in Edinburgh in 1906, he was in Spain and could not attend, but he wrote a long letter of apology, remembering the old days and old friends but hinting at the strain with which he had perpetually to live. They are all ministers, and he has chosen another path in life, a more public and at first glance more exciting one, but they should not envy him.

> Sometime you feel doubtless that the congregation, the little parish, the daily round hardly affords elbow-room. But a little taste of this bitter bread, and a little climbing on the steep stairs of the literary profession make for contentment with the manse, and even with the Deacon's Court. I do not say that I regret anything. The 'calling' was and is too strong for that. But I know well that I was serener-minded when two sermons dominated my week. Give thanks then all of you.[34]

Crockett's later books, especially those dealing with contemporary life, suggest that there were many possibilities which in better circumstances and with other publishers he could have explored successfully. Unfortunately, right from the start he was linked with religious periodicals and publishing houses. The *Christian Leader* gave him his start. Robertson Nicoll, editor of the *British Weekly*, the *Bookman*, the *Expositor* and other periodicals published by Hodder and Stoughton, suggested that he collect some of his *Leader* stories; the publisher he found was T Fisher Unwin, who had been Hodder and Stoughton's London salesman before setting up on his own in 1882.[35] *Woman at Home* which published many of his short stories after his first success was another Hodder and Stoughton enterprise, edited by Annie S Swan. By Crockett's time Hodder and Stoughton had moved away from its early years as a firm which tended to concentrate on the moral, the improving and the religious; the second generation of its managers and editors were more liberal-minded;

> in the intervals of expansion Hodder-Williams moved into general publishing with a large list of cheap novels, but the firm remained under the stigma of being a 'religious' publisher because of its backlist.[36]

Some of this stigma attached itself inevitably to Crockett; *Good Words* which serialised *The Men of the Moss Hags* was a magazine of the same earnest type. For a while, when the *Cornhill*, the *Windsor* and the *Graphic* took him up, there seemed to be a chance of his escaping, and the first three of his books for children, *Sweetheart Travellers*; *Sir Toady Lion* and *Sir Toady Crusoe* were handled by Gardner, Darton and Company, specialists in that field. Had he been able to consolidate this secular connection and free himself from the religious press entirely, it would almost certainly have improved his work. But he was never a rich man and had many calls on what income he had.

Circumstances, the dangerous swiftness of his rise to popularity, his temperament, his failing health, the need to write often and sell immediately for quick returns to provide for his wife and family, the style in which he and his family lived in his first palmy days, possibly the habits into which he had fallen while writing for a market whose literary standards were not high, all combined to bring about a decline. He slipped back to the *British Weekly* and the *People's Friend*, never fully developing his talent for lighthearted historical romance, mildly satirical comedy, sharp exposure of realistic working-class conditions and unsentimental direct depiction of social injustice and hardship. In his haste he lost his critical judgement; one of the saddest things in his later books is the way he lets his characters talk to one another in the current slang, in the hope perhaps that he could inject into these stories the freshness they lacked. One reads the conversations in *Sandy's Love Affair*—a book which conspicuously lacks his vivid description—with increasing irritation at the trifling chatter which passes between the stock figures of snobbish young ladies, brash young cads and vivacious girls. At the same time one feels sorry for the sick man who is turning out this stuff with the best of intentions in his later clouded years.

Mistakes abound even in his early work—possibly the mistakes of proof readers in not picking them up, but they should not have been there in the first place. Meg Kissock is introduced in *The Lilac Sunbonnet* as the servant maid at the Dullarg when she is the favoured and faithful servant maid at Craig Ronald. As time goes on, errors become more common; in *Kit Kennedy*, Sheriff Nicoll who sends Christopher Kennedy to prison has changed his name to Sheriff Maclean when the prisoner is discharged. Alistair French who witnesses the wedding of Lilias and Kennedy has become Nick French at the end of the book. MacWalter is described as coming from Sandhaven in Chapter II, the fishing village from which Christopher Kennedy also comes; but MacWalter has become a Yorkshire merchant in Chapter XIV. It would be depressing and tedious to list all the small but irritating discrepancies, but there are likely to be one or two in every book.

Even the geography of Galloway is not adhered to closely. It follows no logical pattern. One must conclude that Crockett selected names from his memory or the Ordnance Survey Map at random because he liked them for their sound. A wood in Wigtownshire may turn up in the middle of the Stewartry if he needs a good name. Galloway and Bordershire, Kentigernshire and Cheviotshire, are in no way comparable to Hardy's carefully mapped Wessex. Crockett's towns are jumbled together just as he fancied at the moment—Lockermaben, Cairn Edward, Newton Edward, Netherby Junction, Kirktown, Kilgour, Drum, Drumnith, Drumfern, Port Andrew. Cheviotshire or Bordershire seems at one time to be in England, at another in Scotland; in one book it stretches all the way across Scotland, in another it has shrunk to what seems to be the district of Newcastle. If he had made the town and shire names consistent, how much more solidity would his Galloway and North of England books have shown.

To some extent, by avowing his dislike of a serious purpose, he doomed himself to be criticised. He chose to be a teller of tales as a reaction against the Novel of Purpose, but he reacted too far. Sometimes without intending to he achieved more than a yarn—*The Grey Man, Cleg Kelly, Vida, Princess Penniless* and the best of his short stories. Sometimes the yarn carries serious comment implicit in its own events and conclusions—*The Raiders, Cinderella, Silver Sand*. In *The Lilac Sunbonnet* he used the narrative and characters to externalise his own dilemma, hiding the ideas under the guise of a plot. On the other hand, in *Kid McGhie* the element of the sensational overpowered the undoubtedly serious sober theme of Mr Molesay and the penny dreadful almost invalidates the central figure. An exciting narrative can carry comments and values embedded in it here and there, not consistently running through as one theme—*The Cherry Ribband* illustrates different attitudes towards Calvinism though the adventure is pre-dominant. In historical romances this method succeeds most convincingly because we did not live in that particular period and can more readily be beguiled into accepting improbabilities. Indeed, perhaps we in the late twentieth century are too hard on Crockett writing in the nineteenth; our times are harsh and violent, but before 1900—before 1914—life was violent and harsh in a cruder more incredible way than in our more sophisticated days when science and psychology add a ghastlier, more subtle quality to evil than Crockett could have foreseen. It is too easy to blame him for telling tall tales when old newspapers hold the same brutality and melodrama in their files.

His originality was a great strength. Rider Haggard's vast caverns of assorted dead bones become monotonously similar, as do the joyful discoveries which enable his adventurers to escape. In Crockett, the sea-cave in *The Raiders*, the dark pungent warmth of Sawny Bean's den, the cold smooth whispering waters of the cave that is the grave of the Vardarellis, even the cave wherein lie the coffins of the dead Black Douglases in *Rogues' Island*, are all distinct and different. He seldom repeated himself.

He was a teller of tales, but that he continued to the end of his life writing diversely and copiously in spite of growing ill-health and partial exile from the country he knew and loved best, spurred by that most unromantic of necessities, the need to make money for his family, demands respect. He never allowed himself the luxury of self-pity or regret—'the calling was, and is, too strong'—but soldiered on doing what he had himself chosen to do, without looking back.

As time went on, his books did not do well. In letters sent by his agent A P Watt to Hodder and Stoughton, who had acquired all his copyrights, negotiating the royalties to be paid on cheap editions of already published six-shilling books—the shilling editions, the sixpennies, the sevenpennies—there occurs several times with slightly varying wording the note that

> the above-mentioned royalties will be placed in the first instance against that portion of the advance which is still unearned.[37]

The books in question, *Princess Penniless* (1908), *Rose of the Wilderness* (1909) and *The Dew of their Youth* (1910) had in their six-shilling editions sold so poorly that they had not earned the amount advanced to Crockett before publication, and he must make up the difference by forfeiting part of the payments earned by later cheaper editions, and this even although previously, in 1908, he had had to agree to a reduction in advance payment from £500 to £400. The amounts by which this reduced advance had been unearned can be seen plainly in a written slip included by Hodder and Stoughton among the photostats of their Crockett agreements. It is noted as

> Overpaid Crocketts including 'Ione March'

and goes on to list the sorry story;

Ione March	not overpaid	earned	£ 2. 18. 9	in 1908–9
Stickit Minister	overpaid		118. 4. 1	
Deep Moat Grange	,,		71. 18. 2	
Pss Penniless	,,		28. 1. 4	
Dew of their Youth	,,		133. 19. 8	
Pernicketty Town	,,		199. 17. 11	
Rose of Wilderness	,,		96. 3. 4	
Total amount overpaid			£648. 3. 6	Oct 1912

In view of these figures, one understands why, in May 1911 and October 1912, Crockett was obliged to sell many of his cherished books in the saleroom at Sotheby's. The catalogues of these sales are in the Hornel Collection at Broughton House, Kirkcudbright, and present a conspectus of the astonishing range of Crockett's book collecting. The titles listed are of incunabula as well as first editions and whole sets of nineteenth-century contemporaries, natural history as well as folklore and exploration, a copy of the *Breviarum Romanum* as well as *Naphtali, or the Wrestling of the Church of Scotland*, fifty-nine volumes of *The Studio* as well as twenty-seven volumes of the *Reports* of the Historical Manuscripts Commission. There are seventeen volumes of Burton's *Arabian Nights* in the Kamashastra Society Edition, Elzevir Editions of Caesar's *Works* (1635) and Terence's *Comedies* (1635), Joseph Ritson's *Caledonian Muse* (1821), Archenholz's *History of the Pirates, Freebooters and Buccaneers of America* (1807), G P R James's *Works* in one hundred and ninety-six volumes, Bewick's *History of British Birds*, first editions of Jane Austen's novels, Defoe's *A System of Magic, or the History of the Black Art*, a first folio Shakespeare, the *Satiricon* of Petronius (1677), Chambers *Caledonia* in seven volumes, Elizabethan and Jacobean pamphlets, the *Poësies* of Mallarmé, the *Works* of Malory edited by Rhys and illustrated by Beardsley (1893), the *Oeuvres Complètes* of Rousseau, Voltaire, Victor Hugo, Balzac and Verlaine, thirteen volumes of the *Yellow Book* 1894–1897, the Acts of the Parliament of Scotland 1523–1707, the *Natural History of Selborne*, Whymper's *Scrambles among the Alps 1860–69*, twenty-five volumes of Horace Walpole's letters and memoirs, Whittier's *Life, Works* and *Letters* edited by Samuel Picard, Cromek's *Remains of Nithsdale and Galloway Song* (1880), the *History of the Witches of Renfrewshire* (1877), forty-five volumes of Washington Irving's *Works*, a red morocco *Virgilius* with the arms of a cardinal on the sides and his crest on the spine, dated 1583, fifty-three volumes of Captain Mayne Reid's *Works*, *French Architecture* by Viollet-le-Duc in ten volumes (1875), Camden's *Remains*, Sinclair's *Satan's Invisible World Discovered*, the *Poetical Works* of Henryson and of Dunbar edited by David Laing and of Gavin Douglas edited by John Small, fat volumes of Broadsides and Last Dying Speeches, publications of the Bannatyne Club, the Maitland Club, the Abbotsford Club and the Spalding Club, Richardson's *Works*, in twelve volumes with preface by Leslie Stephen, the *Travels* and other works of Lady Hester Stanhope—on and on the list goes, from the sermons of the Rev William Law to Rabelais, and including first editions and complete sets of nineteenth-century classics like Browning, Thackeray, Carlyle, Ruskin, Clough, Morris, Dumas père and fils, Flaubert, Scott, Dickens and Fenimore Cooper—the last in one hundred volumes, says the catalogue, and all first editions except *The Deerslayer*.

These are items taken at random from the 1911 and 1912 sales only; when the posthumous sale of the remainder of his books took place at Sotheby's in 1915, even greater catholicity of taste was seen, and a significant indication of how he gathered his material; there are an astounding number of bound volumes of cuttings made by Crockett himself on the subjects which interested him:

1. Collection of extracts from Magazines and periodicals, Tracts, Newspaper Cuttings, etc formed by the Novelist relating to Miscellaneous Subjects including Anthropology, Art, Astrology, Bibliography, Botany, Folk song and popular poetry, Hagiology, Monasticism, Ghosts, Gipsies, Social Science, Theology, etc classified and arranged in 31 Volumes bound in half morocco
2. Collection of Extracts ... relating to local biography, Shakespeare, Swift, Napoleon, Pascal, Scott, Goethe, Carlyle, Dickens, Thackeray, Montaigne, Shelley, Keats, Lamb, Stevenson ... in 47 volumes in half morocco
3. Collection of Extracts ... relating to the History, Literature, Religious Manners and Customs, Travel and Exploration, etc in Africa, America, Canada, China and Japan, Great Britain, France, Germany, Australia, Egypt, Scandinavia, West Indies, India, etc ... in 74 volumes in half morocco.

One ceases to be surprised that it took the Milroys six weeks to dust the whole library.

Several letters have survived from his last years which give glimpses of Crockett's battle with illness. One was written from Auchencairn to his cousin Samuel Crockett, then of Castle Douglas, the grandson of Uncle Sam of Minnesota and Glenlochar. Crockett explains that he is confined to his bed and may have to be an invalid for some time.

> The fact is I was never rightly better of the influenza-malaria I had before I came home and I took a severe sore throat with other symptoms and have been laid up since Sunday week. The doctor does not think it serious, but forbids me to work or go out. I am also on the lightest diet—'slops' indeed, and no solid food of any kind. However I hope to have better to report, and also I hope to see your mother (though I can't speak much) on Friday—I should like to have a talk with you too before I go. I mean to be here most of the autumn if I get better and settled to work. At present I can't do much, but I hope this nasty relapse will soon pass away.[38]

He concludes by asking his cousin to see if the local chemist can provide him with 'Terebinthese, a kind of gum for kidney complaints' and some bottles of Vichy Celestin, to be sent by the carrier or 'just Davie Gass'. He adds, significantly, that he has an account with the chemist in question. Always, it will be noted, his preoccupation is with his recovery so that he can return to work.

Dr Robertson Nicoll received a letter from Crockett in January 1913, while he was in France, recuperating—but also working, this time for one of his stories set in France, *A Tatter of Scarlet*.

> I have had nearly five months of a serious illness—necessitating an operation. Now I am coming round again, though finding that the simple operation of sitting requires about all the brains I have. I am down here by the Mediterranean chasing the wild Communard of the Midi to his lair (when I am well enough to

do the chasing), and in the meantime writing the first chapters of the book, I had the children with me in relays.[39]

The last two letters are to the Rev William Thomson of Auchencairn, the ones he mentioned in his talk to and allowed to be passed round the Sanquhar Literary Society so that they could see Crockett's beautiful writing. The first is dated 18 October 1913 and headed 'Private Hospital, St André, France'. It apologises for the trouble he has caused his friend in asking for his Bagster's Bible, his Burton's *Anatomy of Melancholy* and three volumes of Montaigne's *Essays* to be found and sent out to him, together with his late Uncle Robert's plaid which ought to have been in a tin trunk, and continues

> I have been through much pain and trouble since I last saw you. An error of diagnosis put my cure back for years, and every grain of the quinine I took was so much irritant poison. I am now, I hope, getting the better of the *enteritis*, but instead of going forth like a strong man rejoicing in his *weight*, I turn the scales at less than you, i.e. between 9 and 10 stones! However there is now hope for me, and I take my best draughts of this fine air and sunshine, sleeping upon the covered balcony every night and sunning myself in the front of the old orchard wall (old Convent of St André, old as Dundrennan and like it Cistercian, but perfect) ...
>
> I hope, if I am stronger, to see you next year. This year I have had to stick to the treatment to keep the candle alight. I have written all my books in bed or on a couch. *But* I have worked and a great comfort it has been.
>
> My daughter is at College in Edinburgh hunting for degrees. Philip has been $3\frac{1}{4}$ years with the *Scotsman* people, and George 3 years in China with the Canton River pirates and such cattle. He is a sub-lieutenant now and as he says, 'No end of a little man.'
>
> Mrs Crockett does not stir from home and Margaret (17) is still at school. But the three children pass every weekend at Torwood.
>
> In the holidays we manage to unite—partly, that is. I am pinned to my rest cure and can't go north on pain of death.
>
> I drink your health in milk—all I have lived on for 13 months![40]

The second letter to Mr Thomson, gratefully acknowledging receipt of the books and the plaid, is dated 1 December 1913, 'Still in Private Hospital, near Perpignan, Pyrenées Orientales'.

> I am still only partly able for work. I have had rather a bad three weeks and have been much confined to my room, which means to bed and couch, all the time. But I have not had such a turn for a year, which ought to make me grateful. Though how much more grateful I should have been not to have had it at all!
>
> On the whole I may call my self content. I can live here with my two windows open and my lungs full of fresh air. Here I can do a little work occasionally, and even when the days are warm and the breezes propitious, rather more than a little.
>
> But early winter always tries me, even here and were I in the North I might as well retire to my little landed property (or 'howking') in Balmaghie Kirkyaird.

> To live and work, however, are great things and permisssion to do both about as much as we have any right to ask of God ...
> I have to keep my son Philip busy contradicting the paragraphs about my being ill, etc. For publishers won't take books from sick authors any more than people will be cured by an invalid doctor. So I say as little as I can about my illness, and my literary agent, Mr Watt, exhorts me to say nothing at all.
> I enjoy the Montaigne very much and above all I am glad to have my old Bible, marked when I still knew a good deal of Greek and even a little Hebrew. I envy you who have kept your classics up. I can read Latin still, because so many chronicles and historical works are written in Latin, but in Greek I could not pass, except in the NT now (by remembrance of the context.) Xenophon would throw me sure and as for Hebrew—I don't believe I know all the letters! ...
> I hope to shake your hand some good day yet to come.[41]

That good day never came, not on this earth. On the 16 April 1914, Crockett died at Tarascon, near Avignon, quietly and suddenly, without pain. Ruth Crockett wrote of it to the MacMillans at Glenhead of Trool on 27 April:

> ... all was over before we knew, he was dead and in this coffin and sent over to this country by this French doctor. Poor Philip had to go and identify the poor dead body, it was terribly hard for the lad. We have not got full particulars yet, we know it was sudden and unexpected, and thank God we know it was very peaceful. My poor husband can have had no idea of it himself.[42]

Unfortunately, the 'full particulars' are not now available for us; Crockett's death certificate, describing him as 'Homme de Lettres', records merely the time and place of his death, since the French practice is not to keep doctors' certificates of death for more than five years.[43]

Crockett's body was brought back to Scotland and travelled by rail to Castle Douglas. There his coffin was taken in procession through the streets to the tolling of the town bell. After the four miles to Balmaghie, there was a simple service in the church before Samuel Rutherford Crockett was laid to rest among the Crockets of Duchrae and Drumbreck. In his introduction to H M B Reid's *The Kirk above Dee Water* in 1895, Crockett had written

> ... there in that high corner I should like to lie, if so the fates allot it, among the dear and simple folk I knew and loved in youth. Let them lay me not far from the martyrs, where one can hear the birds crying in the minister's lilac-bushes, and Dee kissing the rivergrasses, as he lingers a little wistfully about the bonny green kirk-knowe of Balmaghie.

He had moved far away from that quiet country community; the two martyrs, both David Hallidays, are still there, though there is little sign of the minister's lilac-bushes; there he lies, his name and dates and two professions, Minister of the Gospel and Novelist, filling up the last foot of the tombstone he must have known well, under the names of his grandfather and grandmother, his mother, his aunts and one uncle, and one Duchrae cousin who died a child.

The kindest personal comment on Crockett was made by a fellow Free

Church minister, the Rev John Grant of Nottingham, who had at one time held a charge in Midlothian near Crockett when he was still Free Church minister of Penicuik and knew him well, both as friend and colleague. In an obituary article in the *British Weekly*, after vivid recollections of this 'Saul among men', tall and strong and beloved of children, his fellow-minister faces squarely the question, so vexed during his lifetime, of his resignation from the ministry.

> From this ministry, into which the 'three-fold call' and a mother's prayers conspired apparently to carry him, Samuel Rutherford turned aside. By so divesting himself of his sacred office he lost caste with many Scottish folk. Did he do well or ill? Who shall judge? He came to be less clear concerning the call to the ministry than as to the calling he ultimately gave himself to. He chose as he chose who knew best what was best to do ...
>
> Only, I could not judge him unkindly, had I deemed him at fault; he was so generous himself.[44]

To us today, the resignation seems a much less heinous offence than it did in the 1890s and 1900s, but the tribute of Mr Grant can still stand as Crockett's best epitaph: 'He was so generous himself.' Among those who knew him, he

12 Memorial erected by public subscription and unveiled in 1932 by Ruth Crockett at Laurieston. The Queen Mother, then Duchess of York, was a subscriber.

remained a figure to be talked of with affection and passed on to the next generation as someone whom his friends and acquaintances were glad to have known. Not one person seems to have remembered him with dislike or even indifference; all talk and write of him as unique in the eagerness and kindliness of his personality.

As for his reputation as a writer, this is necessarily a more complex judgement. He was not great—he would not have claimed to be great—but he does not deserve to be forgotten entirely, still less to be dismissed as he has tended to be for the past three-quarters of a century. He was a man with a talent for writing, a sharp enjoyment of life, a strong sense of justice, and the need to pass these things on to his readers along with his sense of life's irony, adventure, comedy and absurdity. Over-estimated when he began to write, he has suffered since from continuous under-estimation.

Once again a contemporary—this time anonymously—seems to have expressed a balanced and thoughtful opinion in *The Times* newspaper. After summarising his career without entirely admiring it, the writer ends with a general comment.

> One was amazed at the unflagging cleverness and activity with which he worked his marionettes; but one would have like real people instead—more repose, more thoughtfulness. Yet at his worst Mr Crockett remained an accomplished and versatile showman, and in the periods when he was at his best he was undoubtedly one of the most successful, and deservedly successful, of our popular novelists.[45]

CHAPTER 12

Posthumous Achievements

Crockett's determination to continue writing in spite of illness and partial exile is shown by the five books that appeared after his death. *Silver Sand* was in the press when he died and appeared later in 1914. *Hal o' the Ironsides* came in 1915. *The Azure Hand. A Novel* can be dated only by the Advocates' Library accession stamp in 1917, and *The White Pope* is the same in 1920. *Rogues' Island* came out as late as 1926.

Of these, *Rogues' Island* is of the least interest. Written for boys, it is a nostalgic return to his schooldays in Castle Douglas. The main character, Laurieston, is Crockett himself, organising dim resemblances of his old schoolmates Penman and Maxwell and MacGeorge. They camp on Rough Island and fight with the boys of the town, entertain their old schoolmaster and his daughters and find by accident the burying place of all the dead Black Douglases, their coffins lining the walls of a vast cavern (in a very small island, as we would rather expect). The style is schoolboy slang, tedious and dated. Here and there we glean a little about Crockett himself if we look for it, but the book as a whole, in spite of the boys' cheating their way into a circus and turning by stern treatment a milksop into a decent fellow, at the request of his uncle, is not even of value as a period piece. No boy today would look at it.

Silver Sand is interesting because Crockett has turned full cycle and gone back to *The Raiders*; he has tried to fill in the life of that enigmatic person before he came into the life of Patrick Heron. But the young Silver Sand is out of focus—'out of drawing' as Whistler said of the unfinished portrait.

The Foreword is written by an imaginary schoolmaster, Nathan Crogo, Dominie in Leswalt in Wigtownshire. His tone is apologetic. He is merely the editor of someone else's writing and doubts whether he has done it justice.

> In my frisky youth I could doubtless have allowed the Chronicle to go forth in the more fluent and romantical style in which it was first written, but age steals the poetry out of a man's joints, so blame the rusty jade Time if you find I have not left enough of the flowers of language ... [1]

This sounds like Crockett warning the reader in advance that this story will not be as good as it should be, as it would have been in his younger days, as *The Raiders*. But it has its own interest and excitement. We are back in the times of persecution and Covenanting. Sir Andrew Agnew of Lochnaw, Hereditary Sheriff of Galloway, comes upon a young man trespassing upon his land; challenged, the man announces haughtily that he is John Faa, Lord and Earl of Little Egypt by letters patent issued to his grandfather—king, in fact, of all the gipsies. Sir Andrew, a jovial kindly man who knows all about the gipsy earldom, laughs a little at his haughtiness and says how much he wishes he could employ John Faa as agent and secretary in these dangerous times; Claverhouse is coming to depose him from his sheriffdom and a gipsy's freedom of movement would make him an ideal 'helper'.

John Faa likes this suggestion but he insists upon his rank, which is higher even than that of a Hereditary Sheriff, and makes it clear that he has been well educated on the Continent, in the classics as in other things. If he agrees to serve Sir Andrew, it must be on the understanding that he is to be treated as a gentleman, not as a servant or dependant.

> 'Agreed!' cried hearty Sir Andrew. 'I know quite well who will be master. You shall be as one of mine own house, I promise you.'[2]

But the name John Faa is too well known and has been too often outlawed to be used openly. Sir Andrew knows how Faa has been earning his living and has an idea;

> '...why not call you Silver Sand, which is a good name and one well earned in your business of carrying scythe-sand down from the straths of the mountain lochs where no other dares venture—no, not I myself, the Sheriff with thirty men in armour clinking behind me?'[3]

Now we know who gave Silver Sand his nickname, which we did not know before.

> 'Sir Andrew,' said Silver Sand, 'I wager that you and I by laying our heads together can turn most corners of this crooked way by which we are set athwart this world. A gipsy is not born with any conscience, and if I had suchlike, it must have been gotten from my mother, who was not of the blood of Egypt.'
>
> Sir Andrew looked puzzled, as if a remembrance he could not locate pricked him.
>
> But the young man only smiled and whistled a well-known tune, The Ballad of John Faa ...
>
> 'So you are the son!' said Sir Andrew, suddenly enlightened. 'I knew there was more about you than plain gipsy.'[4]

Now we know what was only speculation before, that Silver Sand was the son of the gipsy who beguiled Lady Casillis from her fine position to roam the world as his wife.

They walk towards Lochnaw, Sir Andrew's castle above the loch. Silver Sand answers Sir Andrew's questions about his education; five years' study with the St Sulpicians at Issy, classical learning from the Jesuits—though this has not made him a Catholic, to Sir Andrew's relief. Indeed, on his return from France, Silver Sand had been impressed at the Brigend of Dumfries and drafted into the service of Claverhouse's dragoons for a while. He had taken part in the persecution of the Covenanters, but deserted some time ago, and is presently being advertised for as a renegade. At this point, those who know *The Raiders* are pulled up sharply. In it, Silver Sand had served as a persecuting dragoon and had become an outcast, anguished by the evil he had done. In this book, there is no torture to twist his limbs, no guilt-racked conscience. How can this John Faa grow into the man Silver Sand we have known before? Crockett has chosen to create him anew, his service with the dragoons passed over lightly. *The Raiders* cannot be repeated. Nathan Crogo's apologetic foreword perhaps reflected Crockett's own apology for any discrepancy as well as for his style.

Crockett's estimate of the Galloway Covenanters is still the same—stubbornness and not religious fanaticism brought them into conflict with the King. But the mood is altogether lighter. Sir Andrew's comments make the King and his edicts things to be laughed at; they bring about precisely what they mean to put down. The gentry hardly bothered with religion until the King interfered.

> 'There's Kenmure now—he's steward depute o' Kirkcudbright, there's Stair and my Lord Galloway. Ye wad think they wad bide wisely at hame and never set their noses over the door cheek. And so they wad if they had been left alane. But I have seen all at the field preachings—aye, even Kenmure and wise Lord Stair, President o' the Court o' Session. What do the like o' them want hearkening to Sandy Peden? When he was minister of Old Luce, would they have stirred from their chimney corners to hear him? Not they! No, nor were they more than occasional attenders at their parish kirks when served by their own ministers. Once a year on Communion Sabbath was as often as ye wad see either o' them in the front o' the gallery ...
>
> The Sheriff laughed as at a gay reminiscence.
>
> 'And I have seen Stair with his feet fair water-logged standing miserable as a cat on a rainy day and thinkin' dootless o' the comforts o' Carscreuch as he listened to Semple's "Thirdly, my brethren"! Ha! Ha! What brought him out there? What sent him to a lodging of one room in a Dutch garret—nothing but the order of the King that henceforth he had not the right to think for himself what he liked, or worship as and when he pleased!'[5]

It is this optimistic bluff personality of Sir Andrew which sets the tone of the book and gives it a flavour totally different from that of *The Raiders*. He is known everywhere as 'the Sherra'—as was the kindly moderate Sir Walter Scott. The persecutors, the Lags, Bruces, Grahams, Earlshalls, are about their bloody work off-stage: we hear of cold-blooded shootings and come upon one lad shot down as he dug potatoes, but these things are taken in the stride of the main characters.

Sir Andrew has to hide away in the Gled's Hole, a cunning cave dug by his son under a huge flat rock. The Rev Walter Dunning is hiding in the Doocot, a cave halfway down a perilous cliff, his food brought to him by Mirren McNoah, the daughter of one of his elders. We are delighted that Crockett has once more returned to his Galloway landscape of rock and heather, boulders and craggy mountains, the wide stretches of the Solway or the North Channel, the sea breaking on the black rocks. The mingled plots work themselves out against this bright familiar background, without asking for deep anguish from the reader or from any of the characters.

The central plot is the eternal triangle of Silver Sand and the two women who love him, the gipsy and the lady. Now that he has come back to Scotland, he takes up his duties as judge, protector and leader of all gipsies, and stands surety in court that Jasper Stanley and his gipsy tribe have not killed the two dragoons whose bodies have been found. Juliana, Jasper Stanley's daughter, has never known a man so courteous and gentle as John Faa, and she exercises the Romany right of all gipsy women to do the 'asking' if she finds a man who pleases her and he is free to marry her. Somewhat naturally, Silver Sand hesitates, but Juliana understands why. Crockett makes her put her plea in terms of the seasons, appropriate for a gipsy girl of the free outdoor life.

> 'Consider,' she said. 'I do not ask for recognition or to be received among your grand folk. You saved us from the gorgiko law and you are hand in glove with the head judge of these parts. You are learned in all the learning of their wise men, as befits the Prince of Egypt. You sit at his table and you talk with him of things high and strange, which Juliana Stanley never heard of nor could understand. All this is right and proper for you. It is your winter under the roof, and clipped about with walls. But you will need your summer also. Then you will yearn for the tent pitched in the glade among the birches, the trout streams running briskly, where you can be free as the birds overhead or the great white clouds sailing by. Then, too, you will begin to bethink you of the girl who is waiting for you with fire bright and pan clattering, the scent of the fried bacon and bread, and all the love she has been keeping for you since you and she were hand-fasted and she gave you her word.'[6]

Silver Sand, without loving her, cannot shame her before her tribe by refusing; he grants her request and they are considered as married by the gipsies. Gradually the wandering uncertainty of the gipsy life takes hold of him and he finds himself happy with Juliana, but always with an unease in his mind which he cannot dispel.

He was wise in his unease. When he meets Lilias Agnew, Sir Andrew's niece, at the Castle of Lochnaw where she is staying with her aunt Lady Agnew, the other half of his nature comes into play. She is entirely the opposite of Juliana. The gipsy girl is dark, Lilias is fair, with hair like ripe August wheat, and eyes that are blue and mock him with teasing Irish carelessness. She is a lady born and educated; she is related to some of the ladies he had known in France. She and Silver Sand are able to talk of France and its elegant ways; Lilias is homesick for her happier times there.

> A maid in this dear drear land has never anything she wants—or at least she has it not for long. In France she has her heart's desire, especially if she be married—*after*, I should say. But here, it is only big boots stamping, spurs jingling, and tender consciences fleeing. Who would have suspected either you or the Sheriff of a liking for the Shorter Catechism? Yet there you are off like

the wildest Whigs to the dens and caves of the earth, leaving us poor women with only our finger-nails to bite—and a poor meal we make of them! Never a thought for us so that you can conscientiously disobey the King![7]

The Covenanters and their beliefs are neatly stood on their heads by a witty woman; 'conscientiously disobey the king' sums their position up with wicked accuracy. Through serving Sir Andrew, Silver Sand often sees Lilias and falls under her bright spell; in spite of his will, he has come near to forgetting Juliana with this *gorgio* woman who belongs to that other world of his, the world of gaiety and music and books and women with fine dresses and laughing voices. This is Silver Sand's predicament, to be a man belonging to two worlds, unable to free himself from either.

Juliana, when Silver Sand is away on Sir Andrew's business, still serves her husband by collecting the dues he is owed by all the gipsies. She brings the money to him, disguised as a young man, Julius Stanley, and has to be introduced to Lilias as Silver Sand's secretary. Lilias takes a fancy to this handsome youth, and Juliana, guessing that Silver Sand and she are almost in love, is forever praising Silver Sand, talking of his bravery, pressing Lilias to love him. It is Juliana's joy to give him his heart's desire, even if it means that she will sacrifice her own.

Silver Sand spends most of his time when he is not at Lochnaw up at the gipsy camp—the Raiders' camp, high up in the Dungeon of Buchan. There he welcomes not only the Scottish and English gipsies but also any of the Wanderers, the oppressed ministers and Covenanters, who make their way up into the high inhospitable hills. He refuses no man shelter, though he knows he is bringing danger upon himself and his clan.

> 'Sir, hearken unto me,' said the ousted minister of Kells, to Silver Sand, 'we are a trial to you, and more than a trial, a danger. But because you have been sorry for us, the least of his little ones, you shall receive ten fold in the Day of Judgment, the reward we are too poor to offer you in this life!'[8]

The Covenanting thread is worked into the life of Silver Sand when he is a young man—not quite as in *The Raiders* but still as an important factor. It does indeed lead him into danger. One day, he ventures down too far, carrying provisions to a hiding place on the south side of the Merrick. On the way back, he is taken prisoner by the dragoons and set on a mare, with his legs tied under the horse's belly, ready to be taken to Dumfries as a rebel.

Juliana sets off disguised again as a young man with a small band of gipsies to rescue him. They come upon the dragoons when they have just heard that James II has been deposed and William of Orange invited to take the throne of Great Britain and Ireland. The persecutions are over and these lesser persecutors are left not knowing what to do. Juliana takes her chance, steals close and cuts Silver Sand's bonds. He is free. But on the way back to the Dungeon, Juliana is quiet and remote. When they reach the Dungeon of Buchan and safety, she slips to the ground, fainting, and before midnight her son is born—another John Faa, to carry on the gipsy kingship. Juliana knows that she herself cannot live but is in an ecstasy of happiness in giving John Faa his heir; she knows that he will never forget her. She had not told him she was to bear his child because she knew that their time together would be short and wanted to make it as long as she could. They talk together quietly. She talks of religion and brings out two little dumpy books, the Old and New Testaments, which she had been given by a tinker who used to stay with the gipsies—John Bunyan. The link with *The Raiders* is made in that moment— Silver Sand showed Patrick the two little books that could be carried in the neuk of a plaid. Now we know who has given them to him. Her mind wanders a little, talking of the Duchrae Bank and Mount Pleasant, mixing them with *The Pilgrim's Progress*, and so, talking of her love and with her arms about his neck, Juliana dies, leaving John Faa with his first-born son. She had known from the first that he could be hers only for a while and is content that he has grown to love her.

But there had grown up strong feeling between Lilias and Silver Sand, although he had been too cowardly to confess that he was married by gipsy law. When, very belatedly, he confesses to her that the young man Julius is his wife Juliana in disguise, Lilias is angry; she declares that Juliana must be a forward minx and cannot understand how she can have wished her husband to love another woman. After Juliana's death her pride is softened. She had not understood.

> 'Poor Juliana,' she murmured. 'I may call her that now? She won the gift of gifts, the good she asked for, but to enjoy it she had but short time. Her sweet little world, all of her own making, came so soon to an end!'

Silver Sand blames himself for his blindness and ignorance, but Lilias says it would have made no difference; it was God's will. Then suddenly she offers Silver Sand her hands in friendship.

> 'Make the boy a good man,' she said quickly, 'make him like Sir Andrew. Let him be simple and true. Bring him up far from the world. You and I, Silver Sand, are spoilt by Paris. We can never taste clean spring water again.'[9]

The generous imaginative understanding which Crockett gives to Lilias is a memorable characterisation. There are several layers of meaning in her first reaction—grief; regret; forgiveness; a little envy, perhaps; the realisation that Juliana had created a little world around Silver Sand through her love, finding her joy in anticipating his wishes; the acknowledgement that she, Lilias, could not have matched the sweetness of spirit which gave all and asked so little; and finally the sadness that it lasted—and could have lasted—only for such a short time.

She thinks ahead of what the child's future may be, and in an impulsive offering of friendship links herself and Silver Sand in the same unworthiness compared with the honest sheer goodness of Sir Andrew. Up to this moment, readers may have been thinking of Sir Andrew with affectionate amusement; he is devoted to his wife Jean Hay in a comic elderly way; he is inclined to shrug his shoulders at the loss of his jurisdiction to Claverhouse; he is just a kindly easy-going old baronet. When sophisticated Lilias suddenly says these things of him—that he is a simple, true, good man, a worthy example for any father to ask his son to follow—it is a revelation. The words in which people speak of him return to our minds.

> 'There is no man like Sir Andrew;' was often said of him everywhere, and indeed he had a way with him which indicated that he was aware in a jovial fashion of his deserts, and possessed a habit of command which was not lessened by the consciousness of two hundred and fifty years of hereditary jurisdiction. But he was a joyous man by nature, being what was called in Galloway 'jocose,' a quality which enabled him without loss of dignity to mingle mercy with judgment on his days of 'justice aires.'[10]

Unlike the youthful Silver Sand, he had no need to stand upon his rank; he was respected for himself and exerted authority without seeming to.

> Ah, a broad buirdly man was Sir Andrew, and a master of all about him. For though he seemed easy to take a liberty with, the lairds and great folk who were under his jurisdiction had not found it either safe or profitable to meddle with the Sheriff.[11]

He is brave and optimistic without minimising the danger in which he stands.

> 'We will provide, never fear,' Sir Andrew said cheerfully. 'The blast is too strong to last. The *bensil* blows down too many trees. They will tire of it, and besides—the life of a man is no more than the breath upon his lips ... at least they will have to 'head me in the Grassmarket if they catch me,' said Bluff Sir Andrew. 'I am too big a fish for any of their barn-end courts-martial. You, James, and you, Silver Sand, would get the short shrift from one of Earlshall's firing parties, but I should require a Privy Council decision and an escort of gentlemen to convoy me down to the Grassmarket like my Lord of Argyle.'[12]

He settles himself as comfortably as he can in the Gled's Nest;

> Sir Andrew was bodily comfortable in the Gled's Nest in the High Wood of Lochnaw. He had several volumes of divinity which he adjudged appropriate to the occasion, besides (what suited him better), on a well-hidden shelf, half a dozen volumes of plays, including Shakespeare, with Beaumont and Fletcher, and the two small folios of Ben Jonson.
> But he was uneasy about these if any visitor called suddenly, and would drop any one of them which he happened to be reading into the meal barrel, or behind Jean Hay's kebbuck of Galloway cheese.
> Then he would fall to *Knox's Reformation* or the last treatise of Mr McWard printed in Holland with the most furious and convincing zeal.[13]

He is no fanatic but a moderate and civilised gentleman who has sufficient sense of what is expected of him to provide himself with suitable Covenanting reading, but at the same time follow his own tastes as a cultured man of the world.

Crockett seldom writes of ideas, but he expresses through Juliana, Lilias and Silver Sand, the idea of a man caught between two worlds, with an insistence which suggests that he had thought of it deeply. Neither world is ideal; Juliana's world is too simple, though Lilias points back to its lovely simplicity with envy when she says that she and Silver Sand 'can never taste clean spring water again'. Lilias's world is too brittle and shallow to be wholly satisfactory. It is Sir Andrew who is set squarely and firmly in the position of a truly good man, the *honnête homme*, honourable, upright without being priggish, reasonable, courteous, kindly and fair.

There could be a very personal reason for Crockett's delineating in such detail Silver Sand's predicament. He himself had been forced by circumstances to live in two worlds. Born and bred a Galloway peasant, education had made him a Free Church minister but an unsettled one, with unorthodox views on literature, on life and especially on the injustice the rich inflicted on the poor; he was virtually a Socialist before socialism could be tolerated. Yet he enjoyed worldly pleasures like book collecting, photography, astronomy, travel, Alpine climbing, wine and good food. When success through his writing came, he removed himself and his family from the Manse to a large house standing in its own grounds, with servants and gardeners and many luxuries, even before he faced the necessity of resigning his ministry. He was thrust into a world of literary rivalry with other writers which had its unhappiness and bitterness. Like Silver Sand, he was trying to live in two worlds. He could not return to Little Duchrae; it had gone. He could not live in the literary world with jealousies and hostile critics; he was too honest and boyish to enjoy social gatherings and literary chit-chat. He would rather be in his library with the maid saying that he was not at home. No intermediate position existed for him, but he could create a Sir Andrew for Silver Sand and Lilias, just as he had bestowed wealth and legacies upon Ralph Peden and Winsome Charteris.

After the high point of Silver Sand and Lilias coming together in love and understanding, the story moves into adventure and is fairly quickly at an end. Lilias brings young John Faa down from the Dungeon of Buchan to be baptised by the Rev William Dunning, out of his refuge in the Doocot for the occasion; Silver Sand opportunely arrives just in time to be present.

He had been determined that his son should be brought up either as a gipsy or as a gentleman, not as one hovering between the two. He in the end has no say in the matter. His brother Hector Faa, a story-book gipsy with golden earrings and a red sash over his doublet and hose, kidnaps the child and so the heir of the Faas leaves Scotland just as his father had done. Word comes from Hungary to say that he will be well looked after; he has been taken from Hector into good hands, to be brought up a tzigane among the tziganas.

There is one last adventure; a renegade gipsy and a villainous Irishman kidnap Silver Sand and torture him to find where the Faa riches have been hidden. A McKitterick comes upon them and heaves one of them into the sea; the other, Grey Roger, contrives to fight on with daggers. A shot is fired across the ravine—Lilias stands astonished at what she has done. There is a pistol smoking in her hand; her shot has saved Silver Sand. Grey Roger is thrown down into the suck of the sea far below; to round things off, it is he who committed the murder of the two dragoons at the beginning of the book for which the Stanleys were being blamed.

After this it is only a matter of time and Silver Sand's recovery before he and Lilias are married by Mr Dunning; Lilias, having saved Silver Sand's life, has shown herself almost as worthy and devoted as Juliana. Bailie, one of the Border gipsies, prophesies that Silver Sand will come back to Scotland:

> Rejoicing yet sorrowing you shall return, and you shall die among your own people that they may escape. Soldiers shall hem them about, but you who are of the blood royal of Egypt, shall die an old man, but more gloriously than any of your fathers and of a death longer to be remembered.[14]

This is a prophecy of the end of *Dark o' the Moon*. But that is far ahead; Silver Sand and his wife leave Scotland for Italy and sunshine and happiness, allowing the last word to Nathan Crogo, who says that there is much left to be told about Lilias and Silver Sand and young John Faa (was Crockett preparing the way for a sequel?) but that he is tired and glad to rest, contemplating his favourite text

> which I have printed in large letters, so that it may sink into the hearts of all, as it has into mine, after knowing Silver Sand and my dear patron Sir Andrew, DEAL COURAGEOUSLY, AND THE LORD SHALL BE WITH THE GOOD.[15]

That, from II Chronicles 19: 11, is as near a 'Moral' as Crockett ever allowed himself to pronounce.

Hal o' the Ironsides followed in 1915; it was not necessarily written after *Silver Sand* as there seems little chance of discovering in what order Crockett's posthumous works were composed, but it has little of the complexity of its predecessor and is an adventure story of Cromwellian days which could have been written for boys.

As usual, Crockett chooses imaginary personages for his principals; he credits the Parliament man Edmund Ludlow with a nephew, Hal Ludlow, and invents an imaginary Lady Molly Woodham for him to marry in the end. Hal is a young man with money to spare and a tendency towards 'petticoating' which in Puritan eyes is only the first step towards 'chambering' and 'wantoning'. He is dismissed and stripped of his insignia. Eager to redeem himself in Colonel Cromwell's eyes, he rides to the eastern part of Ely where in Hog Lane there live the 'peculiar people', Anabaptists, ancestors of our Baptists; he knows them well and hopes to enlist from among them the beginnings of a troop of his own.

The Hog Laners are known to be on the Parliament side; they are shoemakers by trade and have made boots for Cromwell's troops of the Eastern Association. They are a surly and argumentative sect; Crockett in his description of them reminds us of the Marrow Kirk, for it is a characteristic of Puritanism, both Scottish and English, that there never was a sect, no matter how small and narrow, but it contained in it a kernel of something yet smaller, narrower and more bitter. As in the Holy Place there was a Holy of Holies, so in the exalted company of Hog Lane there was an inner sect of Enthusiasts ready to split and re-split infinitesimally till some fiery Gossip Joan should define the future prospects of the world's salvation: 'There are only John and me that are of the Elect, and I'm none so sure of John!'[16]

Hal succeeds in enlisting a troop and drills them until they are able to join the main body of the Eastern Association. He has gone some way towards reinstatement in his much admired and beloved Colonel's eyes, especially when, with the help of a gipsy girl, Neña la Fain from the marshes, he and his troop are able to drive off a Royalist attack on the villages of Gedney and French Drove and capture their leader, Captain Dick Lucy of Charlcote.

Cromwell is seen through Hal's eyes, as a stern courageous leader of men with no subtlety in the picture, no sign of conflicts. He is a family man, kindly although strict, but has no doubts about his purposes. For background, Crockett has studied the English countryside well; he can describe the Fens with their reeds and rushes, alders and willows, ooze and slub, filled with ducks, plovers, heron and lapwings among the rank grasses, the water carrying marsh fever even to those accustomed to the perpetual dampness and chill; Ely by moonlight with its gables and bee-hive-topped staircases, shutters tightly closed against the night air, strangely silent and eerie; Chelmsford market square, its wooden-fronted houses bulging out over their lower storeys, sunlit and busy, the carts creaking and jostling as the waggoners shouted at one another in anger. He has a clear picture of the fowler's hut in which Neña lives with an old man, Jack Wassailer, a Huguenot, really Jacques Oiseleur, helping him with his trade of selling fish, plovers and ducks in the market.

He manages the English speech well; it is not Wardour Street but suggests its period by its careful use of vocabulary belonging to that time, with no admixture of modern locutions which would break the illusion. And he knows the current terms; 'Candlishers' and 'Camdeners' are followers of the Royalists Charles Cavendish and Lord Camden. The metal helmets of the Ironsides are called 'pots'. They are fined twelve pence if they are caught swearing. A 'forlorn' is a reconnoitering party which sets out to find as much information as it can, unsupported by the main body. The Royalists call Cromwell's men the 'Ameners' and Baptists 'Dippers'; Cromwell himself is 'the Huntington brewer' and his Ironsides 'the brewer's draymen'.

Hal and his Hog Lane troopers gradually gather recruits until they are up to the number of the others; Hal is made a Captain and Zered Tuby his Lieutenant, and they gain respect by their discipline and their courage. Hal grows a hardened commander. Danbury Towers is a mansion which is being held for the King by Lady Molly Woodham, Hal's childhood playmate, with a garrison of young Royalists. She recognises Hal disguised as a waggoner at Chelmsford market and saves him from being forced into Prince Rupert's service by claiming that she needs a good stout servant. Taken to Danbury by Lady Molly and her Royalist friends, Hal memorises the defences, and the Hog Laners capture it easily. Lady Molly is safely established with Cromwell's family. The Hog Laners go from one small affray to another; they are fairly successful but never as successful as they had hoped. The enemy is finding out their plans in advance. A shot is fired at Hal one day as he lies on the grass reading; his 'pot' deflects it, but Zered examines the splintered edge. The bullet is exactly the same as all the others used by the Hog Lane troop, made in their own bullet-mould. Zered says nothing but keeps careful watch thereafter.

Hal is ordered to enter Oxford as a spy to discover what he can about the King's forces and their plans. This he does with the help of Neña la Fain. She disguises him as Melchior the Mage in strange flame-coloured silk embroidered with cabalistic signs, and herself as his slave boy Sidi. Melchior keeps to scraps of Latin and a few words of foreign-sounding English; Sidi does most of the magic which he performs, while he invokes Heth, Toth, Astoroth and Demagorgon; he is a great success. Prince Rupert and his brother Prince Maurice are also in Oxford, with Maurice's mistress Lady Lulu—a most unfortunate name for the lady which may have sounded less comic in Crockett's time. She takes a fancy to Melchior and babbles to him all he wants to know about the plans and preparations of the Royalist army, not without a great deal of very voluptuous lovemaking. She follows Hal when he leaves Oxford, and becomes caught up, terrified, in a battle. Hal places her in the keeping of one of his sergeants, Doe Royds, with orders to take her back to Oxford. When the fighting is over and the Hog Laners have destroyed the enemy artillery, Doe Royds rejoins them. Hal is suspicious; what has he been doing and where is Lady Lulu? His answers are too glib and false. Royds tries to escape but Hal has him arrested. In the presence of Cromwell and Ireton, he is searched; out of his pocket there falls a white object into the grass; when found, it is a woman's forefinger with a ruby ring upon it, cut off at the joint. In other pockets and his holster more jewels are found. It is he who is the traitor and has stolen from the woman he has been detailed to protect. They find Lady Lulu dead, with two deep stabs in her breast and her white dress stained and disordered. Without saying so, Crockett conveys that she has been raped as well as robbed and killed.

Two graves are dug. The Lady Lulu is gently and kindly laid to rest in honourable burial. Doe Royds in contrast suffers an uncommonly horrible punishment.

> A post made out of a felled tree was driven deep into the ground at the head of the second grave, and upon this Doe Royds was seated, his legs closely tied about the wood and his arms pinioned behind his back. The badges of his rank were torn from his sleeve and destroyed. And then in an impressive silence, the regiment formed three sides of a hollow square facing towards the post. All the western sky was red like blood, and facing it the Sergeant-Major of the Hog Lane Troop sat immovable on his post, looking in the direction from which his doom was to arrive. Helmet on head, corsleted and breast-plated, he waited, an

erect and soldierly figure. His face showed no emotion, and he neither vaunted nor wavered. He merely sat silent and looked death in the face—so great a thing is personal courage.

From the other side of the deep grave Cromwell, surrounded by his officers, watched the execution of the traitor and slaughterer of women—the first in the new army.

'Hog Lane,' he commanded, 'clear your name!'

The troopers were gathered at the upper end of the enclosure like men about to ride a tournay. At the word of command they put their horses in motion, riding one by one towards the doomed man, and as they passed at full speed each sword struck a full stroke. A long hollow moaning sound broke from the Cambridgers, massed black against the red sunset. But Hog Lane did not pause nor hesitate. As each horseman went whirling by, striking and disengaging his arm, another was hard on his horse's heels. Nor did they cease till all that had been Doe Royds had tumbled piecemeal into the grave, the head with the helm still firm upon it, arms, legs, trunk all piecemeal, and the clean, kindly earth pushed down to hide the horror.

Only the haggled and blood-stained post remained for a memorial, dripping a ghastly viscous dew upon the trampled earth and speckled grass.[17]

This may or may not have happened in Cromwell's army, but Crockett had perfectly good Biblical precedent for it, as he tells us in the name of the chapter, 'The Hewing of Agag'. In I Samuel 15: 13 the killing of the King of the Amalekites is briefly dealt with:

And Samuel said, As thy sword hath made women childless, so shall thy mother be childless among women. And Samuel hewed Agag in pieces before the Lord in Gilgal.

Crockett's restraint makes the horror all the more effective. He gathers the detail slowly, suggesting the deliberate preparation for this most terrible execution. The felling of the tree, the seating of Royds upon it, the tying of his legs and arms so that he cannot move, all slow careful actions, lead up to the stripping of the badges and the irony of giving the man his full rank, Sergeant-Major of the Hog Lane Troop, as if to emphasise the honourable position he had so foully disgraced. There may even be a sardonic pun in the phrase that he 'sat immovable upon his post'.

The troopers are gathered 'like men about to ride a tournay': a tournay is a light-hearted trial of strength among men of nobility and honour. The Cambridge troops feel the horror; they cannot help groaning as the horses race towards their goal, impelled by their riders. Crockett spares us no grim detail; even when the dismembered corpse had 'tumbled'—how deliberately clumsy and undignified a verb—'piecemeal'—how economically that word conveys the untidiness of the shattered body—into the grave and been covered over by the merciful ordinariness of the soil, there is the ugliness of the stump left, bloody and cut by the swords as they have shorn through Royds and left deep hacks in the wood.

Meanwhile Neña la Fain knows that her part in Hal's fortunes is over. Yet some good has come to her; when Jack Wassailer had been near death with malaria, she had sought help from Hal and received it; he had brought a doctor out through the fens to the fowler's hut with the 'Jesuit's bark'—quinine. Jack and Neña are moved to Osea Island in Essex where they can ply their trade in wild-fowl and fish in a dry and pleasant climate.

Naseby and victory follow. Hal and his troop have fought well as part of the New Model Army. At a State Banquet given by his father, the State Commissioner, a rich merchant who has become richer still by being a contractor for the army, Hal sits as an honoured guest; he has been made a Colonel—Cromwell has long since been General. A message is brought to Hal that a young lad insists on seeing him, and has been placed in his chamber to wait until he comes. It is Lady Molly in disguise, jealous of what she has heard of Neña the gipsy girl. She succeeds in compromising herself in Hal's bedroom so thoroughly that Hal has to marry her, which he is by no means averse to doing. John Milton's second wife, a pretty young girl, comes to help dress the bride.

Hal o' the Ironsides is a lively story with strong fast narrative, full of the trampling of horses, the laughter of men and the planning of battles. It is good, competent, but not distinguished. There is much action but little thought, except perhaps when Cromwell for a moment near the conclusion looks down on the Thames from London Bridge.

> 'Can any man cleanse that?' Cromwell's voice came to Hal's ear like that of a man meditating in a solitary place. 'Once it came from a crystal spring, up on a hillside, cupful by cupful. The lambs drank and were satisfied. So narrow it was that in play they leaped across it. Now who can span it, who can touch it without being soiled? Such is our life. God gave it. He alone can cleanse it. Out yonder (he flapped a riding gauntlet in the direction of the sea) is cleansing. A mile or two of salt water and all this flood of impurity and shame shall be cleansed—its filth and our sins sunk in the deep sea of his forgetfulness.'[18]

It may be Oliver Cromwell who speaks, but it sounds very much like Samuel Rutherford Crockett, once more affirming his hope of and belief in the universal salvation of mankind, no matter how sorely it has perplexed the kindness of God.

The Azure Hand. A Novel, dateable only by the Accession Stamp of the Advocates' Library in Edinburgh as 11 September 1917,[19] comes as a complete surprise. It is a detective story, the last form which one would have expected a man of Crockett's temperament to have had the patience to work out. It is a Scottish detective story, its minor characters talking with Scottish accents and its whole flavour Scottish. It shows that Crockett must have read enough of this popular form to know most of the tricks of the trade and be confident enough to add a few of his own. It is not altogether serious; it is a skit upon the detective story rather than a serious attempt to add a new masterpiece to the *genre*, yet it adheres fairly faithfully to the rules, departing from them—excusably—only once, and uses many 'whodunnit' clichés, exaggerating without making the parody so outrageous as to be ridiculous. Since it is a rare book, difficult if not impossible to find in the second-hand and antiquarian booksellers' shops, it may perhaps be permissible to summarise it at greater length than other more important books written by Crockett, simply because it is so extraordinary that it should have been written at all. It opens with magnificent abruptness.

It was Susan who saw him first.

Susan Sim is the under-housemaid at Dent House, a large late-Victorian mansion set in its own grounds, with lawns and parterres and a conservatory, a classic setting for British detective novels.

Susan goes into the library one morning, armed with dustpan and brush. She finds it heavy with pipe-smoke, the blinds still drawn down, and Mr Patrick Fenwick-Dent, her employer and the owner of Dent House, sitting dead in his armchair with a strange grey smile upon his face. Very naturally, she darts back into the hall and calls 'Richard!' to the butler. Mr Fenwick-Dent is dead and marble-cold. Richard calls from a window to Adams, the under-gardener who is working outside, to come in. Adams cannot; the Garden Port, the door from the library into the garden, is locked. Richard lets him in, making him take off his boots and walk in his rig-and-furrow stocking soles to save the carpet. Susan in the meantime faints. Richard locks her into his still-room so that she will be safe and quiet and locks himself and Adams into the library so that they can investigate without being disturbed.

> 'It's just no possible!' gasped Adams, 'he's as quiet as if asleep.'
> 'Touch him!' commanded the butler. But Adams shrank back.
> 'This will be a job for the police, I'm thinking,' he murmured, as if he feared to awake someone. 'Oh, what will her ladyship say?—and Miss Dent and young Miss Aymer?'
> 'That's what we have to think about, Adams—who is to break it to the ladies? Then the police coming about the house, and all the inquiries—I don't like that, Adams.'
> 'Is it natural?' suggested Adams, standing with his legs wide apart and regarding the still figure in the chair as if he were meditating a problem of his profession. 'Or has he—has he committed . . . ?' But this angered the old servant.
> 'Ye are an incomer,' he said severely, 'tis well seen that ye know little of my master. I have served him forty year—aye, forty three year man and boy. A clearer-headed man never stepped—never a cross word between us all that time. Hear ye that? Mind that when they come to ask you, Adams. Draw up the blind, Adams!'[20]

By the light of a sunny morning they examine the room. They find two toddy glasses, one by Mr Dent's chair suspiciously wiped quite clean, the other on a little smoking-table on the other side of the fireplace holding dregs of what Richard sniffs and pronounces to be whisky. On the light-coloured hearthrug there is a blue stain as if a mittened hand had been pressed on it.

Richard does not trust the police; they will cause trouble. Before he can decide what to do, Aymer Valentine, the dead man's niece, comes downstairs and raps on the door; she wants to know why it is locked. They hastily throw a black-and-white checked plaid over the silent figure in the club chair and try to keep her out, but she laughingly ducks under Richard's arm and passes him into the room. She snatches the plaid from the chair, cries out to her Uncle Patrick and kneels by his side. When she feels the icy cold of his hand she rises again and looks at Richard and Adams, and back again. Now that Miss Aymer is there, Richard sends Adam off in the trap for the police and the doctor. He asks Miss Aymer to break the news to Mr Dent's wife and daughter. She hesitates; she will tell Miss Rachel, but someone else would be better for Mrs Dent. We wonder why.

Richard himself remains thoughtfully in the library, looking at the second tumbler. It has left a wet ring on the surface of the table which fits none of the glasses or tumblers in the sideboard. He shakes his head. This is too much for him. Locking up again, he sets out for Laverock Hall nearby, where Mr Fenwick-Dent's oldest and closest friend lives. He is Wilfred Thorald, a retired Judge from India—a nabob, one might say. He may be able to advise from legal knowledge.

Dent House and Laverock Hall sit high on a ridge overlooking the Lochar Moss, a large wide marshy area at the east end of the Solway Firth, into which Lochar Water winds and flows. The nearest town is Quarrier, an ancient Royal Burgh, county town of Kentigernshire, which calls itself the 'Queen City of the South', boasts old-established woollen mills, an important weekly market, a railway junction and an automobile factory. This is Dumfries, whose football team is still called 'Queen of the South'; the automobile factory is Penman's garage.

The name of the Indian Judge is borrowed from Torthorwald, a village a few miles north-east of Dumfries on the road to Lochmaben and Lockerbie, pronounced locally Torr-thorrald. The Lochar Moss is just the Lochar Moss, as it always has been.

Judge Thorald is a lean man of sixty-one who dresses like an old-fashioned dandy; a man of distinction, he wears the out-moded long-waisted Victorian coats which show off his still youthful figure and his endless array of flower-embroidered silk waistcoats. He has had a brilliant legal career in India and wears the button of the Légion d'Honneur; now he is merely a JP but has sufficient weight in the community to have had his old friend Colonel Hector Hampden-Jones, late of the 25th Gurkhas, appointed Chief of Police. In the Judge's waistcoat pocket he carries a gold snuff-box full of his favourite Tunisian cigarettes; he takes out and looks at the snuff-box over and over again every day. On the lid is delicately enamelled a miniature portrait of a woman who closely resembles Aymer Valentine, Mr Dent's niece. The Judge is rumoured to have in his youth wanted to marry Bessie Netherholm, the first Mrs Dent. He immediately accompanies Richard to Dent House.

Aymer has been breaking the sad news to Rachel Dent, only daughter of the dead man, an unhappy sullen unattractive woman in her thirties who has become estranged from her father since his marriage to a step-mother five years younger than she is. The second Mrs Dent is a fluffy frivolous heartless woman who has married her husband only for his money. She is a Londoner, and incorrigibly flirtatious, but finds little opportunity for flirting beside the Lochar Moss. The sound of hysterics from upstairs indicates that the news is being broken to her by her lady's-maid Sylvia Granger.

Aymer, the pretty vivacious niece, lives with them as a kind of supplementary housekeeper; Mrs Dent resents her and often demands that she be sent away, but Aymer has brought great happiness to her uncle's later years, his happiest moment being when in the evenings Aymer comes to tell him all that has been going on—'riddling the day' they call it. Also in the household are Richard Hissy the butler, Connel the first housemaid, Sylvia Granger the lady's-maid, Sue Sim the second housemaid, Tomlinson the gardener who lives in the Lodge, Adams the under-gardener, the cook and several other servants who are of no importance in the story.

Colonel Hampden-Jones arrives, stout, ruddy-faced and white-moustached; he hopes to get everything settled before the city detectives put in an appearance. He is an elderly duffer, bullied by his wife, his four daughters and the Judge. The azure stain is fading; fussily he cuts out its shape in blotting paper as evidence. He cannot see anything to suggest that a crime has been committed at all. The Judge points out the discrepancy between the wet ring and the glasses and tumblers in the house. The Colonel concludes that the murder has been committed by someone in the house. The Judge shows him scaps of paper he has found in the wastepaper basket which when put together read 'I propose to call upon you tomorrow night . . .'[21] The Colonel concludes that the murder has been committed by someone outside the house. He admits, with some semblance of truth, that he is no Sherlock Holmes.

Richard in a little while appears, introducing a slight supple young man with dark eyes, Detective-Lieutenant Luiz Perez Grant,[22] sent by the old-established firm of Edinburgh solicitors McMath, McMath, Lindsay and McMath, who manage the late Mr Dent's affairs. The Crown Office, the permanent body of officials responsible for the public prosecution of crime in Scotland, has been in touch with them, and agrees that the investigation must be handled with delicacy. Grant is to be in charge and be provided with accommodation in the house and every facility. He first takes Judge Thorald to be the Chief of Police, but the Judge 'with a slight smile of appreciation' indicates the Colonel, and introduces himself by name to make his own position clear as an old family friend.

The detective immediately bows with pleased astonishment. He is honoured to meet Judge Thorald. He has read his articles in the *Asiatic Review* (no doubt when studying for the Calcutta Bar, to which he has been called) and will be most interested to hear his opinions on the present case as investigations proceed. He has studied with interest Thorald's judgements on the Upper Bengal gangs and especially his interpretation of the evidence in the poisoning cases at Serampore and Meerut.

The Judge purrs. He has thought of himself as completely forgotten, his ancient reputation

> unknown to all save a few old Indian 'returned empties' like himself dibbled sparsely here and there along South Coast health resorts from Eastbourne to Torbay.[23]

Colonel Hampden-Jones thinks differently. He is less than civil to Grant, who to him is a policeman with the effrontery to look like a gentleman. He is also of mixed blood; the Colonel can tell. His father may be Scots, but his mother ... ? When Grant is taken by Richard to the room allotted for his use, Aymer's old nursery still with her toys and rocking-horse, the Colonel explodes.

> Why, he's a black man—a nigger. I could see the milk-opal on the finger-nails of him. You can smell the tar-brush a mile off. Do you think that I have been all these years in India for nothing? And he has the—the dashed impertinence—to—ugh, Thorald, for three ha'pence, I'd kick him down the stairs![24]

This comic racialist prejudice—deliberately comic—rumbles all through the book until in a moment of rage the Colonel refers to Grant as 'that Crown Office Christy Minstrel'.[25]

The reader's eyebrows inevitably are raised at this point. It is a little surprising that the detective from Edinburgh should have had time to consult with the Crown Office and McMath, McMath, Lindsay and McMath and yet be on the doorstep of Dent House so very soon after the discovery of the crime. The Colonel's anxiety to get on with the investigation quickly before the city detectives put in an appearance prepares us for this to some extent. What is much more odd is that a detective should investigate a crime while at the same time acting on behalf of the family through its solicitors.

Crockett was possibly writing *The Azure Hand* while he was abroad. He must have realised that the situation was anomalous, so he surrounds Grant's appearance with so much angry argument and polite persiflage, racial ill-feeling and criss-cross argument, smooth learned references and angry bluster, that we are quite bewildered and accept everything in order to get on with the story. It is agreed that Grant is to be present at the Procurator-Fiscal's examination of witnesses—the Scots equivalent of a coroner's court; he will sit in the background, taking no part, but noting all on behalf of the family.

> The Fiscal's examination achieved itself with the maximum of fuss and the minimum of results not already attained, which is the general outcome of these functions.[26]

The body has shown no sign of poison of any kind after it has been submitted to analysis, but it is murder, not suicide. Most of the female staff go into hysterics when asked any questions. Sue and Richard answer with clarity. Connel demands that they go upstairs and search her box if they think she had anything to do with it—or else hang her at once. Adams particularly distinguishes himself.

> He had been one of the first called into the library. He had been left alone with the body on more than one occasion, and he had in his mind that 'whatever he said might be used against him'—a formula which he had once heard applied by the local policeman to a tramp-poacher charged with assault. He began with the categoric declaration, 'I am not guilty of this crime,' pro-

nouncing the words slow and staccato, and he could not be cured of the idea that he had to hold up his right hand all the time.

'And to this I swear.'—he added to each well-considered and non-committal reply[27]

Mrs Dent goes into hysterics in her boudoir once more and refuses to come down at all—'Tantrums!' says her maid Sylvia from behind her back, silently mouthing the words to the Judge. His blandishments succeed; after helping her to make up her face nicely he leads her down to the dining room in a long trailing cream-coloured robe.

Grant watches from the shadows in the corner where he has stationed himself. Her poor husband, her poor dear husband, is all she can think of; she had seen him last on the afternoon of the Day, in her dressing room where they always had their quarrels—not that they ever quarrelled, only disagreed—'picked bones one with the other'—in a friendly way. They never quarrelled—'*except about that minx.*'[28] Grant notices that the Judge presses her shoulder, and she immediately explains that the 'minx' was a dismissed servant about whom they differed. Grant wonders and so do we.

Her husband had meant to go out for a walk on the moors with his daughter. He was sorry that she had not felt well but glad she was up to entertaining the two young men who were coming for tea—friends of theirs, a young man home from touring the world with his tutor.

'Mr William Leslie Bowles and Mr Mark Hill—gentlemen staying at the Dent Arms in Quarrier' whispered the Judge, 'I know them.'[29]

The Fiscal asks if her husband had in fact gone walking with his daughter. He had not. He had gone with his niece, Aymer Valentine.

The next witness is Rachel Dent. When questioned, she stared, stubbornly ill-humoured, at the floor. Yes, she had been going for a walk with her father over the moors on the afternoon before his death, but 'that Other' had spoiled things. She had been supplanted in her father's affection by 'that Other' and cried out in sudden fury 'I could kill ... ', then stops herself, saying that she had promised not to say things like that. 'That Other' is not Aymer: it is the one who had taken her father's love from her and had sent Aymer out with her father so as to have Marcus Hill all to herself over the tea-table.

'She hates Aymer as much as I hate her—the evil woman, the supplanter, the *murderess!*'

The chill, contained fury with which the last word was dashed in the face of all about the table, daunted even the Fiscal, albeit well seasoned to all manner of family hatreds and misunderstandings.[30]

Rachel breaks into hysterical accusations of her stepmother and in the end calls for Aymer, who leads her gently to her room. Aymer herself is the next witness; when the time comes, the Judge goes to bring her down.

And then, in his heart of hearts, the Judge felt the rasp of Scott's goodbye to

Lockhart: 'Be a good man, Lockhart—nothing else will serve you when you come to this!' He had come to a very terrible '*this*'—and he had not the right to speak to this young girl. No matter, he would defend her—whatever it might cost himself, or others.[31]

We wonder what terrible '*this*' the Judge had come to. Why had he no right to speak? Only his age?

Aymer comes in like a breath of fresh air after her cousin. She thought she was the last to see her uncle alive. He did not need much sleep and often read until late. He had worries, too, which kept him awake but she did not know what they were. He did not speak much of himself. She often saw him walking in the garden when it was moonlight. She is angered by the Fiscal's question about expectations from her uncle's will; she expected nothing. Now she would have to work, as a housekeeper, cook, tablemaid—she is qualified to do these things.

The question from the Fiscal about her expectations had been prompted by Grant; he sends up another note which makes the Fiscal frown, but he asks the question the note suggests. Would Aymer be surprised if she found that her uncle had left her most of his fortune? Aymer replies that she would not believe it. It was understood that she earn her own living until ... she blushes. The Fiscal understands; until she marries. On the night of the murder, she had seen a lantern being waved in a gap in the trees on the estate, but she had no idea by whom or why.

The official inquiry at last over, Grant suggests to the Judge a visit to the two young men at the Dent Arms, Hill and Bowles. The Judge says he is too tired but he will be interested in Grant's thoughts after the visit. He stalks off haughtily, and Grant watches him with amusement.

> 'Holy Saint Christopher,' he muttered under his breath, 'I will bet a sovereign the old bird's jealous!'[32]

—jealous, that is, of Marcus Hill's relationship with Aymer. When Grant gives his account of the visit to the Judge, the two men sitting at ease in Laverock Hall, smoking Tunisian cigarettes from the snuff-box, he says they seem good enough fellows, the pupil with not too much brain, the tutor inclined to be aggressive. Marcus has said frankly without being asked that he had been in the Dent woods on the night of the murder. The Judge is visibly startled. Is there, Grant asks, any motive either of the young men can have had for the murder? The Judge stretches himself comfortably and tells Grant he is being commonplace; the most brilliant crimes are committed for intellectual satisfaction or to add to life's interest; great criminals need no motive. Grant agrees, but Marcus is not of this type; he is more likely to be interested in pretty servants at Dent House, or one of the ladies.

Thorald reviews the three possibilities. Rachel would be no attraction to anyone. Mrs Dent was a nervous invalid, bored, silly, selfish; she could well be flirting with Marcus or Bowles or both, but she is not a strong enough character to take to murder. There is a pause when it comes to Aymer. The

Judge shows Grant his snuff-box with the miniature; it is, he says, the likeness of another Aymer long since dead but never forgotten. He has trained himself to be a man without a heart, merely a brain, but has not succeeded in regarding Aymer without feeling. He is biased in her favour; he tells Grant this, he says, to put him on his guard. He knows Aymer to be utterly incapable of committing murder, but nevertheless

> The most out of reach of suspicion, the person most improbable, the highest in rumour of innocence—these are the persons to be suspected. That is the modern code of the *policier*.[33]

By *policier* here the Judge means policeman or detective, but we cannot help remembering that *roman policier* is the French name for a detective story.

Thorald gives it as his opinion that Mrs Dent will accuse Aymer of the murder, firstly because she is jealous; Marcus comes to see Aymer, not her, and she knows it; secondly, because of the will. He adds that Mr Fenwick-Dent had had an obsession about wills; he had made one every three months during the last few years. The Judge had been consulted about at least half-a-dozen. A few of the earlier ones had been properly drawn up by his solicitors; others had been drafted in holograph and not signed. More are found tucked away in old books in Mr Dent's library. Mrs Dent has triumphantly produced a will dated February of the current year in which nearly all Mr Dent's money and possessions are left to her. Rachel has equally triumphantly produced a will dated June of the current year in which nearly all Mr Dent's money and possessions are left to her. Grant himself has found stuffed into the tobacco jar in the library a will dated on the day of the murder in which nearly all Mr Dent's money and possessions are left to Aymer.

Meanwhile the Chief of Police is in trouble. His wife demands that he find out what is going on at Dent House and tell her about it; she is being humiliated at the tea-tables of the Quarrier ladies because she cannot give them all the details. She is sure one of the women committed the murder, probably Aymer Valentine because her name sounds like something out of a play. A few days later the unfortunate Chief of Police has another encounter. Marcus Hill calls upon him, to complain about being spied upon by lots of policemen. He is not going to be treated like a hen-house thief. His luggage at the Dent Arms has been searched twice, and his pupil, Billy Bowles, has had his searched once.

He empties out the contents of his pockets on the Colonel's desk—notebooks, sketches, letters, sprigs of white heather donated by the Colonel's daughters, a silver-hafted penknife, several fountain pens, a watch, a gold cigarette case with a monogram, a cycling map, a pipe and tobacco pouch, a ring full of various keys, a letter of credit with a photograph to identify him as the owner, a passport for Russia and Siberia, another for the Turkish dominions, coins from several countries and a purse. His final sarcastic statement is that there is a whole trunkful of photographs but the police have already devoted an entire evening to rummaging through them.

Mrs Hampden-Jones has seen Marcus arrive from an upstairs window. She disapproves of him; she thinks some of her daughters are unsuitably interested in him—a mere tutor—as indeed they are. She now comes sweeping in, looking at the pile of objects on the desk through her lorgnette, demanding what this rubbish is. Marcus replies with chilly politeness that it is all his property, brought to save it from being pawed by plain clothes policemen. He politely escorts her to the door and puts her out. Her daughters, listening, dance and rejoice with unseemly joy.

The two young men, Marcus and Billy, have been travelling round the world together and had settled for a while at Quarrier because it was a good quiet place in which to study seriously. William Leslie Bowles—Billy—is a Ward in Chancery, and Marcus in charge of his health and his education at the behest of the Lord Chancellor, who has advised the tutor to lick the cub into shape. They behave towards one another like two amiable bears. Billy wants to know why they are staying on here; Marcus replies in dreamy tones that he has met her on the beach after he had been swimming. Billy for a horrible moment thinks that 'she' is Mrs Dent, but is assured that this is not so; 'she' pours out tea at Mrs Dent's tea-table; she is Aymer, and he loves her, and she loves him.

> 'Marcus,' said his pupil, 'I would not be so rotten conceited for all the girls in three continents.'[34]

Billy suddenly asks if this was why Marcus was out in the Dent woods at the time of the murder. Marcus answers loftily that he had been merely composing a sonnet about Aymer. Left alone, Marcus murmurs to himself that he *has* seen something Mr Detective-Lawyer Grant might be interested in; they would have to wait and see who came out ahead. Crockett has broken a rule; Marcus has withheld information from the police; Crockett withholds it from the reader.

Sue and Adams all this while have been meeting from time to time in the shelter of the laburnums by the toolshed. They are a typical Scots couple, not given to sentimental speeches. They are also practical; if Connel leaves, as she is threatening to do, Sue will be promoted to head housemaid and a higher wage, four pounds more, she says, and that means saving ...

> 'For the furniture,' said Adams the acquisitive, and the sudden grip of his arm nearly lifted Sue off her feet.[35]

This is the closest to a verbal proposal that he has ever made—or ever will make. Sue is delighted. Tomlinson the gardener may be leaving; all this murder business is too much for his nerves, in which case Adams may be promoted and be given the Lodge to live in. Their wooing proceeds in terms of the Lodge needing a new range, new wallpaper (Sue could put it on herself) and a new double ash wardrobe with bevelled mirrors and two drawers below that Adams has bought. The Judge passes without seeing them. Adams remarks that he was said to have been 'a starcher for the lasses in his day'[36] and that Miss Aymer might do worse than marry him even now. Sue merely laughs.

The Judge has been on his way to another session with Grant, this time in the library at Dent House, with drinks and cigarettes from the inevitable gold snuff-box. Marcus has been cleared of suspicion; another man has admitted to using the stable lantern in the Dent woods. Grant has not been surprised; it was all too simple,

> too much the regular thing, the Rural Policeman's Primer, in fact—footprints on the soft places of the lawn, cross in the heel of left boot, photograph of the murderer in the victim's clenched hand, cuffs with name and address on the washstand, and fingerprints in red all over the place.[37]

He also reports to the Judge that Aymer and Marcus are conducting a correspondence by means of letters hidden in a squirrel's hole in an oak tree overlooking the Lodge lane. For a moment the Judge is displeased; he does not want to believe it. They cannot be. Aymer is under surveillance. But Grant explains: Rachel Dent collects the letters and puts the replies in the arboreal post office.

> The Judge sat for a long moment without smoking, gazing steadfastly at the miniature, then he shut up the box with a snap and put it back in his waistcoat pocket.
> 'I am a fool,' he said; 'what else can I expect?'[38]

Grant has another small success to report—the fingerprints he has photographed, from the will. The Judge had worked with Bertillon at the Anthropometric Institute in Paris and knows something about such things. Alas! the fingerprints have been made by gloves—suede gloves—and are of no value whatsoever as evidence. Grant is cast down and leaves. He is chary of showing any more evidence. Later he watches Rachel make her way back to Dent House with a letter in her pocket (which he had already read and replaced) and makes his way to Laverock Hall where he finds the Judge sitting out-of-doors, asleep. Without opening his eyes, the Judge says 'Good of you to come, Grant. Bring round that chair over there.'[39] He has guessed at Grant's wounded feelings.

What Grant has to show this time are scraps of paper, five sets in all, with the same message on them: 'I propose to call upon you tonight.'[40] One of them is perfectly normal, the one found in the wastepaper basket; the others are different but with an odd resemblance; they all bear the same message, as if practising. Thorald diagnoses that they are the work of two people working together, sharing the task of making individual characters in the words. Suddenly he asks where the papers have been found. They were in Rachel Dent's bedroom. The inference may be that she and Aymer are conspiring together. The Judge asks himself in anguish 'What have I done?'

Strange things have been happening at Dent House. Grant finds himself liking and being liked by Aymer. He has seen Rachel Dent go into the library by the Garden Port, yet when he enters immediately afterwards, the room is quite empty. The supper tray left for him by Richard one evening in the library has had the stopper removed from the decanter. Grant pours some of the liquid into a small flask to be sent for analysis and empties the decanter into an outside drain. The next morning he is awakened by Sue Sim in hysterics; she has seen Miss Rachel's wraith go into the library and disappear. The decanter is full once more. Analysed, both samples of the liquid are shown to be poisoned.

He is now convinced that Rachel administered the poison to her father. She has been taken ill, Aymer says. Under protest, she opens the bedroom door and Grant sees Rachel lying rigid on her coverlet, with the key of the Garden Port in her hand attached to a leather strap of Indian manufacture. He resolves to arrest her once this illness passes, and summons two men with a car to assist him. It is a fine autumn day; the car is in position; Rachel has gone to the Heather House, the little summer house where she often sits sketching; all is in readiness—but the arrival of the entire Hampden-Jones family disrupts the plan, especially when Grant is button-holed by the Colonel.

It is late afternoon before he is free. Miss Dent had been at the tree, his men report, but she seems nervous. So is Grant; the arrest must be made but he will thereafter be regarded as a traitor, a spy, by Aymer.

> They waited so, in the quiet of that October close of day. There was no sound but the rooks noisily cawing their way homewards from the early ploughed fields, still fat from their vegetable feast of the harvest and now more boisterous than ever with abundant animal food out of the red-brown up-turned furrows.
>
> After they had passed, there fell a surprising quiet. The birds went to their deeper retreats. The sun began to dip, and a blue haze invaded the valleys, appearing as it seemed from nowhere. The wind fell suddenly. The hush was almost painful. Still they waited. But yet could not wait much longer. The twilight would come and after that the dark.
>
> A look of fixed resolution—almost the look of a forlorn hope leader, came over Grant's face. It was the last call of duty and he obeyed. He touched Sergeant Howard on the arm and the two of them advanced towards the Heather House.
>
> There was still a lingering ray of sunlight on the summit of the little knoll. Grant pushed the door open. Miss Rachel was sitting there, smiling gently. Before her was a white-spread rustic table, with two cups upon it—empty.
>
> She was quite dead.
>
> And on the rug upon which her feet were placed, slowly fading away—they saw the print of an azure hand.[41]

Crockett is using his local landscape and his familiar birds to build up the tension of waiting. Grant is anxious—'the hush was almost painful'. It must be Miss Rachel. She hates her step-mother. She thinks she has inherited her father's possessions by the will she has produced. She is unbalanced, not to be trusted. She has threatened to kill Mrs Dent. It must be Miss Rachel. However uncongenial, his duty must be done. There are more emotions at play here than in the classic detective novel in which the detective is not personally involved with his suspects. Grant's action when it comes is quiet and controlled; a mere touch on the subordinate's arm. Then comes the anticlimax. The main suspect, on the point of arrest, has been herself murdered. It is the classic detective-story cliché.

Next comes something which is uniquely Crockett, perhaps uniquely Scottish—the almost feudal rage which the two deaths cause in Quarrier. A well-known and respected family has been twice attacked, and the police have done nothing. The country people are filled with terror; the townspeople rise up in rage. Grant has foreseen something like this and has brought in reserves, but the mob breaks through the cordon; the grass and flower beds are black with them and the Territorials have to be called out. The police wield their truncheons but in a discreet way; they are the forces of law. Two young men with cudgels and revolvers lay about them with no such scruples—Marcus and Billy. Adams is in charge of a three-inch diameter hose with which he sends a forty-foot jet towards the mob's leaders. Judge Thorald in his clear light voice, a Browning automatic pistol in his hand, threatens to read the Riot Act. Gradually the angry crowd begins to drift away, their rage dying and their enthusiasm ebbing at this vigorous defence. Tomlinson has fled in terror and will not be back; Sue and Adams may find that the Lodge is vacant sooner than they had expected.

Meanwhile Marcus has been frustrated by being prevented from seeing Aymer; letters are not enough. He is restless and desperate. He goes for a walk in Dent woods, and meets Mrs Dent's maid Sylvia Granger, who declares that she has a message for him. Marcus's hopes are dashed; it is only that Mrs Fenwick-Dent would be glad to see him at Dent House any afternoon. Sylvia knows the situation, and her own vanity makes her try to tempt the young man by talking kindly of Aymer and rousing him to notice her own charms. She does not look or sound like a waiting-maid. Marcus is moved by her friendliness to kiss her—not really her, but Aymer. He must kiss someone. She walks away triumphant, and Marcus finds that Judge Thorald has been a witness to this, amused at the spectacle. Almost immediately Grant comes on the scene, and the Judge tries to share his amusement with him. Grant however feels for Marcus's embarrassment, and considers the Judge a spiteful old monkey. When Marcus tries to go off on his own, Grant stops him; they are both young men who have played the fool, Grant in trying to arrest the wrong suspect, Marcus in being inveigled into kissing a mischievous maid. Because the Judge has been crowing over Marcus, Grant is anxious to make little of the incident.

> And as they strolled Quarrier-wards Marcus opened his mind to Luiz Grant. That is, in part, for he was not yet ready to confess all he knew. Nevertheless he told the detective enough to alter his mind considerably, and the outcome of that talk between the tall hedges was of the gravest and most serious.[42]

Marcus is not yet prepared to tell Grant whatever it was that he had seen on the night of the murder, but he is revealing enough of his own honest nature and his love for Aymer to clear them both of any iota of suspicion.

Triumphing in his malice, the Judge proceeds to visit the ladies of Dent

House. In the presence of Aymer and Sylvia Granger, he tells Mrs Dent that Marcus has been caught kissing Sylvia. Mrs Dent is infuriated. Aymer turns pale. But the Judge has not counted on Sylvia's liking for Marcus. Rather than be a means of hurting him she throws a letter and two ten pound notes on the floor contemptuously, saying that the Judge had bribed her to make advances to Marcus. The Judge is so astonished he lets his cigarette go out. To soothe his damaged ego a little, he visits Marcus and Billy, trying to placate Marcus by suggesting that Mrs Dent may have engineered the whole thing herself. He goes on to charm them with stories of mysterious India, tale after tale of his former triumphs, smoking and playing with the snuff-box. They listen entranced. He then departs with a final wave of his gold-topped cane; he has made up for his defeat.

The only love affair progressing in any way satisfactorily is that of Sue and Adams. Adams has been promoted and is now living in the Lodge. Sue, not wishing to desert Connel, will be a housemaid by day and come down to the Lodge to be a wife during the evening and night. There is nothing to stand in the way of their wedding. The Judge obligingly offers them Laverock Hall for the ceremony and the usual Scottish accompaniment of a festive meal and dancing far into the night. The Judge and a few friends will look in and the barn is available for the dance. And so it is arranged, but Aymer will not speak to Marcus during the dancing. The bride and groom slip away unseen in the traditional manner to go to their new home. Adams is just fumbling for the key when Sue sees a light in the Heather House. She insists that they go and see what it is. Marcus is sitting with the stable lantern in a kind of daze; before him there is a large tumbler of some hot steaming liquid. He is about to drink it when Sue dashes it from his hand. The glass shatters, but some of the liquid falls to the ground. It slowly spreads in the familiar blue stain. Marcus mumbles something incoherent about the butler, a jolly good fellow, but he is not drunk; he has been drugged. As a result of this inexplicable experience, Marcus loses his memory completely.

It is decided that Mrs Dent, Aymer and Sylvia be removed to Fenwick Wester, one of the Dent properties in the next county, for their own safety. It is a fine old peel tower, with a slabbed courtyard and thick stone walls solidly built by the Carlyles of Ecclefechan. In their absence, Grant is able to search Dent House thoroughly but finds little except the false back to the boot cupboard which had enabled Rachel to seem to disappear while merely using a short cut.

Grant decides that character, not clues, will be the solution; mere circumstantial clues had led him to suspect wrongly Miss Rachel and had almost caused his own removal from the case as a failure. There are two possible butlers, Richard and the Judge's, Bailey. Richard might have served tea to Miss Rachel on the fatal afternoon in the Heather House; he might have had a grudge against Marcus. Bailey?—Bailey always looked at the Judge with fear in his eyes. Grant admits that Thorald is his superior in wits as well as experience, but he is at least as likely a suspect as faithful Richard Hissy.

Aymer and Mrs Dent settle comfortably at Fenwick Wester. The will has been administered and Aymer has inherited, but Mrs Dent does not mind; all she has cared about is that Rachel should be cut out. Sylvia, on the other hand, is not very welcome; she has, after all, kissed Marcus. She is very soon dismissed and sent back to Dent House under a cloud. On her way, walking, with her bag and waterproof, she meets Grant who politely takes the bag and waterproof from her and prepares to walk back with her. Sylvia fiercely tells Grant that she can be of service to him; her people are gipsies from India, where she has met Judge Thorald. He brought her to Scotland, and placed her in the service of Mrs Dent, but since then has scarcely looked at or spoken to her; Aymer is all he thinks of. Sylvia declares that she is the same kind of outcast as Grant is, neither one race nor another. Grant says that he is not a man to love or hate.

> 'Love—love,' laughed the girl. 'Man of the East, I will love you till the stars dance and the sun goes out if you will help me to my desire. You and I do not want little blue forget-me-nots out of ditches, and messages dropped in the cracks of trees. We have not the English sentiment about a dropped handkerchief, but a strong man's arms are a strong man's arms, and a woman's lips, her lips—till they belong to the strong man!'[43]

The two plight their strange Oriental troth; she will bring him success by forwarding his career; he will give her in return protection. Grant saw at once that

> Sylvia Granger was his needful weapon—he adroit and subtle, she seasoned and tempered to his hand. So, when they had made their bargain and become thirled to each other—the woman to her man, it came about that Luiz Grant, slipping back into the folk of his mother, silently handed Sylvia the gipsy her own bag and waterproof, and stalked on towards the House of Dent, a good twenty yards before her. And Sylvia Granger followed meekly after, also according to the manner of her people.[44]

It is the gipsy wife all over again; Sylvia has 'asked' and Grant has accepted.

Marcus's lost memory remains a problem. Billy does not wish his tutor to be dismissed and concocts letters to the Lord Chancellor about his own sterling virtues which he makes Marcus copy out.

> 'I am much pleased with the progress of my pupil during these last months. . . . The quiet of this neighbourhood and the steady application to a definite course of study has put him well ahead of many young men of his age in point of scholarship. I cannot too much praise his regularity and the instinct of obedience which actuates it. Yet he is full of spirit, and I am sure will turn out a real Empire-Builder.'
>
> 'That,' said Billy to himself, 'will fetch the old man, confound me if it doesn't . . .'[45]

Billy thereafter acts constructively; he persuades the youngest of the Hampden-Jones daughters, Kitten, to sign on with him for a course of evening classes in Analytical Chemistry three times a week,—thus furthering his own education in his own way, one which involves working at experiments with Kitten alone in a quiet part of the laboratory.

Marcus dimly remembers an invitation from someone to pay a call at Fenwick Wester. He also dimly remembers where Fenwick Wester is. He borrows the inevitable stable lantern from the Dent Arms and sets off to walk there, telling no one. Fenwick Wester is set on the flats of the Lochar Moss. Caerlaverock Castle stands a few miles to the east and the ruins of Sweetheart Abbey in Galloway to its west.

> The whaup whinnied all day about it. The plover-bleat was its most familiar sound—that and the silent swishing of ten thousand wings as the rook population soared their ways twice a day down to the tidal Solway flats or up to the newly ploughed lands of Ruthwell and Half Morton.[46]

It is a long distance, and night is beginning to fall. The 'hungry cold' of Lochar is coming down, so savagely chill that the minds of those caught out in it are paralysed. Local people know not to venture. Aymer is busy tending her aunt—serving her supper, brushing her hair, making sure that she is warm and comfortable. Mrs Dent is very drowsy and content:

> I'm so tired, dear. Say my prayers for me, Aymer—I promised my poor dear husband not to forget them![47]

Aymer goes to her own room, and out of the window she sees a light flickering up and down as if signalling near one of the quicksands for which the Solway is notorious. Hastily she throws on a shawl and runs out into the cold to see who has been trapped.

It is, of course, Marcus and the stable lantern, caught firmly and unable to pull himself free. The danger, or the cold, or merely the exigencies of the plot, has restored his memory. He calls to Aymer to go back; she will only be caught too.

> 'Not a bit of it,' Aymer responded cheerfully, 'I am on good sand—a whole ridge of it. If you had not been such a fool you would have come this way too. You can see where it runs into the bank at the other side. Stand ready to catch the end of my shawl.'[48]

She tells him to throw away the lantern, fall flat on the water and spread his coat to take his weight. The shawl is of Catalan silk, rough like unbleached linen and strong as a rope; her Uncle Patrick had brought it home to her from his travels. Marcus is able to catch it;

> he rose for a moment to the surface, she could see him black and dripping against the fleecy clouds. He threw from him as far as he could the stable lantern, which hit the bank and rolled down again with the musical jingle of pebbles.
>
> 'You have kept the lantern all the time,' she called out angrily, 'and you very nearly lost your life because of it.'

She took the two ends of the scarf-shawl over her shoulders and began to walk away from Marcus. Her feet sank so deep that she had hurriedly to draw them out of the slippers she had worn, and widening her elbows and bending forward, she gave the real 'fetch-him-awa' heave of the Lochar fisherman, so that the feet of Marcus 'fetched away' with a sudden jerk, like a tree that is being dragged by the roots out of soft ground.[49]

The sharp detail of this, and indeed of all the natural description through *The Azure Hand*, make the light-hearted parody and exaggeration very vivid; it is Crockett on his home ground, remembering the ways and scenes of the Solway. The scornful comments from Aymer—'If you had not been a fool, you would have come this way too'; her angry 'You have kept the lantern all the time ... and you very nearly lost your life because of it'—portray a practical Scots lass, hauling her lover out of the treacherous sand very ignominiously.

After this Aymer and Marcus are of course reconciled. He calls the Judge 'an old baboon' and asks indignantly what he was doing outside the Garden Port on the night her uncle had been murdered. He, Marcus, had told the police at once that *he* had been there, and why he had been there. He had seen the Judge, but thought that it was none of his business to tell tales on him. And then, concludes Marcus with feeling, he sets his butler to lure him to the Heather House and tries to poison him.

Aymer, as soon as she has heard all this, packs him off immediately to tell Grant; this is what Marcus, out of a schoolboy sense of honour, has been keeping to himself. Marcus is indeed an ass. Billy, though relieved that he is not dead, tells him so—a silly dunderheaded ass—but, finding that Aymer and Marcus are all set for their wedding, goes off to see his godfather, a gouty old Earl, and makes him promise to persuade the Lord Chancellor to consent to his marrying Kitten Hampden-Jones.

Once Grant has heard Marcus's story, his suspicions rest squarely on the Judge; they have been veering in that direction for some time. He writes a long report to the Crown Office and despatches it, then goes to Laverock Hall. He has a long-standing invitation to see the laboratory in which Thorald conducts his scientific experiments. He is received graciously and made welcome with a comfortable armchair and the Tunisian cigarettes. What puzzles him, he says, is why the murderer took such trouble with notes and scraps of paper, wet marks made by unidentified tumblers, boot cupboards with false backs and blue stains all over the place. The two men spar politely with words underneath which they test one another's cunning. Grant comments flatteringly on the Judge's knowledge of poisons, a compliment Thorald waves modestly aside, saying that he is only a dabbler. Grant persists:

> ' ... you had a good deal of experience with poisons, especially the rarer Indian varieties—the sort that is entered as "snake-bite" by the family in the returns.'
>
> The Judge smiled.
>
> 'A little,' he said, tapping the snuffbox, without, however, taking it out of his

pocket. 'They order that sort of thing better over there. But then, I was born behind the scenes.'[50]

The conversation passes to Sylvia Granger. The Judge has put two and two together and guessed that Grant and Sylvia have come to an understanding. Grant reverts to being a gentleman; gentlemen do not discuss ladies who are not present. The Judge smiles sardonically and suggests that they now view the laboratory, ushering Grant through a strong door with a massive brass lock into a huge scientifically constructed room filled with all manner of experiments set up on tables, little hissing stills and small glowing furnaces. Grant takes an armchair and another Tunisian cigarette. The Judge begins to tell Grant of his struggles to rise high in his profession, the Indian climate which had left him delicate, his reluctance to marry because India was no place to take a woman—and the woman who had promised to marry him had in any case changed her mind and married Fenwick-Dent, his best friend. He is preparing whisky and sodas for himself and Grant, producing a 'Hermos' flask and pouring hot steaming liquid into each glass to warm them up—the room has become chilly. Both drink as the Judge continues talking, but as soon as the Judge sees that Grant has drunk, he alters his manner. His face becomes hard;

> It grew set and implacable and his laugh was no longer gay, though he laughed.[51]

He tips some of his drink and then of Grant's on the carpet; the familiar blue stains appear. Grant stares in horror. He has to listen to the Judge's story of how he had carried out the two murders; his vanity insists that Grant hear of his cleverness, even though they are both poisoned and will die within two hours. He has intercepted Grant's report to the Crown Office; his secret will die with them both but Grant must hear it. When Grant tries to grapple with him the Judge sprays him with a stickly liquid which makes his mind clear although his body is paralysed.

Thorald's light confident narrative proceeds; Grant had separated him from Aymer—no one could do that and live and once he allied himself with Sylvia, Thorald knew he was defeated; Grant was hunting with the Judge's hound, trained for his purposes but now working against him. He had tapped on the Garden Port that night, been admitted as so often before, and poured whisky and soda, adding the poison—Indian of course and undetectable. Dent had fallen forward out of his chair and by putting out his hands as he fell made the first stain on the rug himself. This had given Thorald the idea; he deepened the stains into one in the shape of a mittened hand with suede gloves. Dent had to die on that night; Thorald had seen the will in Aymer's favour which must be the final conclusive will. He wanted Aymer to be rich and happy. Rachel was eliminated because she had helped Aymer and Marcus send one another letters. Because of the wedding he had had to employ Bailey to deal with Marcus, but Bailey was a blunderer; Marcus survived.

Thorald lights another cigarette and pushes the snuff-box over to Grant.

He is enjoying telling Grant the story because he alone, ambitious and proud, will understand his deeper motive.

> You are a man after my own heart, and the real criminal is neither of us but the Government of India which retired a man like myself, in the flower of my age, with a private income and a liberal pension, in addition to the greatest knowledge of subtle poisons under the sun—a knowledge too which he may not use legitimately ... [52]

He sees that Grant is growing sleepy; that will never do; he must hear all. Thorald staggers to his feet, and approaches Grant with a hypodermic syringe. He stands above him elegant and suave as ever. There is a sharp noise from outside. Thorald tries to walk towards the door, but stumbles and falls down near where he had been sitting. He smiles up at Grant. 'Clever Sylvia,' he murmurs, but she will not be able to get in unless she uses dynamite. There is another much louder noise and the door falls inwards. Sylvia has used dynamite. Thorald pulls down Grant's sock and the needle touches his skin, but Sylvia darts in and snatches the needle away. He smiles at her and bids her welcome 'with his last piece of airy insolence'. '*Ave atque vale*, as they taught Grant to say at the Calcutta University', he says, and gives them a sardonic blessing, regretting that he will not be able to attend their wedding. He raises his hands in the mocking gesture, wet as they are with the spilt liquid, and folds them across the flowered waistcoat which as always he is wearing. They leave two long-fingered delicate azure stains in the shape of his hands across the empty pocket in which for so long the gold snuff-box with the miniature of his lost love has been kept—his lost love, the first Mrs Patrick Fenwick-Dent.

He, of course dies, as he has intended to. Marcus's account of how Grant escaped death is the best—and the breeziest. Sylvia

> 'burst in the door with lyddite or something and found the old chap just ready to jab him. You see he wanted him to hear all about it—how he had tricked him and everybody. And so he gave Grant another poison to keep his head clear. Well, the Judge's stuffs were rum. He did not quite understand them himself, and one poison neutralized the other—as you drink whisky when you are snakebitten—or inject permanganate. At least that's the nearest the doctors can come. But if the old chap had been alive he could have told them a lot they don't know. They say that in those presses of his he had all sorts of deadly poisons—things that are not in the pharmacopoeia.
>
> Well, anyway, I went to his funeral, and there was nobody who would say a prayer—so being a Presbyterian Covenanter ... '
>
> 'A pretty Covenanting Presbyterian you are!' said Billy scornfully, 'first I've heard of it!'
>
> 'I am though,' said Marcus; 'doesn't show on me much maybe, but that's because it is so deep down!'
>
> 'Deep fiddlesticks!'
>
> 'At any rate I said as good a prayer as I could for the old sinner. I had a kind of right. He tried to poison me once, but then he was cracked, and I had got to square up somehow.'

'You mean that your prayer was such an uncommon thing that it might prejudice the Authorities!' said Billy.

'No, I don't mean anything of the kind. On the contrary I trouble the Authorities so seldom that they might very likely pay more attention to this one!'[53]

And so, with a final dash of Presbyterianism laced with universal salvation, the story comes to an end with two prospective happy marriages. Marcus is, of course, a parody of Crockett, with his pockets full of travel souvenirs and Siberian passports and the cycling map; it is pleasant to consider that he made himself the amorous silly ass whose idiotic silence confused and held up the whole investigation. The whole story is extraordinarily funny, with Mrs Hampden-Jones sweeping in and out abusing her husband, Sue and Adams planning their wedding with all the attendant wardrobes and wallpaper, and the Judge with his vanity, his gold snuff-box and gold-topped cane perhaps the most comic character of all, an old-fashioned dandy with a fondness for the ladies, tolerated as a tame old pet who has once been distinguished but has dwindled into a poseur.

There is a shortage of suspects, the strongest criticism of this detective story; and Mr Fenwick-Dent is too amiable a character to be an ideal murder victim; but Crockett stiffens his story with copious and entertaining detail in order to make it seem solid, with all the rich inconsequence of real life. One senses throughout the enjoyment which he has felt in making up this complex and yet consistently accurate plot. For once he has concentrated on fitting everything in neatly and hurrying us over any hiccup in the plot with his enthusiastic enumeration of irrelevant encompassing information. The device of making the Judge, so authoritative a commentator on the detection, himself the murderer is one which later detective writers were to hit on for themselves. Crockett tells us from the first that Thorald is an expert on convicting poisoners but obfuscates this with his affected mannerisms, his apparently well-meaning interference, his foolish old man's love for Aymer, his garrulous conceit and his long-past reputation for forensic wisdom which only the Goanese detective Grant can appreciate. The Judge and Grant are neat foils for one another, and the gipsy-bride syndrome which Crockett carries over from *Silver Sand* ensures that the Judge's plot to use Sylvia as his catspaw turns out to be his undoing—and only the Judge and Grant can be expected to realise just how and why.

An interesting advertisement at the end of this, the one and only edition of *The Azure Hand*, is for another of Hodder and Stoughton's publications, a book called *No Man's Land* by 'Sapper', author of *Men, Women and Guns, Sergeant Michael Cassidy* and *The Lieutenant and Others*. These are all war stories—the Kaiser War is still going on—but the next generation, in which Crockett might have played a part had he not died in 1914, is already established. Bulldog Drummond is on the way, with dialogue not any more sophisticated than the amiable leg-pulling and bantering with which Crockett endows his young men.

An even greater surprise is to come. Dated 2 February 1920 by the Advocates' Library Accession Stamp, there appeared another posthumous Crockett publication, *The White Pope, called the Light out of the East*, a thoughtful and sustained essay in what one could call theological science fiction, accepting Edmund Crispin's definition:

> A science-fiction story is one which presupposes a technology, or an effect of technology, or a disturbance in the natural order, such as humanity, up to the time of writing, has not in actual fact experienced.[54]

One would guess that *The White Pope* was written after Crockett had read Fr Rolfe's *Hadrian the Seventh A Romance*[55] which appeared in 1904 and tells the story of George Arthur Rose, an eccentric Englishman frustrated for twenty years by his failure to be accepted as a priest by the Church of Rome. *Hadrian* is just the sort of unusual, intermittently sensational and often very funny book that Crockett would have enjoyed.

George Arthur Rose has always been denied his desire for priesthood on the grounds that he has no Vocation. One day a bishop whom he knows calls upon him, bringing with him a senile Cardinal-Archbishop, whom he addresses as 'Yments' which Rolfe alleges is the English pronunciation of 'Your Eminence'. The decision has changed; Rose is to have his wish. When he goes to Rome, after passing speedily through all the stages towards priesthood, he finds that he has to his astonishment been elected Pope. It is an imaginative wish-fulfilment based on Rolfe's own weird life-story.[56]

In *Hadrian the Seventh* this startling election has come about after much dispute and chicanery among the Sacred College of Cardinals, who cannot agree upon a new Pope because of dissention between factions in Vatican politics. They compromise by electing George Arthur Rose because he is a safe pawn—or so they think. He turns out to be an implacable reformer, forcing the Princes of the Church back to the original simplicity of Christ. He names himself Hadrian the Seventh because the only previous English Pople was Hadrian and he wishes to assert his Englishness; he does not really like Roman Catholics. It is the Faith he cares for, not the Faithful. He rejects the Papal apartments in the Vatican as being too red, too ormolu, too rococo, and chooses instead for his use a suite of attics, ordering that they be papered with plain brown wrapping paper. For his desk he demands a common scrubbed kitchen table, and orders Bramah Locks from Bond Street, so that his secrets may be locked away. He rejects all luxuries except smoking, which he regards as a necessity. He confounds the administrators by putting his own original ideas into action. He creates Cardinal-Deacons out of two Scottish priests (one of them from St Gowff's), three English priests, one American priest and a Welsh Bishop who has been his friend. Remembering that Castle Gandolfo is the Pope's summer residence, he goes there, to think over his plans for the future.

He condemns the pomp, ritual and expense of cathedrals. He issues an *Epistle to All Christians* removing at a stroke every barrier between the Church of Rome and all other Christian denominations and stressing the importance of the individual soul. He issues a Bull, *Regnum Meum*, declaring that 'My kingdom is not of this world' so that he renounces all claim to temporal power. The clergy are to be ministers, not masters; they must live so as to give an example to the people rather than try to persuade by preaching. To every outraged objection, he (having studied Scripture well during his twenty long years of waiting) quotes Christ's own words which cannot be gainsayed; the theologians have no answer. He is fulfilling the Pope's other title, the Servant of the Servants of God.

The book works out in cunning detail the effect of this new Pope on national and international relations, showing the reactions of socialists, anarchists, kings, Kaiser Wilhelm II, the President of the United States, the Japanese Emperor, ruling representatives both lay and ecclesiastical throughout the entire world, and a miscellany of ordinary people living their ordinary lives. The book ends when Hadrian is assassinated by a figure left over from George Arthur Rose's troubled and sensational past.

It is obvious without going any further that Hadrian the Seventh's views on returning to the simplicity of Christ are very much in line with Crockett's own. In Crockett's *The White Pope* many of the structural ideas of Rolfe's book are adopted, but the content is very different. Crockett is in earnest; there is none of the flickering humour and satire that Rolfe employs. Crockett loves both the Faith and the Faithful. Rolfe keeps the scene firmly in Rome; he understands and enjoys playing with the complexities of Vatican ceremonial and theologico-political argument. Crockett moves out into the open air and relies on narrative of journeys through the Italian countryside and beyond; instead of going to Castle Gandolfo, his Pope goes secretly and alone to the Italian district of Apulia where Crockett had set his tale of brigands, the Vardarelli, in *The Silver Skull*. He makes full use of the scenery and the Mediterranean seascapes among which he had travelled himself so often.

His first-person narrator is Lucas Cargill, a Scotsman, once a well-known London journalist whose life, for some personal reasons never explained, is in ruins and who is near despair. Under the bare sun-baked rocks of Mount Trastevera, where even the mud is cracked in the blinding heat, he sees a strange quiet compelling figure.

> The mists were spinning themselves out of the lower valley as from a ropewalk, when I first saw him come up with them out of the Unseen ...
> He was of no great height, clad in a robe of some fine white stuff, all in one piece from his neck to his feet. I took him for a priest of some Order I had never encountered. Very gentle as to the eyes—so I thought—his face like soft ivory, with few lines and a look of youth upon it. Yet no mantling blood as of a young man, no ardours of life, no square strengths of sex about the lips, no proud outlook in the eyes—nothing of all that.
> Yet at first I did not see the eyes. They were turned from me. He was gazing up towards the mountain summit behind me to the right. But I marked instead his dress, and vaguely I said to myself that I had seen something like it somewhere in a picture. But I could not recall the exactness of it, and the thing troubled me, as such trifles will.
> For one thing, if he were a priest, there was no rivulet of little ball-shaped buttons cascading down his front as on a *soutane*. All was plain-woven, in one piece like a stocking. I think it must have been put on over his head. The skirts

were wringing wet with the valley mist. But above many capes of white shed the drops from his shoulders to the ground. In his hand he held a shepherd's staff with a curved head on which he leaned a little wearily.

Save for a white skull-cap his head was bare, his hair still mostly black. Youthful hair it was, silvering only in streaks. He held his head high and the cap prevented me from seeing whether he was tonsured or not. About him the driving valley clouds blew thinner, fuming away into lawny nothingness on the higher slopes.[57]

Into the hard sterile landscape there comes this calm figure of cool whiteness, his robe not stiff like linen but soft as if made in one piece out of soft wool; he comes up out of the valley and his robes are soaked and dripping with water, the image of life. He sees Cargill and is not surprised, greeting him as if he has been expecting him.

'My brother,' he said, holding his hand towards me with a strange gesture which was clearly not that of hand-shaking, 'I am hungry—I would eat!'[58]

Cargill hastens to share with him Sicilian wine and black country bread, but even while he is eating, his eyes and his mind are elsewhere. He asks for somewhere to sleep and Cargill points to his bee-hive hut; the stranger says that enemies who would be glad to kill him are looking for him and asks Cargill to keep watch. Seeing the wonder in Cargill's eyes he tells him his name.

'I will tell you,' he said, 'men call me the Pope—the White Pope!'

Cargill cannot believe this but the stranger persists.

I am he whom they made Pope in Rome. They crowned me yesterday—or was it the day before—or last week? I forget. I am weary. Leave me![59]

Cargill believes that the man must be mad, but the calm serenity of his bearing has caught him entranced. He watches as the man sleeps, until a woman comes, going up to the bee-hive hut and looking within. Cargill runs to stop her. She answers in English that she is Mary Orloff, the man's mother, and that he is indeed the Pope. She found a small waif of four or five singing 'as the Monks do' over a poor man's grave, and had taken him home and brought him up as her son. He had grown up to be a holy man, first a priest, then the head of the Order of the Holy Sepulchrians, then a Cardinal at thirty-three, and now Pope. He had slipped away quietly from Rome after his enthronement and she alone had known and followed him, she feared against his wishes.

He is Brother Christopher—although a Cardinal he had kept his simple name—and has been elected because the French and the Austrians could not agree on a candidate. Brother Christopher tells the story in his own mystical words in Chapter IV, but later Cargill hears a racier version from an outsider, a diplomat, with whom he has been at school at Fettes College in Edinburgh.

The three, Cargill, Mary Orloff and Brother Christopher, go down to the village of Appiano for the woman's possessions—nearly all of them her son's clothes—which she had left in the inn. The village people recognise Brother Christopher as a holy man and ask for his blessing. His words are plain and simple:

> In your hearts alone will ye find God. They are his temples. In your lives you must show Him, if at all. This is too high for you—long it was too high for me. But it is the only True Word. Do not forget, even if now you fail to understand. ... In the incense and the lifted wafer have ye found Him? Did he enter your hearts at the tinkle of the bell? I tell you 'No'! But in the silence, when ye saw your sin great before you and repented, then God filled your hearts.[60]

The village priest, a shabby little man in a dirty *soutane*, calls out in anger that he is a blasphemer, a charlatan; Christopher looks at him and something

> seemed to pass from one to the other like the glitter between the poles of an electric battery.[61]

The priest, Vergas, is subdued and believes, sullenly, but unable to deny the White Pope's rare authority.

Two groups are looking for the White Pope, the army of the King of Italy under General Cipriano, and a party of greedy renegades led by the inn-keeper of Appiano out to make what they can from him. When the army finds him in the rocky foothills, the White Pope paralyses their weapons with a quiet gesture of benediction. When the greedy renegades come to take him, he sweeps them away into destruction by awakening the volcano Trastevera into eruption and engulfing them in its smoke and fire. When the army still tries courageously to approach, the White Pope with a movement of his hand opens a gaping fissure in the rock from ten to thirty feet wide which they cannot hope to cross. As Cargill has said earlier,

> From this time forth we waded through the raw stuff of miracles. I do not attempt to explain.[62]

Then the narrative becomes slow and second-hand, as if Crockett has for the moment run out of power. He introduces a story he has told elsewhere, 'Maria Perrone, Murderess and Saint'[63] and deals with a crowd who are accusing Maria's daughter of murdering her husband; a Venetian woman is the chief accuser and the White Pope knowing that she is the true felon, as he knows all things, says that there is a packet of poison in her dress. It falls to the ground before the crowd, and the Venetian woman falls too, writhes a little, then dies. God, says the White Pope, has avenged.

At the lighthouse on the Tremiti Islands where Maria and her husband had lived, the White Pope and his small company await a British ship *Istria* of the Red Funnel Line which will take them to Southampton. It comes and they board in almost regal style, although the Clydeside engineer grumbles at the delay; his run has been spoiled and they are to take in coal at Malta. Malta is buzzing with rumours about the White Pope and is thought too dangerous; the British Mediterranean Fleet intervenes and escorts them to Marseilles. He who had left Rome to escape pomp is being treated as one of the great ones of this world.

The news of the White Pope has spread, by Morse and Marconi, submarine cable and land telegraph, throughout France and beyond. People of all nationalities are crowding to Marseilles, even a few English pilgrims clinging to their reluctance to speak to their fellow-travellers, except for the women who could not help talking to their neighbours on the journey. The visit to Marseilles is described through the eyes of Cargill's friend M. Merlou, custodian of the Provençal Museum, a sceptic and free-thinker, whose balcony is high above the old port. He and his wife see all the trampling and rush along the wharves and the streets below. He is correcting the proofs of his article on the 'Scepticism of Pascal' but he cannot help watching, and his wife Jeanne whom he had thought a free-thinker like himself is weeping with joy and has produced a rosary. She is praying. The White Pope is a tall man standing in the boat taking him ashore; he rejects the cathedral and also the platform erected to receive him by atheists and socialists; he will speak to the people from the hillside on which stands Sainte Marie de la Garde.

His voice has a strange quivering quality, 'a timbre as of a smitten bell when the sound is dying away';[64] he speaks French as he speaks all languages, with a slight foreign accent. His message is plain and simple as it has always been:

> ...each true man is the Church of the Living God—each man the shrine of the spirit that dwells in him, the Son of God, who was the only perfect Temple of God upon the earth. But, even as the Christ, we also are Temples not made with hands, and Who or What is worshipped therein depends on ourselves ...

He points to the church and the cathedral and declares that they shall

> no longer be things apart, sacred, but places where each shall speak to his fellows the best he hath in his heart. And if there be nothing there to speak, let him be silent. If the churches are left empty, let them be hospitals, filled with the sick or the homeless. And as for the women who frequent them now,—let their worship be service, and help, and the giving up of self.[65]

John Greenleaf Whittier has indeed left his mark.

The White Pope condemns the symbols of the Sacred Heart and the Crucifix: they are external things. Mary, the mother and good housewife of Nazareth, is a fine thing, loving and simple like their mothers and his own, but the priests have made an Immaculate Conception out of her, a thing they do not understand themselves. The face of the Man of Sorrows is better than any symbol. The ecclesiastics, the bishops and great churchmen, scowl sullenly.

The Freemasons and socialists smile knowingly. But their turn is to come. It is a worse evil to teach nothing of religion, to destroy the faith of simple people, and give them no God, no belief. This creates crime and wickedness; this is the sin of the politicians. Both groups listen in sour discontent and go away muttering angrily. Only the ordinary people remain, but even they do not understand; the message is too simple, too plain; only the women catch a glimpse of it.

Back on board the *Istria*, the little party around the White Pope sail on towards England. The fame of the White Pope is spreading to Japan, to Russia, to Asia, to America. News is coming of revival meetings throughout the United States; a certain famous entrepreneur is on his way to offer 60,000 dollars a week to speak in Gospel Halls—Major Pond, we must guess. But the White Pope is not to reach Southampton. A thick white silent mist comes down upon the ship, and an Italian warship the *Trombetta* circles the *Istria* and makes her heave to by a shot across her bow. The officers have orders to transfer the White Pope and his company to the Italian ship. They are taken on board. The King of Italy, Albert Emmanuel (a Crockett invention) awaits them along with Terni, the late Pope's secretary. The King hesitates for a moment, then kneels. Terni holds back, still unwilling.

> Then there ensued a battle of looks between them. Terni stood erect and frowning, a black cliff of a man, and the influence of the White Pope played about him like morning sunshine. Yet I could not imagine such a man giving way like the others.[66]

But although Terni does not kneel, his face is different; he has been changed by the light of the White Pope, in his own way. He obeys.

A British destroyer and two cruisers are now pursuing the *Trombetta*; and the Italian officers are not afraid but worried. The White Pope reaches out his forefinger and sweeps it through an arc from the destroyers to the two cruisers. They instantly stop, swinging off course, issuing clouds of steam, propellors helplessly tangled. They have been put out of action by three different accidents. By the time the British ships have recovered and are bombarding Spezia, the White Pope, the King and the Pope's followers have sped down the coast by train and are in Rome. The King has heard Brother Christopher's simple message—that man must remove the symbols of cross and altar and Sacred Heart and go back to Christ, a carpenter of Galilee who had neither pomp nor ceremony.

> The King tottered and recovered himself. The right hand of the Pope was outstretched towards him. And I, Lucas Cargill, bear witness that I saw something resembling pale lightning pass between them and illumine the King's face—like the flicker which runs before a footstep on wet tidal sand it was.[67]

The next step is to face the College of Cardinals. Seated on the great throne of St Peter, the King and Cardinal Terni standing a little behind, one on each side, like servants, the White Pope explains why he has had to go apart for a while to consider his power and his mission. Now that he has returned they must obey him. They cannot depose him; their own doctrine of infallibility made that impossible.

This is a very simplistic Protestant attitude; Rolfe is much subtler. He knows the Vatican terms:

> If we be Pontiff, We will not, and if We be pseudo-Pontiff, We cannot, depose Ourself.[68]

Some of the Cardinals kneel in obedience, others do not. The White Pope's compelling influence moves invisibly over them, and one by one they yield. Next come the people, the multitude who flood into the vast pavements in front of St Peter's once the soldiers let them pass. They were hoping perhaps for a miracle but can only listen hushed to the marvellous ringing voice:

> Ye men of Rome, ye must wait for the strange last things. Words cannot move you. Ye have heard thirty centuries of them and have lost the power to discriminate. The Word and the Way are become as the hum of bees among the summer lime trees. They only make you drowsy ... [69]

Wherever the vision of the White Pope will be carried out, it will not be in Rome—he will not be there.

Time passes bringing strange events. The Turks begin to move far away to the east, towards Asia, leaving Syria north of Damascus free of their control; there soon is not a pasha between Beirut and the Persian Gulf. There are strange disappearances; chiefs of great state departments are suddenly no longer at their posts, some soldiers have gone, sailors, doctors and surgeons, together with many ministers of religion and one prelate. No lawyers are missing so the cabinets of most countries are able to continue to rule. Rumours spread of great building and agricultural activity, especially in the regions of Palestine and Syria. The railways from Jerusalem to Jaffa are greatly increased in number. Ships are sent out towards these eastern lands but none of them return, yet no country is at war.

Cargill has been as puzzled as anyone else, but one day he and his companions are summoned to go to Jerusalem. They land at Jaffa and go on by train. Shiploads of rich soil have been landed at the Palestine seaports and carried up into the towns and bare hills, so that the desert rocks are planted with trees. Orchards and forests are already in being, feathery with green leaves, and the grey rocks show only here and there. There is no bustle, no noise of orders being given or commands shouted. Everyone is working as if his heart and love were in what he is doing.

> Then we came in sight of Jerusalem. Only the flaming blue of the sky behind us was still the same. For lo! we stood up and saw a city framed in greenery, where formerly not a tree had been visible. It had become a city of palaces. Where the desolate top of Mount Zion had been pared off to make the external cemeteries, a vast building of marble shone, pure and simple in its form, but colonnaded like a Greek temple. Yet it was no temple, only the dwelling of men.

> Looking down we could see within the flash of spraying fountains, while men, dressed in white, went and came by a hundred doors. Of the pinnacled Mosque of Omar there remained no sign, nor could I even distinguish the grey crumbling ruins of the Church of the Holy Sepulchre. White marble was everywhere, new and fresh. There were no dwellings of the wealthy, so far as I could make out, but everywhere houses built like caravanserai, each with rows of habitable chambers about, all of them opening on a central court in which were fountains and gardens.[70]

This is where the statesmen and leaders who have disappeared from countries all over the world have been taken. The council rule this New Jerusalem from the cool opalescent spaciousness of their meeting place; each man serves for a while, then when his task is done passes on into a new existence. There is no crime, no politics, no temples or places of worship. There is no need for them; to live is to worship. The twelve men of the council constantly change; some go 'when the light is upon their faces'[71] and they have proved their worthiness of the truth. Over all presides the White Pope, only he is now known by the other Papal name, 'Servant of the Servants'. Criminals who have proved intractable have been placed in reservations where the Servant's ambassadors visit them and make them into good citizens; the totally impenitent and evil are kept isolated, sterile, in perpetual quarantine from the radiant community.

Above all, the New Jerusalem is a place of light; since the coming of the Servant,

> the arid harshness of sunlight had been arrested—as it were by an invisible translucent dome over the whole series of hills on which stands the New Jerusalem ... a mild radiance was all that struck upon you. More strange still—every corner of the darkest room was filled with that radiance. The air had become a luminous medium, and on the hottest day you breathed it without exhilaration, yet with a clear cool wholesome pleasure, as if it would serve you to all eternity.
>
> Thus the city had no need of the sun or the moon to lighten it, but from the dwelling of the Servant, once the White Pope, there came the stillness of radiance, the glow of peace.[72]

The language has become even more strongly Biblical than in other parts of the book but even without that hint one would be reminded of St John:

> And I saw no temple therein, for the Lord God Almighty and the Lamb are the temple of it. And the city had no need of the sun, neither of the moon, for the glory of the Lord did lighten it, and the Lamb is the light thereof.[73]

Crockett has visualised the Biblical New Jerusalem not as a sudden miraculous creation from an external divine power by way of trumpets and vials and beasts as in Revelation but as an actual locality still here on the humble earth; in his fiction he occasionally pokes fun at eccentric people who struggle to make meaningful conclusions about the vials and beasts and the end of the world. His vision is of humanity still on the humble earth working humbly at their own tasks with their own skills to bring about a gradual process through the grace and guidance of the Servant to create the New Jerusalem for themselves, starting where the dry arid dusty old Jerusalem has stood for weary centuries. Water and light, the gentle elements, when wielded as the Servant wields them, are the conductors of the divine; man himself is divine and needs only to be touched by the Servant to become aware of this. There is no tension, for Crockett is writing of the Omnipotent at work; the interest is in seeing how the author will manipulate personages and events of the nineteenth and twentieth centuries to carry out the purpose of the new creation.

Individual members of the Council are not all identifiable at this distance in time. Lord Cairo, his black moustache looking odd among the radiance of white robes, remembering his days as a young lieutenant when he conducted digs under Mount Zion, is Kitchener of Khartoum. The Scottish Shepherd with the broad high forehead is John MacMillan of Glenhead of Trool. The great preacher with the white hair is Dr Alexander Whyte. The others are too vague; could the French scientist be Paul Curie? The American ex-President Theodore Roosevelt? The young student fresh from college, blushing to find himself in such company, a projection of Crockett himself as he once was? One unexpected personage entrusted with the recalcitrant cardinals when they finally come suing for mercy is a darkish man with a slight beard of naval cut[74] whom Cargill does not at first recognise. He is Nicholas II, once (as he says himself) Csar of all the Russias, given his place in the new dispensation of peace and light because, in the early years of his reign, he did his best to work for peace among the nations of the world. He appealed dramatically for disarmament to all the world, Europe, America and Asia, and brought about a conference at The Hague in 1899 which agreed on rules for warfare—The Hague Convention—and led to the formation of the International Court of Justice there,[75] a fact of which Crockett is well aware, since he is interested in Russia, and which most of us have forgotten. Crockett could not have foreseen the Russian Revolution and the cellar at Ekaterinburg—though it is interesting that he makes Nicholas II say 'I summoned two Peace congresses, yet fought all my life.'

Time continues to pass. Gradually the light spreads over the entire world 'like the continuous glow of radium' (though presumably without its dangers) until all the world is a garden; the Sahara became like Sharon, the icy lands of the Esquimaux the granaries of all mankind. When all is going well, when the divine idea has taken fast hold on the world and is able to run on its own impetus, the work of the Servant on earth is done. The day comes when he is again received into Heaven. One Easter morning Cargill, the first of his disciples, is with him on the Mount of Olives; suddenly

> the pearly light was all about me, but I was alone. The White Pope was not for God had taken him.[76]

Then, and then only, does Cargill realise that he has been in the company of the Blessed, of Christ, Who has once more returned to His Father.

It is interesting to see the imagery with which Crockett was working during what may have been his last years. He has taken the structure out of Rolfe's satirical book and made out of it something gentle, hopeful and at the same time clear. Remembering the seas and landscapes of his travels, the Italian mountains and valleys, the lighthouse of the Tremiti Islands, the great arena of St Peter's Square, the flat white roofs of Jerusalem, he has depicted the journeyings of the White Pope with a restraint and delicacy with which one would not have associated him. The miracles are spectacular, but the means by which they are brought about are quiet almost imperceptible movement of hands or fingers, in no way like divine thunderbolts launched in anger. His New Jerusalem does not appear as the result of a miracle at all; it is built by human hands using spades and trucks and planting trees with effort and labour, under the inspiration of the divine idea. He achieves the vision of St John by means of man's efforts irradiated by the rich light of the White Pope, slowly growing from faith and love. His Paradise on earth bears no likeness to the Victorian idea of Heaven, with golden crowns being cast down on a glassy sea. It is still this transient earth, when trees have to be planted and tended, and the White Fleet of cruisers and ships of war are still necessary.

> There are lawless folk yet upon the earth. We must make ourselves strong while we are making the Evil weak. We must write the decrees of Peace with an iron pen. Afterwards (he lifted up his arms with a great gesture of blessing) there shall be no need of Armies, navies, police, they shall have passed away, become forgotten and obsolete as chain mail—their very organisation a lost art. But in the meantime, and till the Fulness of the Glory, we have need of them.[77]

Women have less to do with this new creation on earth than men; they are of the heart, says the White Pope; men are of the head. There are no women on the Council, not because they are not good enough, but because they are better and know the truth immediately.

Some of Crockett's prejudices remain, to add salt to his vision. The middle-men of the earth who have earned money by making others work for them are sent to practise agriculture and live on the labour of their hands. The rich and idle, having tired of their cars and aeroplanes, are sent to study and pass examinations in mechanics and work happily on the railways or on the White Fleet, a transport system for the whole world. No Paradise would have been complete for Crockett on earth without trains.

Human mortality is not forgotten; perhaps Crockett's long illness was what turned his thoughts towards death and made him describe it in his New Jerusalem; it is called 'The Feast of the New Life', nothing to be feared but a falling asleep among flowers in transition to the next stage in our existence. What has disappeared entirely is the strife he had dealt with so mockingly among his ministers, elders, and Covenanters—the argument for the sake of confuting one's opponent instead of seeking the truth, the conflict which leads to anger and not to the light. Crockett's New Jerusalem is the abode of active abundant creative peace, perpetually renewing itself, never resting, never ending.

The White Pope is not a great book. It is uneven, spending too much time on the events through which Brother Christopher gathered together his disciples, then giving them little to do and letting them drop out of the story entirely. The narrative is not continuous; it hops from chapter to chapter, omitting events which we would like to have explained in more detail, bringing the characters back through Gibraltar on board ship without our having been told that they have left the Mediterranean, leaving vital links out without the elaboration which would have made them convincing. There is evidence of hasty composition, an eagerness to get the basic story on to paper without close attention to its details. If *The White Pope* were among the last of Crockett's writings—the very last—this would explain a great deal. He has conceived a visionary future and is drafting it quickly, meaning perhaps to return and work over it again, filling in the gaps, adding later the connections and explanations. Trifles are given great prominence, but more important events are passed over with disappointing thinness. It is like the first draft of a book that the author was never to finish. At times, there are passages which sound like ideas from his old sermons—good ideas, but ideas which require more vivid externalisation to be satisfactory and more careful exposition to be imaginatively exciting.

Yet *The White Pope*—a book very hard to find, like *The Azure Hand*—is worth reading if only for the unexpectedness of its extension to Crockett's range. The pantheism which he had found in George MacDonald, the quietism he had found in Whittier, the wider, more generous experience of life which he had found in his physical and literary travels, all contradicted the Calvinism in which he had been brought up; they combined at the end of his life to produce this picture of the goodness to which man could rise at the beckoning of God. There is no doctrine of Election, no Effectual Calling, nor any attempt to deal with these familiar concepts from the Shorter Catechism. No doubt it is because his imagination has been set going by Rolfe's *Hadrian the Seventh* that Crockett concentrates on the defects of the Church of Rome and on them alone. It is an easy target, picturesque and colourful, but his concentration on only one area of Christendom makes the book lop-sided and unfair. Most disappointingly, there is no one at all who can be related to the dour dogmatic Calvinism in which he was brought up. We would like to have seen a few Geneva gowns herded into compassion and the light along with the cardinals. But perhaps the omission is itself a condemnation; he ignores Calvinism as if it had no consequence, and the Council in their radiant robes and inspired faces bear no resemblance to a Kirk Session or a General Assembly of the Church of Scotland. There is no disputation, no wrangling, no secessions or disruptions. It might have been a more interesting book if there had been.

There is only one sign in his very early years that this bright creation of peace and harmony, gentleness combined with strength, goodness as a natural flowering of the human mind, has been latent in his imagination from the beginning:

> ...the Sabbath came with its sense of another world altogether. Clearer almost than anything else there comes back to me the remembrance of these Sabbath

morns at the farm, when the sense of 'hallowed days' was in the very air. I seem to get my clearest hints of what the solemn gladness of the New Jerusalem will be from these sweet still Sabbath mornings of my youth ... [78]

The genesis of *The White Pope* perhaps lies in Little Duchrae and those half-submerged memories; given the stimulus of Rolfe, the undramatic slow gentle fantasy could have arisen from them. It is pleasant and at least possible to think so.

Publishers and dates of first editions of Crockett's works

POETRY
Dulce Cor, being the Poems of Ford Berêton (Kegan Paul and Co: London, 1886)
Valete, Fratres! dedicated to his fellow-students by the author of *Dulce Cor* (David Douglas: Edinburgh, 1886)

COLLECTIONS OF SHORT STORIES AND SKETCHES
The Stickit Minister and Some Common Men (T Fisher Unwin: London, 1893)
Bog-Myrtle and Peat Tales Chiefly of Galloway gathered from the Years 1889–1895 by S R Crockett (Bliss, Sands and Foster: London, 1895)
The Stickit Minister's Wooing and other Galloway Stories (Hodder and Stoughton: London, 1900)
Love Idylls (John Murray: London, 1901)
The Bloom o' the Heather (Eveleigh Nash: London, 1908)
Young Nick and Old Nick Tales for the Year's End (Stanley Paul and Co: London, n.d. Advocates' Library Accession Stamp 1910)

NOVELS
The Raiders, being Some Passages in the Life of John Faa, Lord and Earl of Little Egypt (T Fisher Unwin: London, 1894)
The Lilac Sunbonnet (T Fisher Unwin: London, 1894)
Mad Sir Uchtred of the Hills (T Fisher Unwin, Autonym Edition: London, 1894)
The Play-Actress (T Fisher Unwin, Autonym Edition: London, 1894)
The Men of the Moss Hags, being a History of Adventure taken from the Papers of William Gordon of Earlstoun in Galloway and told over again by S R Crockett (Isbister and Co: London, 1895)
A Galloway Herd (R F Fenno and Co: New York, 1895)
Cleg Kelly Arab of the City (Methuen and Co: London, 1896)
The Grey Man (T Fisher Unwin: London, 1896)
Lads' Love An Idyll of the Lands of the Heather (Bliss, Sands and Foster: London, 1897)
Lochinvar (Methuen and Co: London, 1897)
The Red Axe (Smith, Elder and Co: London, 1898)
The Standard Bearer (Methuen and Co: London, 1898)

The Black Douglas (Smith, Elder and Co: London, 1899)
Kit Kennedy: Country Boy (James Clarke and Co: London, 1899)
Ione March (Hodder and Stoughton: London, 1899)
Joan of the Sword Hand (Ward, Lock and Co: London, 1900)
Little Anna Mark (Smith, Elder and Co: London, 1900)
Cinderella: a Novel (James Clarke and Co: London, 1901)
The Firebrand (Macmillan and Co: London, 1901)
The Silver Skull (Smith, Elder and Co: London, 1901)
The Dark o' the Moon being certain further Histories of the Folk called 'Raiders' (Macmillan and Co: London, 1902)
Flower-o'-the-Corn (James Clarke and Co: London, 1902)
The Adventurer in Spain with illustrations by the author and Gordon Browne (Isbister and Co: London, 1903)
The Banner of Blue (Hodder and Stoughton: London, 1903)
The Loves of Miss Anne (James Clarke and Co: London, 1904)
Strong Mac (Ward, Lock and Co: London, 1904)
Maid Margaret of Galloway. The Life of her whom Four Centuries have called the 'Fair Maid of Galloway' (Hodder and Stoughton: London, 1905)
The Cherry Ribband (Hodder and Stoughton: London, 1905)
Kid McGhie: A Nugget of Dim Gold (James Clarke and Co: London, 1905)
The White Plumes of Navarre: A Romance of the Wars of Religion (Religious Tract Society: London, 1906)
Little Esson (Ward, Lock and Co: London, 1907)
Me and Myn (T Fisher Unwin: London, 1907)
Vida, or the Iron Lord of Kirktown (James Clarke and Co: London, 1907)
Deep Moat Grange (Hodder and Stoughton: London, 1908)
Princess Penniless (Hodder and Stoughton: London, 1908)
The Men of the Mountain (Religious Tract Society: London, 1909)
Rose of the Wilderness (Hodder and Stoughton: London, 1909)
The Seven Wise Men (Hodder and Stoughton: London, 1909)
The Dew of Their Youth (Hodder and Stoughton: London, 1909)
The Lady of a Hundred Dresses (Eveleigh Nash: London, 1911)
Love in Pernicketty Town (Hodder and Stoughton: London, 1911)
The Smugglers. The Odyssey of Zipporah Katti being some Chronicles of the last Raiders of Solway (Hodder and Stoughton: London, n.d. Dedication dated 1911)
Anne of the Barricades (Hodder and Stoughton: London, 1912)
The Moss Troopers (Hodder and Stoughton: London, 1912)
Sandy's Love Affair (Hutchinson: London, 1913)
A Tatter of Scarlet. Adventurous Episodes of the Commune in the Midi 1871 (Hodder and Stoughton: London, 1913)
Silver Sand (Hodder and Stoughton: London, 1914)
Hal o' the Ironsides (Hodder and Stoughton: London, 1915)
The Azure Hand. A Novel (Hodder and Stoughton: London, n.d. Advocates' Library Accession Stamp 1917)
The White Pope, called 'The Light out of the East' (Books Limited: Liverpool, n.d. Advocates' Library Accession Stamp 1920)

BOOKS FOR CHILDREN

Sweetheart Travellers. A Child's Book for Children, for Women and for Men. Illustrated by Gordon Browne and W H C Groome (Wells, Gardner, Darton and Co: London, 1896)

The Surprising Adventures of Sir Toady Lion with those of General Napoleon Smith. An Improving History for Old Boys, Young Boys, Good Boys, Bad Boys, Big Boys, Little Boys, Cowboys and Tomboys. Illustrated by Gordon Browne (Gardner, Darton and Co: London, 1897)

Red Cap Tales stolen from the Treasure Chest of the Wizard of the North which Theft is humbly acknowledged by S R Crockett (Adam and Charles Black: London, 1904)

Sir Toady Crusoe. Illustrated by Gordon Browne (Wells, Gardner, Darton and Co: London, 1905)

Red Cap Adventures being the Second Series of Red Cap Tales stolen from the Treasure Chest of the Wizard of the North which Theft is humbly acknowledged by S R Crockett (Adam and Charles Black: London, 1908)

Sweethearts at Home (Hodder and Stoughton: London, 1912)

Rogues' Island (Faber and Gwyer: London, 1926)

MISCELLANEOUS

Raiderland. All About Grey Galloway, its Stories, Traditions, Characters, Humours. With illustrations by Joseph Pennell (Hodder and Stoughton: London, 1904)

My Two Edinburghs: Searchlights through the Mists of Thirty Years. With drawings by Gordon Mein (The Cedar Press: London, 1909)

Notes

Chapter 1 pp 1 to 15

1. 'A Word of Introduction', H M B Reid, *The Kirk Above Dee Water* (Castle Douglas, 1895) p xiv.
2. Most reference books, and the memorial erected to Crockett at Laurieston in 1932, give his year of birth wrongly as 1860. This was his own fault. Pre-1914 editions of *Who's Who* which he could have checked give 1860.
3. Crocket family tradition attested to by Professor John Crocket Smyth, Johnstone, Renfrewshire, grandson of William Crocket, headmaster of Sciennes School, Edinburgh, and therefore Sam's great-nephew.
4. Thomas Cochrane, *Fifty-One Years in the Home Mission Field and Reminiscences 1826–1898* (Edinburgh 1898). Appendix Note E. '... my little church at Laurieston ...', p 134.
    'Among the elders there was Mr Robert Crockett, near relative of Mr Samuel Rutherford Crockett, who had not yet set forth on the stage of time. But my Mr Crockett was quite as distinguished in our narrow sphere. He wooed the Muses with considerable aptitude and success, while his knowledge of Presbyterian polity was so profound as to cause his neighbours to maintain that should it, through an inconceivable chance, be some day missing, my elder could restore it in detail. Mr Crockett used to drive me in his gig on my visits to the people.'
    Mr Cochrane's ministry in Laurieston was during the late 1840s. pp 63–4.
5. Letter from Samuel Crockett in Minnesota to John Crocket, Mains of Duchrae, 18 February 1860 in the possession of Professor J C Smyth and kindly lent.
6. Letter from Samuel Crockett to John Crocket, 18 October 1860 in the possession of Professor J C Smyth.
7. 'A Galloway Herd' by the Author of 'Ministers of Our Countryside' (Rev S R Crockett) *Christian Leader* X, No. 513—XI, No. 552, October 1891—July 1892. This serial was never reprinted in Great Britain but an edition in book form, presumably pirated, appeared in the United States in 1895 published by R F Fenno & Company, New York, followed by others in New York and Chicago.
    Crockett used much of the material from *A Galloway Herd* in *Lads' Love* and some chapters are reprinted in *Bog-Myrtle and Peat*, 1895, pp 169–94.
    The 'What is a kiss?' incident occurs in Chapter X, (3 December 1891), p 1158.
8. *Cleg Kelly Arab of the City* (London, 1896), Adv XXXVII, p 248.
9. 'A Galloway Herd', *Leader* X, p 1158.
10. *Raiderland: All About Grey Galloway its Stories Traditions Characters Humours*, with illustrations by Joseph Pennell (London, 1904) pp 48–9.
11. *Raiderland*, p 26.
12. *Raiderland*, p 22.
13. *Raiderland*, p 197.

14 'A Galloway Herd', *Leader* X, p 1158.
15 Ibid., XI, p 129.
16 *The Christian Leader. A Weekly Record of Religious Thought and Work*, ed Rev W Howie Wylie; Glasgow Price One Penny. First published 4 January, 1882.
17 'A Galloway Herd', X, p 1109.
18 Harper, *Crockett and Grey Galloway* (n.d. Preface 1907) pp 16–19.
19 'A Galloway Herd', X, p 1109.
20 Ibid., X, p 1158.
21 Ibid, X, p 1110.
22 Ibid., *Leader* XI, p 130.
23 'Stray Memories of a Galloway Farm', *The Workers' Monthly*, ed Rev S R Crockett II, pp 8–9. See also *Raiderland*, p 29.
24 *Rogues' Island* (Faber and Gwyer: London, 1926) p 13.
25 Ibid., p 293. See also 'A Galloway Herd', XI, p 34.
26 *Raiderland*, p 21.
27 'A Galloway Herd', XI, p 442.
28 *Bog-myrtle and Peat Tales Chiefly of Galloway gathered from the Years 1889–1895* by S R Crockett (London, 1895) p 184.
29 R H Sherard, 'S R Crockett at Home', *The Idler* VII, July 1895, pp 800–1.
30 *Raiderland*, pp 36–7.
31 'A Galloway Herd', XI, p 442.
32 *The Dew of their Youth* (London, 1910) p 148.
33 *Raiderland*, pp 36–8.
34 Marion MacMillan, 'S R Crockett' MS. 11/8 Hornel Library, Broughton House, Kirkcudbright. p 9.
35 *Raiderland*, p 36.
36 *The Grey Man* (London, 1896) p 184.
37 *Kit Kennedy: Country Boy* (London, 1899) p 320.
38 'Stray Memories', p 9.
39 'A Galloway Herd', XI, p 34.
40 *Raiderland*, p 32.
41 Ibid., p 29.
42 'A Galloway Herd', XI, p 490.
43 Ibid., XI, p 58. See also *Bog-Myrtle and Peat*, p 194.
44 Harper, p 25.
45 'Stray Memories', p 10.
46 Harper, p 27.
47 'A Galloway Herd', XI, p 34.
48 *Raiderland*, p 56.
49 Ibid., p 122.
50 Harper, pp 46–8.
51 Sherard, 'S R Crockett at Home', p 806.
52 *Raiderland*, pp 32–3.
53 'Stray Memories', p 11.
54 *Raiderland*, p 110.
55 Harper, p 50. See also *Raiderland*, pp 115–6.
56 Letter from S R Crockett to Mrs Jeannie Crocket, 19 June 1898, in the possession of, and kindly lent by Mrs Nan O'Brien, Londonderry, Northern Ireland.

CHAPTER 2 pp 16 to 28

1 *My Two Edinburghs. Searchlights through the mists of Thirty Years*, with drawings by Gordon Mein (London, 1909), p 8.

NOTES

2. Ibid., p 9.
3. 'Ministers of Our Countryside. Edited by Saunders McQuhirr of Drumquhat' 'The Biography of an Inefficient', *Christian Leader* X, p 996, 15 October 1891.
4. *Bog-Myrtle and Peat*, p 282.
5. R H Sherard, 'S R Crockett at Home', *The Idler* VII, July 1895, p 809.
6. Diary of William Crocket in the possession of his grandson Professor J C Smyth and kindly lent.
7. Edinburgh University Calendar 1879–80, p 187.
8. Sherard, 'S R Crockett at Home', pp 808–9.
9. Ibid., p 808.
10. Ibid., pp 808–9.
11. Harper, *Crockett and Grey Galloway*, p 61.
12. Ibid., p 54.
13. 'Heston' (John Rae) and 'Theodore Mayne' (J G Carter): 'Sons of the South: S R Crockett', *The Gallovidian*, II No. 6. Summer 1900, Dalbeattie, p 45.
14. Harper, p 125.
15. *My Two Edinburghs*, pp 13–14.
16. Sherard, pp 809–10.
17. Harper, p 74.
18. *The Autobiography and Letters of Mrs Margaret O W Oliphant* ed Mrs Harry Coghill (1899) pp 234–9.
19. Harper, p 74.
20. Sherard, pp 810–11.
21. Anon, 'The Making of a Writer'. Hand-dated 22/1/94, Penicuik Cuttings SRC p 81. (For Penicuik Cuttings see note to Chapter 3). See also Harper, p 75.
22. Letter from Miss Joyce Collyer to the author, 6 May 1978.
23. Sherard, p 811.
24. *Dulce Cor, being the Poems of Ford Berêton* (London, 1886). The pseudonym defies explanation.
25. 'Memory's Harvest', stanza 3 *Dulce Cor*, p 2.
26. Ibid., p 7.
27. (S R Crockett) 'Alexander Whyte as I knew him. By one who owes him more than he will ever pay' *Leader*, Christmas and New Year 1891.
    This unsigned article can be attributed to Crockett because it is one of a number of 'Pen Portraits of Eminent Divines' pasted into a small notebook by Crockett himself as his contributions to the series. The notebook is in the Ewart Public Library, Dumfries. See Chapter 3, Note 21.
28. Rev N M Walker, *Chapters from the History of the Free Church of Scotland* (Edinburgh n.d.) p 81.
29. Thomas Cochrane, *Fifty-one Years in the Home Mission Field* (Edinburgh, 1898) p 107.
30. *Cleg Kelly Arab of the City*, pp 134–7.
31. Anon, 'Death of Mr S R Crockett', *Peebleshire Advertiser and County Newspaper*, 25 April 1914.
32. Samuel Picard, 'The Student Life of S R Crockett: his correspondence with J G Whittier', *The Independent* New York, 5 October 1889, Vol 51 26666. Extract from Letter.
33. (W R Nicoll) 'The Correspondence of Claudius Clear', *British Weekly* LVI (30 April 1914) p 121.
34. Information kindly provided by Mrs Mary McKerrow of Edinburgh, descendant of the Smiths of Netherholm.
35. *Raiderland*, p 3.

36 Information kindly given by Miss Pearl McDowall, Kirkton, Dumfries, and communicated to the author by Mr William McDowall, Sussex, 11 November 1973.
37 *Midlothian Journal*, 24 April 1914 in Penicuik Cuttings. SRC, pp 54–5.
38 Penicuik Cuttings Free Church, p 8 3/12/1886.

Chapter 3 pp 29 to 51

Much of the information about Crockett's life as a Free Church minister in Penicuik is available only because the late Mr R E Black during his life collected in more than one hundred and forty books of cuttings a mass of detail about every aspect of life in Penicuik and district. These provide a rich quarry for local historians.

Some of the items are entire articles from periodicals; others, two or three line strips taken from newspapers which have ceased publication and left no files. Without Mr Black, many of the events chronicled would have been forgotten or survive only in oral tradition. What I have called the 'Penicuik Cuttings' are their printed record.

Mr William W Black of Penicuik allowed me free and generous access to his father's work, especially the two books—Book 18: S R Crockett (apart from Free Church Connection) and Book 57: Free Church Penicuik (South UF)—which directly relate to Crockett. I have also consulted the one covering the Mauricewood Pit Disaster. These, supplemented and corroborated by people in Penicuik who remembered Crockett or had heard their parents or grandparents talk of him, have enabled me to form a picture of his work there, as well as of his later life at home and abroad.

I thank Mr William Black once more for allowing me to use his father's collections and add to that my gratitude to that father whose patience has left to Penicuik a unique record of its past. The 'Penicuik Cuttings' are now deposited in Penicuik Public Library under the classification 'Black's Papers' and available for consultation.

1 Penicuik Cuttings 57, p 9.
2 *Christian Leader* VIII, 14 February 1889, pp 96–7.
3 Ibid., 7 February 1889, p 87.
4 *Midlothian Journal*, 24 April 1914 in Penicuik Cuttings 18, p 55.
5 *Works of Robert Louis Stevenson*, Skerryvore edn, ed Sidney Colvin Letters III, (1926) pp 56–7.
6 Ibid., pp 193–6.
7 Preface, 2nd edn, *The Stickit Minister*.
8 S R Crockett 'Stevenson's Letters', *Bookman* XVII, December 1899, p 74.
9 *Leader* XI, 21 April 1892, p 382.
10 (S R Crockett) 'Adventures of an Itinerant Evangelist in Three Kingdoms' *Leader* XI, 25 May 1892, p 421.
11 W Robertson Nicoll, *Success*, 5 October 1895, p 183.
12 Penicuik Cuttings 57, p 31.
13 Harper, *Crockett and Grey Galloway*, p 85.
14 Anon, 'Pen-Portraits of Eminent Divines 159 S R Crockett' *Leader* XII, 25 May 1893, pp 494–5.
15 'Ministers of Our Countryside IX Some Sermons by the Rev Angus Strong of the Martyrs' Church, Cairn Edward, Muscular Christian' *Leader* XI, 10 September 1891, p 877. Reprinted as 'Cairn Edward's Kirk Militant' in *Bog-Myrtle and Peat*, p 411.
16 *Scotsman*, 9 September 1899, p 7, Col. 7.
17 'The Respect of Drowdle', *The Stickit Minister's Wooing* (London, 1900) pp 339–40.

18 'In the Matter of Incubus and Co', *Vox Clamantium The Gospel of the People* by writers, preachers and workers. Brought together by Andrew Reid (1894).
19 *Vida, or the Iron Lord of Kirktown* (London, 1907).
20 *The Workers' Monthly*, A Magazine for Sunday School Teachers and all Christian workers, ed by the Rev S R Crockett (Gall and Inglis, Edinburgh).
21 Notebook of cuttings in the Ewart Public Library, Dumfries, all from 'Pen-Portraits of Eminent Divines', put together by Crockett.
    138   Prof A B Davidson
    139   Principal Rainy
    140   Rev W H Goold
    141   Rev H D Rawnsley
    142   Dr James Moorhouse, Bishop of Manchester
    143   Rev Dr Alexander Maclaren of Manchester
    145   Rev George Adam Smith
    146   Prof W Gordon Blaikie
    147   Rev John McNeill
    148   Rev James Stalker
    150   Prof John Laidlaw
An article 'Alexander Whyte as I Knew Him' from the Christmas and New Year Extra of the *Leader* 1891 is also included.
22 W Robertson Nicoll, *Success*, 25 October 1895.
23 R H Sherard 'S R Crockett at Home' *The Idler* VII, July 1895, pp 812–14.
24 'A Day in the Life of the Rev James Pitbye', *The Stickit Minister*, pp 147–8.
25 John Buchan, 'Nonconformity in Literature', *Glasgow Herald*, 2 November 1895.
26 *Leader* XII, 31 August 1893, p 830.
27 John Greenleaf Whittier, *Collected Poems* II (Macmillan, 1888) p 97.
28 Reproduced in Harper, pp 105–7.
29 *Leader* XII, 31 August 1893, p 830.
30 (W Robertson Nicoll) 'The Correspondence of Claudius Clear' *British Weekly* LVI, 30 April 1914, p 121.
31 Harper, pp 123–4.
32 Information kindly given by Mrs W Christie, Wolverhampton, daughter of Elizabeth Shanks.
33 *The Play-Actress*, pp 66–8.
34 *Standard*, 24 October 1894.
35 See Note 18.
36 Introduction, *Annals of the Parish* (Edinburgh and London 1895), xvi.
37 Ibid., xxv.
38 Andrew Lang, *Brahma. In Imitation of Emerson Faber Book of Comic Verse* compiled by Michael Roberts 1942, p 233.
39 The artist E A Hornel was interested in Sam Crockett right from the start. His 'Crockettiana' are in Broughton House, Kirkcudbright, which he gave to Kirkcudbright as a bequest.
40 Dan Kennedy, 'S R Crockett's Centenary', *Ayrshire Post* 3 April 1959, p 18.
41 Marion MacMillan, 'S R Crockett' MS. 11/8 Hornel Collection.
42 Letter to the MacMillans, 27 April 1894, Hornel Collection.
43 Letter to the Macmillans, 14 August 1894.
44 *Standard*, 6 June 1894, p 6.
45 Letter to the MacMillans, 6 June 1894, Hornel Collection.
46 Letter to the MacMillans, 27 April 1894.
47 Sherard, pp 797–8.
48 *Raiderland*, p 105.

49 Information kindly given by Mrs W Christie.
50 This version of Crockett's statement is a composite; for different texts see *Standard*, 6 January 1895; *Kirkcudbrightshire Advertiser*, 23 April 1914. Obituary; *Scotsman*, 21 April 1914: Obituary; Penicuik Cuttings 18, pp 91, 95.
51 'The Seven Wise Men' supplement to *Sunday at Home* November 1907, pp 1–35. Reprinted in *The Bloom o' the Heather* (1908) pp 79–167, and as *The Seven Wise Men* RTS (London, 1909).
52 Undated letter from Mrs Marion Crocket to William Crocket probably 1894 or 1895 kindly lent by Professor J C Smyth.
53 T H Darlow *William Robertson Nicoll: Life and Letters* (1925) p 123.
54 *Letters of J M Barrie* ed Viola Meynell (1942). Barrie to Quiller-Couch, 25 March 1896, p 10.

CHAPTER 4 pp 52 to 70
1 George Blake, *Barrie and the Kailyard School* (1951) p 13, 15 et passim.
2 'Ensamples to the Flock', I Peter 2:3.
3 'Ensamples to the Flock', *The Stickit Minister*, p 207.
4 'Ministers of Our Countryside', *The Christian Leader* X (1891).

    I 'A Day in the Life of the Rev James Pitbye', 16 July, p 671.
    II 'The Three Maisters Peter Slees, Ministers of the Parish of Couthy' 23 July, p 675.
    III 'Trials for License by the Presbytery of Pitscottie', 30 July, p 719.
    IV 'The Rev Thomas Todd, Late Probationer', 6 August, pp 743–5.
    V 'The Tragedy of Duncan Duncanson, sometime minister of the Parish of Shaws, deposed for Drunkenness' 13 August, pp 781–2.
    VI 'The Stickit Minister', 20 August, pp 791–2.
    VIII 'The Courtship of the Rev Allan Fairley of Earlswood', 3 September, p 853.
    X 'The Glen Kells Short Leet', 17 September, pp 905–6.
    XI 'Why David Oliphant remained a Presbyterian', 24 September, pp 911–12.
    XIII 'The Rev John Smith of Arkland Prepares his Sermon', 8 October, p 977.
    XV 'Hugh Haliburton's Last Congregation' ['Accepted of the Beasts'] 22 October, pp 1022–3.

The Christian Leader XI (1892).

    XVIII 'Boanerges Simpson's Encumbrance', 25 August, pp 809–10.
    XXXX 'The Minister of Scaur Casts Out With His Maker', 1 September, pp 818–20.

5 'Congregational Sketches', *The Christian Leader* X (1891).

    I 'John Black, Critic in Ordinary', 5 November, p 1068.
The Christian Leader Christmas and New Year Extra 1891 'A Knight Errant of the Streets An Edinburgh Story', pp 4–5.

The Christian Leader XI (1892).

    III 'The Candid Friend', 7 January, p 19.
    IV 'Cleg Kelly, Mission Worker' 28 January, p 80. (to be continued)
'Cleg Kelly, Mission Worker II The Night School' 17 March, p 256.

NOTES

         'Progress of Cleg Kelly III The Fight in the Poliss Yard', 24 March, p 285.
- X   'The Lammas Preaching', 14 July, pp 651–2.
         'A Midsummer Idyll', 4 August 1892, pp 729–30.
- XII   'Ensamples to the Flock', 22 September, pp 891–2.
- XIII   'The Siege of M'Lurg's Mill', 11 November, pp 1050–1.
- XXV   'The Split in the Marrow Kirk', 29 September, pp 1243–4.

The Christian Leader Christmas and New Year Extra (1892).

         'The Tutor of Curlywee', pp 33–4. The story was told by Sir James Caird of Cassencary of John Bright, Minister of Education. See *Gallovidian* II, Summer 1900, p 46.

The Christian Leader XII (1893).

- XV   ' "The Heather Lintie", being a review of the poems of Janet Balchrystie of Barbrax', 2 February, pp 113–4.

6   *Raiderland*, p 36.
7   'The Lammas Preaching', *The Stickit Minister*, p 81.
8   'The Courtship of Allan Fairley', ibid., pp 129–30.
9   'The Three Maister Peter Slees', ibid., p 121.
10   'Boanerges Simpson's Encumbrance', ibid., pp 160, 161.
11   'The Progress of Cleg Kelly', ibid., pp 200–1.
12   'Ensamples to the Flock', ibid., pp 212–3.
13   'The Tragedy of Duncan Duncanson', ibid., p 95.
14   Ibid., p 105.
15   Kurt Wittig, *The Scottish Tradition in Literature* (1958), pp 200–20.
16   'The Stickit Minister', p 7.
17   Ibid., pp 10–11.
18   Ibid., p 11.
19   Ibid., p 12.
20   Ibid., pp 12–13.
21   Ibid., p 14.
22   Ibid., p 14.
23   Registry of Births, Deaths and Marriages, Register House, Edinburgh.
24   *Poetical Works of William Nicholson*, ed Harper, 4th edn. pp 11–12. 'The Black Dwarf's Bones' *Horae Subsecivae*: John Brown 2nd series, Alexander Trotter, *East Galloway Sketches*, p 53.
25   'Accepted of the Beasts', *The Stickit Minister*, p 18.
26   Ibid., pp 17–18.
27   Ibid., p 19.
28   Ibid., p 20.
29   Ibid., p 20.
30   Ibid., pp 25–6.
31   'The Lammas Preaching', ibid., p 82.
32   'Boanerges Simpson's Encumbrance', ibid., p 159.
33   Ibid., p 163.
34   ' "The Heather Lintie" ', ibid., p 46.
35   Ibid., pp 48–59.
36   'The Three Maister Peter Slees', ibid., p 121.

37 'John Black, Critic in Ordinary', ibid., p 246.
38 (W Robertson Nicoll) 'The Correspondence of Claudius Clear', *British Weekly* XIII, 6 April 1893, p 385; William Wallace, 'Minor Notices', *The Academy* XLIV September 1893, p 251.
39 Sir George Douglas, 'The Stickit Minister and some Common Men' (Review) *Bookman* IV, August 1893, p 146

CHAPTER 5 pp 71 to 97
Chapter numbers as well as page references have been given for the benefit of readers who may be using later editions than the first or early ones.

1   R H Sherard, 'S R Crockett at Home', *The Idler* VII, p 814.
2   (W Robertson Nicoll) 'The Correspondence of Claudius Clear', *British Weekly* XVI, 18 October 1894, p 409.
3   John Hepburn Millar, 'The Literature of the Kailyard', *New Review* XII (January–June 1895) pp 384–94. For two comments on his character, see 'The Late Mr J Hepburn Millar, LLD' *Scots Law Times* 23 February 1929, and 'A Pen Portrait', *The Scotsman* 14 February 1929, p 8.
4   John Buchan 'Nonconformity in Literature', *Glasgow Herald* 2 November 1895, p 4.
5   George Blake, *Barrie and the Kailyard School* (1951), pp 47–8, 51.
6   'S R Crockett at Home', p 814.
7   *The Lilac Sunbonnet*, Ch I, p 13.
8   Ibid., Ch III, p 30.
9   Ibid., Ch XXIII, p 186.
10 Ibid., Ch XXIII, p 189.
11 Ibid., Ch XXVI, p 207.
12 Ibid., Ch XXVI, p 207.
13 Ibid., Ch XI, p 104.
14 Ibid., Ch XIV, pp 127–9.
15 Ibid., Ch XXIII, p 185.
16 Ibid., Ch XVIII, p 147.
17 Ibid., Ch IX, p 83.
18 Ibid., Ch XV, p 134.
19 Ibid., Ch XVI, p 141.
20 Ibid., Ch I, p 12.
21 Ibid., Ch II, pp 27–8.
22 Ibid., Ch XXV, p 202.
23 Lawrence, *The Rainbow* (Penguin Edn 1966).
24 *The Lilac Sunbonnet*, Ch. XXI, p 165.
25 Ibid., Ch XIII, pp 120–21.
26 Ibid., Ch XIII, p 122.
27 Ibid., Ch VII, pp 59–60.
28 Ibid., Ch XXIX, pp 236–7.
29 Ibid., Ch XXXIV, p 281.
30 Ibid., Ch XXXV, p 297.
31 Ibid., Ch XVIII, Ch XX, Chapter Titles.
32 Ibid., Ch I, p 18.
33 Ibid., Ch X, p 89.
34 Ibid., Ch V, p 44.
35 Ibid., Ch XXVI, p 214.
36 Ibid., Ch VII, pp 63–4.

37 Ibid., Ch XXX, p 251.
38 Ibid., Ch XXX, p 254.
39 Ibid., Ch I, p 14.
40 Ibid., Ch I, p 16.
41 Ibid., Ch XXVII, p 219.
42 Ibid., Ch XXVII, p 220.
43 (S R C) 'Personal Reminiscences of John Greenleaf Whittier', *Christian Leader* XI, 8 September 1892, p 880.
44 *The Lilac Sunbonnet*, Ch XXXII, pp 264–9.
45 Ibid., Ch XXXII, p 269.
46 Ibid., Ch XXXVIII, pp 321–2.
47 Ibid., Ch XXXVIII, pp 322.
48 Ibid., Ch XXXVIII, pp 326–7.
49 Ibid., Ch XXXVIII, p 326.
50 Ibid., Ch XXXVIII, p 326.
51 Ibid., Ch XLII, p 348.
52 Anon, 'The True Story of Mr Crockett's Kirk of the Marrow', *British Weekly* XVII, 1 November 1894, p 25.
53 Anon, 'Mr Crockett's Marrow Kirk and the Rev Andrew Lambie', *British Weekly* XVII, 10 January 1895, p 192.
54 *The Lilac Sunbonnet*, Ch I, p 14.
55 Ibid., Ch XXXVIII, p 325.
56 James Grant, *Old and New Edinburgh* (n.d.) II, p 95.
57 Francis Russell Hart, 'Scott and the Novel in Scotland', *Scott Bicentenary Essays*, ed Alan Bell (1975) p 73.
58 Francis Russell Hart, *The Scottish Novel A Critical Survey* (1978) pp 118–9.
59 *The Lilac Sunbonnet*, Ch XXXIV, p 280.
60 Ibid., Ch XIII, pp 114–5.
61 Ibid., Ch XXI, pp 166–7.
62 George MacDonald, *Robert Falconer* (1868) Ch XVIII, pp 243–4.
63 *The Lilac Sunbonnet*, Ch XXXIII, p 273.
64 Ibid., Ch X, p 89.
65 Ibid., Ch XXXV, p 300.

CHAPTER 6 pp 98 to 140
1 *The Raiders*, Ch XXXVI, pp 309–10.
2 Ibid., Ch XXXIX, pp 331–2.
3 Ibid., Ch VIII, p 81, Ch XIV, pp 131–2.
4 Ibid., Ch XXXII, p 272.
5 Ibid., Ch XXXV, p 296.
6 John Nicholson, *Historical and Traditional Tales* in Prose and Verse connected with the South of Scotland. (Kirkcudbright, 1843)
7 *Castle Douglas Miscellany*, letter from S R Crockett, 4 December 1893 to his cousin William Crocket asking him to lend him 'the copy of the Castle-Douglas Miscellany which I know your father bought at Joseph Train's sale ... There are many of Train's articles in it and it would be a rich treasure trove for me.' The letter was kindly lent by Professor J C Smyth. Joseph Train was the Castle Douglas Excise Officer and antiquary who was the friend and correspondent of Scott and provided him with Galloway material.
8 *The Scots Magazine*, letter from S R Crockett to his cousin William Crocket in which he says that, 'I got a set of the Scots Magazine (1728–1877) at Stillie's

sale and a copy of Train's History of the Isle of Man'. The letter was kindly lent by Profesor J C Smyth.
9   Robert Simpson, *Traditions of the Covenanters*, or *Gleanings among the Mountains*. Edinburgh (n.d.)
10 *The Raiders*, Ch II, p 22.
11 Ibid., Ch XV, p 143.
12 Ibid., Ch XVI, p 149.
13 Ibid., Ch XVII, p 152.
14 Ibid., Ch XXII, p 195.
15 Ibid., Foreword, pp 11–12.
16 Ibid., Ch I, p 13.
17 Tam Lin: Child, *English and Scottish Popular Ballads* (1898) 39.A.37: I, p 342.
18 *The Raiders*, Ch I, p 13.
19 Ibid., Ch I, p 14.
20 Ibid., Ch I, p 16.
21 Ibid., Ch I, p 18.
22 Ibid., Ch I, p 19.
23 Ibid., Ch I, pp 19–20.
24 Ibid., Ch I, pp 20–1.
25 Ibid., Ch IV, p 37.
26 Ibid., Ch II, p 26.
27 Ibid., Ch II, p 24.
28 Ibid., Ch II, p 27.
29 Ibid., Ch III, p 28.
30 Ibid., Ch III, pp 28–9.
31 *Raiderland*, p 115.
32 *The Raiders*, Ch IV, p 40.
33 Ibid., Ch VI, p 62.
34 Thomas Hardy, *The Return of the Native*, (1878).
35 Lord David Cecil, *Hardy the Novelist* (1943, repr. 1967), p 117.
36 G T Ferguson, 'The Prototype of Silver Sand', *Gallovidian* XI, Summer 1907, pp 125–7.
37 *The Raiders*, Ch XVI, p 149.
38 Ibid., Ch. VIII, p 80.
39 Ibid., Ch VI, p 63.
40 Ibid., Ch VI, p 64.
41 Ibid., Ch VI, p 65.
42 Ibid., Ch VI, p 64.
43 Child, *English and Scottish Popular Ballads* 200. B. 5–6, IV, p 66.
44 *The Raiders*, Ch XXIV, p 217.
45 Ibid., Ch XXXI, p 270.
46 Ibid., Ch XXXII, p 271.
47 Ibid., Ch VI, p 65.
48 Ibid., Ch XXXV, p 298.
49 Ibid., Ch XV, p 137.
50 Ibid., Ch XI, p 99.
51 Ibid., Ch XVI, p 146.
52 Ibid., Ch XVII, p 154.
53 Ibid., Ch XVII, p 155.
54 Ibid., Ch XVII, p 155.
55 Ibid., Ch XVII, p 156.
56 Ibid., Ch XXXV, p 298.

57 Ibid., Ch XLII, pp 357–8.
58 Ibid., Ch XLII, pp 359, 360, 361.
59 Ibid., Ch XLV, p 383.
60 Ibid., Ch XLIV, p 375.
61 Ibid., Ch XLV, p 381.
62 Ibid., Ch XLV, p 382.
63 Ibid., Ch XLV, p 383.
64 Letter from Crockett to Mrs Garden, 18 July 1894, National Library of Scotland 2245.
65 Anon, 'Books of the Week "The Raiders"' (Review) *Scotsman* 5 March 1894.
66 *The Raiders*, Ch XLV, p 385.
67 Ibid., Ch XLV, p 384.
68 Ibid., Ch XLVI, p 394.
69 Ibid., Ch I, p 14.
70 Ibid., Ch XI, p 99.
71 Ibid., Ch XII, p 107.
72 Ibid., Ch XV, p 142.
73 Ibid., Ch XXV, p 221–2.
74 Ibid., Ch XXV, p 224.
75 Ibid., Ch XXIX, p 253.
76 Ibid., Ch. XXIX, p 254.
77 Ibid., Ch XXX, p 262.
78 Ibid, Ch XXXI, p 266.
79 Ibid., Ch XL, p 334.
80 Ibid., Ch XLII, p 352.
81 Anon, 'Books of the Week', 'The Raiders' (Review) 5 March 1894 *Scotsman*.
82 Anon, 'The Raiders' (Review) *Bookman* VI, April 1894, p 20.
83 Anon, 'New Books—The Old Romance' (The Raiders) *St James's Gazette* XXVIII, 29 March 1894, p 5.
84 Andrew McCormick, 'S R Crockett's First Visit to the Glen', *Words from the Wild Wood* (Dalbeattie and Glasgow, 1912) pp 72–3.
85 *Raiderland*, pp 141, 143 note.
86 Nicholson, *Tales*, p 48.
87 C H Dick, 'The Highlands of Galloway' *Gallovidian* XI. Autumn 1909, p 135.
88 Nicholson, *Tales* 'The Murder Hole' pp 54–5 note.
89 Marion MacMillan, 'S R Crockett' MS.11/8 Hornel Collection, Broughton House.
90 Andrew Lang, *The Gold of Fairnilee* (1889) pp 49–50.
91 Sir John Sinclair, *The Statistical Account of Scotland* XII (Edinburgh, 1794) pp 610–11 note.
92 Thomas Hardy, *Far From the Madding Crowd* (1896) Preface v *Tess of the d'Urbervilles. A Pure Woman* (1895) Preface to the Fifth and Later Edns xi–xii, *The Return of the Native* (1895) Preface v *The Woodlanders* (1912) Preface vi.
93 *Far From the Madding Crowd*, I, pp 168–9.
94 *The Raiders*, Ch XL, p 335.
95 FMC, I, p 310.
96 *The Raiders*, Ch XLII, p 353.
97 FMC, I, p 40.
98 *The Raiders*, Ch III, p 32.
99 FMC, I, pp 270, 271.
100 *The Raiders*, Ch XXXVIII, p 323.
101 FMC, II, p 176.

102 *The Raiders*, Ch XXV, p 223.
103 FMC, II, p 84.
104 *The Raiders*, Ch XLIII, p 367.
105 FMC, I, p 89.
106 *The Raiders*, Ch XXI, p 187.
107 FMC, I, p 86.
108 *The Raiders*, Ch XXI, p 198.
109 Ibid., Ch VI, p 61.
110 FMC, I, p 105.
111 Ibid., II, pp 102–3.
112 *The Raiders*, Ch IV, pp 36–7.
113 Ibid., Ch VII, p 73.
114 Ibid., Ch XI, pp 101–2.
115 Ibid., Ch XVIII, p 167.
116 Ibid., Ch XI, p 104.
117 Ibid., Ch XIII, pp 114–5.
118 *Raiderland*, p 62.
119 *The Raiders*, Ch XL, pp 338–40.
120 Ibid., Ch VII, p 72.
121 Ibid., Ch XXXVIII, pp 325–6.
122 Ibid., Ch XX, pp 180–1.
123 Cecil, *Hardy the Novelist*, p 129.
124 *The Raiders*, Ch XXVII, p 243.
125 Ibid., Ch XXVII, p 235.
126 Ibid., Ch XXVII, p 242.
127 Ibid., Ch XXVIII, p 245.
128 Ibid., Ch XXVIII, p 245.
129 Ibid., Ch XLVII, p 400.
130 Ibid., Ch XLVII, pp 400–2.
131 Ibid., Ch XLVIII, p 409.
132 George Blake, *Barrie and the Kailyard School* (1951), p 15.
133 Ibid., p 51.
134 *The Raiders*, Ch XXXII, p 273.
135 Ibid., Ch XXII, p 199.
136 S R Crockett, 'The Apprenticeship of Robert Louis Stevenson', *Bookman* III, March 1893, p 181.

CHAPTER 7, PART I, pp. 141 to 159
1 Letter to John and Marion MacMillan, 18 September 1895, Hornel Collection.
2 'Theodore Mayne' and 'Heston', 'Sons of the South: S R Crockett', *The Gallovidian* II, Summer 1900, pp 40–6.
3 Letter from Crockett to Daniel Mowatt, kindly lent by Mrs Elizabeth Mowatt, Bridge of Allan, Stirling.
4 Harper, *Crockett and Grey Galloway*, pp 161–2.
5 Crockett, 'Introduction', *Annals of the Parish*, John Galt ed Meldrum Blackwood 1895–6, xix.
6 Crockett, 'Scottish National Humour', *Contemporary Review* LXVII April 1895, p 529. For those who have not been dosed with it, Gregory's Mixture, also known as Gregory's Powder, was a compound made principally from rhubarb by the eighteenth century Edinburgh Dr Gregory. Its taste was exceptionally unpleasant, but it remained in use well into the twentieth century.

7   Ibid., p 530.
8   *An Adventurer in Spain* (London, 1903) pp 342–4.
9   Ibid., p 345.
10 'The Raiders', Correspondence *Academy* XLVI, 24 November 1894, pp 423–4.
11 *The Raiders*, Ch XXV, p 224.
12 *The Men of the Moss Hags* (London, 1895), Ch III, p 31.
13 Ibid., Ch IV, p 38.
14 Ibid., Ch XIV, p 107.
15 Ibid., Ch XXX, pp 221–2.
16 Ibid., Ch LII, pp 375–7 Wodrow, *History of the Sufferings of the Church of Scotland* (Glasgow 1828–30), Ch III, p 472.
17 *Men of the Moss Hags*, Ch LVI, p 398.
18 Margaret Warrender, *Marchmont and the Humes of Polwarth* (1894) p 34.
19 *Men of the Moss Hags*, Ch LIV, p 390.
20 'A Word of Introduction', Rev H M B Reid, *The Kirk Above Dee Water* (Castle Douglas 1895), x.
21 *The Standard Bearer*, Ch X, p 82.
22 Ibid., Ch XXX, p 264.
23 Ibid., Ch IX, p 79.
24 Ibid., Ch XIII, p 114.
25 *The Dark o' the Moon* (London, 1902), Ch XLVIII, p 417.
26 *The Banner of Blue* (London, 1903), Ch V, p 47.
27 *The Cherry Ribband* (London, 1905), Ch XVII, p 112.
28 Ibid., Ch XXXV, pp 259–60.
29 Ibid., Ch XVIII, p 119.
30 Patrick Walker, *Six Saints of the Covenant*, ed Hay Fleming (1901), Ch I, p 49.

CHAPTER 7, PART II, pp. 159 to 185
1   William Robertson, *The Kings of Carrick*, A Historical Romance of the Kennedys of Ayrshire (London and Glasgow, 1890) p 17.
2   *The Grey Man*, Ch I, p 8.
3   Ibid., Ch I, pp 10–11.
4   Ibid., Ch L, p 344.
5   Robertson, p 51.
6   *The Grey Man*, Ch XXVII, p 180.
7   Ibid., Ch VI, pp 37–8.
8   Ibid., Ch XI, pp 75–6.
9   D C Macnicol, *Robert Bruce Minister in the Kirk of Edinburgh*, Banner of Truth Trust (Edinburgh Paperback Reprint, 1961) p 38.
10 *The Grey Man*, Ch XII, p 90.
11 Ibid., Ch IV, p 26.
12 Ibid., Ch XIII, p 92.
13 'A Galloway Herd', *Leader* XI, pp 103–6.
14 *The Grey Man*, Ch VI, p 36.
15 Ibid., Ch III, p 20.
16 Ibid., Ch II, p 14.
17 Ibid., Ch XIV, p 101.
18 Ibid., Ch XX, p 141.
19 Ibid., Ch XXV, pp 174–5.
20 Robertson, pp 56–7.
21 *The Grey Man*, Ch XXIX, pp 198–9.

22 Robertson, pp 72–4.
23 *The Grey Man*, Ch XXXIII, p 226.
24 Ibid., Ch XXXV, p 235.
25 Ibid., Ch XL, pp 270, 272.
26 Harper, *Rambles in Galloway* (Edinburgh, 1876) pp 124–5.
27 *The Grey Man*, Ch XLIV, p 299.
28 Ibid., Ch XIII, p 96.
29 *The Black Douglas* (London, 1899), Ch III, p 25.
30 *Maid Margaret* (London, 1905), Ch XLVI, pp 387–8.
31 Ibid., Ch II, p 10.
32 Ibid., Ch XXVI, p 218.
33 Ibid., Ch XXI, p 181.
34 Ibid., Ch XXIII, p 198.
35 Ibid., Ch XXIII, p 198.
36 Ibid., Ch XLIX, p 411.
37 Letter from Crockett to Egan Mew, 16 November 1897. National Library of Scotland, 10,993.
38 Letter from Crockett to James Thin, 2 December 1898. National Library of Scotland, 10,993.
39 *The Red Axe* (London, 1898) Ch I, p 3.
40 Ibid., Ch I, p 7.
41 *Joan of the Sword Hand* (London, 1900), Ch XIV, p 93.

CHAPTER 8 pp. 186 to 201
1 (WRN) 'Rambling Remarks by the Man of Kent', *British Weekly* XVII (18 April 1895) p 416.
2 Ethel Corkey, *David Corkey A Life Story* (n.d.) pp 46–9.
3 *Cleg Kelly*, Adventure I, p 5.
4 Ibid., Adv II, p 11.
5 Ibid., Adv III, pp 22–3.
6 Ibid., Adv XLVII, p 317.
7 Ibid., Adv XLV, p 302.
8 Ibid., Adv VI, pp 48–9.
9 Ibid., Adv X, p 72.
10 Ibid., Adv XI, p 80.
11 Ibid., Adv XI, pp 80–1.
12 Ibid., Adv XII, pp 84–5.
13 Ibid., Adv XII, pp 85–6.
14 Ibid., Adv XII, p 89.
15 Ibid., Adv XII, p 91.
16 Ibid., Adv XIII, p 94.
17 Ibid., Adv XIII, p 97.
18 Ibid., Adv XIV, p 100.
19 Ibid., Adv XIV, p 101.
20 Ibid., Adv XV, p 114.
21 Marion MacMillan, 'S R Crockett', MS.11/9 Hornel Collection, Broughton House, Kirkcudbright, p 9.
22 *Cleg Kelly*, Adv XXX, p 211.
23 Ibid., Adv XXXIV, p 229.
24 Ibid., Adv XLVII, p 320.
25 Information from the late Mr James Milroy, retired railwayman, whose father and grandfather had been Crockett's gardeners.

26 *Cleg Kelly*, Adv XLVIII, pp 327–28.
27 Ibid., Adv XLVIII, p 332.
28 Ibid., Adv LV, p 393.
29 Ibid., Adv LVIII, p 429.
30 Ibid., Adv LV, pp 395–6.
31 Ibid., Adv LIX, p 433.
32 Ibid., Adv LX, p 439.

CHAPTER 9 pp. 202 to 216
1 *Lads' Love* (London, 1897), Ch XXIX, pp 295–6.
2 *Kit Kennedy* (London, 1899), Ch I, p 8.
3 Ibid., Ch VI, p 39.
4 Ibid., Ch VII, p 50.
5 Ibid., Ch XVII, p 115.
6 Ibid., Ch XXI, p 146.
7 Ibid., Ch II, p 18.
8 Ibid., Ch III, p 20.
9 Ibid., Ch III, p 21.
10 Ibid., Ch XXXII, pp 217–8.
11 Ibid., Ch XI, p 74.
12 Ibid., Ch XI, p 75.
13 Ibid., Ch XII, p 84.
14 Ibid., Ch IV, p 32.
15 Ibid., Ch XXXII, p 220.
16 Ibid., Ch XXXIII, p 222.
17 Ibid., Ch XXXV, p 241.
18 'J R', Correspondence *Scotsman*, 17 September 1954.
19 *Kit Kennedy*, Ch LIV, p 381.
20 Ibid., Epilogue, p 382.
21 Ibid., Ch XLVII, p 347.
22 Ibid., Ch XXXI, p 211.
23 Ibid., Ch XLIV, pp 319–20.
24 Ibid., Ch XLIV, p 321.
25 Ibid., Ch XLV, p 323.
26 Ibid., Ch XLV, pp 323–4.
27 Ibid., Ch XLV, p 324. Romans 14: 4. 'Who art thou that judgest another man's servant? To his own master he standeth or falleth. Yea, he shall be holden up, for God is able to make him stand.'

CHAPTER 10, PART I, pp. 217 to 237
1 *Cinderella* (London, 1901), Ch XIV, p 104.
2 Ibid., Ch XXIII, p 159.
3 Ibid., Ch XL, p 282, Psalm 35.
4 Ibid., Ch XL, pp 282–3.
5 Ibid., Ch XLIII, p 316.
6 Ibid., Ch XXII, p 152.
7 Ibid., Ch XLI, pp 287–8.
8 Ibid., Ch XXXIX, p 278.
9 *The Loves of Miss Anne* (London, 1904), Ch VI, p 84.
10 Ibid., Ch VII, pp 103–4.
11 Ibid., Ch VII, pp 101–2.

12 Ibid., Ch XXIV, pp 395–6.
13 *Cinderella*, Ch XXXIII, p 233.
14 Ibid., Ch XLIX, p 347.
15 Ibid., Ch L, p 358.
16 Ibid., End Paper, p 374.
17 *Kid McGhie: A Nugget of Dim Gold* (London, 1905), Ch VI, p 89.
18 Ibid., Ch VI, p 88.
19 *Poems of Matthew Arnold*, ed Miriam Allott 2nd edn (1979) p 531. 'The Good Shepherd with the Kid'.
20 *Kid McGhie*, Ch III, p 42.
21 Ibid., Ch IV, p 54.
22 Ibid., Ch XXVII, p 359.
23 Anon, 'The Decline of Mr S R Crockett', *Scottish Review* II, 24 May 1906, p 571.
24 Janet Adam Smith, *John Buchan a Biography* (1965) pp 171–2.
25 *Kid McGhie*, Ch IV, pp 49–50.
26 Ibid., Ch VIII, p 114.
27 Ibid., Ch XV, p 194.
28 Ibid., Ch VI, p 87.
29 Ibid., Ch VI, p 92.
30 Ibid., Ch XXI, p 283.
31 Ibid., Ch XXI, p 275.
32 Ibid., Ch XXX, p 399.

Chapter 10, Part II, pp. 237 to 252
1 *Rose of the Wilderness* (London, 1909), Ch, XXIII, p 279.
2 Loc. cit. vii.
3 *Vida, or the Iron Lord of Kirktown*, Ch V, pp 41–2.
4 Ibid., Ch XXI, p 192.
5 Ibid., Ch XXII, p 212.
6 The Barlocco Mining Company was founded after Crockett's death and continued to mine barytes until 1920. See *Auchencairn and District*: a Collection of Information factual, legendary and speculative about the area ed A Gray and H Parson (1977).
7 *Vida*, Ch XXXVI, p 340.
8 Ibid., Ch XVIII, pp 149–50.
9 Ibid., Ch X, p 81.
10 *Princess Penniless* (London, 1908), Ch V, p 25.
11 Ibid., Ch X, p 60.
12 Ibid., Ch XXIV, pp 151–2.
13 Ibid., Ch XXV, p 157.
14 *Love in Pernicketty Town* (London, 1911), Ch V, p 34.
15 Ibid., Ch IX, p 73.
16 Ibid., Ch XV, p 126.
17 'A Cry Across the Black Water', *Bog-Myrtle and Peat* pp 27–46.
18 Wemyss Reid, *William Black A Biography* (1902) p 141.
19 *A Tatter of Scarlet* (London, 1913), Ch XXVIII, p 215.
20 Robert Lee Orr, *Lord Guthrie A Memoir* (1923) p 158.

Chapter 11 pp. 253 to 284
1 'Scottish National Humour', *Contemporary Review* LXVII, April 1895, p 529.
2 Ibid., p 531.

NOTES

3 Letter from Mrs William Christie to the author, 22 July 1979.
4 Introduction, *Annals of the Parish* 1895–96, xl–xlii.
5 Henry Cockburn, *Memorials of his Time* (Edinburgh, 1895) p 48.
6 'Scottish National Humour', *Contemporary Review* LXVII, April 1895, pp 531–2. See also *Raiderland* pp 93–4.
7 *Dumfries and Galloway Standard*, 24 January 1895, 6.
8 *Penicuik Cuttings*, SRC 5. For confirmation of Major Pond's offer, see Harper p 132.
9 Morton Cohen, *Rider Haggard His Life and Works* (1960) pp 214–5.
10 Catherine Robertson Nicoll, *Under the Bay Tree* (1934) pp 75–6.
11 Annie S Swan, *My Life* (1934) pp 86–7.
12 *Under the Bay Tree*, pp 75–6.
13 Ibid., pp 30–1.
14 (WRN) Notes of the Week, *British Weekly*, LVI, 23 April 1914.
15 *Under the Bay Tree*, p 77.
16 Andrew Maclaren Young, Margaret MacDonald, Robin Spencer, Hamish Miles, *The Paintings of James McNeill Whistler*. Published for the Paul Mellon Center for Studies in British Art by Yale University Press, New Haven and London, 1980, Catalogue No 453, 199–120. The Grey Man Portrait of S. R. Crockett (Plate 434) is a photograph of Crockett from the *Bookman*. Whereabouts of the painting unknown.
17 Elizabeth Robins and Joseph Pennell, *The Life of James McNeil Whistler* 2 vols, 1908 (New Rev edn, 1921) pp 330–1.
18 Whistler Correspondence, Glasgow University Library.
19 Donald R P Mackintosh, 'Is Crockett Forgotten?', *Border Life* IV, 7 July 1969. The author was told the anecdote by Winifred Gunn, daughter of Dr Gunn of Peebles; she was a close friend of Maisie Crockett, who told her the story. For report of the dinner, see *The Scotsman*, 29 November 1899, 9.
20 Anon., Maid Margaret (Review) *Scottish Review*, 3 August 1905, 68.
21 Anon., The Cherry Ribband (Review) Penicuik Cuttings SRC 16.
22 Anon., 'Stamps and Stickiness', *Academy* LXXIII, 3 August 1907, p 742.
23 Letter from Crockett, July 1902, National Library of Scotland, 8887.
24 Letter from Crockett, December 1903, National Library of Scotland, 8887.
25 Photostats of correspondence between A P Watt and Hodder and Stoughton concerning Crockett's contracts. Letter from Watt to Robertson Nicoll. Kindly provided by Messrs Hodder and Stoughton.
26 Letter from Mrs William Christie to the author, 22 July 1979.
27 Penicuik Cuttings, SRC 93.
28 Harper, p 115.
29 Letter from Crockett to J M Austin, Dalbeattie General Improvement Committee, Town Clerk's Office, Dalbeattie, Department of Mss. and Rare Books, Edinburgh University Library.
30 Letter from Crockett to John Geddie, Hornel Collection, Kirkcudbright.
31 Harper, p 87. The article describing the meeting with Gladstone is one written by Crockett under the pseudonym 'Lancelot Strong': 'A First Meeting with Gladstone', *Women at Home* III, October 1894–March 1895, pp 409–15. For identification of 'Lancelot Strong' as Crockett, see Lorna 'The Woman's World', *British Weekly*. Memories of S R Crockett, LVI, 23 April 1914.
32 Rev William Thomson, 'Reminiscences of Samuel Rutherford Crockett'. A talk given to the Sanquhar Literary Society 1935, pp 13–14. The late Mrs Ruth Sandilands, Mr Thomson's daughter, allowed the author to make a photocopy of this talk.

33 Letter to John Geddie, National Library of Scotland 10,993.
34 Anon., 'The Late Mr Crockett and a New College Anniversary', *The Scotsman*, 25 April 1914, 8.
35 John Attenborough, *A Living Memory Hodder and Stoughton Publishers 1868–1975* (1975) pp 21–2.
36 Patrick Scott, 'The Business of Belief: the Emergence of "Religious" Publishing', *Studies in Church History*, VIII Sanctity and Secularity, ed Derek Baker (1973) p 223.
37 Letters from A P Watt to J Hodder-Williams, 22 December 1910, 9 June 1911 and 11 October 1912, kindly supplied in photostats by Messrs Hodder and Stoughton.
38 Letters from Crockett to 'Cousin Sam' 20 September 1911 kindly lent by Miss Joan Hastings Crockett, 'Cousin Sam's' daughter.
39 Letter from Crockett to Robertson Nicoll quoted in (WRN) 'The Correspondence of Claudius Clear', *British Weekly* LVI, 30 April 1914, p 121.
40 Letter from Crockett to the Rev William Thomson kindly lent by the late Mrs Ruth Sandilands and now in the Department of Mss. and Rare Books, Edinburgh University Library.
41 Letter from Crockett to Rev William Thomson now in Edinburgh University Library.
42 Letter from Ruth Crockett to Marion and John MacMillan, Hornel Collection, Kirkcudbright.
43 Photocopy of death certificate and letter of explanation from the Bureau du Secrétariat General, Mairie, Ville d'Avignon, France, 24 January 1973.
44 John Grant, 'Vale, Frater!', *British Weekly* LVI, 30 April 1914, p 119.
45 Anon., 'Mr S R Crockett', *The Times*, 22 April 1914, 10 Obituary.

CHAPTER 12 pp. 285 to 327
1 *Silver Sand* (London, 1914) Foreword p 5.
2 Ibid., p 15.
3 Ibid., p 15.
4 Ibid., p 16.
5 Ibid., pp 28–9.
6 Ibid., p 61.
7 Ibid., p 91.
8 Ibid., p 201.
9 Ibid., p 238–9.
10 Ibid., p 17.
11 Ibid., p 19.
12 Ibid., p 106.
13 Ibid., p 109.
14 Ibid., p 311.
15 Ibid., p 308.
16 *Hal o' the Ironsides* (London, 1915) p 19.
17 Ibid., pp 276–7.
18 Ibid., p 297.
19 The Advocates' Library in Edinburgh has been a copyright library since 1710; it merged into the National Library of Scotland in 1925. It is likely that any book bearing the Advocates' Library date stamp 11 September 1917 was published by that date and probably in that year.
20 *The Azure Hand* (London, n.d.) pp 16–17.

21 Ibid., p 43.
22 The rank of Detective-Lieutenant may sound unfamiliar but it existed in the detective branch of the Scottish Police in its early days. In 1898 the 41st Report of the Inspector of Constabulary for Scotland recorded that there were two Detective-Lieutenants in the whole of Scotland, so that it must have been a fairly exalted rank; it came immediately below that of Detective-Superintendent and above that of Detective-Inspector. This no doubt explains why Grant was able to command such support, albeit unwilling, from Colonel Hampden-Jones, who should perhaps have been designated Chief Constable. The rank of Detective-Lieutenant ceased to exist in July 1948.
23 *The Azure Hand*, p 49.
24 Ibid., p 53.
25 Ibid., p 251.
26 Ibid., p 56.
27 Ibid., pp 56–7.
28 Ibid., p 61.
29 Ibid., p 62.
30 Ibid., p 66.
31 Ibid., p 68.
32 Ibid., p 74.
33 Ibid., p 83.
34 Ibid., p 113.
35 Ibid., p 118.
36 Ibid., pp 119–20.
37 Ibid., pp 121–2.
38 Ibid., p 123.
39 Ibid., p 136.
40 Ibid., p 140. This is an error but an improvement. The note as first described (p 43) read 'to-morrow night'.
41 Ibid., pp 182–3.
42 Ibid., p 213.
43 Ibid., p 265.
44 Ibid., p 266.
45 Ibid., p 268.
46 Ibid., p 276.
47 Ibid., p 282.
48 Ibid., p 284.
49 Ibid., p 285.
50 Ibid., p 301.
51 Ibid., p 305.
52 Ibid., p 310.
53 Ibid., pp 313–14.
54 Edmund Crispin, Introduction *Best S-F Science Fiction Stories* (1958) ed Edmund Crispin.
55 Fr Rolfe (Frederick Baron Corvo), *Hadrian the Seventh A Romance* (1904 Republished in Phoenix Library 1929). References are to the 1929 edition.
56 A J A Symons, *The Quest for Corvo An Experiment in Biography* (1934).
57 *The White Pope* (Liverpool, n.d.) pp 9–11.
58 Ibid., p 12.
59 Ibid., p 15.
60 Ibid., p 32.
61 Ibid., p 34.

62 Ibid., p 65.
63 'Maria Perrone, Murderess and Saint' *For Our Soldiers* ed C J Sutcliffe Hyne (1900).
64 *The White Pope*, p 151.
65 Ibid., pp 155–6.
66 Ibid., p 189.
67 Ibid., p 201.
68 *Hadrian the Seventh* (Phoenix Edition) p 168.
69 *The White Pope*, p 217.
70 Ibid., pp 226–7.
71 Ibid., p 235.
72 Ibid., pp 231–2.
73 The Revelation of St John the Divine 23: 22–3.
74 *The White Pope*, pp 245–6.
75 Robert K Massie, *Nicholas and Alexandra* (1968) pp 64–5.
76 *The White Pope*, p 253.
77 Ibid., p 233.
78 'Stray Memories of a Galloway Farm', *The Workers' Monthly* ed S R Crockett, II (1891) 9.

Index

This is a single index of names and subjects.
Works by Crockett are italicised. Articles in titles have been ignored in filing order.
[c] following a name indicates a Crockett character.

Adam, Robert   167
An Adventurer in Spain   147
Agnew, *Sir* Andrew [c]   285-92
Agnew, Lilias [c]   288-93
Alexander, William   256-7
Alick (Muckle Alick) [c]   9, 196-8
Anderson, Walter [c]   6-7, 10-11, 166, 196
Anne of the Barricades   250-1
Armour, Lilias [c]   204-6, 208-10, 212-13
Armour, Margaret [c]   204, 207-8
Armour, Matthew [c]   204-8
Arnold, Matthew   228-9
Auchencairn   1, 14, 273, 280
Auchterlonie, Willie   viii, 141-2, 145
Ayrshire   159-77
   see also *The Grey Man*
The Azure Hand. A Novel   285, 297-315, 326

Balchrystie, Janet [c]   55, 66-7
Bank House, Penicuik   47-8, 96, 197, 262, 270
The Banner of Blue   155-6
Barclay Church, Edinburgh   28
Barrie, J M   18, 20, 38, 47, 51-2, 67, 72, 202, 251, 257, 261
   Crockett on   45
   Peter Pan   3, 196
   The Twelve Pound Look   217
Bass Rock   156-8
Bean, Sawny   163-4,166, 171-3, 175, 278

Beardsley, Aubrey   41, 260-1
Big Smith [c]   24-5
The Biography of an Inefficient   16-17
Bismarck, Otto von, meeting with   20-1
Bisset family [c]   212-15
Black, R E   viii, 50, 334
The Black Douglas   142, 177, 185
   see also   Maid Margaret
Black, William   250
Blake, George   52, 73, 81, 138
The Bloom of the Heather   260
Bog-Myrtle and Peat   16, 197, 260, 331
Bowles, T G   263-5
British Weekly   243, 245
Brown, George Douglas   63, 65
Browne, Gordon   143
Browning, Robert   249
Bruce, *Maister* Robert   162-4, 174, 176
Buchan, John   38, 73, 123, 138, 155, 233, 251

Cairn Edward Church Militant   33-4
Cameronianism   242-3
   of Crocket family   1
   defined   3, 5, 6
   kindliness of   10
Cargill, Lewis [c]   317-24
Carlyle, Thomas   245, 265-6
Cassells family [c]   247-9
Castle Douglas   11-12, 14
Celie, *Miss* [c]   57, 188, 191, 195-6, 199-200

351

Charteris, Winsome [c] 71-87, 90-6, 252
The Cherry Ribband 156-7, 184-5, 266, 277
'Christian Leader' (later 'Scottish Review and Christian Leader') 32, 36-8, 71, 233, 237, 256, 260, 276
'Christian World' 228, 232
Christopher, *Brother* [c] 317-26
Church, Mrs E M 180-2
Cinderella 9, 217-23, 227-8, 277
Claudius Clear *see* Robertson Nicoll, W
Cleg Kelly Arab of the City 3, 9, 24-5, 142, 148, 186-201, 213, 217, 235, 277
    see also Kelly, Cleg [c]
Colvin, Sidney 260-1
Congregational Sketches 37
Copland, John 273
Covenanters 98-9, 117-18, 148-53, 157, 175, 184-5, 221, 253, 287, 289
    influence on Crockett 1, 2, 5-6, 11, 41
    see also Men of the Moss Haggs, The Raiders, Silver Sand
Crocket, Annie (mother) 2, 3, 5, 11, 13-14, 20, 22, 62, 204, 262
Crocket, Bob (uncle) 5, 9, 12, 196, 281
    see also Alick [c]
Crocket, Mary (grandmother) 2-14, 204, 207, 252, 272
Crocket, Robert (second cousin) 1, 2, 3, 5, 9, 13, 14
Crocket, William (cousin) 11, 16, 18
Crocket, William (grandfather) 1-14, 204, 207, 226, 272
Crockett, George (son) 143, 275, 281
Crockett, Maisie (daughter) 37, 47, 142-3, 266, 267, 275, 281
Crockett, Margaret (daughter) 143, 275, 281
Crockett, Philip (son) 275, 281, 282
Crockett, Ruth (née Milner) (wife) 33, 47, 73, 141, 142, 147, 267-8, 273, 274, 281-2
    as author 38, 186, 191-2, 195, 198, 217
    as character 146
    see also Milner, Ruth

Crockett, Samuel Rutherford
LIFE
appearance 12, 14, 29, 30, 33, 259
    'Vanity Fair' caricature 262-5
arts student 16-20
astronomy as hobby 143
Ayrshire, visited 141
birth 3, 331
book collecting 19, 66, 262, 279
children 47, 142-3, 275
    see also Crockett, George, Maisie, Margaret, Philip
Christian socialism of 43, 186
courtship 21-2, 26, 147
death 274, 282
divinity student 22-7
epitaphs 1, 283
family history 1-15
fighting, enjoyment of 11, 12, 25, 34, 209, 275
golf viii, 141-2, 144-5
in Heidelberg 20-1
Holland, visited 141
ill-health 267, 274, 280-2
income 18, 21, 142, 251, 263, 276, 278-9
Italy, visited 141
journalism 18-19, 21, 23, 25
justice, sense of 52, 284
in London 20, 141
library of 96, 262, 267, 270
marriage 28
mechanical gadgets, love of 32, 267
ministry of 27-52, 96, 270, 283
mission work 23-5, 30, 34-5, 52
name changes 25-6
nature, interest in 37, 47,
in Oxford 20
personality of 33, 101, 283-4
philately 143, 249
photography 143, 262
politics of 44
as preacher viii, 30, 32
railways, love of viii, 12, 197-8
reading
    early 5-6, 12, 13
    at university 17, 19
Russia, interest in 324
St Andrews, holidays in 141-2
schooling 11, 12, 14

stamp collecting 143, 249
and theatre 42
see also The Play Actress
trains, love of viii, 12, 197-8
travels 20-1, 28
wife see Crockett, Ruth
LITERARY WORK
   children's books 143, 146, 276, 285
   comedy, use of 227
   contemporary settings
      city and country 217-37
      industrial 238-50
      Paris under the Commune 250-1
   on creative process 146, 256
   as critic 44-5
   detective novel see *The Azure ...*
   evangelism treated 247
   exaggeration 17, 19, 129-34
   gardening, market, treatment of 199
   ghost story 260
   gipsies in *see* Faa, Hector [c]; Silver Sand [c]
   as historical romancer 141-85, 217
   history, use of 155-6, 177, 179, 180
      see also Covenanters
   humour of 68-9, 139, 150
   on humour 258-9
      see also Scottish National Humour
   journalism 18-19, 21, 23, 25
   as lecturer 259
   market gardening, treatment of 199
   mining, knowledge of 35
      see also Mauricewood Pit; mining
   mischievousness of 42, 201
   New Jerusalem, vision of 323-7
   on novel 147
   on 'Novel of Purpose' 147, 201, 242, 277
   poetry 19, 22, 27, 30-1, 272
   postcards, influence on 253-5
   posthumous publications 285-327
   publishers 276
   railways in 196, 234-5, 243, 325

readership of 256
realism of 251
on realism 147-8
ridiculous, sense of 30, 52, 120, 127, 200, 227, 256
science fiction, theological *see The White Pope*
Scots, use of 55, 60-2, 138-9, 175, 256-9
on serialised novel 142
servants, portrayal of 9, 42, 206
sexuality, treatment of 79-83
shorthand, use of viii
social security, treatment of 244
supernatural, use of 93, 133-4, 249
tourism, influence on 253-5
tragedy, treatment of assessed 67
trains in 196, 234-5, 243, 325
typewriters, use of viii, 35, 47
visualisation, power of 128-35
women, treatment of 71, 217, 251-2, 325
Cromwell, Oliver 293-7
Culzean Castle 167

Dark o' the Moon 153-5
   see also The Raiders
Deep Moat Grange 249
The Dew of their Youth 8, 252
Dick of the Isle [c] 154
Dickens, Charles 180, 203, 230, 247
Dillingham, Edith [c] 243-6, 252
Douglas, *Sir* George 69
'Dracula', influence of 177
Dulce Cor 22, 26, 30-1, 272
Dumas, Alexander 134, 149
Duncanson, Duncan [c] 59, 202

Edinburgh 186-95, 204, 212-17
   Barclay Church 28
   Crockett's student days in 16-27
   University in 1870s 18
see also Cleg Kelly
Ellison family [c] 156-8

Faa, Hector [c] 109, 117, 153-4, 292
Faa, John [c] see Silver Sand [c]
Faa, Joyce [c] 153-5
Farrish, Ebie [c] 18, 92-3

354 INDEX

Fox, George 40
Fraser, Robert [c] 60-2
    see also The Stickit Minister
Free Church, Penicuik 28
    see also Crockett, Samuel Rutherford, ministry of

Galloway
    in Crockett's work 141-59
    early influence on Crockett 1-15
    people of, character of 149
see also Auchencairn; Castle Douglas; Heston Island; Little Duchrae
A Galloway Herd ix, 3, 6-7, 37, 71, 166, 196, 202, 260, 331
Galt, John 44-5, 116, 162, 257,
    Annals of the Parish, Crockett's introduction to 45, 258
Gibbon, Charles 250
Gibbon, Lewis Grassic 66
Gladstone, William Ewart, meeting with 272
Gordon, Mary [c] 152-3
Gordon, Sandy [c] 148-52
Gordon, Wat [c] 149-50, 152
Gordon, William [c] 148-52
Gosse, Edmund ix, 260-1
Gottfried, Hugo [c] 183
Grant, *Detective Lieutenant* Luiz Perez [c] 300-10, 312-15
Greatorix family [c] 71
Greatorix, Agnew [c] 75-7, 84-5, 93, 95
Greene, Graham 235
Gregory's Mixture 147, 342
The Grey Man 48, 141-2, 159-77, 185, 266, 277
Grindlay, *Mr* (later Grindling, Walter) [c] 43-4, 238-9
Grysland, Ivie [c] 156-8

Haggard, H Rider 129-30, 175, 260, 278
Hague Convention 324
Hal o' the Ironsides 285, 293-7
Hamilton, Hugh [c] 62-4
Hammerton, *Sir* John 267
Hardy, Thomas 38, 107, 109, 123-8, 134-5, 225
Harper, Malcolm, McL 271-3
Hart, F R 90-1

Harte, Bret 38
Heron, John [c] 105-6, 138
Heron, Maxwell [c] 153-5
Heron, Patrick [c] 99-113, 115-22, 124-8, 131, 133-9, 149, 153-4, 175
    as 'Crockett minus' 101
Heston Island 14, 100, 121, 273
Hill, Marcus [c] 302-6, 308-15
Hogg, James, influence of 114-15, 257
Hope, Anthony 182
Hornel, E A 249

Ione March 142, 217-18, 227, 252
Isle Rathan 14, 100, 103-6, 121, 128, 130

Jack, *Rev* Robert T 50
James VI, *King* 175-6
James, Henry 38
    Crockett's dislike of work of 146-7
Joan of the Sword Hand 142, 182-4

Kailyard School vii, 52, 72-3, 146, 251, 259, 267
    origin of name 72
Kavanagh, Vara [c] 191-200
Kelly, Cleg [c] 52, 54, 57-8
    see also *Cleg Kelly ...*
Kennedy, Christopher [c] 204-5, 209-14
Kennedy, Kit [c] 197, 200
    see also *Kit Kennedy ...*
Kennedy, Launcelot [c] 161-76
Kennedy, Marjorie [c] 162, 164, 166-9, 171-6
Kennedy, Nell [c] 162, 164, 166, 169-75
Kennedy, *Sir* Thomas [c] 160-2, 165, 169-71, 174
Kid McGhie A Nugget of Dim Gold 25, 228-37, 266, 277
Kilpatrick, Anne [c] 223-7, 252
Kirk on the Hill 5, 10, 240, 253, 255
Kissock, Meg [c] 71, 77, 84, 91, 94-5, 277
Kit Kennedy: Country Boy 8, 14, 18, 142, 203-17, 277
    see also Kennedy, Kit [c]
Kitchener of Khartoum, *Lord* 266, 324

Lad's Love 9, 142, 202, 331
The Lady of a Hundred Dresses 249
Landsborough, Betty [c] 204, 206, 213
Lang, Andrew 47, 122-3
Laureates of Labour 37
Lawrence, D H 79-82
Lennox, Maisie [c] 149-52, 252
Levellers, Galloway 153-4
The Lilac Sunbonnet 9, 36, 42-3, 54, 69, 71-98, 120, 138, 142, 146, 148, 203-4, 214, 238, 253, 277
literary agent, profession of invented 260
Literary Vignettes 37
Little Duchrae 2-11, 76, 107, 203, 207, 243, 253-4, 268, 292, 327
Little Esson 249
Livingstone, David 211
Lloyd George, David 244
Lochinvar 141
see also Men of the ...
Love Idylls 260
Love in Pernicketty Town 246-9
The Loves of Miss Anne 219, 223-7
Ludlow, Hal [c] 293-7

MacClellan, Quintin [c] 152-3
MacDonald, George 31, 92-6, 225, 229, 235, 326
MacGeorge, William 12, 14, 18-19, 22, 249, 271, 285
McGhie, Kate [c] 152
McGhie, Kid see Kid McGhie ...
McKill, Hector [c] 43-4, 238-9
Maclaren, Ian 32, 52-3, 72, 206, 209, 250-1, 257, 261
M'Lurg, Leeb [c] 53-5, 58-9, 104, 209, 252
MacMillan, John 45-7, 121, 130-1, 141, 268, 324
MacMillan, *Rev* John [c] 99, 105, 152, 154-5
MacMillan, Marion 45-7, 122, 141, 268
McQuhirr, Alexander [c] 142, 202
McQuhirr, Mary [c] 6-8, 10, 252
McQuhirr, Saunders [c] 6-8, 10, 60-2, 142, 202
McTaggart, Clemmy [c] 224-7
MacWalter, Walter [c] 205-9, 212-13

Mad Sir Uchtred of the Hills 41, 138
Maid Margaret 177-9, 266
see also Black Douglas
March, Ione [c] 217-18
see also Ione March
Marie Stuart 19-20
Marrow Kirk 54, 73-8, 83, 85-90, 94-5, 293-4
Marsden-Smedley, John Bertram 20-1
Mauricewood Pit, Penicuik 238
disaster 34-5, 43, 240-2
see also mining
Maxwell, *Lady* Grizel [c] 98-100, 109, 120, 138-9
Maxwell, *Sir* Herbert 46, 271-2
Maxwell, May [c] 99, 103-4, 106-7, 111-12, 115-20, 134, 138, 153, 252
Maxwell, Richard [c] 98, 110, 120
Maxwell, William 12, 14, 285
Me and Myn 249, 267
Men of the Moss Hags 46, 142, 148, 151-2, 161, 174, 253, 256
see also Covenanters; Lochinvar
Millar, J H 72-3, 76, 80-1, 238
Milner, George 21-2, 26
Milner, Ruth 21-2, 26, 28
see also Crockett, Ruth (wife)
Milroy family viii, 50, 143, 270
mining
Crockett's knowledge of 35
impact on environment 241-2
lives of miners 43-4, 238-40
see also Mauricewood Pit
Mischief, May see Maxwell, May
Molesay, Archbold [c] 228, 230-3, 235-7, 251, 277
Morris, Tom 141, 144
Mowdiewort, Saunders [c] 71, 77, 90, 94, 95, 120
Murder Hole, Loch Neldricken 99, 118, 121-2, 135, 139, 154, 253, 255
Mure, James of Auchendrayne 160, 162, 167-8, 170, 173
Mure, John of Auchendrayne 159-60, 162, 164, 166, 169-70, 173, 175

New Naturalists 37
Nicholas II, *Csar of Russia* 324
Nicholson, William 122, 135, 164
Nicoll, William Robertson see Robertson Nicoll, W

Oliphant, *Rev* David [c]   43-4

Paris under the Commune   250-1
Peden, Alexander   156-7
Peden, Ralph [c]   71, 73-88, 90-8, 105-6, 204
Peebles   270
    described   273
Pen Portraits of Eminent Divines   37
Penicuik   27-35, 50
    described   273
see also   Bank House; Crockett, Samuel Rutherford, ministry of; Mauricewood Pit; Wellington ... School
Penman, Andrew S   12, 14, 241, 271, 285
Pennell, Joseph   260, 265, 268
'People's Friend'   203-5, 213, 219, 238
'Le Petit Parisien'   147-8
Pilkington   28
The Play Actress   41-2, 186, 218
Polwart, Harry [c]   154
postcards, Crockett's influence   253-5
Princess Penniless   243-6, 277

Quakers   40
Quharrie [c]   99, 104, 107-8, 112, 114, 137

Raiderland   6, 44, 107, 256, 268
The Raiders   9, 14, 21, 40, 46, 69, 71-2, 98-140, 146, 148-9, 155, 175, 177, 253, 259, 277-8, 285, 287, 289
    contemporary critics on   120
see also *Dark o' the Moon*; *Silver Sand*
Raiders Bridge   133, 253-4
Rainy, *Principal*   27, 36, 50, 220
The Red Axe   142, 182-3
Red Cap Adventures   143
Red Cap Tales   143
The Respect of Drowdle   35
Richards, Frank   142, 263
Rigg, Reston [c]   247-9, 252
Robertson, William   159-60, 169, 171, 173
Robertson Nicoll, William   26, 32, 36-7, 41, 46-7, 51, 68-9, 71-2, 78, 84, 92, 156, 261-2, 268, 276, 280

Rogues' Island   278, 285
Rolfe, Frederick William   316-17, 322, 325-7
Ros, Amanda McKittrick   138
Rose of the Wilderness   237-8
Ross, Adrian [c]   246-9
Ruff, General Theophilus [c]   198-201
Rutherford, *Rev* Gilbert [c]   41

Salvesen, Hubert [c]   243-6, 252
Sandy's Love Affair   249-50, 276
'Sapper'   233, 238, 251, 315
Scots language, Crockett's use of   55, 60-2, 138-9, 175, 256-9
Scott, Sir Walter   98, 105, 109, 115-16, 120, 147, 152, 257-8, 287
    Crockett's adaptations of   143
Scottish National Humour (lecture)   44, 256-9
Setoun, Gabriel   256-7
The Seven Wise Men   viii, 50
Shakespeare, William   138, 147
Shanks, Elizabeth   viii, 42, 48, 257, 268
Sherard, R H   17, 18, 20, 36
Silver Sand [c]   99-101, 104, 107-20, 122, 126-7, 135-7, 139, 154-5, 175, 285-93
    'Crockett plus'   101
    name explained   286
    two worlds of   292
Silver Sand   277, 285-93
The Silver Skull   180-2, 185, 317
Simpson, *Rev* Boanerges [c]   55-7, 64-7
Simpson, Marjory [c]   156-7, 184-5
Sir Toady Crusoe   143, 146, 238
Sir Toady Lion   13, 143, 146, 275
Skinner, Ebenezer [c]   16-17
Smith, Big [c]   24-5
The Standard Bearer   152-3, 155
Stanley, Juliana [c]   288-90, 292-3
Stevenson, Robert Louis   29-31, 38, 40-1, 45, 57, 98, 105, 109-10, 115-16, 120, 138, 160, 203, 257, 261
    Crockett on   140
The Stickit Minister and Some Common Men   27, 36-8, 40, 45, 52-70, 74, 141, 146, 186, 202, 260, 263
The Stickit Minister's Wooing   142, 260
Stirling, Hester [c]   219-23